SUBSTANCE ABUSE ASSESSMENT, INTERVENTIONS AND TREATMENT

DRUG USE AND ABUSE

SIGNS/SYMPTOMS, PHYSICAL AND PSYCHOLOGICAL EFFECTS AND INTERVENTION APPROACHES

SUBSTANCE ABUSE ASSESSMENT, INTERVENTIONS AND TREATMENT

Additional books in this series can be found on Nova's website under the Series tab.

Additional e-books in this series can be found on Nova's website under the e-book tab.

Substance Abuse Assessment, Interventions and Treatment

Drug Use and Abuse

Signs/Symptoms, Physical and Psychological Effects and Intervention Approaches

Marie Claire Van Hout
Editor

nova publishers
New York

Library of Congress Cataloging-in-Publication Data

ISBN: 978-1-62618-232-5

Library of Congress Control Number: 2013932900

Published by Nova Science Publishers, Inc. † New York

Contents

PREFACE

The use and misuse of drugs is a major social, health, political and economic issue globally. This book presents a series of chapters encompassing the following key areas of interest.

Chapter 1 explores the impact of drug use during pregnancy and appropriate methods of intervention. Studies across socioeconomic lines indicates the importance of focusing on this public health problem, due to its characteristic physical, emotional and mental developmental problems occurring in children born from mothers who abused drugs during pregnancy.

Chapter 2 discusses the impact of parental drug addiction on the child, in terms of prenatal effects, unhappy childhoods, parental neglect, absenteeism and abuse, poor educational experiences and outcomes, the role reversal where the child assumes the paternal role, and potential child development of problematic substance use. Recommendations are made with regard to supporting children and teenagers during a parents' recovery process, the development of parental skills and renewed parent-child bonding.

Chapter 3 reports on how improvements in positive child outcomes can result from interagency working between child protection and addiction treatment providers. Results from the Irish experience highlight significant gaps in the knowledge base with regard to child outcomes and types of professional learning required to develop improved interagency practice competence. Specifically, processes must be embedded in inter-agency work which supports the human relational and policy/practitioner related tensions which exist between child protection, addiction treatment and other activity systems.

Chapter 4 presents prospective practitioners' views on youth work and drug education tactics in Hong Kong, with specific interest in distinguishing between social work and teaching majors intentions to work in the drugs field, their attitudes towards youth drug users, and levels of satisfactions with education and training in the field. The chapter presents information on the present holistic approach to addressing youth drug use, dependence and treatment in Hong Kong.

Chapter 5 explores the relationship between drug use and sex work. Sex workers represent a particularly risky group in terms of problematic substance use. Particular attention is devoted to environmental, social and structural factors in two countries namely the Netherlands and Ireland with distinctive policies around sex work and drugs respectively.

Chapter 6 presents a physico-psycho-socio economic focus on the use of the mind altering plant known as Khat *'Catha edulis Forsk (Celastraceae)'* native to East Africa and the Arabian Peninsula. Use of this '*Flower of Paradise*' predates the consumption of coffee with the chewing of Khat leaves practices for social, psychological, cultural and religious reasons.

Chapter 7 discusses the common over the counter drug codeine which represents an interesting quandary in terms of its regulated status, with individuals varying in their metabolism of codeine, estimation of safe dosages, and dependence potential. Although effects are milder than heroin, codeine abuse potential remains of concern, with physical dependence occurring with regular use over a short period of time.

Chapter 8 discusses the psychosocial consequences of marijuana use in terms of relaxation, enhancement and coping motives and associated outcomes. Life enhancement and relaxation motives are associated with positive use outcomes of marijuana. Negative outcomes relate to the use of alcohol and a number of health problems, with coping motives and transitions in use also modestly related to experiencing more negative effects. Being female and being married are significant predictors of less positive experiences of use. Recommendations are made with regard to future research directions focusing on reported role fulfillment and role conflicts at different stages of the cannabis career.

Chapter 9 reports on the molecular genetic mechanisms of addiction involving the ΔFosB Gene. Many transcription factors have been identified and an overwhelming amount of evidence suggests that ΔFosB pathways represent one of the genetic mechanisms in where drugs of abuse can produce stable genetic states of expression in the brain that directly contribute to addiction. The chapter presents detail on the effects of amphetamines, cocaine, nicotine, and opioids on ΔFosB pathways and the effect these pathways have on the brain.

Chapter 10 provides an up-to-date review of studies regarding the role of stress in the development of addiction to psychostimulant drugs in these animal models. Stress is a risk factor for the initiation and maintenance of drug consumption and for relapse after detoxification periods. The physiological responses to stress and the relationship between the brain systems involved in addiction and stress are described, followed by the SA and CPP animal models of addiction and the different kind of stressors used in experiments using these models, with special reference to social defeat stress. Results of studies showing how different stressors modify the acquisition and reinstatement of SA and CPP, and studies that have evaluated the capacity of different drugs to reduce the effects of stress on the acquisition and reinstatement of SA and CPP, such as NA, CRF, kappa, DA and hypocretin antagonists are discussed. The chapter concludes by presenting potential treatment approaches based on these studies.

Chapter 11 examines gender and mental health service provision in Ireland with particular reference to alcohol related disorders and sensitivity of care. The theoretical and empirical literature in relation to gender, mental health care provision and alcohol related issues is explored. Drinking alcohol is considered a gendered activity and impacts upon gender sensitivity and mental health care provision. Gender differences exist and the literature suggests that there is less social acceptability for women with alcohol related problems as traditional codes of femininity are seen to be broken, and such behaviour patterns are largely viewed as deviant. Lastly,

Chapter 12 presents a review of Motivational Interviewing and its use within the clinical context. Clients' internal experience of discrepancy has been significantly related to therapeutic outcomes in MI sessions (alongside some other therapist behaviours). Its origins and observations around future use of this model conclude.

I hope that you enjoy reading this book, and that it contributes to your understanding of drug use, abuse, dependence, intervention and treatment.

Marie Claire Van Hout

Marie Claire Van Hout, Ph.D.

In: Drug Use and Abuse
Editor: Marie Claire Van Hout

ISBN: 978-1-62618-232-5

Chapter 1

ILLICIT DRUG USE DURING PREGNANCY – EPIDEMIOLOGY, EFFECTS AND WAYS TO INTERVENE

Zaino Petersen*
Alcohol and Drug Abuse Research Unit,
Medical Research Council, South Africa

ABSTRACT

Substance abuse in pregnant women is an ongoing problem in various parts of the world. Studies across socioeconomic lines indicate the importance of focusing on this public health problem, due to its characteristic physical, emotional and mental developmental problems occurring in children born from mothers who abused drugs during pregnancy. The continued abuse of drugs also causes financial strain on both the abusers and the health care system, with drug using mothers and their offspring often needing specialized care as a direct result of their addictions. A fact even more disconcerting is that it seems that women of reproductive age are increasingly abusing drugs, with females of childbearing age constituting approximately 30% of the substance addicted population in some countries. Determining the prevalence of drug use among pregnant women based on their self-reports often proves unreliable due to the stigma attached to substance abuse and the embarrassment associated with using while pregnant. The legal consequences of drug use also create a fear of being punished and loosing custody of their babies, which again reinforces determination to hide their drug using status. In light of the telling epidemiology and the detrimental effects of drug use during pregnancy, pregnancy specific interventions aimed at rehabilitating drug using women has become a public health necessity across the world.

Keywords: Pregnancy, illicit drugs, addiction, effects of drugs, substance abuse interventions

* Corresponding Author. Alcohol and Drug Abuse Research Unit, Medical Research Council, South Africa. Email: zainonisa.petersen@mrc.ac.za.

INTRODUCTION

The abuse of illicit drugs (as well as alcohol, tobacco and prescription drugs) during pregnancy has become a public health issue in various countries. It has detrimental effects on pregnancy outcomes and childhood development. Illicit drug use during pregnancy also negatively affects the neurological development and overall health of babies (Wagner, Katikaneni, Cox and Ryan, (1998). In the United States, 4% of all pregnant women have been reported to be using illicit drugs such as marijuana, cocaine, ecstasy, other amphetamines and heroin (Koren, Hutson and Gareri, 2008). A study in South Africa conducted at antenatal clinics also found 15% of pregnant cigarette smokers to have used illicit drugs during pregnancy, and alarming figure given that this was not the focus of the study (Everett-Murphy et al., 2010). Another study in Toronto found that 37 out of 600 (6.25%) infants born across three metropolitan hospitals tested positive for cocaine (Ryan, Ehrlich and Finnegan, 1987). As a result of these high rates, women are often not truthful about their drug use as they fear being exposed for putting their unborn babies at risk. A study at Midwife Obstetric Units in South Africa found almost 9% of pregnant women testing positive for using at least one illicit drug, while only 3.6% of this sample truthfully self-reported to be using (Petersen-Williams, Parry, Mathews and Jordaan, 2012). Similarly, another study (Friguls et al, 2012) report that only 2% of their sample reported illicit substance use, while 16% tested positive, indicating the extent to which women underestimate their drug use. Consequently, the information we have about the prevalence of drug use during pregnancy and the type of drugs used, is often inaccurate (Addis, Moretti, Ahmed Syed and Koren, 2001). The accurate reporting of drug use, however, is a vital component for selecting appropriate antenatal clinical management necessary for both the mother and the unborn child. In the absence of appropriate treatment and counseling, most women will be unable to overcome their addiction on their own (Petersen, Nilsson, Steyn and Emmelin, 2012).

While tobacco smoking during pregnancy is the leading preventable cause of poor pregnancy outcomes in many countries, studies show that pregnant women who smoke are more likely than those who do not, to use other illicit drugs (Gaalema, Higgins, Pepin, Heil and Bernstein, 2012). As in many other studies across the globe, the most commonly used illicit drug during pregnancy in the US is marijuana, with high rates of usage also among South African pregnant women (NSDUH, 2007; Petersen, Steyn, Everett-Murphy and Emmelin, 2010; Hayatbakhsh, Kingsbury, Flenady, Gilshenan, Hutchinson, and Najman, 2011). Another drug that seems to be preferred by pregnant women is methamphetamine, with several studies in the US, South Africa, the Czech Republic and others demonstrating the increase in the use of this drug in the general population and among pregnant women (Arria and Wish, 2006; Slamberova and Charousova, 2008; Petersen et al., 2012). In Australia, a recent study found opiates (46.8%) to be the most commonly used drug during pregnancy, followed by 23% of pregnant women using amphetamines (Abdel-Latif, Oei, Craig, Lui, NSW and ACT NAS Epi Group, 2012).

Despite these alarming statistics, pregnancy is regarded as the window of opportunity for women to deal with their drug addiction. In the absence of caring for themselves, women are concerned about the effects their drug use will have on their offspring. Women who quit or reduce their substance use often cite their pregnancy as the determining factor to change their behavior, with 65% of women in one study citing pregnancy as a motivator for seeking care and receiving treatment (Jackson and Shannon, 2012).

THE EFFECTS OF USING DRUGS DURING PREGNANCY

The use of illicit substances during pregnancy has potentially serious clinical effects on fetal development and the continued development of the neonate and child (Kennare, Heard and Chan, 2005). The extent of harm caused by using illicit drugs during pregnancy varies, and is often dependent on the types of drugs, the frequency of use and whether its use continues throughout pregnancy. Given the fact that women who use illicit drugs also most likely drink alcohol and smoke tobacco, it is often difficult to ascertain which of these substances are responsible for specific outcomes.

Women also often use more than one illicit drug, making it hard to determine the effects of specific drugs. Furthermore, drug addiction is often associated with poor nutrition, disturbed sleep patterns, basic self-neglect and risky sexual behavior, all of which are not conducive to a healthy pregnancy. Table 1 presents a list of commonly used drugs during pregnancy and its effects on the fetus and neonate. The most common effects by type of substance will be discussed here.

Amphetamines (ecstasy) and Methamphetamine (speed, crystal meth, and ice, crank): Amphetamines are synthetic, highly addictive and mood altering drugs which is used illegally, and legally as a prescription drug. Amphetamine and methamphetamine acts as a central nervous system stimulant. The use of these drugs increased drastically in recent years (Parry, Plüddemann, Myers, Wechsberg and Flisher, 2011). A few studies have aimed to determine the effects of amphetamines and methamphetamines in children exposed to these drugs prenatally.

While many of the outcomes for these two types of drugs are similar, one study found congenital heart defects and a skeletal defect called clubfoot to be more common among infants exposed to ecstasy (MDMA, 2007). Prenatal ecstasy exposure also predicted poorer infant mental development (Singer, Moore, Min, Goodwin, Turner, Fulton and Parrott, 2012). Heavily exposed infants suffered a delay in motor development, with infants having poorer than normal motor quality at the age of four months, coupled with lower milestone achievement (Singer, et al, 2012).

Another commonly abused type of drug is methamphetamine, also known as speed, ice, crank and crystal meth. Various studies have found intra-uterine growth retardation to be more common among women using methamphetamine during pregnancy (Smith et al, 2006 and 2012).

The use of this drug during pregnancy also increases the risk of pregnancy complications, such as premature rupture of the placenta leading to premature birth, and low birth weight. While the long-term effects of these drugs requires further investigation, many studies have found that infants exposed prenatally and who were born prematurely are at risk of experiencing learning and attention deficits during the early school-going age (Smith et al., 2012). Immediate effects after birth may include withdrawal-like symptoms such as jitteriness, drowsiness and breathing problems.

Table 1. Illicit drugs commonly used by pregnant women and its possible effects during pregnancy and after birth

Drug	Possible effects
Marijuana	Compromised fetal growth Low birth weight Premature labour Withdrawal symptoms: Persistent crying Disturbed sleep patterns Trembling. Possible learning problems Problems paying attention
Methamphetamine	Increased heart rate Decreased levels of oxygen Birth defects, such as cleft palates Dependence on or addiction to methamphetamines Tremors Sleep problems Excessive crying and extreme irritability Muscle spasms Feeding difficulties Abnormal reflexes Mental and physical disabilities Decreased motor coordination and learning difficulties later in life
Ecstasy/other amphetamines	Miscarriage Impaired motor control Impaired milestone achievement Birth defects (congenital heart disease and clubfoot)
Heroine/other opiates	Increased risk of infection in the fetus Low blood sugar Bleeding within the brain Poor fetal growth Premature rupture of the membranes Birth defects Greater risk of HIV due to the mother sharing needles Low birth weight Premature birth Increased risk of sudden infant death syndrome (SIDS) Withdrawal symptoms
Cocaine	Miscarriage Premature labor Low birth weight Smaller heads, smaller brains and affected mental development. Labor and delivery complications Placental abruption Mental retardation, cerebral palsy, visual and hearing impairment. Birth defects Poor motor ability Feeding difficulties and sleep disturbances.

Marijuana (cannabis): This is a central nervous system depressant and hallucinogen, most commonly smoked, but also ingested. Some studies have concluded that the effects of this drug included low birth-weight, preterm labour, small for gestational age and admission to a neonatal intensive care unit after birth (Hayatbakhsh, Flenady, Gibbons, Kingsbury, Hurrion, Mamun and Najman, 2012). However, another study found no significant relationship between marijuana use and low birth weight, but indeed a relationship between prenatal marijuana use and deficits in school achievements. Long-term effects include emotional and behavioral problems, with exposed infants being more prone to depression at the age of ten (Gray, Day, Leech and Richardson, 2005).

Cocaine and crack cocaine: This is a substance derived from the coca plant and it too acts as a central nervous system stimulant. In addition to low birth weight, placental problems, premature labour and behavioral deficits, cocaine exposed babies could be born with smaller than average heads, which could be indicative of smaller brains and therefore decreased intellectual abilities (Bateman and Chiriboga, 2000). Other studies have suggested that prenatal cocaine exposure could also increase the risk of having birth defects (Vidaeff and Mastrobattista, 2003).

Heroin (H, horse or smack): This substance belongs to the class of drugs known as opiates. It acts as a central nervous system depressant and analgesic most commonly injected. The most noted effect of heroin use is the withdrawal symptoms newborns present immediately after birth; these include fever, irritability, trembling, vomiting, diarrhea, persistent crying and even seizures. The severity of these conditions depends on the extent of the mother's use during pregnancy (Briggs, Freeman and Yaffee, 2005).

Ways to Intervene

Given the prevalence of drug use during pregnancy, interventions to improve birth outcomes by dealing with the addiction before and while pregnant, is a necessity. In light of the high prevalence of drug use among the general population, the US administration recommends improved ways of dealing with the issue. The National Drug Control Strategy (2012) proposes reaching women when they attend prenatal care, thus ensuring early intervention. This also creates opportunities for the referral of drug using women for appropriate substance abuse treatment. The report suggests that these steps need to be a part of routine prenatal care.

While some addictions require only behavioral change therapy, others require detoxification and replacement therapies. Pregnant women with a heroin addiction for example needs to be weaned off the drug by means of methadone treatment, and not be forced to stop using abruptly, which could be very dangerous for the unborn. Methadone maintenance has proven to have definite advantages for the pregnant women and the fetus and should be a priority in heroin using pregnant women (Mactier, 2011). While the newborn will experience withdrawal systems after birth, this can be safely managed and outweighs the effects of continued exposure to the drug prenatally. Regardless of this side effect, methadone-exposed babies have higher birth weights than babies born to women who continue to use heroin.

As described earlier, illicit drug use is often associated with tobacco smoking and the abuse of alcohol. In many settings, smoking cessation services are already offered to pregnant women, and this could be the ideal opportunity for health care providers to educate and counsel women on drug use as well (Petersen, Nilsson, Steyn, Emmelin, 2012). In the absence of biological testing for drugs, women often hide the fact that they are using drugs. However, in a client-centered setting where women play an active role in their rehabilitation and do not feel judged for their drug use, women may be more willing to disclose their substance use (Petersen, Nilsson, Everett and Emmelin, 2009; Ordean and Kahan, 2011). There is also a need for a shift from fragmented service to more integrated services. When women require different services spread across various sites (antenatal care, addiction counseling, HIV testing and treatment, TB care) they are more unlikely to adhere to all appointments (Ordean and Kahan. 2011). This paper by Ordean and Kahan (2011) is evidence of the role of a comprehensive service model in improving prenatal visits, reduced drug use throughout pregnancy and significantly improving maternal and neonatal outcomes. Health providers should also be aware of the increased risk for contracting HIV among methamphetamine and other stimulant users, which reinforces the importance of interventions addressing both substance use, risky sexual behavior and HIV (Parry, Plüddemann, Myers, Wechsberg and Flisher, 2011;).

Conclusion

This chapter highlighted the public health dilemma of drug abuse during pregnancy. While some information is available on the effects of different types of drugs, more drug-specific research is required to fully understand the contribution of different drugs to pregnancy outcomes and how to deal with each respectively. This is an evident problem in various sectors of society, which requires culturally specific interventions. While drug use during pregnancy is a reflection of the rates in the general population, we need to understand why certain drugs are becoming more prevalent in certain countries. Prevention and education in the general population, with a specific focus on women approaching their reproductive age thus need to be a priority. A move towards integrated services is also necessary to increase the chances of women presenting for antenatal care and benefitting from substance abuse treatment and counselling.

References

Abdel-Latif, M.,E., Oei, J., Craig, F., Lui, K., NSW and ACT NAS Epidemiology Group. (2012). Profile of infants born to drug-using mothers: A state-wide audit. *Journal of Paediatrics and Child Health.* Article first published online: 25 APR DOI: 10.1111/j.1440-1754.2012.02471.x

Addis, A., Moretti, M.E., Ahmed Syed, F., and Koren, G. (2001). Foetal effects of cocaine: an updated meta-analysis. *Reprod. Toxicol. 15*(4), 341-369.

Arria, A.M., and Wish, E.D. (2006). Nonmedical use of prescription stimulants among students. *Pediatr. Ann.* Aug, *35*(8), 565-571.

Briggs, G.G., Freeman, R.K., and Yaffee, S.J. (2005). Drugs in Pregnancy and Lactation 7th edition. Philadelphia, PA, Lippincott Williams and Wilkins.

Friguls, B., Joya, X., Garcia-Serra, J., Gómez-Culebras, M., Pichini S., Martinez S.,…Garcia-Agar, O. (2012). Assessment of exposure to drugs of abuse during pregnancy by hair analysis in a Mediterranean island. *Addiction*; *107,* 1471–1479.

Gray, K.A., Day, N.L., Leech, S., and Richardson, G.A. (2005). Prenatal marijuana exposure: effect on child depressive symptoms at ten years of age. *Neurotoxicol. Teratol.* May-Jun, *27*(3), 439-48.

Hayatbakhsh, M.R., Flenady, V.J., Gibbons, K.S., Kingsbury, A.M., Hurrion, E., Mamun, A.A., and Najman, J.M. (2012). Birth outcomes associated with cannabis use before and during pregnancy. *Pediatr Res*; *71*(2), 215-219.

Hayatbakhsh, M.R., Kingsbury, A.M., Flenady, V., Gilshenan, K.S., Hutchinson, D.M., and Najman, J.M. (2011). JM. Illicit drug use before and during pregnancy at a tertiary maternity hospital 2000-2006. *Drug Alcohol. Rev.*, Mar; *30*(2) 181-187.

Jackson, A., and Shannon, L. (2012). Examining barriers to and motivations for substance abuse treatment among pregnant women: does urban-rural residence matter? *Women Health.*, *52*(6), 570-586.

Kennare, R., Heard, A., and Chan, A. (2005). Substance use during pregnancy: risk factors and obstetric and perinatal outcomes in South Australia. *Aust NZ J. Obstet. Gynaeco, 45*, 220–225.

Koren, G., Hutson, J., and Gareri., J. (2008). Novel methods for the detection of drug and alcohol exposure during pregnancy: Implications for maternal and child health. *Clin. Pharmacol. Ther. 83*(4), 631-634.

Mactier, H. The management of heroin misuse in pregnancy: time for a rethink? (2011). *Arch. Dis. Child Foetal. Neonatal. Ed.* Nov, *96*(6), F457-60. Epub 2010 Jun 28.

Minnes, S., Lang, A., and Singe, L. (2011). Prenatal Tobacco, Marijuana, Stimulant, and Opiate Exposure: Outcomes and Practice Implications. *Addict Sci. Clin. Pract.* July; *6*(1), 57–70.

Myers, B., Petersen, Z., Kader, R., and Parry, C.D. (2012). Moving beyond access: towards a quality-orientated substance abuse treatment system in South Africa. *S. Afr. Med. J.* Jun 28, *102*(8), 667-668.

National Drug Control Study (2012). Executive office of the President of the United States.

Ordean, A., and Kahan, M. (2011). Comprehensive treatment program for pregnant substance users in a family medicine clinic. *Can. Fam. Physician*, *57*:e430-435.

Parry, C.D., Plüddemann, A., Myers, B., Wechsberg, W.M., and Flisher, A.J. (2011). Methamphetamine use and sexual risk behaviour in Cape Town, South Africa: a review of data from 8 studies conducted between 2004 and 2007 *Afr. J. Psychiatry.* Nov, *14*(5):372-376.

Petersen Williams, P., Parry, C., Mathews, C., and Jordaan, E. (2012). Maternal substance use among women attending Midwife Obstetric Units in the Cape Metropole, South Africa. Presented at the 30th International Congress of Psychology, Cape Town, South Africa, July 2012.

Petersen, Z., Nilsson, M., Everett, K., and Emmelin, M. (2009). Possibilities for transparency and trust in the communication between midwives and pregnant women: the case of smoking. *Midwifery*, Aug, *25*(4):382-391.

Petersen, Z., Nilsson, M., Steyn, K., and Emmelin, M. (2012). Identifying with a process of change: A qualitative assessment of the components included in a smoking cessation intervention at antenatal clinics in South Africa. *Midwifery.* Oct 1. doi:pii: S0266-6138(12)00151-9. 10.1016/ j.midw.2012.07.016. [Epub ahead of print].

Petersen, Z., Steyn, K., Everett-Murphy, K., and Emmelin, M. (2010). Pregnant women's responses to a tailored smoking cessation intervention: turning hopelessness into competence. *Glob. Health Action*. Dec 14, *3*.

Reproductive Toxicology Center. MDMA. Updated 3/1/07.

Ryan, L., Ehrlich, S., and Finnegan, L. (1987). Cocaine abuse in pregnancy: effects on the fetus and newborn. *Neurotoxicol. Teratol. 9*(4), 295-299.

Singer, L.T., Moore, D.G., Fulton, S., Goodwin, J., Turner, J.J., Min, M.O., Parrott, A.C. (2012). Neurobehavioral outcomes of infants exposed to MDMA (Ecstasy) and other recreational drugs during pregnancy. *Neurotoxicol Teratol.* May-Jun, *34*(3), 303-310.

Singer, L.T., Moore, D.G., Min, M.O., Goodwin, J., Turner, J.J., Fulton, S., Parrott, A.C. (2012). One-year outcomes of prenatal exposure to MDMA and other recreational drugs. *Pediatrics*. Sep, *130*(3), 407-413.

Smith, L.M., LaGasse, L.L., Derauf, C., Grant, P., Shah, R., Arria, A…Lester, B.M. (2006). The Infant Development, Environment, and Lifestyle Study: Effects of Prenatal Methamphetamine Exposure, Polydrug Exposure, and Poverty on Intrauterine Growth. *Pediatrics*, *118*(3), September, 1149-1156.

Smith, L.M., Paz, M.S., LaGasse, L.L., Derauf, C., Newman, E., Shah, R.,…Lester, B.M. (2012). Maternal depression and prenatal exposure to methamphetamine: neurodevelopmental findings from the infant development, environment, and lifestyle (ideal) study. *Depress Anxiety*. Jun, *29*(6), 515-522.

Substance Abuse and Mental Health Administration. (2007). Results from the 2006 National Survey on Drug Use and Health: National Findings. Office of Applied Studies, NSDUH Series H-32, DHHS, Publication No. SMA 07-4293, Rockville, MD.

Vidaeff. A.C., and Mastrobattista, J.M. (2003). In Utero Cocaine Exposure: A Thorny Mix of Science and Mythology. *American Journal of Perinatology*, 20(4), 165-172.

Wagner, C. L., Katikaneni, L. D., Cox, T. H., and Ryan, R. M. (1998). The impact of prenatal drug exposure on the neonate. *Obstet. Gynecol. Clin. North Am., 25*, 169–94.

In: Drug Use and Abuse
Editor: Marie Claire Van Hout

ISBN: 978-1-62618-232-5

Chapter 2

THE EFFECTS OF PARENTAL DRUG ADDICTION ON THE CHILD

Rebekah Brennan*
School of Health Sciences, Waterford Institute of Technology

ABSTRACT

Parental substance misuse and dependency impacts on their children in a profound and far reaching manner. Prenatally the physiological effects of drug use may include fetal abnormalities, neonatal withdrawals, transmission of blood borne viruses, and poor nutrition. Children of drug abusing parents are more likely to experience unhappy childhoods, with family life characterised by violence, neglect, parental absenteeism and abuse. The child of a drug addicted parent is likely to receive inadequate education through transcience between different schools, poor attendance and a lack of parental involvement in their child's progress.

Reversal of familial roles may occur where the child adapts a paternal role over their drug dependant mother or father. Teenagers are particularly vulnerable to parental addiction exposure, leading to escapist behaviours such as alcohol and drug abuse, sexual experimentation and criminality. While recovery from addiction is the desired outcome for any parent dependant on drugs, transition to recovery is often a lengthy, disconcerting and traumatic juncture for children.

Relapse during the beginnings of recovery is common causing disappointment and broken trust. Skills training in the areas of re-building the parent child dyad is key when parents are in the post treatment phase. The effects of parental drug abuse during childhood have many negative ramifications for emotional and social functioning in adulthood. In this regard, substance abuse in the home can be viewed as a social and generational issue. Further research is needed into child reporting of subjective experiences in a drug using home, with longitudinal progress recording to inform family support initiatives and interventions.

Keywords: Family, addiction, children, recovery

---

* Email: rebekahbrennan@live.ie.

Introduction

Family systems theory underpins the majority of modern family therapy modalities (Dore, 2008; Broderick, 1993). Central to this approach is the hypothesis that a persons behaviour must be contemplated within the familial context and as symptomatic of a wider dysfunction (McHale and O'Sullivan, 2008). The family is typically structured according to a unique set of rules, roles and norms, each deserving of due consideration when addressing one member's poor functioning (Sim and Timothy, 2007; Galvin, Dickson and Marrow, 2006). The role of the family in the treatment of substance abuse is crucial. Substance misuse has a negative influence on family routine, tradition and "*status quo*" (Copello, Velleman and Templeton, 2005). Each family member is affected (National Advisory Committee on Drugs (NACD), 2011). The link between substance use and criminality, homelessness and domestic violence means that the family environment of the drug abuser is often stressful and unpredictable for other family members (Caetano, Nelson and Cunradi, 2001; Barber and Crisp, 1995; World Health Organization (WHO), 1993; Powers, 1986). Families living with substance abuse lack autonomy, cohesion, ability to express and experience increased conflict (Clair and Genest, 1986; Moos and Moos, 1984; Moos and Billings, 1982; Filstead, McElfresh and Anderson, 1981). A collaborative family involvement in the recovery of the substance abuser can improve recovery outcome (Copello et al, 2005). Conversely, a lack of cohesion within the family construct is associated with poor service retention and treatment outcome (Meyers, Miller, Hill and Tonigan, 1999). The impact of parental substance misuse on children and family is dynamic and influenced by many factors (Arria, Moe and Winters, 2010). This chapter will describe the effects of parental drug abuse on the child, young person and family, looking at what occurs during active drug addiction, the transition to recovery period and during recovery.

Methods

For this chapter the search terms "parental drug abuse", "effects of drug abuse on children" "prenatal effects of drug abuse" "drug abuse in the home" "families effected by drug abuse" "addiction in the home" "the drug addicted parent" "children of drug addicted parents" "addicted family in recovery" "parents in recovery" "children of parents in recovery from addiction" were entered into electronic databases EBSCO Host, Science Direct and Google Scholar restricted to results dated 1960 to 2012. This systematic search for articles on this topic produced 2702 results. The articles were studied, screened for relevance and duplicates removed, with 80 articles used for the purposes of this chapter.

Active Addiction

Drug abuse defines the user's life through time spent procuring substances, periods of intoxication and periods of recovery (Lussier, Laventure and Bertrand, 2010; Das Eiden, Edwards and Leonard, 2002). All else, including the needs of family members and children is likely to come second to the relationship with drug addiction (Crnkovic and DelCampo,

1998). The parental prioritisation of drug abuse is often first evident during pregnancy. Maternal drug use is associated with fetal abnormalities, neonatal withdrawals, transmission of blood borne viruses, and poor nutrition (Advisory Council on the Misuse of Drugs (ACMD), 2003). Fetal alcohol exposure is linked to the development of childhood behavioural and emotional dysfunction including poor social skills and learning difficulties (D'Onofrio et al, 2007; Kelly, Day and Streissguth, 2000). Maternal abuse of cocaine is also linked to learning and behavioural problems postnatally (Singer et al, 2004; Chasnoff, Burns, Schnoll and Burns, 1985). Opiate exposure prenatally can lead to many physiological outcomes in infants including abstinence syndrome (ACMD, 2003) which is characterised by disordered feeding and sleeping behaviours and excessive crying (Zuckerman, 1994). This in itself can create a difficult early parenting experience with indaquate maternal aftercare and support (Keen and Allison, 2001). Parents who substance abuse are also more likely to experience parental stress and feel unable to cope (Kelley, 1998).

As childhood progresses, the negative impact of parental substance abuse on the care giving environment is significant (Barnard, 2003). Parental drug abuse is associated with a lack of maternal interaction and an absence of closeness in the parent child dynamic (Penning and Barnes, 1982; Brook, Lukoff and Whiteman, 1980; Braucht, Kirby and Berry, 1978; Kandel, Kessler, and Margulies, 1978). An authoritarian and punitive approach to parenting is linked with parental drug abuse (NACD, 2011; Hien and Honeyman, 2000; Burns, Chethik, Burns and Clark, 1991; Bauman and Levine, 1986). Typical also is a neglectful parenting style which places the child in an extremely vulnerable position (Barnard and McKeganey, 2004; ACMD, 2003). Children of drug abusing parents are more likely to experience unhappy childhoods (Velleman, 2004; Velleman, 2002) characterized by unreliable and inconsistant parental behaviour (Jarmas and Kazak, 1992; Jones and Houts, 1992; Roosa, Sandler, Beals and Short; 1988; West and Prinz, 1987). Episodic violence is common (Black, Bucky and Wilder-Padilla, 2005) and children tend to prematurely adapt a sense of responsibility (Cleaver, Unell and Aldgate, 1999). Reversal of familial roles may occur where the child adapts a hypervigalent role, watching over the parent through fear of overdose and a deeply ingrained sense of endangerment (Howe, 2005; ACMD, 2003). Children growing up in environments such as these describe feelings of intense fear and helplessness (ACMD, 2003; Hogan and Higgins, 2001) as they are exposed to traumatic scenes of adult intoxication and criminal acts in their home (Hogan and Higgins, 2001). Parents who abuse drugs are also more likey to maltreat their children physically (NACD, 2011). Children are often isolated from avenues of help and support through fear of punishment, being taken into care or through wishing to remain loyal to their families (Velleman,Templeton, Reuber, Klein and Moesgen, 2008; Buckley, Holt and Whelan, 2007). The diversion of household income from essential grocery and heating bills to drug procurement means that the childs basic needs are often neglected (Bauman and Dougherty, 1983; Rosenbaum, 1979). This gives rise to feelings of insecurity and abandonment in the child (ACMD, 2003; Hogan and Higgins, 2001). Substance abusing parents are often missing from the home for hours or days at a time (Kolar, Brown, Haertzen, and Michaelson, 2004; Hogan and Higgins, 2001). Parental absence can also be attributed to imprisonment (Beckerman, 1998) and through social services placing the children into care (Nair et al, 1997). Inadequate education often results from transcience between different schools (Barnard, 2007), poor attendance (ACMD, 2003) and sparse parental involvement in their childs progress in school (Hogan and Higgins, 2001). This has the added effect of depriving the child of a potential safe haven outside a disordered home, or a social outlet to develop peer relationships and skills. This can generate feelings of resentment and rage, with far reaching emotional impact. The ramifications of these distressing early experiences include long lasting negative emotionality (Cleaver et al, 1999) and conduct and behavioural difficulties (West and Prinz, 1987; Nylander, 1979; Robins, 1966;).

A childhood spent in the chaotic world of substance abuse can be the genesis of a very difficult adolescance and early adulthood (Clark, Cornelius, Kirisci, and Tarter, 2005; Clark, Cornelius, Wood, and Vanyukov, 2004). Modelling and normalisation of drug consumption and a lack of closeness in the parent-child dyad increases the likelihood of a problematic adolescence (Brook, Brook, Gordon, Whiteman and Cohen, 1990). Teenagers are particularly vulnerable to parental addiction exposure (Latendresse et al, 2008; Dahl and Spear, 2004; Biederman, Faraone, Monuteaux, and Feighne, 2000). Adolescants experiencing parental absence may be left to cope with puberty in isolation, generating feelings of low self worth and loneliness. This may give rise to escapist behaviours such as alcohol and drug abuse, sexual experimentation and criminality (ACMD, 2003; Ferguson and Lynskey, 1998). The family as a whole suffers from parental substance abuse with decreased caring and warmth in the home and more incidents of stress and conflict (NACD, 2011). The support of extended family members such as grandparents can be central to children's safety and well being during chaotic periods of drug dependence (Barnard, 2003).

Transition to Recovery

Children of substance abusing parents are acutely aware that drug use is the causal factor for their unhappy existence and wish for their parent to recover so that they can have a "normal" life (Barnard, 2007). However, transition to recovery is often a lengthy, disconcerting juncture for children which can also be traumatic in another form (Arria et al., 2010; Brown and Lewis, 1999). A triggering event such as a drug overdose, the collapse of a relationship (NACD, 2011) or imprisonment (Beckerman, 1998) is likely to precede the decision to seek treatment, causing significant stress and upset for the child. When a parent goes into treatment, most are separated from their children causing further distress. A recovering parent often struggles with internal frustrations and exposed deficits in their parenting skills (Friedman, 2004). An environment of emotional turbulence may exist as the parent processes their own negative emotionality from their addiction (Friedman, 2004). An authoritarian parenting style is associated with parents in detoxification, indicating a desire for control in an unstable period (Bauman and Dougherty, 1983). As the child adjusts to a drug free environment, relapse is a common occurance (Arria et al., 2010). Naturally this can cause huge disappointment, broken trust, lack of confidence and emotional pain (Barnard, 2007). Raised expectancies around abstinence can create anxiety and fear around relapse (Arria et al, 2010). Children may view their parent's love for them as motivating factors for recovery and react badly to relapse, developing defence mechanisms to protect themselves from this eventuality (Barnard, 2007).

Along the continuum of parental recovery, the emotional fall out from active addiction is far reaching and symptoms of early exposure to drug abuse in the home can be seen long after the parent becomes drug free (NACD, 2011). A family may continue to experience unsettled emotions for three to five years after the drug using parent goes into recovery (White and

Savage, 2005). In the early stages of recovery, treatment may involve physiological, behavioural and emotional upheaval as the parent goes through withdrawals and distress (NACD, 2011). Parents are likely to need comprehensive post treatment skills training, e.g. in the areas of discipline and over-indulgence through guilt when rebuilding the parent child relationship (Arria et al., 2010). Children may have difficulty understanding and adapting to the change in roles as the parent attempts to perform in ways they did not before. It may be a challenge for the parent to meet the child's needs during this overwhelming time (NACD, 2011). Parents in established recovery can become absorbed in meetings, new friends and social activities to the detriment of their child at home. Parental absence can cause loneliness, poor engagement with schooling, discipline issues and lack of closeness in the parent child dynamic (Arria et al., 2010). Parents may underestimate the depth of their children's distress and fail to assess their needs accurately, minimising them due to disordered belief systems stemming from their own early life experiences (Devaney, 2008). Despite these difficulties, recovery from addiction has many positive ramifications for the child (Andreas, O'Farrell and Fals-Stewart, 2006; Callan and Jackson, 1986; Moos and Billings, 1982). Stress levels are significantly reduced when a parent stops using a substance (Moos and Billing, 1982). Children generally notice the atmosphere at home is happier. They begin to receive greater parental attention and there are less incidences of frightening events (Barnard, 2007). Paternal recovery from alcoholism is associated with a reduction in difficulties for the child (Andreas et al., 2006). A cognitive and behavioural shift in the family construct results in an altered family environment post treatment (Moos and Billings, 1982). Families of parents in recovery show improved functioning post treatment (Billings and Moos, 1983). Sustained abstinence from substances can have significant positive effect on family and child functioning (Callan and Jackson, 1986; Andreas and O'Farrell, 2007). Families with recovering parents are not hugely dissimilar from families without alcoholism (Moos and Billings, 1983).

CONCLUSION

While some parents who substance abuse are capable of caring for their children and providing an emotionally healthy home life (Hogans and Higgins, 2001), most children of drug abusing parents live in an unreliable and lonely world where they are vulnerable to harm (Barnard, 2007). Research has shown that problematic drug use jeopardises family functioning and has negative impact on a child's health and emotional well-being with far-reaching consequences into their adult lives (NACD, 2011). Each member of the family unit comes under significant stress and damage to their psychological health as a result of substance addiction in the home (Velleman et al, 1993). Each individual entangled in the web of parental drug abuse needs help in relation to this issue (Copello et al, , 2005). An emotionally close, well adjusted family environment with high levels of bonding protects adolescents from problematic societal functioning (Hirschi, 1969). In this respect substance abuse in the home is a social and generational issue (NACD, 2011). Further research is needed into child reporting of subjective experiences in a drug using home, and continual progress recording of these children over time, to garner insight into their long and short term needs (Hogan and Higgins, 2001). There is also a need for more intensive and coordinated family support initiatives (NACD, 2011).

REFERENCES

Advisory Council on the Misuse of Drugs (AMCD). (2003). *Hidden Harm, Responding to the Needs of Children of Problem Drug Users,* London: Home Office.

Andreas, J. B, O'Farrell, T J., and Fals-Stewart, W. (2006). Does individual treatment for alcoholic fathers benefit their children? A longitudinal assessment, *Journal of Consulting and Clinical Psychology, 74*(1), 191-198.

Andreas, J.B. and O'Farrell, T.J. (2007). Longitudinal associations between fathers' heavy drinking patterns and children's psychosocial adjustment. Journal of Abnormal Child Psychology, 35(1), 1–16.

Arria, A., Moe, J. and Winters, K. (2010) Parenting Challanges in Recovery, *Counsellor - The Magazine for Addiction Professionals*, 11, 10-17.

Barber, J.G. and Crisp, B. R. (1995). The 'pressures to change' approach to working with the partners of heavy drinkers, *Addiction, 90*(2), 269 – 276.

Barnard, M. (2003) Between a rock and a hard place: the role of relatives in protecting children from the effects of parental drug problems, Child and Family Social Work, 8(4), 291- 299.

Barnard, M. (2007) Drug Addiction and Families. London: Jessica Kingsley.

Barnard, M., and McKeganey, N. (2004). The impact of parental problem drug use on children: what is the problem and what can be done to help? Addiction, 99(5), 552-559.

Bauman, P. S. and Dougherty, F. E. (1983). Drug-addicted mothers' parenting and their children's development, International Journal of the Addictions, 18(3), 291–302.

Bauman, P. S., and Levine, S. A. (1986) The development of children of drug addicts, The International Journal of the Addictions, 21(8), 849-863.

Beckerman, A. (1998) Charting a course: Meeting the challenge of permanency planning for children with incarcerated mothers. *Child Welfare, 77*, 513-529.

Biederman, J., Faraone, S.V., Monuteaux, M.C., and Feighner J. A. (2000) Patterns of Alcohol and Drug Use in Adolescents Can Be Predicted by Parental Substance Use Disorders, Pediatrics, 106(4), 792-797.

Billings, A.G. and Moos, R.H. (1983). Psychosocial processes of recovery among alcoholics and their families: Implications for clinicians and program evaluations, *Addictive Behaviours, 8*(3), 205-218.

Black, C., Bucky, S., and Wilder-Padilla, S. (1986). The interpersonal and emotional consequences of being an adult child of an alcoholic. International Journal of Mental Health and Addiction, 22(2), 213 – 231.

Braithwaite, D. and Baxter, L. A. (2006) Engaging theories in family communication: Multiple perspectives, Thousand Oaks, California: Sage Publications Inc.

Braucht, G. N., Kirby, M. W., and Berry, G. J. (1978) Psychosocial correlates of empirical types of multiple drug abusers. Journal of Consulting and Clinical Psychology, 46(6), 1463-1475.

Broderick, C. (1993) *Understanding family process: Basics of family systems theory,* Thousand Oaks, California: Sage Publications Inc.

Brook, J. S., Brook, D.W., Gordon, A. S., Whiteman, M., and Cohen, P. (1990). The psychosocial etiology of adolescent drug use: A family interactional approach, *Genetic, Social, and General Psychology Monographs, 116*(2), 111-267.

Brook, J. S., Lukoff, I. F., and Whiteman, M. (1980). Initiation into adolescent marijuana use, *Journal of Genetic Psychology, 137*, 133-142.

Brown, S., and Lewis, V. (1999) The Alcoholic Family in Recovery: A developmental model. New York: Guilford Press.

Buckley, H., Holt, S., and Whelan, S. (2007) Listen to Me! Children's experiences of domestic violence, *Child Abuse Review, 16*(5), 296-310.

Burns, K., Chethik, L., Burns, W. J., and Clark, R. (1991). Dyadic disturbances in cocaine-abusing mothers and their infants, *Journal of Clinical Psychology, 47*(2), 316-319.

Caetano, R., Nelson, M.A., and Cunradi, C. (2001). Intimate partner violence, dependence symptoms and social consequences from drinking among White, Black and Hispanic couples in the United States. *Americal Journal on Addictions, 10,*60 – 69.

Callan, V. J., and Jackson, D. (1986) Children of alcoholic fathers and recovered alcoholic fathers: personal and family functioning, Journal of Studies on Alcohol, 47(2), 180-182.

Chasnoff, I.J., Burns, W.J., Schnoll, S.H., and Burns, K.A. (1985). Cocaine use in pregnancy, *The New England Journal of Medicine, 313*(11),666-669.

Clair, D., and Genest, M. (1986) Variables associated with the adjustment of offspring of alcoholic fathers. *Journal of Studies on Alcohol, 48*(4), 345-355.

Clark, D.B., Cornelius, J.R., Kirisci, L, andTarter, R.E. (2005) Childhood risk categories for adolescent substance involvement: A general liability typology, Drug and Alcohol Dependence, *77*(1), 13–21.

Clark, D.B., Cornelius, J.R., Wood, D.S., and Vanyukov, M. (2004). Psychopathology risk transmission in children of parents with substance use disorders, American Journal of Psychiatry *161*(4), 685–691.

Cleaver, H., Unell, U., and Aldgate, J. (1999) *Children's needs—parenting capacity: the impact of parental mental illness, problems alcohol and drug use and domestic violence on children's development,* London: Department of Health.

Copello, A.G., Velleman, R.D.B., and Templeton, L.J. (2005) Family interventions in the treatment of alcohol and drug problems, *Drug and Alcohol Review, 24*(4), 369-385.

Crnkovic, A.E., and DelCampo, R.L. (1998). A system approach to the treatment of chemical addiction, *Contemporary Family Therapy, 20*(1), 25-36.

D'Onofrio, B., Van Hulle, C., Waldman, I., Rodgers, J., Rathouz, P., and Lahey, B. (2007) Casual inferences regarding prenatal alcohol exposure and childhood externalizing problems, *Archives of General Psychiatry, 64*(11), 1296-1304.

Dahl, R. E. and Spear, L. P. (2004) Adolescent Brain Development: Vulnerabilities and Opportunities. New York : Annals of the New York Academy of Sciences.

Das Eiden, R., Edwards, E.P. and Leonard, K.E (2002). Mother-infant and father-infant attachment among alcoholic families, *Development and Psychopathology*, 14(2), 253-278.

Devaney, J. (2008). Inter-professional Working in Child Protection with Families with Long-Term and Complex Needs, *Child Abuse Review, 17*(4), 242-261.

Dore, M. (2008) *Comprehensive Handbook of Social Work and Social Welfare*, New Jersey: John Wiley and Sons Inc.

Ferguson, D. M., and Lynskey, M. T. (1998) Conduct problems in childhood and psychosocial outcomes in adolescence: A prospective study, *Journal of Emotional and Behavioural Disorders*, 6(1), 6–12.

Filstead, W.J., McElfresh, O., and Anderson, C. (1981). Comparing the family environments of alcoholic and "normal" families, *Journal of Alcohol and Drug Education, 26*(2), 24-31.

Friedman, L. (2004). *From Dads to Grandparents to Parents in Recovery :States' Experiences in Supporting Diverse Populations*, Retrieved from http://www.circle ofparents.org/downloads/CircleofParents_Recovery.pdf.

Galvin, K., Dickson, F., and Marrow, S.R. (2006) *Systems Theory: Patterns and (W)holes in Family Communication*, Thousand Oaks, California: Sage Publications Inc.

Hampton, R. L., Senatore, V., and Gullotta, T. P. E. (2002) *Substance abuse, family violence and child welfare:Bridging perspectives: Vol. 10: Issues in children's and families' lives,* Thousand Oaks, California: Sage Publications Inc.

Hien, D., and Honeyman, T. (2000). A closer look at the drug-abuse maternal aggression link, *Journal of Interpersonal Violence, 15*(5), 503-522.

Hirschi, T. (1969) *Causes a/delinquency*. Berkeley: University of California Press.

Hogan, D., and Higgins, L. (2001) *When parents use drugs: key findings from a study of children in the care of drug-using parents.* Dublin: Children's Research Centre.

Howe, D. (2005) *Child Abuse and Neglect: Attachment, Development and Intervention,* London; Palgrave/MacMillan.

Jarmas, A., and Kazak, A. (1992). Young adult children of alcoholic fathers: depressive experiences, coping styles and family systems, *Journal of Consulting and Clinical Psychology,* 60(2), 244-251.

Jones, D.C., and Houts, R. (1992). Parental drinking, parent-child communication, and social skills in young adults, *Journal of Studies on Alcohol and Drugs, 53*(1), 48-56.

Kandel, D. B., Kessler, R. C., and Margulies, R. S. (1978) Antecedents of adolescent initiation into stages of drug use: A developmental analysis. *Journal of Youth and Adolescence, 7*(1), 13-40.

Keen, J. and Alison, L. (2001) Drug misusing parents: Key points for health professionals, *Archives of Disease in Childhood, 85*(4), 296–299.

Kelley, S. J. (1998). Stress and coping behaviors of substance-abusing mothers, *Journal of the Society of Pediatric Nurses, 3*(1), 103-111.

Kelly, S., Day, N., and Streissguth, A. (2000). Effects of prenatal alcohol exposure on social behavior in humans and other species, *Neurotoxicology and Teratology, 22*(2), 143-149.

Kolar, A. F., Brown, B. S., Haertzen, C. A., and Michaelson, B. S. (1994) Children of Substance Abusers, the life experiences of children of opiate addicts in methadone maintenance. *American Journal of Drug and Alcohol Abuse, 20*(2), 159-71.

Latendresse, S.J., Rose, R.J., Viken, R.J., Pulkkinen, L., Kaprio, J., and Dick, D.M. (2008) Parenting Mechanisms in Links Between Parents' and Adolescents' Alcohol Use Behaviors. Alcoholism: Clinical and Experimental Research 32(2), 322-330.

Lussier, K., Laventure, M., and Bertrand, K. (2010) Parenting and Maternal Substance Addiction: Factors Affecting Utilization of Child Protective Services, *Substance Use and Misuse, 45*(1), 572- 1,588.

McHale, J., and Sullivan, M.J. (2008) Family Systems, In M. Hersen and A. Gross (Eds.), Handbook of Clinical Psychology, Volume 2: Children and Adolescents, Hoboken, NJ: John Wiley and Sons.

McKeganey, N., Barnard, M., and McIntosh, J. (2002) Paying the Price for their Parents' Addiction: meeting the needs of the children of drug-using parents, *Drugs Education Prevention and Policy*, *9*(3), 233-246.

Meyers, R.J., Miller, W.R., Hill, D.E., and Tonigan, J.S. (1999). Community reinforcement and familytraining (CRAFT): Engaging unmotivated drug users in treatment. *Journal of Substance Abuse 10*(3), 1–18.

Moos, R.H., and Billings, A.C. (1982) Children of alcoholics during the recovery process: Alcoholic and matched control families. Addictive Behavior, 7(2), 155-163.

Moos, R.H., and Moos, B.S. (1984) The process of recovery from alcoholism: Company functioning in families of alcoholics and matched control families, Journal of Studies on Alcohol, 45(2), 111-118.

Nair, P., Black, M.M., Schuler, M., Keane, V., Snow, L. and Rigney, B.A. (1997). Risk factors for disruption in primary caregiving among infants of substance abusing women.*Child Abuse and Neglect, 21*(11), 1039-1051.

National Advisory Committee on Drugs (NACD). (2011) *Parental Substance Misuse: Addressing its Impact on Children. A Review of the Literature.* Stationary Office, Dublin.

Nylander, I. (1979). A 20-year prospective follow-up study of 2164 cases at the child guidance clinics in Stockholm, *Acta paediatrica Scandinavica, 276,* 1 – 45.

Penning, M., and Barnes, G. E. (1982) Adolescent marijuana use: A review, *International Journal of Addictions, 17*(5), 749-91.

Powers, R. (1986) Aggression and violence in the family. In Campbell, A., Gibbs, J., *Violent transactions*, Oxford: Blackwell.

Robins, L. (1966) *Deviant children grown up.* Baltimore: Williams and Wilkins.

Roosa, M., Sandler, I., Beals, J., and Short, J. (1988). Risk status of adolescent children of problem drinking parents, American Journal of Community Psychology, *16*(2), 225– 229.

Rosenbaum, M. (1979). Difficulties in taking care of business: Women addicts as mothers, *American Journal of Drug and Alcohol Abuse, 6*(4), 431–46.

Sim, B., and Timothy, U. (2007) The dynamics of family relationship in male adolescent drug rehabilitation (Doctoral Disseration), *Dissertation Abstracts International Section A: Humanities and Social Sciences*, *67*(10), 3983.

Singer, L.T., Minnes, S., Short, E., Arnedt, R., Farkas, K., Lewis, B., Klein, N., Russ, S., Min, M.O., and Kirchner, H.L. (2004) Cognitive outcomes of preschool children with prenatal cocaine exposure, *The Journal of the American Medical Association*, *291*(20), 2448-2456.

Thyer, B. A. (2008) *Comprehensive handbook of social work and social welfare, volume 2: Human behavior in the social environment.* New Jersey: John Wiley and Sons Inc.

Velleman, R. (2002) *The children of problem drinking parents: an executive summary.* Retrieved from http://www.med.ic.ac.uk/divisions/64/execsum 70.pdf.

Velleman, R. (2004). Alcohol and drug problems: an overview of the impact on children and the implications for practice. In Gopfert, M., Webster, J., Seeman, M., (2nd Ed) Seriously Disturbed and mentally ill parents and their children, Cambridge: Cambridge University Press.

Velleman, R., Bennett, G., Miller, T., Orford, J., Rigby, K., and Tod, A. (1993) The families of problem drug users: the accounts of fifty close relatives, *Addiction, 88*(9), 1281-1289.

Velleman, R., Templeton, L., Reuber, D., Klein, M. and Moesgen, D. (2008). Domestic Abuse Experienced by Young People living in Families with Alcohol Problems: Results from a Cross- European Study, *Child Abuse Review, 17*(6), 387-409.

West, M., and Prinz, R. (1987). Parental alcoholism and childhood psychopathology, *Psychological Bulletin, 102*(2), 204-218.

White, W., and Savage, B. (2005). All in the family: Alcohol and other drug problems, recovery, advocacy. Alcoholism Treatment Quarterly, 23(4), 3-38.

World Health Organization (WHO). (1993). *Psychological impact of substance use on families: a literature review.* Geneva: World Health Organization.

Zuckerman, B. (1994)*Effects on parents and children* in VA Williamsburg and D.J. Besharov (eds), *When drug addicts have children: reorienting child welfare's response.* Washington DC: Child Welfare League of America.

In: Drug Use and Abuse
Editor: Marie Claire Van Hout
ISBN: 978-1-62618-232-5

Chapter 3

TRANSFORMING INTER-AGENCY PRACTICE ACTIVITY IN AN IRISH CONTEXT: PRACTITIONER RESEARCH FROM ADDICTION TREATMENT AND SOCIAL WORK AGENCIES

Liam McCarthy and Robert O'Driscoll*
Irish Association of Social Work and Irish Association of Alcohol and Addiction Counsellors

ABSTRACT

Recent national and international literature and Irish tribunal reports suggest that child protection and addiction treatment practitioners can increase positive outcomes for children in care through more effective inter-agency practice. The Irish experience and the analysis in this chapter highlight significant gaps in the knowledge base related to the outcomes for this client group and that little attention has been paid to the types of professional learning required to develop interagency practice competence. Spanning these two dimensions, this chapter studies what and how social work and addiction treatment professionals learn, when doing inter-agency work from within addiction treatment and child protection agency settings. This chapter is based on a medium scale qualitative study, conducted by social work and addiction treatment practitioners and it demonstrates the potential of practitioners to transform their own practice settings. Cultural Historic Activity Theory (CHAT) methodology along with Development Work Research (DWR workshops were used in 2011 as an effective approach, that focused practitioners involved in multi-agency working on behalf of children in care on their own practice activity and gave them a systematic analytical lens with which to reflect on their shared inter-agency activity. Notably the research surfaced a tension between bureaucratic knowledge related to policy and protocol, and practitioner knowledge related to experience and practice, and a dilemma as to how to give appropriate balance

* Acknowledgment is given to co-researchers Miriam Keogh and Patricia Mc Shane, to Arbour House Assessment and Treatment Centre and North Lee Social Work Department for mandating the research project. Acknowledgment is also given to the personnel from the social work and addiction agencies and youth clients who participated in the research and Dr Kennth Burns from the Department of Applied Social Studies University College Cork for his mentoring during the project.

to the influence of both in developing practice. This tension was particularly evident in relation to policies and protocols that give essential shape and structure to inter-agency activities, such as referral procedures, case management and key working practices, these being key processes operating at the boundary between addiction treatment and social work services. A tension also surfaced related to practitioner experiences of the positive and negative dimensions of the relational field encountered in their inter-agency work. Exploring these types of tensions evidenced considerable potential to further transform interagency practice. It is argued that the existing inter-agency architecture needs to be augmented so that the optimal outcome of interagency activity effort can be achieved, and so that practice can be sufficiently dynamic in response to the evolving needs of children in care with alcohol and drug problems. Specifically, processes must be embedded in inter-agency work that tends in an ongoing way to the human relational and policy/practitioner related tensions that exist between child protection, addiction treatment and other activity systems.

Keywords: Cultural Historic Activity Theory (CHAT), Adolescent, Addiction Treatment, Social Work, Inter-agency, Development Work Research (DWR), Reflective Practice, Substance Abuse, Practitioner Research

INTRODUCTION

The Interagency Practice and Outcomes for Teenagers in Addiction and Social Services (IPOTASS research project arose from the shared aspiration of practitioners from addiction treatment and child protection agencies in the South of Ireland to explore what might contribute to improved outcomes for children in the care of the state with substance abuse problems. The project was a two-year medium scale practitioner research project that ran from March 2010 until March 2012.

There were concerns that these children fared less well than children not in the care system and this concern found resonance within the literature. There appear to be serious gaps in the Irish research and statistical literature on child protection and welfare cases that involve substance misuse (Horgan, 2011) similar to the case in the United Kingdom (Forrester and Harwin, 2006), Australia (Dawe, Harnett, and Frye, 2008) and the United States (Drabble, Osterling, Tweed, and Pearce, 2008). Although an analysis of the Child Care Dataset (HSE, 2007) indicates that circa twenty percent of Irish child welfare cases involve a family member abusing alcohol or drugs, internationally this can be anything from 40% to 80% (Drabble, 2007; Drabble, et al., 2008; Green, Rockhill, and Burrus, 2008).

After the publication of a number of reports; Commission to Inquire into Child Abuse 'Ryan Report' (Ryan, 2009), the Roscommon Child Care Inquiry (Helath Service Executive, 2010), A report based on an investigation into the implementation of Children First: National Guidelines for the Protection and Welfare of Children (Ombudsman for Childrens Office, 2010), Cloyne Report (Murphy, Mangan and O'Neill 2010) and Child Death Review Group Report (Shannon and Gibbons, 2012) there was repeated recognition of less than effective interagency working and unreliable cooperation and partnership among those who provide services for young vulnerable children and their families.

There were many cases of poor practice and failures of interacting agencies to communicate and work effectively on behalf of the children identified in these tribunal and investigation reports. A call for increased interagency practice effort currently permeates contemporary Irish policy and practice discourse. Recent policy developments such as the National Substance Misuse Strategy 2009-2016 (Department of Community Rural and Gaeltacht Affairs, 2009) 2009) and Revised Children's First Guidelines (Office of the Minister for Children and Youth Affairs, 2010), service reconfiguration such as the emergence of the new Child and Family Support Agency (Department of Children and Youth Affairs, 2012) and practice change such as the roll out of the Irish National Rehabilitation Framework (Doyle and Ivanovic, 2010), all repeat this call to improve interagency activity.

Literature on Inter-Agency Practice

In the early phase of the research timescale (April to September 2010) a systematic literature search was conducted. The primary search was limited to the English language, with open dates for all countries. The main academic databases (Socio Index, Academic Premiere, Psych Info, JSTOR, CINAHL, Science Direct, Web of Knowledge, Cochrane, OCLC First Search); selected journals (over 80); dedicated web sites to addiction or social work (over 40); and the University College Cork library catalogue were searched. The search produced over one hundred and seventy reports, journal articles or books. An early review of these documents shaped the choices of research aims, questions, methodology, method and research design that was submitted and approved by the relevant Ethics Committee[1] in January 2011.

The literature accessed was significantly weighted with policy, procedure, outcome study and good practice guideline type material as to how to develop and enhance interagency effectiveness, for example (Higgins, 2007) and (Young and Gardner, 2002). The assumptions underpinning policy enthusiasm for such work need to be considered in the light of the reviewed literature that point to flawed communication, conflict between agencies, failures to recognize and understand expertise and professional insularity as some of the contradictions and dilemmas inherent in and between organizations (Watkin, Lindqvist, Black, and Watts, 2009). Some writers, for example Sloper (2004) and Marsh (2006), indicate that there is little evidence to suggest that interagency working improves outcomes for children and families. These perspectives highlight the need to deliberate where and when such work should occur. For example in relation to the Irish context:

> Relating to the lack of theoretical basis is the vagueness regarding the rationale for interagency working. Much current thinking and practice is based on the belief that intractable and complex problems require interagency responses and that interagency working leads to collaborative advantages. However, this appears to draw more on the rhetoric of interagency approaches than on any hard evidence of its effectiveness. Interagency working is seen self-evidently as a good thing, without a full understanding of how it improves upon the existing situation or what targets it is to achieve. (Duggan and Corrigan, 2009, p. 13)

Despite assumed benefits, service providers in the Irish context continue to struggle to build effective collaborations. They have to overcome issues of mistrust, lack of understanding of other systems' values or goals, different or conflicting mandates or

[1] CREC – Clinical Research Ethics Committee for Cork Teaching Hospitals

priorities, definitions of the primary client (McAlpine, Marshall, and Doran, 2001), issues of confidentiality (Richardson and Asthana, 2006), all of which is a cause for concern in collaborative practices (Drabble, et al., 2008; Green, et al., 2008; Green, 2002).

There is substantial international literature outlining the theories, definitions, rationales, structures, models and processes including the weaknesses and challenges that practitioners face when conducting interagency work in child protection and substance misuse treatment (Drabble, et al., 2008; Duggan and Corrigan, 2009; Rubenstein, 2003; Shannon, 2009; Young and Gardner, 2002). In an attempt to work through the problems and barriers that interagency working presents to practitioners, there has been considerable work carried out on developing best practice guidelines and protocols for effective interagency working between community, voluntary and statutory services in Ireland (Blanchardstown-Equal-Initiative, 2004; HSE and C.D.T, 2009). However, there may be a risk that these permanent documentations of work practices could invite practitioners to view their work practices as fixed or a given instead, of being complex, constantly changing practice environments that needs to be open to transformation. Professionals often find themselves having to collaborate with each other and with professionals from other disciplines and services without the requisite skills to do so; they may also have varying scope in terms of including children and families in developing collaborative care plans. In fact Duggan and Corrigan (2009) state that there was a virtual absence in the literature on interagency working of the voice of the child and family. Soan (2006) advocates that if the core reason for action (the child or young person) is not at the vanguard of that action, progress and improvement will be hampered. The emphasis placed upon consensual models of interagency working, and models of good practice, may tend to under-recognise the importance of the internal tensions, dilemmas and contradictions generated by interacting systems as important mechanisms for learning and transforming practice (Engeström, Miettinen, and Punamäki, 1999). Practitioners are the pathways through whom procedural and policy mechanisms become operational. Practitioners bring with them prior learning connected to their professional background and work experiences. They also have different professional traits or perspectives in relation to the aims, roles and responsibilities and timelines (Sloper, 2004). The objectives of their joint work derive from different professional characteristics and agency priorities and remits (Glennie, 2007; Jones, Packard, and Nahrstedt, 2002). These become hugely determining factors in shaping the effectiveness of interagency working. How practitioners learn to do such work and what they are learning as they struggle to enhance their interagency practice deserves to take central focus in this chapter, as such themes remain largely under researched in this jurisdiction.

METHODOLOGY

The choice of methodology in the IPO-TASS project was influenced strongly by the "Learning in and for Interagency Working" project that was a collaboration between the Universities of Bath, Birmingham, Oxford and Longborough conducted was over a four-year period in the United Kingdom (Daniels et al., 2007), a project later replicated in Northern Ireland in 2005 (Gallagher, Kilpatrick, and Carlisle, 2005) by Queens University. Influenced by and an attempt to expand the work of the Universities in the UK and Northern Ireland, we used Activity Theory to inform research methods. Activity Theory is based on ideas that originate in the classical German philosophy of Kant and Hegel, in the influential writings of Marx and Engels, and in Lev Vygotsky's Soviet Russian cultural-historical social psychology, which was further developed by Leontiev and Luria (Engeström, et al., 1999). Activity theory calls the unit of analysis an activity system that consists of object oriented, collective and culturally mediated activity carried out by individual actors or 'subjects' or communities of practitioners (Warmington, 2008). The constituent parts of the activity systems incorporate the 'object of activity' which is what the 'subjects', the social workers and addiction treatment practitioners or the 'community of practice' are working on with children and families in interagency activity. In the activity, 'mediating artefacts'' consist of the signs, symbols, division of labour, tools and rules (physical or conceptual) that guide and shape interagency practice. Activity Theory places an emphasis on the *object* of activity in our case between child protection and addiction treatment services where professionals are often working on and aiming for sometimes differing outcomes. This allowed us to understand through dialogue, the histories of these systems, the multiple perspectives and the network of interacting activity systems involved in the lives of children and families in this setting. This offered a conceptual framework to systematically analyze the complex interactions and relationships between children in the Irish looked after system, their families, and the professionals who are working together on their behalf. It allowed us to provide a theoretical account of the interacting elements of the systems under investigation by choosing multiple members of the activity through whose interpretation; the activity was constructed and conveyed dialogically to us in individual interviews and workshops. These concepts are highlighted below in figure 1, which has been adapted from (Engeström, 2001):

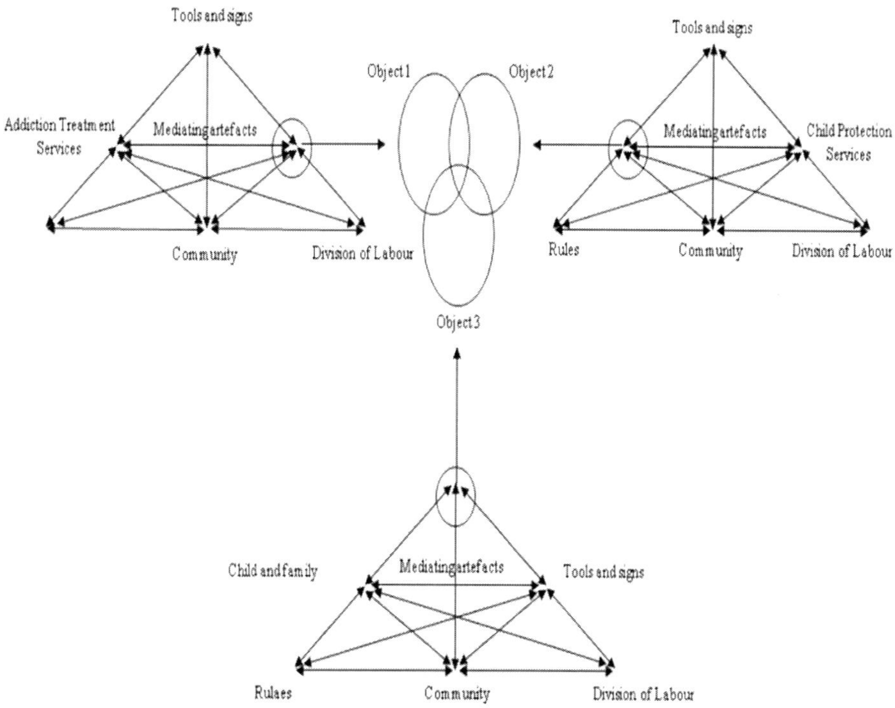

Figure 1. Interacting Activity Systems – Addiction Treatment Services, Child Protection Services and the Child and family.

Activity theory provided the analytical framework for understanding the complex process of systemic interaction but did not provide a theory of how these organizations learn when they interact. Development Work Research (DWR) or the 'Change Laboratory Method' is a methodology for applying Activity theory so as to create expansive learning in workplaces and was developed Yrjö Engeström, Professor at the Centre for Activity Theory and Developmental Work Research at the University of Helsinki in Finland. DWR aims to enquire into currently embedded workplace practices using the links between individual and social dimensions of professional learning and knowledge creation through conceptualising organisations as activity systems, working through developmental contradictions and striving towards co-configuration and knot-working (Engestrom, 2012). Co- configuration is a loosely configured type of multi-agency working where practitioners who wouldn't normally collaborate come together in support of young people and families over extended periods of time. It involves moving beyond the mass customization of services towards reflexively adapting services and practice in response to the ever-changing needs of young people and families. It involves clients in co-designing, co-constructing or co-configuring the services they need (Daniels, et al., 2007). Knot-working (Engeström, 2005) is a way of working that encourages social workers and addiction treatment professionals to come together in an unstable and fast changing, dispersed and partially improvised orchestration of collaborative types of work practices between professionals who would only occasionally interact on behalf of their clients.

The theory of expansive learning can be understood as the construction and resolution of evolving tensions, dilemmas and contradictions that are ever present in complex activity systems and are also embedded in activity when these systems interact (Engeström, 2001; Engeström, et al., 1999).

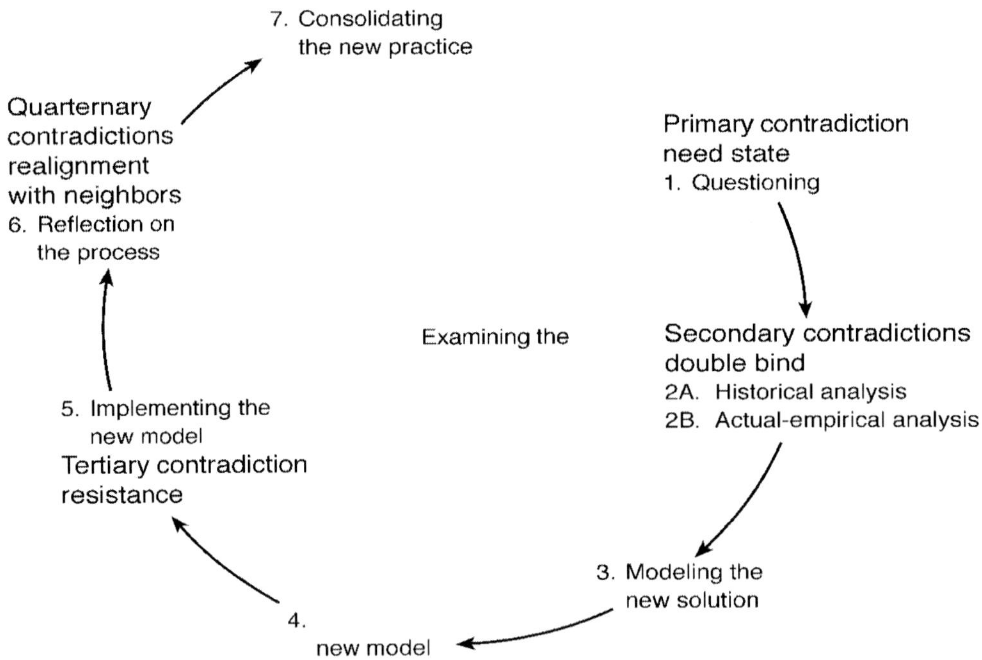

Figure 2. Expansive Learning Diagram from (Engeström, 2001).

Warmington et al. (2004) define expansive learning as meaning the ability of practitioners engaged in an activity to make intelligible, and augment, the object of activity so as they can respond to it in progressively more complex and responsive ways.

In this theoretical framework contradiction, disturbance, dissonance etc. are seen as the leveraging points for change. The methodology therefore aimed to surface and makes explicit the imbalances between components of these interacting activity systems. We employed a Vygotskian 'dual stimulation' approach in which the 'subjects' were invited to a neutral space provided by University College Cork, where practice problems were identified and introduced and participants were also provided with the tools with which to solve the practice dilemmas or a means by which they could construct the tools to solve the problems (Daniels, et al., 2007).

Data Evolution

The first data collection phase of IPOTASS involved conducting interviews with young people in care (n = 3), young people who graduated from care (n = 3) and professionals from child protection and adolescent homeless social work departments (n = 6) and professionals from adolescent outpatient and residential addiction treatment centres (n = 6) in the South of Ireland.

These interviews were transcribed and analysed (circa 15 hours of one-to-one interviews and ten hours of group workshops) and provided baseline data on the experiences of looked after children and the social work and addiction treatment professionals working together on their behalf. This surfaced many of the internal tensions; dilemmas and contradictions (n = 300) that are present in interagency practice but which from an Activity Theory perspective offered potential as the driving force of change. We engaged practitioners (n = 12) in a series of DWR workshops (n = 4) and a further validation workshop (n = 1), conducted during 2011 over a period of nine months.

Here they were provided with 'mirror' data (Warmington, et al., 2004) in the form of a PowerPoint slideshow, that contained utterances from the earlier interviews that reflected the identified tensions, dilemmas, and contradictions that were embedded in their current interagency practices.

Researchers as interventionists provided Activity Theory as a conceptual lens to analyze their work and then worked alongside these practitioners who questioned each other, contested each other's ideas and practices and learned from each other. The invitation to practitioners was to reflect on the many contradictions present in their current inter-agency practice and to embrace the possibilities that these challenges offer in terms of transforming the way they work together on behalf of children in their care. This provided us with the focus that was required to understand the way in which professionals learned with the aid of tools provided by us as researchers. Table 1.below details the data collection and analytical stages over 2011 and 2012.

The DWR phase of the research assisted these practitioners to see potentials in their shared care plans and client trajectories. The complex and ever changing work environments inhabited by professionals involved in child protection and addiction treatment requires a disposition that allows them to engage with complexity, uncertainty and varying levels of distributed expertise across the boundaries of their own organizations (Guile, 2011).

Table 1. Evolution of Data

Phase	Data Instruments	Description
Mid-Jan to mid-Feb '11	Individual Interviews	Individual structured interviews with 12 practitioners and 6 clients (16-20 yrs) – (1 hour for practitioners and 30mins for clients)
	⇩	
By mid-Mar 2011	Analysis 1	Analysis by the Research Team using Activity Theory to select from the interview data quotations that point to concept or contradiction in the inter-agency activity
	⇩	
End Mar '11	First Change Laboratory	Presentation at First Change Laboratory of Research Team selected data for discussion and exploration by practitioners using the Activity Theory tools. Laboratory session is facilitated by members of the research team as researcher/interventionist concepts (2 hour session)
	⇩	
	Analysis 2	Analysis by the Research Team using Activity Theory to select from the First Change Laboratory data (e.g. quotations) that points to concepts and contradictions emergent from the systematic discussion of inter-agency practice.
	⇩	
End Apr '11	Second Change Laboratory	Data is again presented into the session by the research team and similar to Laboratory One, systematic reflection on inter-agency practice is facilitated using the tools of Activity Theory (2 hour session)
	⇩	
	Analysis 3	Repeat of process of Analysis 2
	⇩	
End May '11	Third Change Laboratory	Repeat of process of presentation of data and systematic reflection using Activity Theory tools. (2 hour session)
	⇩	
	Analysis 4	Repeat of process of Analysis 2
	⇩	
End Jun '11	Fourth Change Laboratory	Repeat of process of presentation of data and systematic reflection (2 hour session)
	⇩	
Oct '11	Validation Workshop	Preliminary findings and emerging direction were shared with and processed with the practitioner research participants
	⇩	

Phase	Data Instruments	Description
Sept '11 to May '12	Analysis 5 Parallel Literature Review and data Analysis	Using A Grounded Theory approach, D-Analysis (developed by the UK LIW research team) and Activity Theory, analysis of the entire data transcripts from the four workshops to identify emergent concepts and learning process amongst the practitioners
	⇩	
July '12	Synthesis Workshop	Research Team workshop to synthesise the literature and data analytical processes into agreed key findings for presentation to the field

This disposition involves different levels of mastery of the personal, cognitive and affective structures of professional experiencing of interagency practice. Edwards (2009) suggests that

> Relational engagement with the knowledge and motives of other professionals in the field can produce a form of common knowledge which comprises of a partially shared understanding of what matters for other contributing experts. This knowledge can then mediate responsive professional action (p. 7).

To aim for the latter without the former is she suggests an error. Engaging practitioners in the DWR process offers potential to equip practitioners with what Engeström (1997) cited in Warmington, et al. (2004) calls 'tools for disagreement' that can take advantage of inter-professional tensions and contradictions between collaborating professionals and their clients.

Data Analysis

There were in three main stages to the data analysis process

1. Analysis of the individual interview data - Once the individual interviews were transcribed the research team analysed them using the concepts from Activity Theory. A small selection of practice tensions or contradictions were extracted from that analysis and presented to the first Change Laboratory session for reflection and analysis by the session participants.
2. Analysis between Change Laboratory Sessions - Once the Change Laboratory sessions had been transcribed the research team analysed the transcript using the concepts from Activity Theory and Expansive Learning and a small amount of data was mirrored back at the next session (some selected data from the interview stages was also be presented beyond the first Change Laboratory session). Data for mirroring back was selected that in the research team's view pointed to possible tensions or contradictions between elements of the interacting activity systems or concepts that begin to emerge related to the expansive learning cycle. That analysis was repeated between each of four scheduled sessions. Over 300 tensions within practice were coded from the one-to-one interviews using CHAT Structural coding. On each workshop occasion around 12 pieces of data were mirrored back to the participants.

3. Analysis of the entire series of Change Laboratory sessions - We took two parallel approaches to the analysis of the group transcripts with two researchers working in parallel, one using a Grounded Theory approach (Glaser, 1992; Glaser and Strauss, 1967) and the other a D-Analysis[2] discourse analysis approach. This chapter largely reports on the grounded theory lens on the data.

The grounded theory approach to the data analysis spanned six months and involved three cycles of coding before moving towards construction of a theory as to what was happening in the workshops. We acknowledge a methodological inconsistency in approach between Grounded Theory and Activity Theory in that the former aims for an emergent theory and the latter is an existent theory and as such this is perhaps a limitation. However we did take steps to manage this by ensuring that:

- The researcher engaged in the grounded theory analysis of workshop data avoided accessing the literature until the end of the process
- The same researcher avoided applying CHAT concepts while adopting the Grounded Theory approach

It was in the later stage of analysis that we merged the Grounded Theory emergent concepts with the CHAT framework. We consider that this is appropriate to the research design and allows us to present an interesting picture of what happened through the research process.

DETAILED FINDINGS

A Process of Shared Perceiving

Participants in the research DWR workshops engaged in a process of subjective and shared perception forming (perceiving or 'sense making') of their shared inter-agency practice. This is significant in that the practice activity tensions and contradictions, surfaced by the research and analysis were real practice issues that had not been processed to this point. Within the specific structure of the research context participants engaged in a meaningful real-time systematic analysis and reflection on a range of their 'experiential' practice dilemmas, an example of what (Schön, 2003) calls reflection on action. The perception forming dialogue could be categorised into statements types:

- Assumption statements (i.e. where what was said either named or belied an assumption)
- Value statements (i.e. where what was said either named or belied a value position)
- Motivational statements (i.e. where what was said conveyed the motivations of the person)

[2] The D-Analysis discourse analysis was developed in the LIW study and is detailed in (Edwards, 2009). In that study they developed a protocol to facilitate their analysis of the research data in order to "… identify evidence trails of work based learning …"

- Interpretive statements (i.e. where the person was trying to interpret or reach an understanding)
- Wondering statements (i.e. statements that conveyed the person was wondering about a topic)
- Definitional statements (i.e. where a person's statement conveyed that they had decided on an interpretation or understanding)
- Honest statements (i.e. where a person shared an honest revelation of themselves, their context or practice)
- Evidential statements (i.e. where a person gave evidence from practice experience or information)
- Expressing Feelings (i.e. where a person was naming or conveying their feeling in what they said)

Many of these types of statement relate to the inner world of the practitioner as they struggled to make sense of their experiences in respect of a number of topics of central importance in their inter-agency work. Below in detail we surface the evidence of the transformative potential of processing practitioner experiential knowledge in relation to those central topics, through

- The example of the Referral Process
- The example of the Case Management
- The example of the Client and Carer Voice
- The example of Practitioner Relationships
- The example of Inter-Agency Perspectives

The Referral Process

The process and procedures by which practitioners communicate and effect the movement of a client towards another agency, a referral, constituted a significant amount of the dialogue through the research process. There was strong evidence of divergences between what practitioners understood to be the rationale for referral processes and their perceptions as to current practice. Such was the spread and nature of these, that practitioners consider a review of the referral process as needed and that significant benefit would accrue from such a review. A case could be made for a mapping of the adult rehabilitation Framework (Doyle and Ivanovic, 2010) on to adolescent drug treatment services. There are extracts from the dialogue that support a call for clearer rehabilitation pathways for adolescent clients, clarity around professional roles, clarity around responsibilities for assessment of need and clarity of referral processes.

It was viewed that informed consent is facilitated for the client by going though the referral form with them and that this embeds a value of respectful working with a person. While it was acknowledged that referral forms are completed, clients can still arrive for many reasons without adequate informed consent:

> "I know that's something I would have been mindful of over the years, like, you identify the need, the need is very great, the kid doesn't see it in any shape or form, but yet we can start ploughing into all these different services without listening to what they really want ...we all have our own agenda as services and then ... could we work together as services to go at the pace of the client?"

Despite the existence of a largely operating referral process, informed consent, an essential component of the rationale for such processes, cannot be assumed to be present. In relation to information content it is claimed that properly completed referral forms allow for gathering of statistical information, trigger funding mechanisms, allow for prioritisation of clients, allow for matching with counsellors, and allow for commencement of a dialogue with the client at the receiving agency. Such is the imperative to convey information as a client moves towards a new service, that while problems need to be addressed, it be asserted that:

> "... Referral forms are essential, they're non-negotiable, they have to, they have to be there to keep everybody safe and to see if the person is in the appropriate ..."

That said there were many voices that placed a relative importance on the information conveyed and brought questions as to the degree that written communication can convey all the necessary practice information or nuances in particular circumstances. Ultimately at the receiving agency, commencement of a dialogue is necessary with the client, and while useful, information in forms has limitations in that regard. For one practitioner, in their experience they prioritise the first ten-minute contact with the client over lots of information on file:

> "But you're probably going to learn as much about them in those 10 minutes of speaking with them and meeting and watching their body language and what kind of a person they are. Then they have around 50 pages of referral forms, so as important as they are, just for me, again, in my opinion, they're not as hugely important but I think they would be spending a huge chunk time on ...".

While acknowledging that poorly completed forms can disadvantage clients (e.g. degree of prioritisation, matching with counsellors) there is usually an additional need on referral of a client for compilation of reports from various sources, because referral forms do not hold all the information a particular agency might compile. Further, there was also acknowledgement that there are cases, or information, for which referral forms don't seem sufficient' - there might be information about people that other people might need to know.

> "You know, you might, you know, "he's quite aggressive towards women" or "he hates men" or, you know, something like that, and you just, you think, "Well you know, if I write that down, that's also a judgement ... also with some young people and you would see, almost like a rap sheet, and you know, you might ring somebody and say, "Listen, I'm sending so-and-so to you. I know on paper he looks terrible, but when you meet him, you'll be mad about him"

Referral forms can be inconsistently filled out and cannot obviate the importance of connection and contact with people and, as a written form, cannot convey in full or adequately information that in practitioners' judgement is important.

Practitioners differ in terms of what constitutes the referral process and while largely consented to amongst practitioners, it can have different weight of importance in their respective practices. For example one practitioner found the process of going though the referral with the client, perhaps over a few sessions, as a guide to their dialogue and grounding to their practice. The referral form structure invites practitioners to slow down and reflect on achieving engagement and collaboration. It can convey the referrers' sense of client motivation/readiness for change to the receiving agency and allow sharing of concerns and experience with the client to the point of referral.

> "It reminds you as a professional that there is a need to collaborate with this young person around the referral because they have to buy into it, they have to give you the information, they have to sign up to what you are actually putting forward, so I think that's a very positive thing, and I think it, as I said already, it settles someone like me who may have a busy day, being working, you know and may at times want to get the task completed, you know, and then you look at it and you read it and you say, "Well hold on a second, let's take it a little bit easy here now and let's work on how will I engage with the person around this?"

On the other hand, while not dismissing forms, another practitioner related that

> "Sending a form was too impersonal for me, 'cos like this person might have taken great risks and had really progressed in terms of their ability to trust and to open and to name what they needed, and I felt just sending the form through the post didn't honour them, you know? So that's what I'd like to see, more of a kind of a maybe a physical handover or a, you know, or the care plan, that being transferred in a way that it doesn't just come through the door to somebody"

Fundamentally embedded within the process for practitioners is the value of respect for the client, the family and between practitioners. There was a sense that respect is conveyed when forms are diligently completed and that a properly effected referral is 'only honouring the client'. Referral forms did embed empowerment, inclusion and respect for the client and the form acted as a structure for that empowering and inclusive engagement. However, for all the strengths of the referral process and apart from inconsistencies of completion and different weighting in practice, there remained a sense that forms on their own were not sufficient to effect a referral. A fully respectful process would involve more emphasis on joint engagement with the client and families together with referrer and receiving agency at the point of referral.

Practitioners generally recognize and accept the need and rationale for a referral process. However there was a very strong emphasis in the dialogue on re-centring such a process around:

- Personal accompaniment of the client through the journey
- Embedding within the protocols, routines that make practitioner inter-relationships the priority
- Balancing the need for information with the reality of its actual usage and demands it places on practitioners in demanding work environments

- Sharing understandings of each others practice such that the rationale for the processes are understood and thus garner more practitioner consistency in their use across services

Overall there was support for a significant review of the referral processes between the agencies involved.

Case Management

Case Management also figured prominently in the dialogue, it being understood as the process by which the shared casework is both managed and co-ordinated. The dialogue around Case Management centred on a number of areas and there were differing and strong views in regard to some, notably

- Roles and Responsibilities
- Co-ordination versus management
- Existing Structures

Overall the perspectives on the themes swung between those that suggested a more contingent approach to case management and those that favoured a more fixed approach.

In relation to Roles and Responsibilities a tension existed between practitioners as to the degree any particular profession would supersede another in terms of decision making around a client. There was an assertion that there exists policy level clarity regarding 'someone' being responsible for the bigger picture and sharing it with others [i.e. the policy decision has been made that a single person be identifiable as responsible for bigger picture][2]. For example it was claimed that:

> "It's my understanding that there's ... agreement that social work have decided that it's their responsibility to be the case managers and that that's not something that our service has chosen, that was something that was put on us"

This position contrasted with the desires by practitioners for a holding of the case management roles in a more contingent, fluid and respectful ways. Practitioners understood they had different roles with clients, but where work was shared there was a heartfelt desire that the case management process be respectfully collaborative and responsive. While the importance of a central focal person was largely affirmed, it was viewed as more important that there be a focal person, than importance being placed on the particular profession that occupied the role.

> "So a co-ordinator certainly, but not, I wouldn't give them the role or the title of "case manager", that they are the ones who have to sign off on everything or whatever. Now I certainly would see a role for somebody because it's them, I think it's important that there is

[2] It is notable that in the workshops there was an unquestioned assumption that an Adult Rehabilitation Framework applied to youths. This reflected in the dialogue as a confusion amongst the practitioners as to what decisions had been taken in relation to case management roles.

somebody who is keeping an overall look on everything and that not everybody then has to be doing that, if you know what I mean, that there would be one person"

These examples capture the tension between acknowledging on one hand the need for 'sign off' by someone, and on the other hand aspiring for practice arrangements that foster balance and respect within practitioner relationships. The contrast of terms 'case co-ordination' as against 'case manager' seems to capture the balance in practice that practitioners' desire. In a sense the 'manager' dimension of case management implies a forcing of the elements together or 'make the jigsaw fit the pieces'.

While currently happening, there was a strong sense throughout the dialogue that the inter-agency architecture must robustly support regularity of engagement by professionals together with clients and that agency time priorities must facilitate these process. Such processes would facilitate

> 'Delegating tasks to particular people, I think that would help, it would improve communication and it would also, I suppose, take the spotlight off the one particular person and there could be a collective response to the needs of the child or the young person and their family'

In relation to existing structures the perspectives offered though the dialogue highlights that even within protocol/standardisation of roles, once working relationships are good practitioners find their way of working effectively. Perhaps 'case manager' has become synonymous with power of decision making/veto and this is perceived as counter-productive to 'equality' or 'equality of esteem' within professional relationships.

Confusion was certainly in evidence around the role of the Case Manager, policy decisions that seem to be dictating the direction of this, communication around roles and responsibilities and the degree of scope for a contingent arrangement to working together. There was a shared sense that case management as an approach was needed and beneficial. However, people distinguished between co-ordination and management. The assertion that there exists policy level clarity of decision regarding 'someone' being responsible for the bigger picture and sharing it with others has a sense of the decision as already having been made. The Centre for Effective Services (CES) called this single practitioner with responsibility for the client care trajectory, the 'Lead Professional' (Burke, Owens, and Ghate, 2010, p. 25). While explicating and explaining different types and models of interagency working, types of protocols and best practice around assessment, referrals and accessing appropriate services, there was no recognition in the CES document of the type of practitioner concerns that were highlighted in the research process.

Practitioners in the research had a preference for a more contingent approach to case management and they drew on their practice experience to advocate for more flexibility in roles and collaborative relationships than those envisaged under the new protocols. Here perhaps we have a core source of frustration for practitioners, and perhaps people higher in the order of management - the two worlds of practice and bureaucracy collide - practitioners react to the perceived imposed protocols that in their perspective violates a core knowledge base for them, their practice experience. There is less recognition of this type of policy and practice collision in the literature and we suggest that this is an important consideration in implementing rehabilitation pathways and strategies that require cross departmental or inter-agency collaborations.

Client and Carer Voice

Policy and practice approaches both affirm the importance of client and carer voices in the shaping of client interventions and care pathways. Through the dialogue a clear focus in the discussion related to the importance of the family and carers to recovery from substance use. Practitioners expressed a valuing of both client and carer/family voices in both shaping care planning and the development of policy. However, there was mixed evidence in the research dialogue as to the operation of that principle in practice. The dialogue largely concluding that the system needs to develop ways to support carers, particularly foster carers, to sustain their involvement and support for substance recovering youths. Foster parents, carers and families need support so as they in turn can support young people as it is in their home environment that most of the recovery work happens:

> "it's all very well bringing a person into a treatment centre or treating the person in a community base, but they go home, they go, you know, back into their own places for 99% of the rest of the time, or a lot more than 99% of the rest of the time, and that's where the real work happens ..."

Many centres and agencies emphasise strongly their family work and evidence and affirmation of this is also within the dialogue. And yet practitioners could also say that part of the problem and challenge was:

> "... part of the problem is not hearing, we don't hear their voices often enough and those issues often enough and take those things into consideration often enough and when we are putting policy together ..."

According to Kilkelly and Donnelly (2006, p. 2), in a study she conducted into the legal framework for young people's participation in the healthcare setting, "the state has a legal obligation to listen to young people in the healthcare sector and more importantly, this process in turn, can have a therapeutic effect that is worth harnessing". More specific to the area of drug and alcohol treatment, Cullen (2006)in his '*Report to HSE Regional Drug Coordinating Office – Adolescent Treatment Framework*', also suggested that in developing services targeting adolescents there should be some deeper input from teenagers themselves, their families and the communities they come from. We recognise that including young people and families in services is not without its own challenges.

The need to provide services that protect and are nurturing, offer guidance and implement appropriate controls in contrast with the clients need for autonomy around decision making in line with their level of maturity and responsibility is an inherent contradiction. However, notwithstanding these challenges professionals in the field continuously acknowledged the value in establishing partnerships with young people and carers when developing care trajectories. Care-plans that are co-constructed and involve the young person in setting goals and reviewing progress were perceived to be respectful and honouring of the client.

Practitioner Relationships

In the dialogue participants also broached their experiences of other practitioners – social work and addiction professionals. Contributions in relation to this practitioner relational topic span all of the workshop series. The experience in the workshop and the nature of the dialogue points to the need for practitioners to understand each other, and that where this is not achieved misconceptions, speculation and judging happen. People need to have opportunities to clarify their understanding; not only of each other's role, but also of their experience of the relationships they are involved in when doing shared casework.

Participants in the research workshops were making an effort to be honest about their understanding of their own and the others' practice. In effect participants made effort to work through blocks that had arisen in their relationship with the other over time. Whether these perceptions of the other were fair, accurate, merely perception or inaccurate isn't made clear but they nevertheless operated in practice and had persevered over time. The research workshop space provided the participants with an opportunity to do work that ought to be happening in real time practice settings. Given the fact that these perceptions had accumulated and endured over time a question needs to be asked as to whether the existing inter-agency architecture is adequate to process these types of relational experiences - it is either not operating optimally or its structure is not equipped to deal with these aspects of real practice experiences.

Addiction practitioners have had negative experiences of social work that lead to perceptions and speculations, for example:

- One participant, based on prior experiences speculated as to the experience a child will receive from a particular practitioner. They anticipated weeks of unreturned messages and promises being made to client and then being broken
- Another admitted they personally have a very negative view of the care system

However they also have had counter experiences that challenge their understanding, for example:

- It was acknowledged that there are co-operative and un-co-operative social workers
- Another perspective acknowledged knowing the psychological effect on people of being exposed to the traumatic lives of children and families in jeopardy

Social workers when commenting on their own professions acknowledged both the passion for their work and also their frustrations, for example:

- It was expressed that social workers 'real' interest of social work is for good outcomes for youth. The use of power (e.g. mandating treatment) is contingent on the case needs and hoped for change
- Another clarified that 'pressure of work' operates to create poor contact with other professionals and that to be overloaded is not to be a 'bad worker'
- Another acknowledged that their time was scarce for the remaining thirty percent of cases that involved significant management and inter-agency work

Social workers also held contrary perspective in relation to their addiction colleagues, for example:

- One person speculated that the fact of a high statistic for kids in care doing well would probably shock a lot of people present
- Another acknowledges that addiction professionals would understand the appropriate next steps better than their own profession, allowing for a deeper understanding to be elsewhere than themselves

Within the workshop space, change was evident when participants had the chance to express their perspectives, hear the perspectives of others and process the new experience of their engagement with the professionalism of others. It was interesting that an understanding of the crisis nature of the work and of other agencies emerged as a partial understanding and explanation of their experiences of practice. Practitioner relationships are often driven by crisis:

> "It's generally because something has become undone or has been, is unravelling, or there's some kind of issue or crisis that's, you know, and then we're all chatting to each other and we're all trying to talk to each other and we're all trying to catch each other at half-past three on a Friday afternoon"

Experiences of the other practitioner if mostly done in crisis type situations will leave us with a distorted perspective on them, as we will only have experienced them in a crisis-responsive state. While empathic speculation is helpful to redress and balance these, we will need to actually experience them in other states to rebalance the perspective fully. Creating these opportunities was acknowledged as difficult to achieve in practice.

> "I don't think we pull it out; we don't pull the time out of our working lives either. We're not very good at saying "No" and saying "No, hang on, I'm not seeing eight clients tomorrow or the six the next day" or whatever it is, I'm actually taking two hours out of my time on Thursday to sit with my peers and discuss where we're at as an agency or where we're at as a service"

This suggests practitioners and/or agencies do not prioritise reflection on practice together and its worth noting the distinction here between an individual practitioner reflecting on their own practice and practitioners together reflecting on their joint practice. Practitioners are often problem focused and need to learn to dialogue with other practitioners about process and partial change in tandem with problem solving. An interesting contrast emerged between a strength-based approach and the CHAT approach of surfacing tensions/contradictions and expansive learning approach. What practitioners dialogue about and how they do it is also important and an appropriate balance needs to be maintained in the practitioner conversations. With out a balance being placed on affirmation of what is working well, surfacing and analysing tensions and contradictions could be experienced as counter productive. Add to this an accumulation of perhaps negative experiences of others, the ever present crisis context and it is understandable as to why a culture of such transformative dialogue has not emerged.

Creating such a culture needs support towards releasing the transformative potential of inter-practitioner dialogue.

Inter-Agency Perspectives

Agency and inter-agency dynamics have a significant part in shaping the experiences of practitioners as they relate to each other when they work jointly. Practitioners are saying that significant progress is needed in this regard. As discussed above, practitioners when cast into joint working of cases with practitioners from other agencies must effort to understand the others practice and what shapes that. Each practitioner's practice is shaped significantly by the dynamics within their own agency system. When practitioners meet to work together (at the boundaries of each others agencies), each practitioners' agency dynamics are largely hidden from the other. These dynamics, especially when not fully understood by the person from the agency or where system loyalty and boundaries place limits to their visibility, lead to distortions in the struggle to understand and share practice with the other. The effects of such misunderstandings manifest as misinformation, myth making and blaming of each other. Within the research dialogue participants articulated honestly the presence of these inter-agency effects between practitioners, but also became more honest with each other about the dynamics within their own agencies. While a significant amount of information sharing was done about their agencies, with honesty about their own agency's deficits, there were also significant expressions of pride, affirmation and valuing about their home bases. This research surfaces the proposition that if people only knew the effort that goes on internally in agencies, confidence would be built through that knowing. We argue that such an effort will involve encountering self and others at a level beyond what is currently facilitated by inter-agency processes.

While it is no surprise that any group, organisation or agency will have its own culture, priorities, agendas or personalities it is interesting nonetheless to surface and elucidate that reality. This is especially so given what practitioners say in relation to them and their effect on their inter-agency work. Policy rhetoric urges effective inter-agency work and internal and intra-agency dynamics continue to hold significant sway at practitioner levels on that work. It follows that processes need to be strengthened that facilitate harnessing and mitigating the effects on practice of these agency dynamics. Practitioners in the research dialogue pointed to that reality in their work:

> "I think there's another element to the way we work I think that maybe is not acknowledged and it's that each agency have their own internal agenda which quite often is nothing to do with their ethos or what they're for and it's probably more to do with resourcing ... or whatever ..."

When this practitioner meets with others in their inter-agency work, the practitioners' own agency reality, will impact on the other practitioners, through things like degrees of responsiveness, energy experienced, commitments honoured, effectiveness of communication with others. Without making these dynamics sufficiently visible, other practitioners will experience these effects in their colleagues without knowing its cause. Making such dynamics visible however is not unproblematic. Is it permissible within the culture of the inter-agency work to talk about such dynamics?

> "And sometimes I think that those relationships are missing 'cos we, it's like as if our organisations are families and we can be, you know, we can argue among ourselves inside but when we go outside the door now, we pretend that we're getting on or, you know, ... we put up a great old show ... I think that that's a huge barrier for us in terms of working together as professionals as well because I certainly am quite uncomfortable with being as honest as I would like to be"

The problem with being open, honest and visible is that it needs to be appropriately discerned and safe enough to be so: After all it leads to vulnerability for a while. The problem with not being open, honest and visible is that agencies tend to operate in isolation of each other's reality. This dilemma is indeed a tension within inter-agency working that needs attention – how to be with other agencies in a way that is sufficiently open, honest and visible and at the same time discern what is appropriate and safe in terms of a healthy respect and keeping of an agency's rightful boundary?

The cost however is high in a system where agencies operate in relative isolation of each other - myths and misconceptions occur. For example a myth that had developed in practice: that children in the care system do not fare well. This was challenged and corrected by a participant who asserted:

> "...you were saying about watching the programme about the negativity of children in care. I suppose my primary role now is ... and to my absolute astonishment when I started doing that first, I found, because we normally talk about all the difficult problems and so on and so forth, is I found that the vast majority of children that are in care are actually doing exceptionally well, so I mean that is to put a kind of a balance on it, ... I think it is very important to state at all settings because there is a general belief system that all children in care are eventually going to do rather badly whereas my experience has been absolutely astounding..."

For whatever reason their perception had been created to the contrary, that children in the care system fared badly. Pessimism, negativity and low morale emerge by allowing such perceptions to propagate through the practice field, probably largely uninformed and ungrounded in real data.

Is not this part of the problem assuming that we 'acutely' and accurately know the deficits, or the others shortcomings, when in fact a more systemic and structured analysis is needed – moving from anecdotal to precise knowledge. That is not to say that the care system is fine and that poor outcomes do not occur. Another participant considered that poor outcomes tended not to be acknowledged in a way that allowed learning from practice experience:

> "... I think there's a shying away at times from us all like, that, like, the outcomes [poor] at times we don't acknowledge that in a way that kind of informs our practice differently ..."

It is reasonable to argue that where agencies work in relative isolation a culture is unlikely to be fostered conducive to an inter-professional and practitioner learning. In fact from the evidence we surfaced, where crisis drives practice, where practitioner and agency relational dynamics are not processed adequately a blaming culture is more likely to emerge. Through the dialogue it was acknowledged that blaming of others occurs, and myths get propagated – a degree of self-censure in this regard was advocated as a more productive and relational building approach as was a need to properly represent the reality of agencies.

We argue in this chapter that social worker and addiction professionals need to reflect and spend time communicating role boundaries and limitations. There is good evidence that insufficient is known and shared about the other agency's strategic and operational plans, training, ethos, policies, goals and objectives.

Within the research dialogue there were views that agencies more typically innovate in isolation of others and that agencies don't typically include others in co-construction of internal programmes. Practitioners we met called for less isolation by agencies in the development of the plans and programmes, more joint implementation initiatives and increasing opportunities for agency visits and joint trainings.

> "So ...but we don't necessarily kind of include each other in the building of that or in the construction of that ... I'm coming to realise it more and more is that the training part of it ... but that we do try and kind of develop languages that work for us as agencies with each other and that we kind of maybe do engage in kind of implementing some learning that makes sense for agencies to be involved in..."

However sharing of information and dialogue amongst practitioners is not the whole story! Service gaps and the engagement of management levels as to the impact of these on practice emerged as a significant issue for practitioners. An expressed aspiration for the research project for some participants was that they as practitioners might find a way to articulate their voice to other organisational levels:

> "Because it would be easy to come up with stuff that we can do, do you know, it's the stuff that is going to challenge us and challenge the higher powers ... with some ideas, you know, that challenged the powers-that-be in this research"

It was not the intention in the research project to place the emphasis on system level influences on practice, the aims were to focus on what practitioners were learning as they analysed their practice. That said it is obvious that system deficits and influences impact significantly on practice. For example system impacts create a situation where:

> "I have very rarely met anyone in Cork or any other prison that hasn't actually been in [Treatment Centre3], and actually thinking back, I think the only people that I have actually met in prison would have actually been in Limerick prison and that's only because they're from that area, everybody else would have, they would have been through [Treatment Centre] at some stage during their teens"

Clearly this is a practice knowledge that is beyond the role of an individual practitioner to address. It is knowledge that system managers need to engage with. Practitioners acknowl-

[3] Specific Treatment Centres were not identified

edged the value of empirical research towards influencing department levels and an aspiration held for this research was that it might have such an influence.

Advancing Practice and Competence

Practitioner experiences relate that good and bad things are happening within their existing inter-agency work, practice can be frustrating, agency objectives may differ and that practitioners do work to support each other and benefit the client. The surfacing of these contradictory experiential perspectives in the same practitioner workshop space created the opportunity for the participants to further explore the tensions in their practice. Based on snapshots of inter-agency activity taken in past studies and consistent with this research and activity theory tenets itself, we can confidently anticipate that inter-agency practice activity will ALWAYS have an active complement of tensions, dilemmas and contradictions embedded within its current 'status quo', and these themselves in various stages of resolution and transformation.

In reciprocal relationships with other professionals, practitioners were able to enrich their interpretations of features of their professional worlds and consider a broader range of possible responses to the ever-present contradictions embedded within their practice – they had expansively learnt. This two-fold engagement, with the expertise of their own and other professions, and the relational expertise gained through those interactions, has potential to increase these practitioners' confidence of engagement with the knowledge that underpins specialist practice and their capacity to harness 'distributed expertise' that others can contribute across local systems (Edwards, 2011).

Practitioner Competencies for Inter-Agency Practice Transformation

Notable current literature on the competencies for inter-agency working relates to the concepts of becoming reticulist practitioners (Buckley, 2011) boundary crossers (Kerosuo and Engeström, 2003) and knot-workers (Engeström, et al., 1999). Reticulists are multi-skilled practitioners who can negotiate informal networks of professionals and use influence and personality to create and recreate goals and desired outcomes. These kind of professionals can utilise personal and professional relationships, appreciate organisational power dynamics, are future oriented and can weigh up the pros and cons of different decisions made and the impact that those decision in turn have on the trajectory of the child and family. Intuitively they know when to be diplomatic, when to bargain, be convincing or confrontational and how to be strategic and tactical when required. Being skilled at advancing the interests of the organisation, and balancing those with the interests of those in their care and using discretion and tact are essential characteristics. They are able to frame and reframe dilemmas and challenges and engage with the complexities of the modern social care environment. They can elicit and communicate common sets of objectives and goals and use strategic leverages with different stakeholders in the process.

Knot-workers are professionals who are able to come together around a family in need and work with other professionals towards agreed goals, disentangle when needed, and reform again when the family needs them over differing and sometimes extended timeframes. Boundary crossers are those professionals who can come out of their institutional silos and engage with the expertise of other professionals and hold the discomfort of being outside their familiar work environment, be pedagogical in their practice and recognise the professionalism of others while learning in action from the relational experience of working on shared objects of activity.

Practitioners were asked at the individual interviews "What competencies did you find as particularly useful or needed by practitioners involved in joint practice of this kind?"

> "[a practitioner] but there isn't actually a huge emphasis on me developing myself in terms of, you know, how I engage with other agencies or how I engage with other families"

Significant competencies talked about by practitioners were: being highly organised in their case work; communication and listening skills; having an ability to process other people's perspectives; having initiative, self-awareness and a critical faculty; having an ability to hold/navigate professional, ethical, legal and procedural boundaries; discernment regarding relevant information and perspective sharing; confidence in your own assessment; having an ability and tolerance for holding tension, discomfort and difference; willingness to try new things and negotiate.

Agency placements, inter-agency training and practitioner forums/spaces were mentioned by some as means to address the other identified competence relating to developing a shared understanding of each others practice and professions. Opportunities to join up practice and create bridges, change mindsets, reflect on practice, (re)-surface experiences for reflection and advancement of learning from experience were seen as important so as to build trust and working relationships to be able to access distributed expertise and knowledge among practitioners of different services. Suggestions were made in relation to a percentage of course curricula being devoted to inter-agency work as one possible means to prepare people for what will be a significant aspect of their work.

The competencies surfaced by the research resonate strongly with those from the literature, overall suggesting that current inter-agency practice needs to advance and that the development of practitioners with the necessary expanded competencies is the key component needed to achieve this advance in practice. It is argued in this chapter that in-sufficient opportunities are created within practice to reflect together within and between agencies on joint practice and this tends to diminish collaborative efforts. The shift needed in inter-agency settings is a move away from working from role positions with each other (what am I responsible for) to one of shared responsibility (what can I contribute). As discussed earlier, having a non-crisis relationship with practitioners allows for a healthier communication and clearing of frustrations.

Participants offered ongoing training opportunities, agency visits and spaces like the one experienced in the research as structures through which the types of practice issues encountered could be processed. While shared inter-agency training models with other professionals were valued, they can be hit and miss as regards connecting with each other's work and participation can vary. Practice training placements or agency visits also offer some possibilities for shared understanding. Shared implementation of joint practice change initiatives was also offered as pathway to a shared understanding of 'what was actually implemented[4]'. It was also viewed that because of constantly changing practice environments there is an ongoing regular need for inter-agency practitioner level engagement, development or training.

In complex organisations and activities a mix of these approaches is likely to carry favour. That said they do not all have the same function and objectives. It would seem that some practitioners at least value surfacing of difference, tensions and conflicts as a means for change and moments are habitually lost and no formal structure exits to deliberately catch and look at them – hence the potential of structuring spaces such as DWR workshops into the inter-agency activity architecture - There is merit in advocating for practice reflection space to be replicated (perhaps similar to the DWR space) but on a larger scale. There was however a specific desire that management level be in agreement to meet the need to create structured spaces for practitioners.

Characteristics of Practitioner Spaces for Inter-Agency Practice Analysis and Reflection

Spaces are not created habitually in practice for practitioners and agencies to come together to dialogue and reflect together on their joint practice.

Largely inter-agency practice is characterized by inter-professional crisis encounters that are fraught, where agendas arise and where there it is likely that relationships become strained. By structuring into the practice architecture opportunities for non-crisis type encounters different types of relationships with other practitioners are facilitated. Within the workshops, characteristics of practitioner inter-agency practice analytical and reflective spaces emerged. Characteristics informed by participants' prior experiences and their experience in the workshops.

Practice change will always encounter implementation difficulties and practitioners need spaces together to carry initiatives through. Such is the importance of inter-agency practice to the effectiveness of work with clients, it was viewed that the creation of such spaces ought to have to more priority than that afforded through coffee mornings, open days and other occasions that are often over taken by case priorities. There was an interest amongst the participants to continue beyond the research context discussing ideas because of their interest in change, hearing each others perspectives and stepping outside of working to agendas. While a DWR approach to structuring such a process within the practitioner space would involve a series of more regular (monthly/bi-monthly) sessions with a facilitated process perhaps over one to two years, practitioner spaces need not necessarily follow the pattern of the DWR approach. The argument presented in this chapter is that to optimize and continually transform inter-agency practice activity the process dimension of such work needs to be given attention in the system and characteristics of an approach to that challenge are presented in Table 2.

[4] This idea is interesting because there is a literature on the demands of implementation (Fixsen, Naoom, Blase, Friedman, and Wallace, 2005)

Table 2. Characteristics of a practitioner reflective space

Practice Analytical, Reflective Spaces	Extracts from Dialogue
Purpose Create a practitioner inter-agency space that is 'non-crisis' in character (i.e. there being no immediate pressing needs of a child lessens the immediacy of pressure and reactivity in the practitioner encounters) Facilitate an inter-practitioner dialogue that is 'hats off', affirmative, reflective, strengths based Put issues on the table and proposals to upper levels to contrast the top-down dynamics of many change initiatives	"... there will be some spaces, like I'd like to able to meet colleagues and professionals working in the area in a non-crisis situation because when I am meeting somebody in a crisis situation, everybody is fraught and everybody has an agenda and you are more likely to dislike somebody and it becomes personalised when it's completely unnecessarily but that's the only interaction you have with them" "But as I think, like, I think there is an opportunity to do something like that, to actually put the proposals forward and create a forum of all the disciplines, you know, including the childcare and including the families ..."
Motivation for participation – passion for change A quality of the space was the 'attitude' [presence] of participants in a way very different from the usual practice encounters, in that it facilitated sharing of each others passion for the work, such as values, energy, honesty, feeling	"I think also the attitude that we bring to this group is different because if you think, people volunteered to participate in this research because, you know, we would like to see some changes and positive effects in this so if we come to this group, we are willing to, you know, throw ideas on the table and discuss them, and we are open to look at other services and how they operate and take their points on board because there is no other agenda at work..."
Process and Location Structure process for the reflection and analysis with an importance given to the 'how of facilitation' – the facilitation by the researchers was perceived as neutral and purposeful A quality of the research space was the perceived neutrality of its 'physical location'	"...its physical locations and .... How its facilitated" "I think there's a neutrality about this space too" (in a University and not an agency)
Mandate or Sponsorship Line management would need to be approached for mandate for the 'space' or give it sponsorship Both practitioners and managers need to prioritise practitioner reflective spaces in inter-agency work	"well I think it needs to be sanctioned by or requested by senior management for this to happen ... I suppose the idea would be coming from something like this but getting somebody on board then at a much senior level to say, "Yes, that's a very good idea" and so therefore they want this to happen and they want feedback as well ... "
Fostering Practice Relationships and Communication Desire for a supportive environment amongst practitioners to facilitate communication (e.g. if safety was an issue in a 'safer' research setting it must be a real inhibitor in practice!)	"That's kind of, in many ways, like you know, if this is the theme that emerges in this group setting which is meant to be non-threatening and still people have a problem communicating so it kind of highlights to me that there must be a bigger problem communicating in an interagency setting that really needs to be spelt out ..."

CONCLUSION

The IPO-TASS project was conducted in a similar environment to that faced by the researchers in the LIW study in the UK in 2005. As we stated, currently social practice in the Irish setting is being significantly influenced by policy, evidence based practice and institutional level discourse and developments. Concurrent with reports into the system deficits, system restructuring is imminent for child protection social workers and addiction treatment, and practice will be influenced by the roll out of the National Rehabilitation Framework (Doyle and Ivanovic, 2010), initially for adult services, but likely eventually to significantly shape adolescent addiction services. One of the key recommendations in the framework document asserts that "rehabilitation can only be delivered effectively through inter-agency working based on a continuum of care that operates within the context of enhanced case management and a quality standards framework" (p. 8). That said, the report also acknowledges that interagency working is fraught with difficulties and this resonates with the discourse in this chapter. Economic constraints will further impact on service provision and are likely to prompt further reconfigurations of services and consequent implications for practice. In short, inter-agency practice activity is occurring within systems that are facing dramatic change.

The points surfaced in this chapter in relation to referral process, case management, practitioner relationships and greater inclusion of client and carer have considerable implications for rehabilitation pathways that are highly dependent on interagency working for client progression. We argue that for an optimal implementation and transfer into the inter-agency practice paradigm of initiatives such as the rehabilitation framework it will be necessary to meaningfully engage with the types of issues surfaced in this chapter. The central thesis of this chapter and the evidence from the research is that for the activity systems to be transformed in an ongoing way towards client needs, the existing inter-agency architecture must be augmented by a structure that facilitates the ongoing processing of practitioner experiences of their shared work. The proposed structures for inter-agency practitioner reflective spaces would have characteristics consistent with those outlined in this chapter and our conclusion is that the DWR approach is worth implementing further into the system.

REFERENCES

Blanchardstown-Equal-Initiative. (2004). *Blanchardstown Equal Inter-agancy Inititive - Making Inter-Agency Protocols Work.* Retrieved from http://www.bap.ie/dloads /Making_Inter-agency_Protocols_Work_Oct_ 2004.pdf on 29/9/2010

Buckley, H. (2011). *Supporting Parents, Protecting Children.* Paper presented at the Open Day on 02/09/2011, Bessborough Centre, Cork.

Burke, K., Owens, S., and Ghate, D. (2010). *Learning from experience to Inform the Future - Findings emerging from the initial phase of the Children's Services Committees in Ireland.* Dublin: Centre for Effective Services.

Cullen, B. (2006). *Report to HSE Regional Drug Coordinating Office – Adolescent Treatment Framework.* Dublin: Addiction Research Centre T.C.D.

Daniels, H., Leadbetter, J., Warmington, P., Edwards, A., Martin, D., Middleton, D., Popova, A., Apostolov, A., and Brown, S. (2007). Learning in and for multiagency working. *Oxford Review of Education, 33*(4), 521-538.

Dawe, S., Harnett, P., and Frye, S. (2008). Improving outcomes for children living in families with parental substance misuse: What do we know and what should we do? *Child Abuse*

Prevention, 29. Retrieved from http://www.aifs.gov.au/nch/pubs/issues/issues29/ issues29.pdf on 20/5/2010

Department of Children and Youth Affairs. (2012). *Report of the Task Force on the Child and Family Support Agency.* Dublin: Government Publications.

Department of Community Rural and Gaeltacht Affairs. (2009). *National Substance Misuse Strategy.* Dublin: Department of Community Rural and Gaeltacht Affairs.

Doyle, J., and Ivanovic, J. (2010). *National Drugs Rehabilitation Framework Document - National Drugs Rehabilitation Implementation Committee.* Dublin: Health Services Executive.

Drabble, L. (2007). Pathways to Collaboration: Exploring values and collaborative practice between child welfare and substance abuse treatment fields. *Child Maltreatment, 12*(1), 31-42.

Drabble, L., Osterling, K., Tweed, M., and Pearce, C. (2008). *Pathways to Collaboration Factors That Help and Hinder Collaboration Between Substance Abuse and Child Welfare Fields.* Retrieved from http://www.csulb.edu/projects/ccwrl/Drabble_II.pdf on 20/5/2010

Duggan, C., and Corrigan, C. (2009). *A Literature Review of Inter-Agency Work With a Particular Focus on Children's Services.* Dublin: Children Act Advisory Board.

Edwards, A. (2009). *Improving inter-profesional collaborations : multi-agency working for children's wellbeing.* London:New York: Routledge.

Edwards, A. (2011). Building common knowledge at the boundaries between professional practices: Relational Agency aand realtional expertise in systems of distributed expertise. *International Journal of Educational Research, 50*(1), 33-39.

Engeström, Y. (1997). Coordination, cooperation and communication in the courts: expansive transitions in legal work. In M. Coles (Ed.), *Mind, Culture and Activity: seminal papers from the laboratory of comparative human condition* (pp. 369-388). Cambridge University Press: Cambridge.

Engeström, Y. (2001). Expansive Learning at Work: Toward an activity theoretical reconceptualization. *Journal of Education and Work, 14*(1), 133-156.

Engeström, Y. (2005). *Activity Theory and Expansive Design.* Retrieved from http://projects final.interactionivrea.org/2004-2005/SYMPOSIUM%202005/communication%20material/ACTIVITY%20THEORY%20AND%20EXPANSIVE%20DESIGN_Engestrom.pdf accessed 20/11/2012

Engestrom, Y. (2012). *Center for Activity Theory and Developmental Work Research*, from http://www.edu.helsinki.fi/activity/people/engestro/ accessed 24/10/2012.

Engeström, Y., Miettinen, R., and Punamäki, R. (Eds.). (1999). *Perspectives on activity theory* Cambridge: University Press.

Fixsen, D. L., Naoom, S. F., Blase, K. A., Friedman, R. M., and Wallace, F. (2005). Implementation Research: A Synthesis of the Literature *FMHI Publication 231.* Tampa, FL: The National Implementation Research Network, University of South Florida, .

Forrester, D., and Harwin, J. (2006). Parental substance misuse and child care social work: findings from the first stage of a study of 100 families. *Child and Family Social Work, 11*(4), 325-335.

Gallagher, T., Kilpatrick, R., and Carlisle, K. (2005). *'The Setting up of Learning in and for Interagency Working in Northern Ireland'.* Paper presented at the 6th Annual Conference of the Teaching and LearningResearch Programme, Warwick, 28-30 November 2005.

http://www.academia.edu/965433/The_setting_up_of_Learning_in_and_for_Interagency_Working_in_Northern_Ireland

Glaser, B. (1992). *Basics of grounded theory analysis : emergence vs. forcing*. Mill Valley, CA: Sociology Press.

Glaser, B., and Strauss, A. (1967). *The discovery of grounded theory : strategies for qualitative research*. N.Y. : Hawthorne.

Glennie, S. (2007). Developing interprofessional relationships: tapping the potential of inter-agency training. *Child Abuse Review, 16*(3), 171-183.

Green, B. L., Rockhill, A., and Burrus, S. W. M. (2002). What Helps and What Doesn't: Providers Talk about Meeting the Needs of Families with Substance Abuse Problems Under ASFA. *NPC Research*. Portland.

Green, B., Rockhill, A., and Burrus, S. (2008). *The role of interagency collaboration for substance-abusing families involved with child welfare* (Vol. 87(1)): NPC Research, Portland, OR.

Guile, D. (2011). Learning at the boundary: A commentary. *International Journal of Educational Research, 50*(1), 55-61.

Health Service Executive, and Community Drug Teams. (2009). *Inter agency addiction protocols - Blanchardstown Parts One and Two*. Retrieved from http://www.lenus.ie/hse/handle/10147/120513 on 20/11/2012.

Health Service Executive. (2007). *Children and Families – Analysis of Childcare Dataset 2007*. from PCCC, Performance-Management-Unit [accessed online on 18/5/2010 on HSE Intranet]

Health Service Executive. (2010). *Roscommon Child Care Case - Report of the Inquiry Team to the Health Service Executive*. Dublin: HSE.

Higgins, D. J. (2007). *Cooperation and coordination: An evaluation of the Family Court of Australia's Magellan case-management model.* : Canberra: Family Court of Australia [accessed online at http://www.aifs.gov.au/institute/pubs/magellan/magellan.pdf on 20/5/2010].

Horgan, J. (2011). P*arental Substance Misuse: Addressing its Impact on Children - A Review of the Literature*. Dublin: National Advisory Committee on Drugs (NACD).

Jones, L., Packard, T., and Nahrstedt, K. (2002). Evaluation of a training curriculum for Inter-Agency Collaboration. *Journal of Community Practice, 10*(3), 23-40.

Kerosuo, H., and Engeström, Y. (2003). Boundary crossing and learning in creation of new work practice *Journal of Workplace Learning, Vol. 15* (7/8), 345 - 351.

Kilkelly, U., and Donnelly, M. (2006). *The Childs right to be heard in the healthcare setting: Perspectives of children, parents and healthcare professionals*. Dublin: Office of the Minister of Children.

Marsh, P. (2006). Promoting Children's Welfare by Inter-Professional Practice and Learning in Social Work and Primary Care. *Social Work Education, 25*(2), 148-160.

McAlpine, C., Marshall, C., and Doran, N. (2001). *Combining Child Welfare and Substance Abuse services: A blended model of intervention* (Vol. 80(2)). Rockville, MD: Child Welfare League of America.

Murphy, Y. Mangan, I. and O'Neill, H. (2010). *Report by Commission of Investigation into Catholic Diocese of Cloyne*. Ireland: Department of Justice and Equality.

Office of the Minister for Children and Youth Affairs. (2010). *Revised Children's First Guidelines - National Guidelines for the Protection and Welfare of Children*. Dublin: Government Publication.

Ombudsman for Childrens Office. (2010). *A report based on an investigation into the implementation of Children First: National Guidelines for the Protection and Welfare of Children*. Dublin, Ireland Ombudsman for Children's Office.

Richardson, S., and Asthana, S. (2006). Inter-agency Information Sharing in Health and Social Care Services: The Role of Professional Culture. *British Journal Of Social Work, 36*(4), 657-669.

Rubenstein, G. (2003). Safe and Sound: Models for Collaboration between the Child Welfare and Addiction Treatment Systems. (Legal Action Center, Arthur Liman Policy Institute). Retrieved from http://www.eric.ed.gov/ on 13/5/2010.

Ryan, S. (2009). *Report of the Commission to Inquire into Child Abuse Implementation Report*. Dublin: The Stationary Office.

Schön, D. (2003). *The reflective practitioner : how professionals think in action*. Aldershot: Arena.

Shannon, G. (2009). *Third Report of the Special Rapporteur on Child Protection - A Report Submitted to the Oireachtas*. Dublin.

Shannon, G., and Gibbons, N. (2012). *Report of Independent Child Death Review Group*. Dublin: Government Publications.

Sloper, P. (2004). Facilitators and barriers for co-ordinated multi-agency services. *Child: Care, Health and Development, 30*(6), 571-580.

Soan, S. (2006). Are the needs of children and young people with social, emotional and behavioural needs being served within a multi-agency framework? *Support for Learning, 21*(4), 210-215.

Warmington, P. (2008). *Learning in and for multiagency working*.

Warmington, P., Daniels, H., Edwards, A., Brown, S., Leadbetter, J., Martin, D., and Middleton, D. (2004). *Learning in and for interagency working - Interagency Collaboration: a review of the literature*. Retrieved from http://www.education2.-bham.ac.uk/documents/research/liw/Interagency_collaboration_review.doc on 14/7/2010.

Watkin, A., Lindqvist, S., Black, J., and Watts, F. (2009). Report on the Implementation and Evaluation of an Interprofessional Learning Programme for Inter-Agency Child Protection Teams. *Child Abuse Review, 18*(3), 151-167.

Young, N., and Gardner, S. (2002) Navigating the Pathways: Lessons and Promising Practices in Linking Alcohol and Drug Services with Child Welfare. *Technical Assistance Publication (TAP) Series 27*. Rockville, MD: SAMHSA Publications.

In: Drug Use and Abuse
Editor: Marie Claire Van Hout

ISBN: 978-1-62618-232-5

Chapter 4

THE FUTURE OF HONG KONG'S ANTI-DRUGS CAMPAIGN: PROSPECTIVE PRACTITIONERS' VIEWS ON ENGAGING IN DRUG ABUSE WORK, ATTITUDES TOWARD YOUNG DRUG USERS AND SATISFACTION WITH DRUGS EDUCATION

Kevin Kwok-yin Cheng, Henry Wai-hang Ling and Wing Hong Chui*

Department of Social Work and Social Administration, The University of Hong Kong

ABSTRACT

In the past decade, there has been growing concern about the rise of substance abuse, particularly among young people, in Hong Kong. The Hong Kong Government has adopted a holistic approach to tackling this problem. Social workers from government departments and non-governmental organizations, hospitals that deliver treatment programs for drug abusers, and primary and secondary schools have all been enlisted to prevent drug abuse and rehabilitate drug abusers. Looking toward the future, the next generation of social workers, health care workers, and teachers must be equipped to deal with the increasing challenges of drug abuse. This chapter provides an overview of the drug abuse problem in Hong Kong and the preventative and treatment services that are available. A recent exploratory study that measured the intentions of college majors (N = 721) in social work, nursing, and education to engage in drug abuse work, their attitudes toward drug users, and their satisfaction with the drug education provided by their respective institutions is also reported. The results of this study indicated that social work majors have the greatest intention to engage in drug abuse work and that their attitudes toward drug users are most positive. Conversely, teaching majors have the least intention to engage in drug abuse work, are more negative toward young drug users, and are least

* Corresponding Author. Associate Professor, Department of Social Work and Social Administration, The Jockey Club Tower, The Centennial Campus, The University of Hong Kong, Hong Kong SAR. Email: ericchui@hku.hk.

satisfied with the education and training provided by their institutions. The views of these prospective practitioners provide insight on how substance abuse treatment will take shape in the near future in Hong Kong.

Keywords: Anti-drug campaign, attitude toward young drug abusers, training satisfaction, social work students, nursing students, teacher education students, Hong Kong

INTRODUCTION

The issue of drug abuse, particularly among young people, is a topic of public concern in Hong Kong. Over the past years, the Hong Kong Government has initiated various strategies to tackle this issue. Besides more punitive responses from law enforcement agencies, there have been increased efforts, in co-operation with other agencies, to treat, prevent, and reverse the trend of illegal drug use among young people. These efforts include counseling through social workers, clinical treatments in hospitals, and education campaigns in primary and secondary schools.

This chapter begins by providing an overview of the drug abuse trend in Hong Kong and the holistic approach adopted by the Government, along with other agencies, in response to the rising substance abuse problem among adolescents. It then reports on a recent exploratory study that measured the views of college majors in social work, nursing, and education toward serving drug users and their perceptions of drug abusers and education/training on drugs-related topics. It is felt that college majors in these areas represent the future generation of practitioners who will be directly engaged in work with drug abusers, specifically young drug abusers, therefore their views and attitudes are paramount in shaping future efforts in Hong Kong's anti-drug abuse strategy.

DRUG ABUSE IN HONG KONG: AN OVERVIEW

A drug abuser is defined by the Hong Kong Central Registry of Drug Abuse (CRDA) as

> a person who is known or suspected to have taken any kind of substances in the last four weeks of the time of reporting, irrespective of the number of takings, and the substances harms or threatens to harm the physical or mental health or social well-being of an individual, in doses above or for periods beyond those normally regarded as therapeutic (Narcotics Division, 2012a, p.4).

According to the latest figures published by CRDA, the number of reported drug abusers in Hong Kong decreased from 18,513 in 2001 to 13,252 in 2006, bounced back to 14,241 in 2008, and then trailed off to 11,469 in 2011. Like their adult counterparts, the numbers of young drug abusers, defined as those aged under 21, has also fluctuated over the past several years. In 2006, the number of reported young drug abusers was 2,578; the number reached a peak of 3,474 in 2008 and then declined to 2,811 and 2,006 in 2010 and 2011 respectively (Narcotics Division, 2012a). Nevertheless, the public is very concerned about young peoples' involvement with illicit substances. Approximately 38.0% of drug abusers reported that they started to use illegal substances between the ages of 12 and 15. The mean age of first drug use was 15 for young drug abusers and 18 for all drug abusers, including adults (Narcotics Division, 2012a).

The landscape of the types of drugs popular among drug abusers in Hong Kong has also changed. Since 2007, the number of psychotropic substance abusers (PSAs) has overtaken the number of abusers of heroin, which had traditionally been the most common drug of choice for drug abusers. Currently, for young drug users, the most popular type of psychotropic substance is ketamine, or, as it is known locally in Hong Kong, 'Little K' (K仔), with the second most popular being methamphetamine, or ice, followed by cocaine. In 2011, the number of ketamine drug abusers stood at 3,600 (79.9% of all young drug abusers) and the number of ice users at 528 (22.0%). Another major concern is that the number of multiple drug abusers, meaning people who have taken more than one type of drug in a particular year, the majority of whom abuse two types of drug on the same occasion, has been on the rise (Narcotics Division, 2012a).

The shift from heroin to psychotropic substances has been attributed to the growing dance club scene that began to emerge in Hong Kong in the mid-1990s (Laidler, 2005). This follows the global trend in dance club culture that started in many Western societies and led to recreational drug use among adolescents (Hunt and Evans, 2003). Taking advantage of this growing market, local businesses in Hong Kong converted existing karaoke bars and restaurants into dancing venues. In such venues, young people are able to find a place to "[flee] the home, however temporarily, to engage in a form of leisure – to socialize, listen to music, search for euphoria, and transcend the mundane realities of everyday life, exert their energy through dance, and use alcohol or drugs" (Laidler, 2005, p.1271). Whereas heroin is traditionally associated with lower working class males, drugs such as ketamine or ecstasy represent a more youthful trendy culture (Laidler, 2005). Indeed, most young drug abusers indicated that the reasons for their drug use are due to peer influence, to relieve boredom, and curiosity (Laidler, 2005; Narcotics Division, 2012a).

Compared with other international cities, Hong Kong is the only region where ketamine is the predominate drug of choice for young drug abusers. Laidler and Hunt (2008) posit possible reasons for this phenomenon. First, as noted, the sharp increase in dance venues both in Hong Kong and across the border in Shenzhen, Mainland China, has made ketamine accessible to young people from a range of social classes, especially as it is more affordable than other types of drugs. Second, young drug users do not regard ketamine as addictive, particularly in small dosages. Ketamine is seen as a substance that relieves the stress and boredom of everyday life and allows the user to 'float' or 'feel free.' Ketamine is not limited to the dance scene as it is a drug that is relatively easy to carry and inhale. Over 95% of ketamine users reported sniffing as the most popular method of inhaling the substance (Narcotics Division, 2012a).

Obviously, the perception that ketamine use is harmless is incorrect. In a recent review of 233 hospital cases involving ketamine use in Hong Kong, it was found that most patients experienced impaired consciousness (45%), abdominal pain (21%), lower urinary tract symptoms (12%), and dizziness (12%) (Ng, Tse, Ng, and Lau, 2010). In another review of hospital cases of street ketamine users in Hong Kong, it was observed that drug abusers who exhibited lower urinary tract symptoms also displayed abnormalities in their bladders (Chu et al., 2007). Needless to say, ketamine abuse, like other substance abuse, can have profound adverse effects that severely hamper a person's quality of life.

A Holistic Approach to Tackling Drug Abuse

Given the mounting concerns about young drug abusers, the Chief Executive of Hong Kong, in his policy address in 2007, commissioned the Secretary for Justice to lead an inter-departmental task force to tackle the drug abuse problem in Hong Kong "from a holistic perspective" (Office of the Chief Executive, 2008). The said task force reported that the anti-drugs strategy in Hong Kong follows a five-pronged approach: preventive education and public awareness; treatment and rehabilitation; legislation and law enforcement; cooperation with external bodies, such as authorities in Mainland China and around the world; and further research (Task Force on Youth Drug Abuse, 2008). Here, we focus on the first two approaches.

In the summer of 2008, a territory-wide campaign was launched under the slogan of "No Drugs, No Regrets. Not Now, Not Ever" to educate the public on the consequences of drug abuse. Pop singers and television programs depicting real stories of drug abusers were used as part of anti-drug advertisements (Task Force on Youth Drug Abuse, 2008). Preventive strategies are arguably most evident in secondary school settings, specifically through the controversial use of drug testing. Originally set to be initiated in the 2009-2010 academic year, public outcries over the admission of young drug abusers into hospital emergency departments led to an earlier pilot of a school-based drug testing scheme in the secondary schools of Tai Po District in mid-2009 (Cheung and Lam, 2009). Drug testing includes urine sampling and hair sampling. There are concerns over the scheme including privacy issues, the consent of students and parents, the resources available to carry out the scheme, and the overall effectiveness of drug testing as a preventive strategy. Reviews of overseas drug testing initiatives found school-based drug testing to be ineffective in tackling drug abuse (see Cheung and Lam, 2009; Shek, 2010). During the pilot scheme, 2,495 secondary school students were randomly selected, with 1,975 taking the test in the initial one-year trial period; no confirmed cases of drug abuse were found (*The Standard*, 2010).

The Government is set on implementing drug testing in all secondary schools in Hong Kong (*The Standard*, 2010). However, the Task Force on Youth Drug Abuse (2008) noted that

> many teachers are not that well-equipped with knowledge and skills in delivering drug education to students and handling drug cases effectively. The school management may also be in need of expertise, resources and support from the outside to put in place the right approach and protocol of dealing with antidrug matters on campus (p.46).

Social workers and health care professionals (i.e. doctors and nurses) are at the forefront of the treatment and rehabilitation of drug abusers. In terms of treatment programs, a wide range of interventions exists for different types of young drug abusers with varying circumstances and backgrounds. These can be generally categorized into five types of intervention programs. First, community-based counseling services are provided by the Social Welfare Department (SWD). These services are aimed at assisting drug abusers to abstain from their habits by providing them with relevant information and counseling; 11 of these counseling centers are geared toward psychotropic substance abusers. Medical staff members are on hand in the centers to provide preliminary medical treatment. Second, substance abuse clinics (SACs), which are run by the Hospital Authority (HA), are available for more serious cases. These clinics provide medical treatment, counseling, and even psychotherapy to drug abusers who have psychiatric problems. SACs receive referrals from community-based counseling centers and other health care providers. Third, there are 20 methadone clinics around Hong Kong that provide a service for opiate dependent persons on an outpatient basis. These clinics operate on a voluntary basis for drug dependent people who choose to substitute methadone for drugs in order to help them reduce their cravings. Fourth, there are 40 residential drug treatment centers, rehabilitation centers, and halfway houses that are maintained by 17 non-governmental organizations (NGOs). Half of these are subvented by either the SWD or the Department of Health (DH). These centers offer a variety of different programs for different people. Lastly, there are drug addiction treatment centers (DATCs) run by the Correctional Services Department (CSD) for offenders who are found guilty before a court of law for offenses punishable by imprisonment and who are found to be addicted to drugs (Narcotics Division, 2012b). In addition, social workers and nurses are also a part of the school-based drug testing scheme mentioned above.

Given the variety of personnel, such as social workers, health care professionals and teachers, engaged in the anti-drugs campaign in Hong Kong, there is a need for training to be provided for these workers. Such training has begun to be implemented. For instance, the HA organized a seminar in 2010 that targeted these professionals to enhance their knowledge of different treatment strategies (Narcotics Division, 2012b). A Beat Drugs Fund was set up in 1996 by the Hong Kong Government to fund an assortment of anti-drugs projects by various organizations. In 2010, the Government enhanced the fund by adding an additional HK$3 billion to the capital outlay of HK$350 million. One of the approved projects in 2010 was a training program for social work students organized by the Hong Kong Social Workers Association. This project include workshops on addiction counseling and a practice resource directory (Narcotics Division, 2012c). Starting from the 2008–2009 academic year, NGOs commissioned by the Narcotics Division (ND) provided about 364 on-site training programs for teachers in both primary and secondary schools (Narcotics Division, 2012b).

METHODS

In order to gain an understanding of the attitudes of prospective practitioners toward young drug abusers and the idea of working with them, we conducted an exploratory study surveying tertiary students from social work, nursing, and education majors. Previous studies observed that it would be useful to measure attitudes on certain issues by college majors in the respective field, such as views of criminal justice issues by criminal justice majors, because they represent the next generation of practitioners (Mackey, Courtright, and Packard, 2006). Since the anti-drugs campaign in Hong Kong adopts a holistic approach that involves personnel from a range of expertise, including social work, health, and education, we adopted the same logic and felt that it would be imperative to measure the attitudes of these prospective practitioners.

Participants

This study was conducted as a joint effort between the Hong Kong Social Workers Association and the University of Hong Kong. Students of the three majors from 14 tertiary institutions in Hong Kong were invited to participate in the study in 2012.

A purposive sampling was utilized to ensure sufficient numbers of participants; 900 questionnaires were distributed, and in the end, 721 completed questionnaires were collected by the Hong Kong Social Workers Association.

The response rate was 80.1%, which was a satisfactory level. Prior to the commencement of the questionnaire study, the students were assured that their anonymity and the confidentiality of the data were guaranteed and that they could withdraw from the study anytime if they so desired without any consequences.

The sample was comprised of 383 social work majors (mean age = 24.00), 198 nursing majors (mean age = 22.15), and 135 education majors (mean age = 20.47). The majority of the participants were females (n = 480), with males making up slightly less than a quarter of the sample (n = 143).

The composition of the study sample by majors and measured in percentages is presented in Figure 1, and the composition of the sample by gender is presented in Figure 2.

We were interested in assessing the differences between the three majors in order to determine if there were any differences between the three groups in terms of their intentions to serving drug users in the future, their attitudes toward young drug abusers, and their evaluations of whether their schools or NGOs provided sufficient education and training on drugs-related matters.

Therefore, a series of one-way analysis of variance (ANOVA) were performed using SPSS v.19 for Windows.

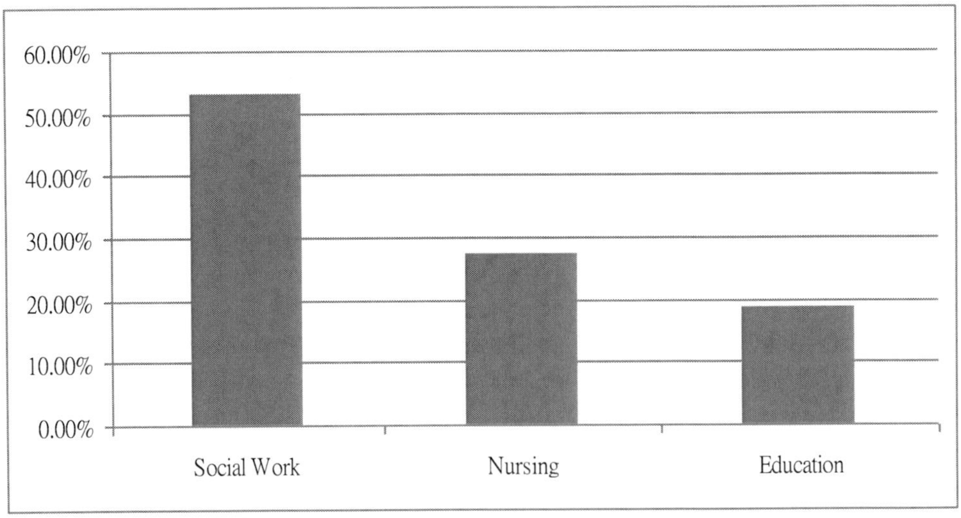

Figure 1. Sample of the Study by Majors (Percentage).

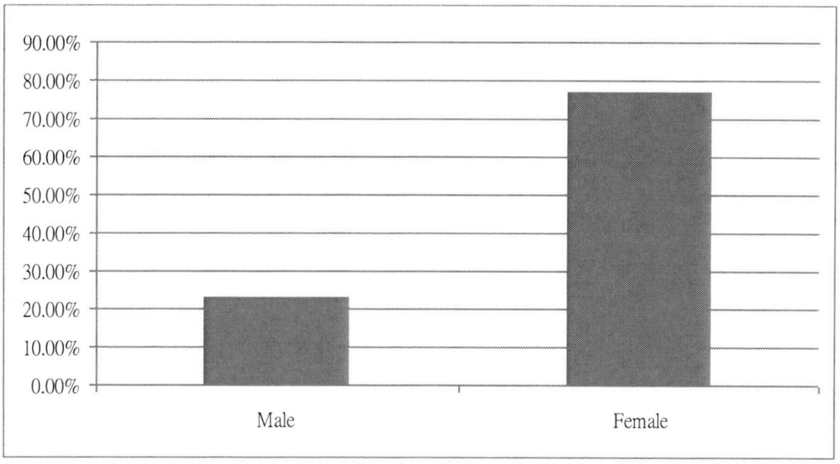

Figure 2. Gender of the Respondents.

Measures

Theory of planned behavior. The theory of planned behavior (Ajzen, 1991) is based on the notion that intentions to perform certain activities can be predicted from the potential participant's attitudes toward the behavior, subjective norm, and perceived behavioral control. It is a popular model for predicting certain behaviors. Over a hundred studies have used the theory of planned behavior to predict various behavioral outcomes, including problem gambling (Wu and Tang, 2012), weight control (Povey, Conner, Sparks, James, and Shepherd, 2000), condom use (Schaalma, Kok, and Peters, 1993), doing exercise (Godin, Valois, and Lepage, 1993; Norman and Smith, 1995; Yordy and Lent, 1993) and volunteerism (Warburton and Terry, 2000). As it was found in previous works that the subscale perceived behavioral control demonstrated poor reliability (Povey, Conner, Sparks, James, and Shepherd, 2000), we changed perceived behavioral control to questions pertaining to self-efficacy, as recommended in the literature (Greenslade and White, 2005; Schaalma, Kok, and Peters, 1993; Terry and O'Leary, 1995). The revised model of the theory of planned behavior is presented in Figure 3.

The first factor, attitudes toward the behavior, refers to the evaluation of the potential participant as to whether the behavior in question is positive or negative.

The subjective norm factor refers to the social pressure to conduct the behavior (e.g. "Most people who are important to me would approve of me serving drug users in the future"). Lastly, self-efficacy is the perceived control that one has over the behavior in question (e.g. "I am confident that I could serve drug users in the future"). The achievement of actually performing the behavior is, in turn, predicated upon the intention to perform the said behavior. An additional three questions measured the participant's intentions (e.g. "It is likely that I will serve drug users in the future"). In this study, we modified the wordings of Greenslade and White's (2005) questionnaire that was used to predict behavior in participating in volunteer work using the theory of planned behavior. We replaced intentions regarding and attitudes toward volunteering with intentions regarding and attitudes toward serving drug users. For example, the original item "It is likely that I will engage in three or more hours of volunteer work per week during the next month" was modified to "It is likely that I will engage in work to serve drug users in the future." Each item was measured on a 7-point Likert scale ranging from 1 (strongly disagree) to 7 (strongly agree).

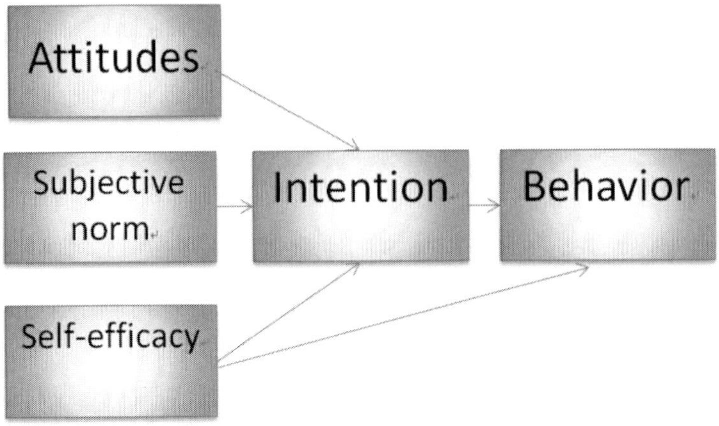

Figure 3. Model of Theory of Planned Behavior.

Chinese Youth Attitudes toward Young Drug Users scale. The Chinese Youth Attitudes toward Young Drug Users scale (Chui and Chan, 2012) is a recent instrument that was developed specifically for the Hong Kong Chinese context. The items of the scale were developed through focus groups with 26 not-at-risk and at-risk (i.e. had come into contact with the juvenile justice system) adolescents. The scale was refined through exploratory factor analysis using responses from 137 secondary school students and was subsequently reduced to 12 items. These items are divided into five factors. The subscales are: perceived relationship with young drug users (e.g. "It is difficult to get along with young drug users"), perceived social relationships of young drug users (e.g. "Young drug users might have friends from the triad gang"), value-judgment perceptions of young drug users (e.g. "Young drug users are self-degraded"), perceived sociological justification for using drugs (e.g. "Using drugs makes a person more courageous"), and perceived psychophysiological rationale for using drugs (e.g. "Using drugs could help one to escape from reality"). A higher score on the first three subscales would reflect a more positive attitude toward young drug users, and a higher score on the last two subscales would be indicative of disagreement with the excuses given for using drugs. Each item was measured on a 5-point Likert scale ranging from 1 (strongly agree) to 5 (strongly disagree).

Drugs Education/Training. Two statements—"My school is able to provide sufficient drugs-related education" and "Non-governmental organizations (NGOs) are able to provide sufficient drugs-related training"—were included to measure the participants' satisfaction with the education and training that they were receiving on drugs-related matters. The purpose was to survey the current landscape in terms of drugs education/training for future practitioners. The two items were each measured on a 7-point Likert scale ranging from 1 (strongly disagree) to 7 (strongly agree).

RESULTS

Theory of Planned Behavior

In terms of *attitudes toward serving drug users*, one-way ANOVA revealed that there were significant group differences between the three groups of majors: $F(2,685) = 8.73$, $p < .001$. Post-hoc Turkey tests found that compared to nursing and education majors, social work majors held significantly more positive attitudes toward serving drug users: $p < .01$; education majors: $p < .01$. There were however, no significant differences between those majoring in nursing and in education.

With regard to *subjective norm*, significant between-group differences were found for the three groups: $F(2,702) = 3.63$, $p < 0.05$. Post-hoc Turkey tests found that compared to social work majors, nursing majors held greater subjective norm: $p < .05$. No difference was found between social work and education majors or between nursing and education majors.

Table 1. Mean scores and SD for the Theory of Planned Behavior subscales

	Mean	SD	Sig.
Attitudes toward serving drug users			
Social work	5.57	0.94	0.000***
Nursing	5.27	0.95	
Education	5.26	0.92	
Subjective norm			
Social work	4.06	0.99	0.027*
Nursing	4.28	0.86	
Education	4.19	0.95	
Self-efficacy			
Social work	4.02	0.84	0.467
Nursing	4.05	0.79	
Education	3.94	0.86	
Intention regarding serving drug users			
Social work	4.14	1.15	0.000***
Nursing	4.11	0.99	
Education	3.66	1.08	

Notes: 1 = strongly disagree to 7 = strongly agree.
Between group sig. *$p < .05$; ** $p < .01$; *** $p < .001$.

With regard to *self-efficacy*, there were no significant between-group differences for the three groups: $F(2,692) = 0.76$, $p = .47$.

Finally, for *intentions regarding serving drug users*, there were significant between-group differences: $F(2,692) = 9.76$, $p < .001$. Post-hoc Turkey tests found that social work and nursing majors had greater intentions to serve drug users compared to education majors: $p < .001$ and $p < .01$ respectively. But there were no significant differences between social work majors and nursing majors. The mean scores and standard deviations (SD) for each planned behavior subscale are presented in Table 1.

Attitudes toward Young Drug Users

As with the theory of planned behavior subscales, ANOVAs were performed for each of the five factors of the Chinese Youth Attitudes toward Young Drug Users scale (Chui and Chan, 2012). For the first subscale, *perceived relationship with young drug users*, ANOVA results showed significant between-group differences: $F(2{,}701) = 57.03$, $p < .001$. Post-hoc Turkey tests revealed social work majors to be significantly more positive with respect to perceived relationship with young drug users compared to nursing majors: $p < .001$ and education majors: $p < .001$. There was no significant difference between nursing and education majors.

The other subscale that displayed significant between-group differences was *value-judgment perceptions of young drug users*: $F\ (2{,}701) = 127.55$, $p < .001$.

Table 2. Total Mean Scores and SD for the CYAYDU Subscales

	Mean	SD	Sig.
Perceived relationship with young drug users			
Social work	10.51	2.15	0.000***
Nursing	8.92	2.11	
Education	8.57	2.29	
Perceived social relationships of young drug users			
Social work	7.63	1.91	0.893
Nursing	7.55	1.95	
Education	7.61	1.92	
Value-judgment perception of young drug users			
Social work	7.35	1.62	0.000***
Nursing	5.32	1.73	
Education	5.33	1.77	
Perceived social relationships of young drug users			
Social work	8.00	1.43	0.686
Nursing	7.89	1.57	
Education	8.02	1.53	
Perceived sociological justification for using drugs			
Social work	6.34	1.55	0.046*
Nursing	6.08	1.65	
Education	6.00	1.61	

Notes: 1 = strongly agree to 5 = strongly disagree.
Between group sig. $^*p < .05$; $^{**}\ p < .01$; $^{***}\ p < .001$.

Again, social work majors held significantly more positive value-judgment perceptions of young drug users compared to nursing majors: $p < .001$) and education majors: $p < .001$. There was no significant difference between nursing and education majors.

The final subscale that showed significant between-group differences was *perceived psychophysiological rationale for using drugs*: $F(2,702) = 3.09$; $p < .05$. Post-hoc Turkey tests revealed that social work majors had a slightly higher perceived psychophysiological rationale for using drugs compared to the education majors: $p < .01$. No significant differences were found between social work majors and nursing majors or between nursing majors and education majors.

With regard to the other two subscales, *perceived social relationships of young drug users* and *perceived sociological justification for using drugs*, there were no significant group differences between the three groups. The total scores and SD for each subscale of the Chinese Youth Attitudes toward Young Drug Users scale are presented in Table 2.

Drug Education/Training

For the statement "My school is able to provide sufficient drugs-related education," one-way ANOVA tests showed significant group differences between the three majors: $F(2,706) = 32.06$; $p < .001$. Post-hoc Turkey tests found that compared to education majors, social work majors significantly felt that their schools were able to better provide sufficient education on drugs-related issues: $p < .001$. Similarly, compared to education majors, nursing majors felt that their schools were able to significantly better provide sufficient education on drugs-related issues: $p < .001$. There were, however, no differences found between social work and nursing majors.

There were also significant group differences with respect to the statement "Non-governmental organizations (NGOs) are able to provide sufficient drugs-related training": $F(2,615) = 9.36$; $p < .01$. Post-hoc Turkey tests revealed that compared to education majors, social work majors significantly felt that NGOs were able to provide sufficient drugs-related training: $p < .01$. No differences were found between the other groups. The mean scores and SD for the two statements are presented in Table 3.

Table 3. Mean Scores and SD for the Views of Drugs Education/Training

	Mean	SD	Sig.
My school is able to provide sufficient drugs-related education			
Social work	3.27	1.40	0.000***
Nursing	3.11	1.33	
Education	2.47	1.40	
Non-governmental organizations (NGOs) are able to provide sufficient drugs-related training			
Social work	4.75	1.28	0.003**
Nursing	4.49	1.19	
Education	4.34	1.23	

Notes: 1 = significantly disagree to 7 = significantly agree.
Between group sig. $*p < .05$; $** p < .01$; $*** p < .001$.

CONCLUSION

In recent years, Hong Kong has witnessed a shift toward the increasing abuse of psychotropic substances, particularly ketamine, by young people. In responding to the mounting public concern over young drug abusers, the Hong Kong Government has adopted a holistic approach in its anti-drugs campaign. This holistic approach has entailed strategies encompassing prevention, rehabilitation, and incarceration as well as cooperation between government departments, community services and experts from the fields of social work, health and education. It is evident that the Government does not believe that drug abuse can be stopped through a single policy or strategy; rather, it believes that the anti-drugs campaign must involve a multi-pronged approach that targets different drug abusers in different circumstances at different stages.

This approach includes counseling services provided by social workers, medical treatment by nurses and doctors, and prevention, even school-based drug testing, by educators. Nonetheless, despite all of these efforts, there is still a long way to go in reversing the trend of young drug abusers. The use of psychotropic substances has regrettably become associated with a trendy youth culture in Hong Kong. Unlike heroin, which has a lot of stigma attached to it because of its connection with low-income working-class males, psychotropic drugs have proliferated due to the dance culture and are viewed as harmless ways to escape from mundane everyday life. There is a need for the next generation of social workers, health workers and educators to carry on the campaign against drugs in Hong Kong.

To this end, we conducted an exploratory study to assess the attitudes of future practitioners in these three fields toward (a) serving drug users in the future, (b) young drug users, and (c) the education/training that they are receiving in relation to drugs. Our results showed that social work majors demonstrated a stronger intention to engage in drug abuse work in the future and held more positive attitudes toward young drug users in general. A possible explanation for this is that social work majors believed that their schools and NGOs provide sufficient education and training in drugs-related matters, as indicated by their responses to our last two items involving drugs education/training.

On the other hand, education majors had the least intention to serve drug users, held more negative attitudes toward the prospect of serving drug users, and greater negative perceptions of young drug users in general. This is a troubling finding because teachers are more often than not the first point of contact with young drug users since these young people will likely be attending school. If they do not have much intention to serve and care for students who abuse drugs, they cannot identify and refer students who are at risk to suitable parties to receive help. Social workers and nurses are often only contacted when there is suspicion that a young person has been engaging in substance abuse and is in need of counseling or treatment. With the controversial school-based drug testing set to become mandatory for all schools in the region, further hostilities may develop between teachers and students. Therefore, more education needs to be given to education majors in order to promote their intentions to serve drug users and reduce their negative attitudes toward them.

Our findings also revealed that education majors found their respective institutions to be the least sufficient in providing them with education/training on drugs-related matters. The warning issued by the Task Force on Youth Drug Abuse (2008) regarding the lack of expertise and training for school teachers was shared by the education majors themselves.

Surely, this is an area where improvement is needed. Increasingly, NGOs are providing on-site training for primary and secondary school teachers (Narcotics Division, 2012b). Although this is indeed a step in the right direction, training during their tertiary school years, before students have commenced their careers as teachers, would equip them for what is ahead.

While our study provides empirical evidence on the perceptions of future practitioners who will be a part of Hong Kong's anti-drugs campaign, several limitations must be acknowledged. We relied on purposive sampling to ensure that there would be a sufficient number of participants in each major. As such, our results cannot be generalized to all tertiary students in Hong Kong. Related to this, participants from certain fields of study that are relevant to the anti-drugs campaign were not recruited. Most notably, students in the field of criminal justice and corrections were neglected. Past studies that measured attitudes toward offenders found law enforcement officers to be more negative compared to those who are more involved in the rehabilitation of offenders, student samples, and the general public (e.g. Kjelsberg, Skoglund, and Rustad, 2007; Melvin, Gramling, and Gardner, 1985; Ortet-Fabregat, Perez, and Lewis, 1993). It would be interesting to compare the attitudes of criminal justice majors toward young drug users with those of the three majors in our study, who are geared more toward rehabilitative work in their future careers.

ACKNOWLEDGMENTS

The authors would like to thank the Hong Kong Social Workers Association for granting them the right to use the data of its project. The project is funded by the Beat Drugs Fund, Hong Kong.

REFERENCES

——— (2012b). *The sixth three-year plan on drug treatment and rehabilitation services in Hong Kong (2012-2014)*. Hong Kong: Hong Kong Special Administrative Region Government.

——— (2012c). Beat drugs fund. Hong Kong. Retrieved from http://www.nd.-gov.-hk/en/beat.htm

Ajzen, I. (1991). The theory of planned behavior. *Organizational Behavior and Human Decision Processes, 50*(2), 179-211.

Cheung, W. H., and Lam, M. Position statement of the Hong Kong College of Psychiatrists on school-based drug tests in Hong Kong: A review of its effectiveness and our recommendations. *Hong Kong Journal of Psychiatry, 19*, 133-136.

Chu, P. S. K., Kwok, S. C., Kam, K. M., Chu, T. Y., Chan, S. W. H., Man, C. W., Ma, W. K., Chui, K. L., Yiu, M. K., Chan, Y. C., Tse, M. L., and Lau, F. L. (2007). 'Street ketamine' – associated bladder dysfunction: A report of ten cases. *Hong Kong Medical Journal, 13*, 311-313.

Chui, W. H., and Chan, H. C. O. (2012). The Chinese youth attitudes toward youth drug users scale: An initial scale development and refinement. *Drug and Alcohol Review, 31*(4), 477-482.

Godin, G., Valois, P. and Lepage, L. (1993). The pattern of influence of perceived behavioral control upon exercising behavior – an application of Ajzen theory of planned behavior, *Journal of Behavioral Medicine, 16*(1), 18-102.

Greenslade, J. H., and White, K. M. (2005). The prediction of above-average participation in volunteerism: A test of the theory of planned behavior and the volunteers function inventory in older Australian adults. *The Journal of Social Psychology, 145*(2), 155-172.

Hunt, G., and Evans, K. (2003). Dancing and drugs: A cross-national perspective. *Contemporary Drug Problems, 30*, 779-814.

Kjelsberg, E., Skoglund, T. H., and Rustad, A. (2007). Attitudes toward prisoners, as reported by prison inmates, prison employees and college students. *BMC Public Health, 7*, 1-9.

Laidler, K. A. J. (2005). The rise of club drugs in a heroin society: The case of Hong Kong. *Substance Use and Misuse, 40*(9-10), 1257-1278.

Laidler, K. A. J., and Hunt, G. (2008). Sit down to float: The cultural meaning of ketamine use in Hong Kong. *Addiction Research and Theory, 16*(3), 259-271.

Mackey, D. A., Courtright, K. E., and Packard, S. H. (2006). Testing the rehabilitative ideal among college students. *Criminal Justice Studies, 19*(2), 153-170.

Melvin, K. B., Gramling, L. K., and Gardner, W. M. (1985). A scale to measure attitudes toward prisoners. *Criminal Justice and Behavior, 12*(2), 241-253.

Narcotics Division (2012a). *Central Registry of Drug Abuse sixtieth report.* Hong Kong: Hong Kong Special Administrative Region Government.

Ng, S. H., Tse, M. L., Ng, H. W., and Lau, F. L. (2012). Emergency department presentation of ketamine abusers in Hong Kong: A review of 233 cases. *Hong Kong Medical Journal, 16*, 6-11.

Office of the Chief Executive (2008). *2007-08 policy address: A new direction for Hong Kong.* Hong Kong. Retrieved from http://www.policyaddress.gov.hk/07-08/eng/policy.html

Ortet-Fabregat, G., Perez, J., and Lewis, R. (1993). Measuring attitudes toward prisoners: A psychometric assessment. *Criminal Justice and Behavior, 20*(2), 190-198.

Povey, R., Conner, M., Sparks, P., James, R., and Shepherd, R. (2000). Application of the theory of planned behaviour to two dietary behaviours: Roles of perceived control and self-efficacy. *British Journal of Health Psychology*, *5*(2), 121–139.

Schaalma, H., Kok, G., and Peters, L. (1993). Determinants of consistent condom use by adolescents: The impact of experience of sexual intercourse. *Health Education Research, 8*(2), 255–269.

Shek, D. T. L. (2010). School drug testing: A critical review of the literature. *The Scientific World Journal, 10*, 356-365.

Task Force on Youth Drug Abuse (2008). *Report of the Task Force on Youth Drug Abuse.* Hong Kong: Hong Kong Special Administrative Region Government.

Terry, D. J., and O'Leary, J. (1995). The theory of planned behaviour: The effects of perceived behavioural control and self-efficacy. *British Journal of Social Psychology, 34*(2), 199–220.

The Standard (2010, September 24). Drug tests set for schools citywide. *The Standard.* Retrieved from http://www.thestandard.com.hk/news_ detail.asp?sid=29695948andart _id=103241andcon_type=1andpp_cat=11

Warburton, J., and Terry, D. J. (2000). Volunteer decision making by older people: A test of a revised theory of planned behavior. *Basic and Applied Social Psychology, 22*(3), 245–257.

Wu, M. S., and Tang, S.K. (2012). Problem gambling of Chinese college students: Application of the theory of planned behavior. *Journal of Gambling Studies*, *28,* 315-324.

In: Drug Use and Abuse
Editor: Marie Claire Van Hout ISBN: 978-1-62618-232-5

Chapter 5

A COMPARATIVE ANALYSIS OF THE DIFFERENT LEGISLATIVE CONTROLS RELATING TO SEX WORK AND DRUG USE IN THE NETHERLANDS AND IRELAND

Dara Losty and Kevin Lalor*

School of Social Sciences and Law, Dublin Institute of Technology

ABSTRACT

The purpose of this chapter is to explore drug use among sex workers in the Netherlands and Ireland and to examine why sex workers relationship to drug use differs in the two countries. Sex workers are considered an at 'risk group' in society, and are thus more likely to become involved in problematic drug use. The environmental, social and structural factors were also analysed to compare sex workers involvement in the sex work industry in both the Netherlands an Ireland. The wider socioeconomic factors, such as poverty, homelessness, employment prospects, educational attainment and their access to health and social services will also be discussed. This chapter will provide a detailed analysis of the nature of drug use and how it serves to socially discriminate the subculture of sex work in the Netherlands and Ireland.

Prostitution is a structural necessity for society and will continue to be universally inevitable all the while sexual repression remains essential to the functioning of society" (Burke, 2009, p. 200).

Keywords: Ireland, The Netherlands, Sex work, prostitution, drug use, legislation, stigma, risk

INTRODUCTION

"Ask anyone what the oldest profession in the world is and the odds are they will answer: Prostitution" (Van der Poel, 1992)

* Corresponding Author. School of Social Sciences and Law. Email: dara.losty@gmail.com.

This chapter will explore drug use among sex workers in the Netherlands and Ireland and analyse if sex workers' relationship to drug use differs in the two countries. It will examine the nature of sex work in Ireland and the legislation which relates to sex work and how policies continue to develop. The same will also be considered in the Dutch context. The environmental factors of sex working and sex workers drug taking behaviour in both countries will be analysed. The degree of drug addiction will be an important part of consideration, as it can often coincide with the extent of risk taking. This is the case as sex workers with a serious drug addiction often work long hours take greater risks with clients and work in more dangerous conditions to fund their problematic drug addiction (Cameron, Gilchrist and Scoular, 2005). The theoretical perspective of sex working and drug use will be outlined, as it is important to develop a greater understanding of the reasons for individuals entering sex work. It is important to provide a theoretical analysis as it can generate a greater understanding into criminal justice practices and also provides a deeper insight into why people engage in certain behaviours (Cote, 2002).

EXAMINING THE IRISH CONTEXT

Irish Legislation Regarding Prostitution

The legislation surrounding the legalities and illegalities of prostitution in Ireland is somewhat misleading as it is legal to exchange money for sex but it is illegal to advertise a brothel or prostitution. It is also the case that soliciting from a vehicle is an offence alongside 'kerb-crawling'. Police use of legal powers in Irish society remains inconsistent in relation to sex work (McCullagh, 1996). The current legislation which governs prostitution in the Irish context is The Criminal Law [1](Sexual Offences Act) 1993. Section 11 of the 1993 Act outlines that selling sex in Ireland is not illegal although loitering and importuning an individual for the purpose of prostitution and living off the earnings of prostitution is illegal [2](Irish Statute Book, 1993). This creates a 'double standard' aspect according to Bacik (2002) as it fails to actively criminalise the selling of sex, although it criminalises public displays of prostitution and has also created a more confrontational relationship between the police and sex workers. It has been argued that sex workers are often faced with an increasing reluctance to report attacks due to the negative experiences they have with Gardaí under the law (Bacik, 2002).Section 7 of the 1993 Act criminalises those who solicit in a public place and it is considered an offence if it is a client, sex worker or a third party (e.g. pimp) [3](Irish Statute Book, 1993). The chief purpose of the Act was to decriminalise male homosexuality and laws governing prostitution were considered a secondary provision of the Act (O'Connor, 1996). Prior to 1883 under the Sexual Offences Act, a member of an Gardaí was required to bear witness in court that a woman was a 'common prostitute', rather than an individual who was loitering for the purpose of prostitution. This was highly flawed as the term 'common prostitute' was regarded as unconstitutional because it was detrimental towards the accused and was also highly discriminatory on the basis of gender (O'Connor, 1996). Laws relating to

[1] Irish Statute Book. (1993). *Sexual Offences Act.* Ireland: Office of the Attorney General.
[2] Irish Statute Book. (1993). *Sexual Offences Act.* Ireland: Office of the Attorney General.Section 11
[3] Irish Statute Book. (1993). *Sexual Offences Act.* Ireland: Office of the Attorney General. Section 7

prostitution have not been renewed since 1993. The chief rationale of existing legislation regarding sex work is to protect society from the public order offences that are traditionally associated with prostitution, despite the changing nature of sex work in Ireland (Department of Justice and Equality: Discussion Paper, 2012).

There has been a growing trend to criminalise the purchase of sex in Ireland which has been reflected in the motion in the Seanad on the 12th of October 2011 which sought for the Governement to consider adopting the Swedish model of sex work legislation (Seanad Debate, House of the Oireachtas, 2011). On the 1st January 1999 the law which prohibits the purchase of sex came into force in Sweden, alongside additional legislation which upholds a zero tolerance policy on all forms of prostitution (Ekberg, 2004). Senator Katherine Zappone noted in Seanad Debate that '*criminal sanctions for the purpose of sex are a proven deterrent to prostitution*' (Seanad Debate, House of the Oireachtas, 2011). The topic was recalled at a later date in the Seanad on the 18th April 2012 which urged the Governement to make a definitive decision regarding whether or not legislation should be enacted similar to that of what exists in Sweden. In another note, Senator Aideen Haydon highlighted in the Seanad debate that we are failing to take into consideration the reasons why individuals choose to become involved in prostitution in the first instance and that '*the way the problem is represented is not indicative of the social issues around prostitution* (Seanad Debate, House of the Oireachtas, 2012). Deputy Kathleen Lynch in the Seanad Debate highlighted that it has been difficult to analyse the effect of the ban in its entirety in Sweden although the prevalence of street prostitution was approximated to have halved since the changes in legislation which signifies a real reduction in prostitution (Seanad Debate, House of the Oireachtas, 2012). The key element of Swedish legislation relating to prostitution is focused on one of the root causes, which is the recognition that by curbing the demand for sex workers it will reduce the size of the already globalised prostitution industry (Ekberg, 2004).

This growing awareness for the need to review existing laws on prostitution became apparent with the implementation of a consultation process which was introduced in July 2012 by Minister for Justice Alan Shatter. Interested groups were invited to submit a discussion paper in relation to the review of existing legislation [4]The Joint Oireachtas Committee on Justice, Defence and Equality (2012) outlined the reasons for this growing need for change by highlighting the changing environment of prostitution in Ireland, with prostitution now moving from outdoor to a more hidden indoor activity. Indoor prostitution is now facilitated by the use of the internet and mobile phones which is making easier for sex workers to arrange meetings with clients. Residing in rented accommodation is also making it increasingly easier to move between different locations. This review will analyse whether or not the existing legislation is amply capable of addressing the criminal behaviour that often coincides with prostitution [4](Department of Justice and Equality, 2012).

The existing legislation is still under review in Ireland and a conference was held on October 13th 2012 which discussed the document on the Future Direction of Prostitution Legislation (2012). The conference took account of the viewpoints of interested parties and members of the public and facilitated an open discussion on all aspects of prostitution in Ireland (Department of Justice and Equality, 2012). There were submissions from many interested Irish organisations such as Ruhama, Sex Workers Alliance, the National Women's

---

[4] Department of Justice and Equality. 2012. *Discussion Document on the Future Direction of Prostitution Legislation*. Department of Justice and Equality.

Council of Ireland and the Immigrant Council of Ireland which were discussed in the conference. There were also speakers from Sweden, which included Pye Jackobson from the Rose Alliance organisation and Jack Verbruggen from the Dutch Ministry of Security and Justice (The Irish Times, 2012). Minister for Justice, Alan Shatter said that a report on the recent public consultation process on the future legislation on prostitution in Ireland will be drawn up by the Joint Oireachtas Committee on Justice, Defence and Equality by the end of 2012 (The Irish Times, 2012).

Irish Legislation Regarding Human Trafficking and Drug Use

The Criminal Law (Human Trafficking) Act 2008 criminalises all types of trafficking as specified in [5]Article 3 of the United Nations Trafficking Protocol. The Garda National Investigation Bureau within Ireland also maintains a separate division which focuses specifically on trafficked persons cases (United Nations Office on Drugs and Crime, 2009). It remains quite difficult to examine the exact extent of human trafficking in the Irish context according to the Report of Department of Justice, Equality and Law Reform and An Garda Síochána Working Group on Trafficking Human Beings (2006). The report also underlines how evidence exists which highlights how eastern European women are being trafficked into Ireland for the intention of sexual mistreatment.

When examining Irish drug legislation it is important to note that illegal drug use is prohibited under numerous Irish drug laws. For example, the Misuse of Drugs Act 1977 and 1984 prohibits the use of non-medical opiates such as heroin [6] (Irish Statute Book, 1984). Section 23 of the Misuse of Drugs Act 1977 allows members of an Garda Síochána to search a person if they are suspected of having controlled and/or illegal drugs in his/her possession without a warrant.

The Nature of Sex Work in Ireland

It is important, first of all, to consider that we are unable to look at prostitution without focusing on the wider economic and social contexts which give rise to it (O'Neill, 1997). According to Irish studies, sex workers are exposed to numerous risks in their living and working lives, and there exists an even riskier environment for those also engaged in problematic drug use (National Advisory Committee on Drugs, 2009). It has been noted how former sex workers are now pursuing sex work due to financial pressure in recent times in Ireland (Ruhama, 2010). According to a study by the National Advisory Committee on Drugs (NACD), many sex workers with children noted that the need to provide for their children meant that they remained working as sex workers due to the easy accessibility of financial rewards. This was also the same for those who were former drug users, although the increasing pressure of maintaining financial stability and providing for their family resulted in

[5] "Trafficking in persons" shall mean the recruitment, transportation, transfer, harbouring or receipt of persons, by means of the threat or use of force or other forms of coercion, of abduction, of fraud, of deception, of the abuse of power or of a position of vulnerability or of the giving or receiving of payments or benefits to achieve the consent of a person having control over another person, for the purpose of exploitation. Exploitation shall include, at a minimum, the exploitation of the prostitution of others or other forms of sexual exploitation, forced labour or services, slavery or practices similar to slavery, servitude or the removal of organs; (Office of the United Nations High Commissioner for Human Rights, 2000)

[6] Irish Statute Book. (1984). *Misuse of Drugs Act.* Ireland: Office of the Attorney General.

a greater risk of relapsing (National Advisory Committee on Drugs, 2009). It was outlined by Ruhama how there was a 9% increase in the number of women utilising their outreach van service, which is an outreach service that travels to known areas of Dublin where prostitution takes place and offers support and hot drinks to sex workers. It was also the case that the women who availed of the outreach service were predominantly Irish and engaging in problematic drug use (Ruhama, 2010).

It has remained a relatively contentious issue to calculate the number of drug users in Ireland actively engaging in sex work due to its highly stigmatised nature in society (NACD, 2009). The clandestine environment of sex work and drug use is often centred in working class areas of high unemployment, low educational attainment and economic marginalisation (Cox, Ryan and Whitaker, 2011). It has been estimated that approximately 80% of women working as sex workers have been subject to some form of sexual abuse in their childhood (Ruhama, 2006). It is also the case that large sums of women become involved in sex work before the age of 18, which raises concerns in relation to young people entering prostitution because they feel they have no other choice (Ruhama, 2006). According to the Irish Escort client survey (2006) 1.2% of those who completed the survey were offered an escort who was 14 years of age, 1.6% were offered an escort who was 15 years of age, 3.2% were offered an escort who was 16 years of age and 9.1% were offered an escort who was 17 years of age. It was also the case that 73% of those surveyed noted that they had been in contact with an escort that they assumed was being forced to work and 81.7% suspected that they had been in contact with an escort that was being abused. These statistics reveal that there is an increased likelihood that some of those involved in the commercial sex trade are suspected to be working against their will and/or may be victims of sex trafficking. It also highlights how there are also individuals involved in the sex industry in Ireland who are under the age of 18.

Advocacy and Sex Work in Ireland

In recent years in Ireland there has been a growing campaign which seeks to legalise sex work in Ireland, such as the belief expressed by the Sex Workers Alliance (SWAI). The SWAI have expressed that if we are to protect sex workers from any additional risks and harms then it is important to encourage a less judgemental and open outlook on what they describe as '*just another service industry*'. They reject the claim that prostitution is simply violence against women, as the reality is that not all sex workers are female and not all clients are male (SWAI, 2012). In a recent study by the Department of Health and Children entitled 'The Irish Study of Sexual Health and Relationships' (2006) it was estimated that 6.4% of the respondents had paid for sex at some point in their life. There was a distinct trend that emerged which suggested that males in the younger age categories were most likely to have paid for sex. Men of all different classes within this study had paid for sex, with those working in the higher professional group maintaining one of the highest percentiles for ever having paid for sex at just under 10%. This small but significant number of individuals who are estimated to have ever paid for sex suggests how there exists a likelihood of individuals who are willing to pay for sex. This may especially be the case as there are now a multitude of routes for clients to come in contact with sex workers, whether it's online or in a chat room or through an agency (SWAI, 2012). According to the Irish Escort Client Survey (2006), 41.7% of those that had used an escort service were between the ages of 25-34, were white (93.7%), had some form of third level education (74.2%), earned €30,000-€40,000 a year (18.3%) and were either living with a partner or married (43.7%).

EXAMINING THE DUTCH CONTEXT

Dutch Legislation Regarding Sex Work

The Netherlands maintains relatively liberal policies regarding sex work and drug use. Sex work was decriminalised in the year 2000 and payment for sex between two consenting adults is not considered illegal. The Netherlands became the first country in the European Union to legalise prostitution (Siegel, 2009). Sex workers also pay income tax and have access to a range of health and social services and the Netherlands recognises adult sex work as a legitimate occupation [7](Netherlands Ministry of Foreign Affairs, 2004). Dutch sex work policy formation incorporates various viewpoints from a number of organisations, most notably politicians, sex workers, civil servants, criminal justice representatives, social workers, members of the Red Thread Prostitute Union, the general public and brothel owners (Kuo, 2002). Through lifting the ban on brothels, it has enabled local authorities to publish regulations overseeing health, safety, working conditions and hygiene for sex workers working in brothels and brothel owners must comply with by-laws in order to qualify for a licence. If brothel owners fail to uphold the conditions of their licence then they can be subject to various penalties such as additional fees, removal of licence and closure. It is also the case that employers working in the sex industry must meet the terms of Dutch labour laws and tax and insurance obligations [5](Netherlands Ministry of Foreign Affairs, 2010). Under Article 273a of the Dutch Penal Code members of the police force maintain the right to request identification records, such as birth certificates and passports in order to determine if the individual is working legally (Kuo, 2002). It has also been the case that a number of illegal immigrants working in the Netherlands as sex workers were confronted with many dilemmas after the Government lifted the ban on brothels. Many illegal immigrants were forced to either leave the country or continue working in the sex work industry in the criminal circuit (Seigel, 2009).

It was estimated by the [5]Netherlands Ministry of Foreign Affairs in 2004 that approximately 5% of all prostitutes were street prostitutes. The sex workers engaged in street prostitution mainly work in ‘toleration zones’. These zones were legitimately established during the 1980’s and 1990’s in order to create a safer environment for sex workers. Members of the police force are located at the entrance of the toleration zones in order to decrease the likelihood of sex workers becoming subject to harm. Members of the police force are not permitted to acquire the names or licence plate numbers of the individuals who enter the zones (Kuo, 2002). These regulations did improve the working conditions of some sex workers, although it fuelled an even greater industry for the trafficking of women, illegal prostitution and illegal drugs, according to Staring and Zaitch (2010). The most significant objective of Dutch policy relating to sex work is to incorporate greater control mechanisms and to put an end to the exploitation of human beings for the purpose of prostitution [8](Netherlands Ministry of Foreign Affairs, 2010). The legislation aids Governmental efforts to tackle organised crime through the establishment of stringent penalties for those involved

---

[7] Netherlands Ministry of Foreign Affairs. (2004). *Dutch Policy on Prostitution: Questions and Answers.* Netherlands: Netherlands Minisrty of Foreign Affairs

[8] Netherlands Ministry of Foreign Affairs. (2010). *Faq about Dutch Policy on Prostitution 2010.* Netherlands: Dutch Ministry of Foreign Affairs.

in criminal behaviour. It targets those more specifically involved in violent behaviour, individuals who exploit minors or who are involved in human trafficking (Siegel, 2009).

Dutch Legislation Regarding Human Trafficking and Drug Use

The trafficking of persons has been criminalised in the Netherlands since 1911. In January 2005 the article 250a of the Dutch Criminal Code was replaced with Article 273a which criminalised all types of trafficking recorded in the United Nations Trafficking Protocol. In 2005 a nationwide plan on trafficking persons was also implemented in the Netherlands (United Nations Office on Drugs and Crime). Article 273a also incorporates the illegality of any form of forced labour, slavery and the trafficking of organs (Staring and Zaitch, 2010).

It is against the law to maintain control over an individual through violence or threat and to keep the victim in a state of dependency. A majority of female sex workers working in the Netherlands are foreign nationals and according to Dutch legislation and many of these are victims of human trafficking as they are coerced or experience some form of exploitation (Staring and Zaitch, 2010). The Dutch Opium Act of 1928 and 1999 distinguish between class A drugs (heroin and cocaine etc.) and class C drugs (marijuana etc.). The decriminalisation of the use of soft drugs and the selling of a maximum of 5 grams is permitted in coffee shops in the Netherlands (Ministry of Justice of the Netherlands, 2011).

The Nature of Sex Work in the Netherlands

There is a perception that exists in the Netherlands that the sex industry is safe due to its legality and regulated nature which makes exchanging sex for money part of the Dutch experience. This creates a high demand for sex work and as a result there exists a constant human supply of male and female sex workers to respond to the growing demand (Shared Hope International, 2007). Gotz, Prins, van de Laar, van Leeuwen and van Veen 2008 mention how a majority of sex workers in 'streetwalker' districts are engaged in drug use and work in unfavourable conditions. It is also the case that there are many forms of sex work in the Netherlands, with the most widely known being window prostitution and in recent years there has been a massive demand for sex workers working in escort agencies. Numerous sex workers also work independently in brothels, sex clubs, sex farms and so on. (Staring and Zaitch, 2010). The Dutch Central Bureau of Statistics (CBS, 2004) estimated that approximately 11.5 thousand sex workers work as escorts or call girls, which highlights the growing trend toward more hidden forms of sex work. It was estimated that the proceeds of the sex work industry in the Netherlands, both legal and illegal, was approximately €660 million (CBS, 2004). The Netherlands is a popular destination for 'sex tourism' due to the promotion of one of the most famous and well known red light districts 'De Wallen'. International and local visitors availing of commercial sexual activity has resulted in an increasing demand in sexual services and the development of commercial sex markets (Shared Hope International, 2012). The Netherland's red light districts are now regarded as normalised destinations where one can participate in a walking tour and sex tourism is now an integral part of the Amsterdam experience (Jeffreys, 2009). It has also been estimated that the extensive advertising and promotion of the Netherland's sex tourism market is far outpacing the existing number of sex workers working in the red light districts (Shared Hope International, 2009). It is also the case that due to the Amsterdam's expanding youth and gay culture and the liberalisation of sex work legislation, it became a sanctuary for soft drug use and the increasing demand created an even greater supply of male sex workers (Zuilhof, 1999).

Advocacy and Sex Work in the Netherlands

The foundation of the 'Red Thread' (De Rode Draad) in 1984 provided information on the rights of sex workers in relation to tax and licensing and their aim was to empower sex workers and also work against the stigmatisation of the sex work industry (The Red Thread, 2011). The World Health Organisation (WHO, 2005) stated that oppressive legislation confines the rights of sex workers and that the criminalisation of sex work contributes to an environment were violence and harassment is tolerated. Through the formation of the Sex Workers Initiative Group Netherlands (SIGN), which consisted of a group of Dutch sex workers and sex worker rights activists, they were able to organise a conference which advocated for the rights of sex workers in Europe in June 2003. SIGN sought for additional support from other sex workers rights activists, sex workers and people involved in sex work organisations in other European countries, which resulted in the establishment of an International Organisation Committee (OC) in January 2004 (Brooks, Ditmore and Koken, 2006). The OC consists of 15 individuals who are sex workers of former sex workers from all over Europe. The extensive lobbying of the Sex Workers Initiative Group Netherlands (SIGN) for over two years resulted in the formation of a new legal international body which is the International Committee on the Rights of Sex Workers in Europe (ICRSE). The ICRSE acts as a foundation for future plans and initiatives through organising conferences and writing consultation papers (Sex Work Europe, 2006). The major themes which appear as part of the ICRSE consultation papers are violence, adherence to appropriate labour laws and migration (Sex Work Europe, 2006). It is also the case that the Red Thread promotes the decriminalisation of sex work and advocates for the rights of sex workers, such as what is expressed by the WHO and the ICRSE. They highlight how sex workers do not need pimps, as they can forward complaints to members of the police force and through enforcing their civil rights they can also pursue matters further to the courts (The Red Thread, 2012).

Examining the Theoretical Framework of Sex Work and Drug Use

Conflict Theory and Functionalist Theory

It has been the case that functionalist and conflict theories expose the intricacies of why prostitution continues to exist within almost every society (Taylor and Thio, 2012). Conflict theory, similarly to functionalist theory, underlines the imbalanced disposition of power and resources within society and thus links deviance to social discrimination and inequality.

Conflict theory stems from the writings of Karl Marx which highlighted how the dominant class control and maintain the power and resources within society and thus instruct institutional rules which uphold their power and dominance (Anderson and Taylor, 2008). When examining sex work from the conflict theory perspective it is important to note that it derives some ideas from feminist theory. Prostitution reflects the ideologies of a patriarchal society, as males are socialised to express dominance over females. Promiscuous females, such as those engaged in sex work, are considered a threat to the moral order, unlike promiscuous males (Taylor and Thio, 2012). Conflict theorists emphasise the notion of social control to deal with deviance and crime within society. *"Social control is the process by which groups are brought into conformity with dominant social expectations"* (Anderson and Taylor, 2008).

Functionalist theory, on the other hand, highlights the inevitability of the existence of sex work within society. This naturalness which prostitution maintains within society in rooted in the notion that the marriage/prostitution dichotomy where married men look for sex (Burke and Selfe, 2001). It was argued that functionalist theory goes so far to note that if a society wishes to conserve the foundation of marriage, then the existence of sex work is important in order to ensure that survival (Burke and Selfe, 2001). Prostitution essentially provides individuals with quick, easy, emotionally detached sexual gratification and provides a sexual outlet for such individuals. It has been argued that the sex industry influences married men to seek prostitutes for 'premarital' 'extramarital' and 'immoral' sex as men are unable to persuade 'respectable' women to engage in 'immoral' sexual relations (Taylor and Thio, 2012).

Stigma and Deviance

It has been noted in previous research that it is important to empower sex workers as they are often subject to stigmatisation which can lead to such individuals adopting a shameful and dishonourable identity within society (Cox, et al., 2011). Those who are stigmatised often experience discrimination by those who are 'unstigmatised' or considered 'normals' which excludes them from societal approval and integration and leads to the internalisation of shame and self-denigration (Goffman, 1968). Goffman (1968) highlights how those who are stigmatised often experience feelings of insecurity and anxiety as they fear that those who are considered 'unstigmatised' will disrespect them and this will result in the stigmatised individual engendering notions of inferiority. Engaging in sex work and consuming drugs are considered imperfections in an individual's character, as those individuals who have obtained deviance through actively engaging in deviant behaviour are failing to conform to societal values (Cox, et al., 2011). It is also the case that for a large number of male sex workers, the stigma associated with male prostitution among peers has contributed in concealing an increasing furtive male sex work industry. Societal homophobic attitudes has also aided in pushing male prostitution further underground and increasing the risks involved in male sex work (Grimes, 2001).

Durkheim believed that acts of deviance were commonplace occurrences because those acts that displease collective norms and societal values are present in all societies and their generic existence points to their universal functionality (McLaughlin and Mincie, 2006).It has been noted that even in jurisdictions were sex work has been legalised, like in the

Netherlands, sex workers continue to be subject to stigmatisation within society. The stigma attached to sex work and the deviant status bestowed upon individuals engaging in drug use has resulted in many sex workers falling between the lines and failing to receive access to health and support services (Cox, et al., 2011). Those engaged in sex work are considered 'immoral' and a threat to the natural and pure existence of femininity and as a result they suffer social marginalisation and 'whore stigma' (O'Neill, 1997). Prostitution was traditionally viewed as immoral and the prostitute was viewed as a corrupt figure whose livelihood was dedicated solely to her lust, which is essentially failing to conform to her pre-determined gender role within society. It has also been argued that prostitution has been held up with notions of gender hierarchy, where female expression of sexuality is in need of male domination (Spector, 2006). The notion exists that 'stigma' is an issue for the idealist as it embodies a political problem of power relations such as the oppression of women (Jeffreys, 2008). Symbols of stigma for sex workers actively engaged in intravenous drug use was scarring from injecting drugs. In Cox, et al (2011) study of drug using sex workers in Dublin, it was highlighted how sex workers made an effort to conceal the scarring through injecting in areas that were inconspicuous to pass as non drug users. They expressed that scarring was the worst legacy of intravenous drug use and as an effort to conceal the scars they would inject in areas like the feet and neck. According to Vanwesenbeeck (2004), sex workers are often stigmatised which leads to increasing levels of emotional distress and exhaustion. They also often engage in distancing strategies or become 'depersonalised' from their client as a coping mechanism.

'Cultural Capital'

It is often the case that sex workers were not considered a resource within society (NACD, 2009) it can have a significant impact on their ability to secure any type of '[9]cultural capital'. The notion of 'cultural capital' emphasises that for an individual to sustain cultural capital they need to maintain certain characteristics that are defined as 'high status signals' by a large sum of the general population. These 'signals' are then defined as 'status markers' for an individual (Lamont and Lareau, 1988). This is also in accordance to Marx's notion of 'Conflict Theory' which noted how the dominant classes have authority which allows them to access the resources within society (Anderson and Taylor, 2010). Due to the power of the dominant classes within society, this gives them immediate access to 'cultural capital', as they maintain 'high status signals' because they are considered the dominant class by the majority. It is often the case that women involved in sex work are labelled as 'promiscuous' and considered a threat to the moral order within society, which seriously effects their access to any form of 'cultural capital' (Taylor and Thio, 2012).

A sex worker's 'cultural capital' also plays a defining role in the type of sex work they are involved in. It is often the case that due to the varying conditions of the different forms of sex work within the industry, sex worker's 'cultural capital' can be vital in establishing a safer form of sex work (Cabezas, Oritz and Valencia, 2010). When an individual maintains

[9] *In Bourdieu's global theoretical framework cultural capital is an informal academic standard, a class attribute, a basis of social selection and a resource for power which is salient as an indicator/basis of class position* (Lamont & Lareau, 1988).

little or no cultural capital they often experience exclusion and isolation and become distanced from 'normal' social ties.

> "Bourdieu argues that cultural capital is used by dominant groups to mark cultural distance and proximity, monopolise privileges and exclude and recruit new occupants of high status positions" (Lamont and Lareau, 1988).

Male Sex Work and Stigma

Male sex workers are also subject to a stigma, as they are labelled both homosexuals and prostitutes (Jeffreys, 2008). This is even more so for those who are also engaged in drug use. Male prostitution and homosexuality have traditionally been perceived as deviant and thus requiring social control. There is also a notion which exists that male sex work is intrinsically not as exploitative or degrading as female sex work, as relations between two men maintain a particular shared equality that is absent between the interactions of male and female sexual encounters. This is not entirely the case. As male sex workers are often subject to stigma and discrimination by members of the public and are thus ashamed to avail of services (World Health Organisation, 2006). Furthermore male sex work is also an area which receives little or no media coverage and due to the lack of awareness services are scarce and service providers are unaware of the needs of male sex workers (Grimes, 2001).

SEX WORK AND DRUG USE

Sex Work and Drug Dependence

Sex work has always been a notoriously dangerous profession and sex workers are exposed to serious risk, such as violence and exploitation. They can also be subject to sexual abuse from clients and sexually transmitted infections (Rekart, 2005). Intravenous drug use is linked to the increase in the spread of HIV among drug using sex workers. Harm reduction measures are known to reduce the level of drug related harm, such as the spread of HIV and sexually transmitted infections, rather than trying to prevent the use of drugs (Cusick, 2005). It is also the case that sex workers who are not involved in illicit drug use are overlooked by harm reduction strategies, thus the wider issues of sex work are failing to be addressed (Cusick, 2005). Access to support services for drug users is a crucial element for rehabilitation and harm reduction and it is also vital that these services are located in catchment areas where drug use is more common. Quigley (2003) notes how networks of methadone clinics in Dublin remain underdeveloped, with some disadvantaged areas continuing to lack any local drug service. It has been noted that prostitution has undergone a transformation from more traditional public forms of prostitution to the more hidden and private spheres such as escort agencies, private parlours and internet prostitution. This form of 'backstage' sex work is often crucial for client satisfaction, as they prefer a certain degree of anonymity and secrecy (Staring and Zaitch, 2010). It is estimated that the use of particular drugs, such as Mephedrone, can dramatically increase sexual arousal and pleasure. In a study by Van Hout and Brennan (2011) they analysed how the drug Mephedrone increased user's confidence, decreased their sexual inhibitions and facilitated intense sexual experiences. Illicit drugs, such a Mephedrone, lead to unsafe sexual practices and also allow individuals to overcome any social inhibitions.

Van Hout and Brennan (2011) noted how prolonged sexual intercourse associated with the Mephedrone drug increased users risk of contracting sexually transmitted infections due to condom tearing.

Unsafe sexual practices among sex workers often coincide with their client's drug taking. It is also the case that clients under the influence of drugs and/or alcohol often demand prolonged or rough sexual intercourse (Graaf, Straver, Vanwesenbeck, Visser and Zessen, 1995). This creates a very risky environment for those individuals engaged in sex work, and even more so for those who work in the sex industry to fund their drug addiction.

Sex Work and Drug Use in an International Context

Various international studies have analysed the co-existence of problematic drug use and sex work. Kouimtsidis, Mosedale and Reynolds (2009) examine in their study how a vicious circle of sex work and illicit drug use existed among female sex workers in London. The severity of drug dependence was often associated with the level of risk taken during sexual encounters with clients, namely non-use of prophylactics.

This has also been statistically related with their financial need (Rekart, 2005). Cameron, et al., (2005) highlight in their study in relation to crack and cocaine use among female prostitutes in Glasgow how women engaged in outdoor prostitution were more vulnerable to violence from clients in comparison to sex workers engaged in indoor prostitution. For many sex workers, drug abuse was a coping mechanism.

In Edwards, Harcourt and Philpot's study on Drug Use by Prostitutes in Sydney (2000), they estimated that marijuana was the most popular drug among the participants of their study and was used as a form of relaxation. It was also the case that prostitutes used amphetamines to keep them alert during night shifts, they also helped them cope with any negative feelings they may have had about their work. In a study by Kramer (2007) examining substance abuse among female sex workers working in escort agencies and on the street in Arizona, she indicated how 59% of the respondents said that they engaged in substance abuse in order to numb the pain of 'turning tricks'. She also highlighted how 29% engaged in alcohol consumption to numb the pain of prostitution and 44% insisted that the only way to turn a trick was to 'get high' prior to sexual encounters.

In Cox, et al (2011) study of sex workers in Dublin, the respondents highlighted how they believed heroin use was viewed as more stigmatising than cocaine or any other drug. Female sex workers response to their work also tends to overwhelmingly negative according to Browne, Khan, Marino and Minichiello's (2003) study with positive experiences of prostitution accounting for only 10% of the overall time spent dedicated to sex work. It is often the case that individuals engaged in sex work are subject to violent behaviour from male clients. According to Farley (2003) this notion is traditionally rooted in the fact that men believe that they maintain an inherent entitlement to sexual access to women and that they can be sexually aggressive in response to female sex workers.

Male Sex Work and Drug Use

There exists a distinct gender structure of the sex working population as a majority of studies focus on the participation of female sex workers in the sex work industry. It is important to note that despite the overrepresentation of women in the global sex trade, a growing number of men are also active in the trade (Kempadoo, 1999). The number of males engaging in sex work is continuing to increase throughout Europe, despite the lack of services and harm reduction facilities dedicated specifically to male sex workers (European Network of Male Prostitution, 2002). Male sex workers are also more susceptible to contracting HIV and other sexually transmitted infections. According to UNAIDS, male sex workers are 19 times more likely to contract HIV than the general population. This is quite startling, considering that only 1 in 10 male sex workers have access to HIV services (UNAIDS, 2009). Smith and Seal (2007) noted how in their study of male escorts in the United States of America that a majority of them engaged in substance abuse regularly, with cocaine and ecstasy being the most commonly used drugs. Approximately one fourth of the respondents in the study reported having serious problems with drug and/or alcohol abuse and stated that their drug habits were seriously affecting their lives. Polidrug use was associated with an increased risk of unsafe sexual encounters with clients and the sex workers' clientele would also often engage in drug use (Browne, Khan, Marino and Minichiello, 2003).

It has been argued in the Irish context that a vast majority of male sex workers become engaged in street prostitution out of necessity and they are predominantly in the younger age category. It is also the case that the vast majority become involved in sex work due to drug and/or alcohol addiction, homelessness and unemployment (Grimes, 2001). There exists no statistical data in Ireland regarding the amount of males engaging in prostitution, or the number of those also engaged in problematic drug use (Grimes, 2001).

The rise in the number of males engaging in problematic drug use in the 1970's and 1980's in the Netherlands resulted in a changing environment for men in street prostitution. For a number of men, this became a way of financing their problematic drug habit, although the extent and type of drug use among male sex workers is highly dependent on the type of sex work they are involved in.

Male escorts and those working in clubs are more likely to engage in smoking cannabis, sniffing cocaine and taking ecstasy (Zuilhof, 1999). Atkinson, Ross, Timpson and William's 2007 study of drug using male sex workers analysed how approximately two thirds of the respondents reported consuming drugs with paying partners. This highlights how the drug consumption of the sex worker alone is not the only thing that is important to consider, but also the drug habits of their respective partners.

CONCLUSION

This chapter has examined the legislation surrounding sex work, drug use and human trafficking in both the Netherlands and Ireland and the nature of sex work in both countries. A theoretical analysis of sex work and drug use was also discussed alongside drug use and sex work from an international context. Research has continued to support the notion that sex workers under the influence of drugs maintain a greater willingness to engage in sexual risk taking in order to fund their drug habit (Cameron, et al., 2005). Sex workers encompass one of the vastly stressed groups within society who often opt for self-medication and engage in recreational drug use as a coping strategy (Edwards, et al., 2000). This chapter has outlined how the fundamental human rights of sex workers continue to be markedly breached, even in the Netherlands were it is a legal profession, as the legal position of the sex worker as an employee as classified by law is complicated to attain in practice (Staring and Zaitch, 2010). It was also important to incorporate how there here has also been a growing recognition of the rights of sex workers throughout Europe and efforts have been made to ensure that their rights are upheld. This is reflected in the establishment of the International Committee on the Rights of Sex Workers in Europe (ICRSE). The ICRSE fight against the negative moral judgements which sex workers are often confronted with.

REFERENCES

Anderson, M.,L., and Taylor, H.F. (2008). *Sociology: Understanding a Diverse Society.* United States of America: Wadsworth Publishing.

Atkinson, J., Ross, M.W., Timpson, S.C., and Williams, M.L. (2007). Characteristics, drug use and sex partners of a sample of male sex workers. *Drug and Alcohol Abuse, 33*, 63-69.

Bacik, I. (Ed). (2002). *Criminal Justice in Ireland.* Dublin: Institute of Public Administration.

Brennan, R., and Van Hout., M.,C. (2011). "Bump and grind": an exploratory study of Mephedrone users' perceptions of sexuality and sexual risk. *Drugs and Alcohol Today, 11,* 93-103.

Brooks, S., Ditmore, M., and Koken, J. A. (2006). Documents by Sex Workers. In Melissa Hope, Ditmore (Ed.) *Encyclopaedia of Prostitution and Sex Work.* United States of America: Greenwood Press.

Browne, J., Khan, M.A., Marino, R., and Minichiello, V. (2003). Alcohol and drug use in Australian male sex workers: its relationship to the safety outcome of the sex encounter. *Aids Care 15(4)* 549-561.

Burke, R.H. (2009). *An Introduction to Criminological Theory.* Devon: Willian Publishing.

Burke, V., and Selfe, D.W. (2001). *Perspectives on Sex, Crime and Society.* Great Britain: Cavendish Publishing Ltd.

Cabezas, Amalia, L., Oritz, D., and Valencia, S. (2010). Latinas, Sex Work and Trafficking in the United States. In Asencio, M. S. (Ed.) *Latina/o Sexualities: Probing Powers, Passions, Practices and Policies.* United States of America: Rutgers University Press.

Cameron, J., Gilchrist, G., and Scoular, J. (2005). Crack and cocaine use among female prostitutes in Glasgow: Risky business. *Drugs, education, prevention and policy, 12*, 381-391.

Central Bureau of Statistics Netherlands (CBS). (2004). *The illegal economy in the Netherlands. Netherlands*: Dutch Central Bureau of Statistics. Retrieved From: http://www.cbs.nl/NR/rdonlyres/3C62D796-A06D-4DBC-9F18-CC2045CD41BB/0/200505X10pub.pdf

Cote, S. (2002). Introduction. In Suzette, Cote (Ed.) *Criminological Theories Bringing the Past to the Future.* United Kingdom: Sage Publications Ltd.

Cox, G., Ryan, P., Whitaker, T. (2011). Stigmatization among Drug-Using Sex Workers Accessing Support Services in Dublin. *Qualitative Health Research, 21,* 1086-1100.

Cusick, L. (2006). Widening the harm reduction agenda: From drug use to sex work. *International Journal of Drug Policy, 17,* 3-11.

De Rode Draad (The Red Thread). (2011). Information for Sex Workers, for questions about your situation and your work. *The Red Thread.* Retrieved from: http:// rodedraad. nl/index.php?id=1649

Department of Health and Children. (2006). *The Irish Study of Sexual Health and Relationships.* Department of Health and Children. Ireland. Retrieved From: http://www.dohc.ie/publications/pdf/ISSHR_Main_Report.pdf?direct=1

Department of Justice and Equality. (2012). *Discussion Document on Future Direction of Prostitution Legislation.* Ireland: Department of Justice, Equality and Defence. Retrieved From: http://www.inis.gov.ie/en/JELR/ Discussion%20Document%20on%20 Future%20 Direction%20of%20Prostitution%20Legislation.pdf/Files/Discussion%20Document%20 on%20Future%20Direction%20of%20Prostitution%20Legislation.pdf

Department of Justice, Equality and Law Reform. (2006). *Report of Department of Justice, Equality and Law Reform and An Garda Síochána Working Group on Trafficking in Human Beings.* Ireland: Department of Justice, Equality and Law Reform. Retrieved From: http://www.justice.ie/en/JELR/THBreport.pdf/Files/THBreport.pdf

Duncan, P. (2012, October 15). Call for Prostitution Legislation to be Reviewed. *The Irish Times.* Retrieved From: http://www.irishtimes.com/ newspaper/ireland/2012/1015 /1224325258155.html

Edwards, J.M., Harcourt, C.L., and Philpot, R.C. (2000). Drug use by Prostitutes in Sydney. *British Journal of Addiction, 84,* 499-505.

Ekberg, G. (2004). The Swedish Law that Prohibits the Purchase of Sexual Services. *Violence Against Women, 10* 1187-1218.

Escort Ireland Client Surveys. (2006). *Irish Escorts Client Survey 2006.* Ireland: Irish Escort Clients. Retrieved From: http://www.escortsurveys.com/irish_ escort_clients_survey_ 2006.html

European Network of Male Prostitution. (2012). *Manual: Tips, Tricks and Models of Good Practice for Service Providers Considering, Planning or Implementing Services for Male Sex Workers.* European Network of Male Prostitution: The Netherlands. Retrieved From: *http://www.who.int/hiv/topics/vct/sw_toolkit/Tips_Tricks_Models_of_Good_ Practice_part_1. pdf*

Farley, M. (2003). Prostitution and the Invisibility of Harm. *Women and Therapy 26(3/4)* 247-280.

Goffman, E. (1963). *Stigma: Notes on the Management of Spoiled Identity.* United States of America: Simon and Schister Inc.

Gotz, H.M., Prins, M., van de Laar, M.J., van Leeuwen, P.A., and van Veen, M.G. (2008). HIV and Sexual Risk Behaviour among Commercial Sex Workers in the Netherlands. *Archives of Sexual Behaviour, 10,* 1-18

Graaf, R.D., Straver, C.J., Vanwesenbeeck, I., Visser, J.H., and Zessen, G.V. (1995). Alcohol and drug use in heterosexual and homosexual prostitution, and its relation to protection behaviour. *AIDS care, 7,* 35-48

Grimes, T. (2001). *Such a Taboo: An analysis of service need and service provision for males in prostitution in the Eastern Region.* Dublin: Eastern Health Board Print. Retrieved

From: http://www.hse.ie/eng/ services/Find_a_Service/Sexualhealth/Gay_ Men's_ Health_Service/Research_Reports/Such_a_Taboo_service_needs_for_males_in_prostitution_Ireland_2001.pdf

Hayden, A. (2012). Human Trafficking and Prostitution: Motion. (Vol 214, No. 12). *House of the Oireachtas Seanad Éireann Debate*. Ireland. Retrieved From: http://debates.oireachtas.ie/seanad/2012/04/18/00007.asp

Irish Statute Book. (1984). *Misuse of Drugs Act*. Ireland: Office of the Attorney General.

Irish Statute Book. (1993). *Sexual Offences Act*. Ireland: Office of the Attorney General. Irish Statute Book. (2008). *Criminal Law (Human Trafficking) Act 2008*. Ireland: Department of Justice.

Jeffreys, S. (2008). *The Idea of Prostitution*. Australia: Spinifex Press.

Jeffreys, S. (2009). *The Industrial Vagina: The Political Economy of the Global Sex Trade*:Canada: Routledge

Kempadoo, K. (1999). Continuities and Change: Five Centuries of Prostitution in the Caribbean. (Ed.) In Kamala, Kempadoo. *Sun, Sex and Gold: Tourism and Sex in the Caribbean*. United States of America: Rowman and Littlefield Publishers Inc.

Kouimtsdist, C, Mosedale, B., and Reynolds, M. (2009). Sex work, substance misuse and service provision: The experiences of female sex workers in South London. *Drugs, Education, Prevention and policy 16,* 355-363.

Kramer, L.A. (2003). Emotional Experiences of Performing Prostitution. *Journal of Trauma Practice, 2*(3/4) 187-197.

Kuo, L. (2002). Prostitution Policy: *Revolutionising Practice through a Gendered Perspective*. New York: New York University Press.

Lamont, M., and Lareau, A. (1988). Cultural Capital: Allusions, Gaps and Glissandos in Recent Theoretical Developments. *Sociological Theory, 6* (2) 153-168.

Lynch, K. (2011). Human Trafficking and Prostitution: Motion. (Vol 210, No. 13).*House of the Oireachtas Seanad Éireann Debate*. Ireland. Retrieved From:http://debates.oireachtas.ie/seanad/2011/10/12/00008.asp

McCullagh, C. (1996). Crime in Ireland: A Sociological Introduction. Cork: University College Cork.

McLaughlin, E., and Muncie, J. (2006). *The Sage Dictionary of Criminology*. London: Sage Publications.

Ministry of Justice of the Netherlands. (2011). *Dutch Drug Policy*. Netherlands: Ministry of Justice of the Netherlands

National Advisory Committee on Drugs. (2008). *Drug Use, Sex Work and the Risk Environment in Dublin*. Dublin: The Stationary Office.

Netherlands Ministry of Foreign Affairs. (2004). *Dutch Policy on Prostitution: Questions and Answers*. Netherlands: Netherlands Ministry of Foreign Affairs.

Netherlands Ministry of Foreign Affairs. (2010). *Faq about Dutch Policy on Prostitution 2010*. Netherlands: Dutch Ministry of Foreign Affairs. Retrieved From http://www.minbuza.nl/binaries/content/assets/minbuza/en/import/en/you_and_the_netherlands/about_the_netherlands/ethical_issues/qa-prostitutie-2010-en.pdf

O'Connor, A. (1996). *Women Working in Prostitution: Towards a Healthier Future*. Dublin: Women's Education Research and Resource Centre. Retrieved From: http://www.drugsandalcohol.ie/5616/1/2030-023Women.pdf

O'Neill, M. (1997). Prostitute Women Now. In A. Scamber and G. Scambler (Ed.) *Rethinking Prostitution: Purchasing Sex in the 1990's*. United States of America: Routledge.

Quigley, P. (2003). Hard Cases in Hard Places: challenges of community addictions work in Dublin. *Drugs, education, prevention and policy, 10,* 211-221.

Rekart, M.L. (2005). Sex-work harm reduction. *British Columbia Centre for Disease Control, 366,* 2123-2134.

Ruhama. (2006). *Uncovering the Misconceptions: The Realities of Legalised Prostitution.* Ireland: Ruhama. Retrieved From: http://www.ruhama.ie/ page.php?intPageID=207

Ruhama. (2010). *Ruhama 2010 Statistics Report.* Ireland: Ruhama. Retrieved From: http://www.ruhama.ie/easyedit/files/2010statsreportruhama.pdf

Seal, D. W., and Smith, M.D. (2007). Sexual Behaviour, Mental Health, Substance Use and HIV Risk Among Agency-Based Male Escorts in a Small U.S. City. *International Journal of Sexual Health, 19(4)* 27-39.

Sex Work Europe (ICRSE). (2006). *Sex Workers Stand up for Rights.* The Netherlands: Committee on the Rights of Sex Workers in Europe. Retrieved From: http://www. sexworkeurope.org/de/about-icrse/ conference-05/conference-press/88-ruth-frost

Sex Workers Alliance Ireland (SWAI). (2012). 33 Reasons why Criminalising the Buyers of Sex is not a 'Solution. SWAI. Ireland. Retrieved From: http://www.sexworkers allianceireland.org/legalissues.html#anchor

Shared Hope International. (2007). *Demand: A Comparative Examination of Sex Tourism and Trafficking in Jamaica, Japan, the Netherlands and the United States:The Netherlands.* United States of America: Shared Hope International. Retrieved From: http://www. sharedhope.org/Portals/0/ Documents/demand_netherlands.pdf

Siegel, D. (2009). Human Trafficking and Legalised Prostitution in the Netherlands. *Temida, 10,* 5-16.

Spector, J. (2006). *Prostitution and Pornography.* California: Stanford University Press.

Staring, R., and Zaitch, D. (2010). The Flesh in Weak, the Spirit Even Weaker. In A. Cauduro, A.Di Nicola, A. Lombardi and P, Ruspini (Ed.) *Prostitution and Human Trafficking: Focus on Clients.* New York: Springer Science and Media.

Taylor, J.D., and Thio, A. (2010). *Social Problems.* Canada: Jones and Bartlett Learning.

UNAIDS. (2009). UNAIDS Guidance Note on HIV and Sex Work. Switzerland: UNAIDS. Retrieved From: http://www.unaids.org/en/media/ unaids/contentassets/documents/unaids publication/2009/JC2306_UNAIDS-guidance-note-HIV-sex-work_en.pdf

United Nations Office on Drugs and Crime. (2009). Global Report on Trafficking in Persons. Switzerland: United Nations. Retrieved From: http://www.unodc.org/documents /Global_Report_on_TIP.pdf

Van der Poel, S. (1992). Professional male prostitution: a neglected phenomenon. *Crime. Law and Social Change, 18,* 259-275.

Vanwesenbeeck, I. (2005). Burnout among Female Indoor Sex Workers. *Archives of Sexual Behaviour, 34,* 627-639.

World Health Organisation. (2005). *Violence Against Women and HIV/AIDS: Critical Intersections (Violence against Sex Workers and HIV Prevention).* Switzerland: Department of Gender Women and Health. Retrieved From: http://www.who.int/gender /documents/sexworkers.pdf

World Health Organisation. (2006). Double *Stigma, Double Challenge: Mental Health and HIV/AIDS in Central and Eastern Europe and the Newly Independent States.* The

MAIDS Project: The Netherlands. Retrieved From: http://www.search4dev.nl/document/362887

Zappone, K. (2012). Human Trafficking and Prostitution: Motion. (Vol 214, No.12). *House of the Oireachtas Seanad Éireann Debate*. Ireland. Retrieved From: http://debates.oireachtas.ie/seanad/2012/04/18/00007.asp

Zuilhof, W. (1999). Sex for Money between Men and Boys in the Netherlands: Implications for HIV Prevention. In Aggleton, Peter (Ed) *Men who Sell Sex: International Perspectives on Male Prostitution and HIV/AIDS*. London: University College London.

In: Drug Use and Abuse
Editor: Marie Claire Van Hout

ISBN: 978-1-62618-232-5

Chapter 6

KHAT-CHEWING PRACTICE: PHYSIO-PSYCHO-SOCIOECONOMIC IMPACTS AND TREATMENT APPROACHES

Kaliyaperumal Karunamoorthi*
Unit of Medical Entomology and Vector Control,
Department of Environmental Health Sciences and Technology,
College of Public Health and Medical Sciences, Jimma University,
Jimma, Ethiopia
Research and Development Centre, Bharathiar University,
Coimbatore, Tamil Nadu, India

ABSTRACT

Mind-altering drugs, especially plants, have always fascinated human beings by its mystic superstitions, magical thoughts and religious rituals. Among the plants khat [*Catha edulis* Forsk (Celastraceae)] is a natural stimulant and it has been used by humans to alter the conscience and the sensorium. Khat consumption is a part of social and cultural fabric of the society in East Africa and Arabian Peninsula. However, over the past two decades, this practice has migrated to all parts of the world by the diasporas, from countries where khat is more commonly used. The fresh leaves of khat are customarily chewed to attain a state of stimulation induced by the psychostimulant component cathinone (natural/herbal ecstasy). Vast numbers of literatures indicate both the positive and negative impact of khat-consumption, however majority of them state about the detrimental practice of khat and its own negative physio-psycho-socioeconomic consequences. The long-term khat-consumption may lead to metabolic disorder as well as to serious ramifications on human health and wellbeing.

In the past, this practice was confined within a few countries as a national issue, but over the past two decades it has been rapidly spreading across the globe due to globalization. Therefore it is not just emerging as a global public health issue but also generates severe negative psycho-socio-economic consequences on the world population,

* Corresponding author Email: k_karunamoorthi@yahoo.com. College of Public Health and Medical Sciences, Jimma University, Ethiopia, Mobile: +251-913-547-847; +91-9600-918-524.

a matter of grave concern. Since khat consumption practice is closely associated with cultural, traditional and religious beliefs, it needs to be approached very cautiously with novel innovative tools. The World Health Organization not only considers the wide-spread habit of khat chewing as a pharmacologically equivalent amphetamine abuse, but has also included cathinone in its list of controlled drugs. Throughout human history, the khat plant remains as a controversy and the khat-chewing practice is still debatable. The present book chapter briefly describes about the khat plant, the history of khat-chewing practice and its prevalence as an age-old practice. Notwithstanding it also deals elaborately on the physico-psycho-socioeconomic impacts of khat chewing practice and its treatment approaches.

Keywords: Drug Use and Abuse, Khat, Khat-chewing, Physico-Psycho-Socioeconomic Impacts

INTRODUCTION

Mind-altering drugs, especially plants, have always fascinated human beings. Surrounded by mystic superstitions, magic thoughts and religious rituals, they have always occupied man's attention. Among the plants used by humans, those able to alter the conscience and the sensorium have drawn special consideration, like, the psychodysleptic drugs, due to their astonishing effects (Delay and Deniker, 1961). The name stimulant can be given to any drug that increases the rate of physiologic function. The term psychostimulant is more specific, referring to compounds that have direct neurological effects, typically: heightened alertness, increased energy, appetite suppression, and sometimes euphoria. This use of psycho-stimulants is widespread and occurs in both recreational and clinical settings. Therapeutic monitoring and screening for use and abuse of these drugs is common in clinical laboratories. Understanding the physiological effects and uses of stimulants will be of value to clinical and forensic laboratory scientists (Foley, 2005).

The use of psychoactive substances in religious and healing rituals, in semi-ritual practices which reinforce social and political bonds, and simply as recreational activity is a universal cultural practice (Steinberg, 2004). In indigenous societies the practice is often governed by an evolved tradition and etiquette that place strictures on misuse (Gebissa, 2004). The use/abuse of psychoactive drugs such as khat leaves are believed to alter one's moods or emotional state either through the sustained release or inhibition of neurotransmitters, thereby enhancing or dampening the response of the individual (Abebe et al., 2005).

Khat is an ancient plant associated with psychological, health and socioeconomic issues on humans. Khat is a plant vastly used in the African continent. The khat-chewing aspect of this plant in particular, is one of the most widespread, longstanding, age-old customs in Eastern and Southern Africa and certain areas of the Arabian Peninsula (Karunamoorthi, Udeani, Babu, and Mossie, 2010). In the last two decades, khat has been regarded as a psychoactive plant taken out of its cultural environment, used in new settings by immigrants. However it has been perceived as an object of abuse and has been targeted for elimination (Carrier, 2007; Grayson, 2008).

Khat abuse and associated health risks are also a growing concern in Europe, North America, Middle-East, New Zealand and Australia as immigrants from African and Arab communities carry the habit of khat chewing (Bhui et al., 2006). In Britain, there are first reports of use by young people of non-migration background which places it in the pathways; toward health risk behaviors among young people in general (Holligan, 2009).

In Islamic countries, alcohol consumption is in general a socially unacceptable practice. But at the Horn of Africa chewing the leaves of the khat tree is both socially and culturally accepted practice. Consequently khat usage is wide spread in the region and the practice has now become the proverbial "door in the wall" – or escape mechanism – that many people use to cope up with the full range of difficult life experiences such as long term unemployment and traumatic life events (Odenwald et al., 2009; Bhui and Warfa, 2007). Since time immemorial, there have been numerous disputes and debates over khat-chewing practices with respect to its positive as well negative impact on society. In recent years, khat-chewing has been observed across all age groups, however its use has been observed to surge among teenagers (Karunamoorthi et al., 2010).

History of Khat Plant

An early written description of khat appeared in Paris in 1697 when Barthelemy d'Herbelot de Molainville traveled to Yemen (translated): "[It] is made with a seed which is unknown to us, which has been forbidden by the doctors of the law in the province of Yemen..., where it originated. ...because it is too strong, and affects the brain" (Krikorian, 1984). It was not until 1975, that United Nations laboratories first discovered the active ingredient of khat to be cathinone, an amphetamine-like substance that has sympathomimetic, euphoric, and mood-altering effects among other health consequences (United Nations Narcotic Laboratory, 1975). The earliest scientific report concerning khat was in the eighteenth century by the botanist Peter Forskal (Baasher, 1980).

Physical Characteristic Features of Khat Plant

Khat is a bushy plant and commonly known as the "Flower of Paradise". It is grown and widely used in the regions extending from Eastern to Southern Africa, as well as on the Arabian Peninsula, particularly in Ethiopia, Somalia, Yemen, Kenya, Malawi, Uganda, Tanzania, the Congo, Zambia, Zimbabwe, Madagascar, and South Africa. Khat grows especially well in moist conditions and is generally cultivated along the mountain slopes, at altitudes of 3500-7000 ft, and can vary in height from 3-15 ft (Figure 1) (Hattab and Angmar-MaÊ nsso, 2000). Distribution is in bundles of stalks with leaves, each weighing in the range of 100-500g (Figure 2). The fresh leaves and stalks exist in different varieties of various qualities. Young yellow leaves from the distal branches appear to be the most desirable among the consumers (Paris, 1958). The leaves from the lower branches are referred to as ''qatal'' and are less desirable.

The khat shrub has two forms, red khat and green khat also known as white khat. There is a distinct user's tendency to prefer red khat over the green khat.

Because the chewers believe that red khat has higher levels of the psycho-stimulating principles than green khat. Khat can be grown in drought-hit-areas where other crops usually fail and also at high altitudes. Khat leaves can be harvested throughout the year and the planting is staggered to obtain a continuous supply.

Figure 1. Author with the well-grown Khat plant of about 6 feet.

Figure 2. Bundle of khat leaves.

MODE OF KHAT-CHEWING

The difference between khat and other stimulant agents is related to the special way in which khat is consumed. Khat leaves are usually chewed but may be smoked, sprinkled on food, or brewed into a tea. Young, fresh khat leaves are chewed and held in the lower buccal pouch unilaterally in a bolus for 3 h or longer. The saliva/leaf slurry is usually swallowed and may party be expectorated (Hattab and Angmar-Maensso, 2000). Chewed predominantly for its pleasurable effects, khat leaves play a major role in social life of the communities who consume it. The young fresh leaves of khat are considered to be the most desirable, presumably due to their higher cathinone content (Toennes, Harder, Schramm, Niess, and Kauert, 2003).

In one study, only 10% of the original alkaloid content remained in the leaves after they were chewed for 1 hour. This study also demonstrated that the oral mucosa play a primary role in absorption (Toennes et al., 2003). Typically, an individual consumes 100-200 g of khat leaves (1 bundle) in a session, and its effect lasts for several hours. The stimulant effects of khat are due to its pharmacologically active ingredients – cathinone and cathine – which are naturally occurring alkaloids that can be extracted from the plant. Cathinone is absorbed through the buccal mucosa and the stomach. After absorption it is metabolically transformed, mainly to norephedrine (Feyissa and Kelly, 2008).

Historical Perspective of Khat-Chewing Practice

It has been believed that the consumption of khat leaves pre-dates the use of coffee and the practice of khat chewing has been prevailed for social and psychological rationales (Karunamoorthi et al., 2010). Khat chewing is a practice that dates back thousands of years in the Horn of Africa and the Arabian Peninsula (Al-Mugahed, 2008). The leaves were chewed by the people in the medieval Islamic sultanates of the southern region of today's Ethiopia as early as the fourteenth century. From there, the khat chewing culture spread to the Horn region along the historic long-distance trading routes that connected Muslim trading states with each other and with the Indian Ocean world. By the mid-nineteenth century, the plant was used for a variety of purposes in the same region that is now Ethiopia. In the Kingdom of Shawa (central Ethiopia) and in Kaffa (southwestern Ethiopia), the plant has been extensively cultivated and used (Beke, 1843; Harris, 1844).

Beginning in the early twentieth century, its consumption was transformed from a luxury enjoyed by the urban elite to a cultural practice performed by a significant portion of the population in the region and, after the 1930s, to a commonplace pastime activity of nearly all social classes, cultural categories and religious affiliations. Khat chewing is a legal pastime and has woven into the social and cultural fabric of Ethiopia, Somalia and Yemen (Odenwald et al., 2005). In the last two decades, khat has migrated from the traditional use regions in the Horn of Africa and the Middle East to Western countries (Carrier, 2007; Gebissa, 2010).

Prevalence of Khat-Chewing

There is no reliable estimate on the prevalence of khat-chewing worldwide, however it has been estimated to be that nearly 5 to 10 million people, predominantly living in the horn of Africa and the Arabian peninsula, most notably including Ethiopia, Somalia, and Yemen (Balint, Ghebrekidan, and Balint, 2009; US Department of Justice, 2003) and from Djibouti, Madagascar, Tanzania and Uganda (Elmi, 1983; Ihunwo, Kayanja, and Amadi-Ihunwo, 2004). Recently this habit has reached to other parts of the world too (Al-Motarreb, Baker, and Broadley, 2002). The use of this drug has also been reported among immigrants of East African and Arabian origin living in Europe and the Americas (Kuczkowski, 2005; Al-Motarreb et al., 2005; Kassim and Croucher, 2006), as a social recreational act and to establish and maintain their cultural tradition and identity (Karunamoorthi et al., 2010).

In Yemen, it is estimated that at least 80% of men, 60% of women, and increasing numbers of children younger than 10, settle down on most afternoons to enjoy a pastime recommended by religious mystics since the 10th century (Kandela, 2000). Recent regional and countrywide surveys reveal that an average of 30 percent of Ethiopians is regular khat chewers (Figure 3) (Belew, Kebede, Kassaye, and Enquoselassie, 2000; Arrafaine, 2004).

The prevalence and socio-demographic correlates of khat use have also been determined in a large house-to-house survey carried out in the rural Ethiopian community of Butajira (Alem, Kebede, and Kullgren, 1999). Khat chewing, particularly in Yemen, is deeply rooted in tradition and is believed to form a basis of social interaction and increased self-esteem. Formerly, khat leaves were used to prepare a tea-like drink (Hattab and Angmar-MaÊ nsso, 2000). Not surprisingly, the Yemenian government has tried to curtail the habit but with little success. In 1972, the Prime Minister of Yemen forbade khat chewing by civil servants and tried to limit the amount of its cultivation, but 3 months later he lost his post (Kandela, 2000).

Khat is unique as a substance of abuse. Unlike other abused substances, khat is highly perishable. The leaves are freshly stripped from the khat trees at dawn and rapidly distributed by airplanes and by organized delivery systems in regions where khat chewing is widespread (Kandela, 2000). Various reasons were given for chewing khat. In Ethiopia, eighty percent of the chewers use it to obtain maximum concentration during prayer. It has been observed to have strong association of Muslim religion, smoking, and high educational level with daily khat chewing. Therefore, khat chewing affects a majority of the adult population of the Butajira district, in particular the most educated and most productive age group (Alem et al., 1999).

Figure 3. Author with the Ethiopian women carrying khat to the market.

BIOCULTURAL PERSPECTIVES OF KHAT CHEWING

Khat-chewing is both a social and a culture-based activity and the effect may last for several hours. It is said to enhance the social interactions, and so khat sessions are frequently used for celebrations (Karunamoorthi et al., 2010). These khat sessions, known in Ethiopia as "barch'a", and in Yemen as "majlis al-qat" (literally "the council of khat"), are informal events. The modern khat-chewers implicate that it boosts up their energy levels, increases alertness, confidence, sense of happiness, thought process, creativity and communication (Hassan et al., 2000). Khat is harvested in the early morning hours and sold in markets in late morning as bundles of twigs, stems, and leaves. Since khat leaves are highly perishable, following the harvest the khat sellers wrap it up with banana leaves to preserve its freshness (Figure 4). Yemenis consider khat sessions to represent important social occasions to meet other people and for the exchange of ideas and information. Although friends and individuals of similar social status gather together, these occasions are frequently open to anybody who wishes to attend, especially sessions which combine weddings, funerals, and political election campaigns. At such gatherings, social class distinctions are forgotten (Raman, 1983). In Ethiopia, khat is commonly used for social recreation. Occupational groups such as motor vehicle drivers and truck drivers, chew khat during long distance trips, in order to keep them awake, and for other different reasons. There is also some specific usage of khat by the special sections of the community; craftsmen and farmers use khat to reduce physical fatigue, and traditional healers to heal ailments (Mekasha, 1983; Kalix, 1984).

Figure 4. An Ethiopian female khat seller wrapping the bundle of khat with banana leaf.

CHEMICAL CONSTITUENTS OF KHAT

The environment and climate conditions majorly determine the chemical profile of khat leaves. Khat is known as a 'natural amphetamine'. The main psychoactive ingredients in khat are cathinone (chemically similar to amphetamine) and cathine, a phenethylamine-type substance isolated from the plant (Figure 5).

The fact that cathinone has a closer structural similarity with amphetamine, and both sharing common pharmacodynamic features, has led to the conclusion that cathinone is the most important active ingredient of khat which causes the major pharmacological effects (Hollister, 1995).

Khat must be transported quickly to its intended market because of its limited shelf life. Fresh khat leaves contain cathinone--a Schedule I drug under the Controlled Substances Act; however, the leaves typically begin to deteriorate after 48 hours, causing the chemical composition of the plant to break down. Once this occurs, the leaves contain cathine, a Schedule IV drug (US Department of Justice, 2003). In addition, khat plants contain chemicals called alkaloids, which serve as narcotics and hallucinogens. In 1975 Cathinone (β-ketoamphetamine) a monoamine alkaloid was found in the khat shrub. Cathinone is closely related to cathine, ephedrine, and other phenethylamines. Cathinone is not very stable and breaks down to produce cathine and norephedrine (Figure 5). Cathinone differs from many other amphetamines in that it has a ketone functional group. Other amphetamines that share this structure include the antidepressant bupropion and the stimulant methcathinone among others.

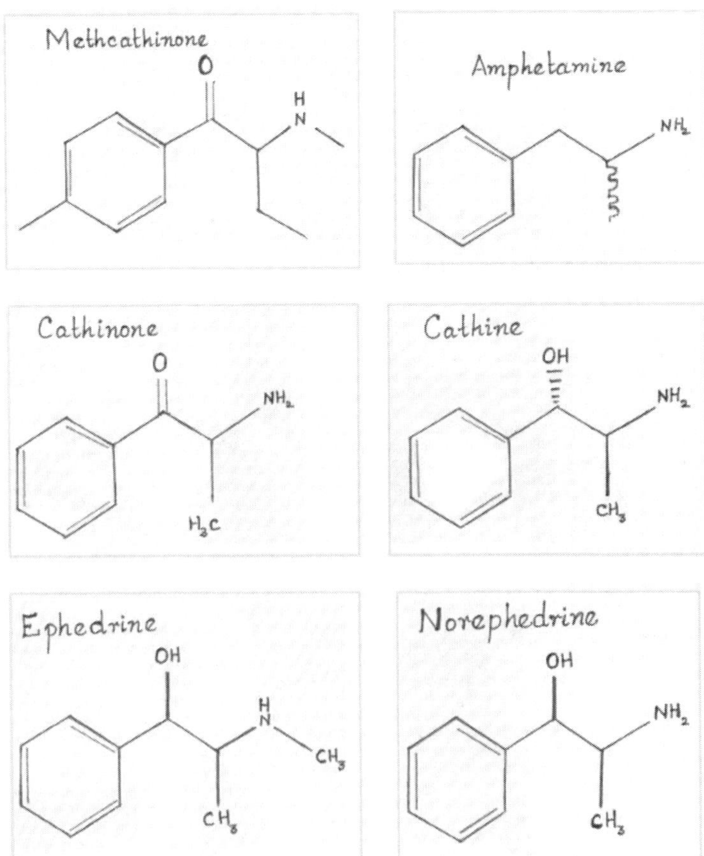

Figure 5.Major chemical constituents of Khat.

MODE OF ACTION

Khat is chewed for recreational purposes and its valued psychostimulant effect is highest when fresh (Baasher, 1980; Elmi, 1983). Fresh khat leaves mainly contain cathinone (United Nation Narcotic Laboratory, 1975), an alkaloid thought to mediate the main psychostimulant effects (Kalix, 1992). The aforesaid explains the users' preference for the fresh khat (Guantai and Maitai, 1982; Schorno, Brenneisen, and Steinegger, 1982). Cathinone, like amphetamine, acts by releasing catecholamines from presynaptic storage sites and subsequently inhibit their uptake, thereby increasing temporal and spatial presence of these neurotransmitters (dopamine [DA], serotonin [5-HT] and noradrenaline [NA]) at the presynaptic receptors (Safer and Krager, 1998; Krause, Dresel, Krauser, Kung, and Tatsch, 2000).

Psychostimulants and other drugs that inhibit uptake of 5-HT into the presynaptic nerve terminals increase serotonergic neurotransmission by enhancing its synaptic concentrations (Kimani and Nyongesa, 2008). Khat chewing over a prolonged period has been reported to produce a number of adverse consequences, ranging from psychiatric disturbances to damage to the major organs of the body (Hoffman and Al'absi, 2010]. In addition, long-term khat chewing has been associated with neurological disorders too (Morrish, Nicolau, Brakkenberg, and Smith, 1999).

EFFECTS OF KHAT-CHEWING

The use/abuse of psychoactive drugs such as khat leaves are believed to alter one's moods or emotional state either through the sustained release or inhibition of neurotransmitters, thereby enhancing or dampening the response of the individual. Cathinone stimulates an excessive production of dopamine, which controls feelings of pleasure and happiness, in the human brain. This can lead to a variety of short-term effects, including hallucinations, bizarre thoughts, schizophrenia, high blood pressure, rapid breathing, lethargy, mild depression, nightmares, and heightened alertness. The drug also can make users more aggressive, inflate their egos, and cause them to be irrational and irritated, which may lead to unusual behavior, such as increased arguments, reckless actions, and violence. The effects of chewing khat, which can vary by user and it may not show up for 3 or more hours, but then may last for several hours. Cathinone can be found only in fresh khat leaves. Older leaves contain the substance cathine, which is less sought after by chewers. Notably, cathine lacks the euphoric effects of cathinone. Its main effects are a moderate degree of euphoria, leaving the user cheerful and talkative, followed by mild depression (Kandela, 2000). Most chewers used khat to gain good level of concentration for prayer. Some chewers reported that khat intake results in increased energy levels and alertness, enhances imaginative ability and the capacity to associate ideas, and improves the ability to communicate.

INDECISIVE LEGALITY OF KHAT

Khat used to be sold in the past in restricted areas but now is sold freely on the open market in the major cities of Ethiopia or elsewhere without any interventions. Khat, a plant containing the active principle, S-(-)-cathinone, is often chewed in Ethiopia without any restriction by law enforcement officials (Figure 6).

On the contrary, the plant active principle, S-(-)-cathinone is a schedule I of the controlled substance Act (according to the United Nations Drug and Crime control, 1975). Cathinone's derivative, cathine is also a schedule IV psychomimetic drug.

In Canada and parts of the European Union, khat possession is illegal (WHO Expert Committee on Drug Dependence, 2006). In Australia, to import khat, a license and permit are needed by the Australian Quarantine and Inspection Service (Australian Government, 2009), whereas in the United Kingdom, khat possession and use are legal. In the United States, fresh khat is a schedule I drug under the Controlled Substances Act, defined as having a high potential for abuse and not currently accepted for medical treatment (US Department of Justice, 2003).

To date, human research involving khat has been limited by low participant numbers; thus, whether khat chewing is dangerous and addictive or rather a way of life that lacks serious long-term health effects for the user remains controversial.

In the EU, the starting point for controlling psychoactive substances is the two UN treaties, the Single Convention on Narcotic Drugs of 1961 and the Convention on Psychotropic Substances of 1971, which between them list nearly 250 substances to be controlled by all signatories under their national drug legislation. The psychoactive substances in khat, cathine and cathinone, are listed in Schedule III and Schedule I respectively of the 1971 convention; it follows that they are also therefore controlled in all EU Member States (Griffiths et al., 2010). The plant khat is not controlled at UN level. In 2006, the WHO Expert Committee on Drug Dependence critically reviewed khat and recommended not to schedule it in the UN conventions, since the level of abuse and threat to public health was not significant enough to warrant international control (WHO Expert Committee on Drug Dependence, 2006).

Figure 6. Ethiopian Khat trader selling the khat leaves in the market.

PSYCHOLOGICAL IMPACTS OF KHAT CHEWING

Khat-Chewing and Neurological Disorder

In recent years khat induced psychosis (serious mental illness) has become more common. This may follow consumption of exceptionally potent material, when taken in excess or in a predisposed individual (Hassan, Gunaid, and Murray-Lyon, 2005). Studies show that khat is functionally used by people with Posttraumatic Stress Disorder (PTSD) and other mental disorders to achieve temporary relief from their symptoms (Bhui et al., 2003; Odenwald et al., 2009); and that excessive khat use is associated with the development of psychotic symptoms which may be brief or persistent (Odenwald et al., 2009; Odenwald, 2007; Warfa et al., 2007). Odenwald et al. (2009) recently illustrated the causal mechanism for khat-induced paranoid symptoms among combatants. Furthermore, there is initial evidence that early onset of khat use in life and excessive khat use might be a substantial risk factor for the development of schizophrenia-type disorders (Odenwald et al., 2005). The chronic use of khat has also been associated with the development of hypertension (Halbach, 1972), psychosis, cognitive impairment and disabling neurological illness (Morrish et al., 1999). Khat is also linked to relapse or deterioration of pre-existing chronic psychotic disorders (Bhui et al., 2003; Bimerew, Sonn, and Korlenbout, 2007). Furthermore khat chewing seems to complicate the management of pre-existing serious mental illness. Preliminary data on sixty-five psychotic male patients who were admitted for psychiatric care in Sana'a due to symptoms uncontrolled by treatment have been analysed (Hassan, Gunaid, Ali, and Shehab, 2003). They indicated that khat chewing in psychotic patients was likely to be associated with disturbance of mood and behaviour, aggravation of delusional symptoms and diminished response to anti-psychotic therapy (Hassan et al., 2005).

Effects of Khat-Chewing on Learning and Memory

A study investigated the effects of fresh khat extract on learning and memory in CBA mice and has shown that khat extract has selective effects on spatial learning and memory, with low dose having no effect on learning but impairing memory, whereas high dose impairs learning but improves memory. However, the mechanism by which khat induced strong effect on learning and memory needs to be elucidated. In addition, there is need to investigate the effect of post-training administration of khat extract on spatial learning and memory and further explore the effect of this widely used psychostimulant on learning and memory using other paradigms (Kimani and Nyongesa, 2008).

SOCIO-ECONOMIC IMPACTS OF KHAT CHEWING

The influence of khat chewing is not only linked with health-related problems but also with household economic welfare. There are good economic reasons for limiting the use of khat. It has been estimated that 40% of irrigated farmland is given over to khat cultivation, overtaking coffee and cereal farming. Even the poorest families admit spending up to 50% of their income on the leaves (Kandela, 2000). The potential adverse effect is diversion of income for the purchase of khat, resulting in neglect of the essential commodities of the family, leading to family discord and divorce (Kalix, 1984; Mekasha, 1983; Zein, 1984; Pantelis, Hindler, and Taylor, 1989). Khat fuels the local informal economy and is indeed "green gold" for many farmers and traders. However, khat chewing has drained the resources away from the regional economies to the producer regions, and has diverted the khat-chewers from more productive activities. It also drains the household income considerably and affects not only the khat-chewer, but also his/her entire family, society as well as the country at large. Khat-chewing practice not only induces psychiatric morbidity and adverse health effects, but also leads to criminal involvement and disturbance of public disorder too.

Nationally, diversion of resources toward the production or importation and marketing of khat has a negative impact on the economies of khat consuming countries. Baasher (1980), estimates that in cities of Somalia and Yemen, a consumer spends about 25% of his daily earnings on khat and that the extensive cultivation of khat results in the decreased production of other more essential crops like cereals, which indirectly promotes malnutrition related illness among the community in the khat growing areas (Murad, 1983). In addition, Bin Sallam (2004) estimated that $10 million to $26 million dollars are spent daily in Yemen on purchasing khat. Furthermore, this rather large economic expenditure limits the availability of financial resources needed for protecting and improving people's health and wellbeing (Regional Committee for the Eastern Mediterranean, 1961). It is well known that khat chewing is highly prevalent in Yemen, and the general population has a positive perception of the habit (Al-Motarreb et al., 2005). Yemenis have chewed khat for nearly 700 years, and all previous attempts to curb the habit have failed (Baron, 1999; Whitekaer, 1999). In fact, there is evidence that the habit has been spreading rapidly in Yemen in recent years, becoming a socially acceptable behavior for women and even children (Baron, 1999; Yemen Times, 2006).

Khat-Chewing and Loss of Productivity

In Sana'a, where the normal hours of work are between 8am and 2pm, people frequently leave work soon after midday in order to purchase the best leaves from the market. During the afternoon almost every person in the street is observed to have khat branches wrapped in plastic tucked under their arm, in preparation for an evening of relaxation (Kandela, 2000). The profits from growing khat are huge and far greater than those of growing coffee, resulting in large plantations of mature and well-established khat crop growing.

Indeed, nearly three decades ago the practice was quite confined to older men or members of Muslim communities who used it in lieu of alcohol on religious grounds, which posed limited public health and socio-economic threat. However, in the recent years, the production and consumption of khat in certain African states have risen dramatically and several million people using khat in a daily basis, has raised public health concerns. Within the last decade the hitherto little known psychoactive substance of khat has emerged as a regional and international issue and has caused alarm among policy makers and health care professionals. Besides damaging health, khat has been observed to cause adverse psycho-socio-economic effects on many other aspects of life, including the loss of thousands of acres of arable land and billions of hours of work (Ageely, 2008).

PHYSIOLOGICAL IMPACTS OF KHAT CHEWING

Khat-chewing and Gastrointestinal Tract

In the gastrointestinal tract, the astringent characteristics of the tannins in khat accounts for periodontal disease, stomatitis, oesophagitis and gastritis (WHO Advisory Group, 1980). Delay to intestinal absorption contributes to some degree to malnutrition. Tannins and norpseudoephdrine contribute to constipation, the most common medical complaint of the khat user. In a randomized controlled trial, Heymann et al. (1995) reported a delay in gastric emptying after chewing khat, which was attributed to the sympathomimetic action of the cathinone.

Makonnen (2000) reported that khat produced constipation in mice and an antispasmodic action on guinea-pig isolated ileum. The antispasmodic effect of khat extract was observed to be similar to that of d-amphetamine. Khat chewing has also been shown to be a risk factor for duodenal ulcers (Raja'a, Noman, Al-Warafi, Al-Mashraki, and Al-Yosofi, 2000). The oral consumption of khat by people of Arab Peninsula has been linked with oesophageal carcinoma (Gunaid et al., 1995). Accordingly, human genotoxicity caused by khat chewing was ascertained by the occurrence of micronucleus in exfoliated buccal and bladder cells of khat consumers (Kassie, Darroudi, Kundi, Schulte-Hermann, and Knasmuller, 2001).

Khat-Chewing and Loss of Appetite

Khat tends to diminish appetite leading to malnutrition in extreme cases, and can cause hypothermia and hyperventilation. Despite having the physical limits to the amount that can be chewed, a few people have acute damaging side-effects (Kandela, 2000). It is known that amphetamine-like compounds affect appetite centrally, by acting in the arcuate nucleus of the hypothalamus, but cathinone also has effects on gut motility which may compound this effect (Heymann et al., 1995).

Khat-Chewing and Cardiovascular Physiology

Cathinone increases heart rate and blood pressure through norepinephrine release from peripheral neurones similar to amphetamine (Kalix, 1992). Regular khat chewing is associated with elevated mean diastolic blood pressure (Tesfaye, Byass, Wall, Berhane, and Bonita, 2008). Controlled human studies have shown increases in arterial blood pressure after chewing khat coinciding with increased plasma cathinone concentrations (Widler, Mathys, Brenneisen, *Kalix, and Fisch,* 1994). Cardiovascular complications from cathinone use may therefore be similar to those of amphetamine. The temporal relation between use of amphetamine (Bashour, 1994) or its analogue, "ecstasy" (3,4-methylenedioxy-methamphetamine, MDMA) (Henry, Jeffries, and Dawling, 1992; Kuczkowski and Benumof, 2003), and myocardial ischemia/infarction and dysrhythmias, respectively, is well documented. Myocardial ischemia/infarction could be precipitated by the increased myocardial oxygen demands, from cardiac stimulation and peripheral vasoconstriction by cathinone and coronary vasoconstriction (Kuczkowski, 2005). Researchers studied the impact of khat chewing on cardiovascular physiology and demonstrated that khat chewing is a potential risk factor for myocardial ischemia (Al-Motarreb, Al-Kebsi, Al-Adhi, and Broadley, 2002).

Khat-Chewing and Cancer

The habit of chewing khat has prevailed for centuries among populations in the regions where it has been grown, and its use is gradually spreading to other parts of the world. Khat chewing is associated with harmful effects and pathological conditions in various organ systems as well as in oral tissues (Al-Habori, 2005). People who chew khat for prolonged periods have been found to have a higher incidence of head and neck cancer when compared with those who do not chew khat (Soufi, Kameswaran, and Malatani, 1991; Nasr and Khatri, 2000).

Some people claim that khat has medicinal effects in, for example, diabetes and asthma. However, recent studies suggest links with cases of oral and gastrointestinal malignancies and some cases of lymphoma. But it is not yet clear whether these cases can be attributed to the use of khat or the increased use of chemical fertilizers to improve the yield. One thing is certain, even if medical evidence is forthcoming about ill effects of the substance; it is unlikely to have any significant impact on the extraordinarily widespread use of khat, which is such a fundamental part of everyday life in Yemen (Kandela, 2000).

Khat-Chewing and Sexuality

The effect of khat on human reproduction remains as an area of considerable interest (Mwenda, Arimi, Kyama, and Langat, 2003). Ethical concerns limit the nature of experimentation on khat using human subjects. Relatively few studies have addressed possible effects of khat on reproductive function and these have mainly focused on male animals since the recreational use of khat is more prevalent in men than women (Al-Motarreb et al., 2002a). Limited studies that have been done provide conflicting results, with some investigators suggesting that khat increases sexual desire and can be used as an aphrodisiac (Islam et al., 1990). In contrast, alternative findings suggest khat may have the opposite effect, and may result in impairment of sexuality (WHO Advisory Group, 1980).

Islam et al. (1990) reported loss of libido and decreased semen output in people who chew khat. In addition, deleterious effects of khat on semen parameters including sperm morphology have been observed in khat addicts, especially those who have consumed khat for a long time (El-Sshoura et al., 1995). Cathinone was responsible for the decrease in testosterone concentration (Balint et al., 1991).

Through its effect on the male reproductive system, the drug leads to progressive estrangement between husband and wife. Khat has attributed for one out of two divorces in Djibouti (Kalix and Braenden, 1985). Long-term and regular consumption of khat may also lead to progressive and diminished sex performance, leading to sexual impotence in male (Dalu, 2000).

Khat-Chewing and Pregnancy

Pregnancy is an important event during a woman's reproductive life. The mother as well as her fetus's are extremely sensitive to external stimuli. Like tobacco smoking, khat chewing during pregnancy can have a severe adverse effect on the baby's health and wellbeing (Abdul Ghani, Eriksson, , Kristiansson , and Qirbi, 1987; Eriksson, Ghani, and Kristiansson, 1991). In Yemen, a recent study has well-documented a high prevalence of khat chewing during pregnancy. This study implicated that disadvantaged women (in terms of education, wealth or health care utilization) are more likely to chew khat during pregnancy than other women (Khawaja, Al-Nsour, and Saad, 2008). A few other studies have investigated the prevalence, and adverse effects, of khat chewing in pregnant women in Yemen and beyond (Mwenda et al., 2003).

Several studies documented a number of negative reproductive health consequences and adverse pregnancy outcomes of khat chewing, including lower lipoid, sexual impotence, and inhibition of utero-placental blood flow, leading to a teratogenic effect and the impairment of fetal growth (Mwenda et al., 2003). Although Yemeni women frequently complain of poor lactation (Hassan et al., 2005; Luqman and Danowski, 1976), it is not established empirically whether this is due to khat chewing. A recent case report has documented chest pains, tachycardia and hypertension after a session of khat chewing by a pregnant woman (Kuczkowski, 2005).

Khat-Chewing and Lower Birth Weight

Lower birth weight was also found to be associated with khat chewing (Hassan et al., 2005; Mwenda et al., 2003; Abdul Ghani et al., 1987). However, there is no significant association between chewing khat and still birth or congenital malformations (Eriksson, Ghani, and Kristiansson, 1991). It is well-established that low birth weight is a known risk factor for both perinatal and young infant death; hence, khat chewing may be a contributing factor to infant mortality (Mwenda et al., 2003). In Yemen, infant mortality has been relatively high. The infant mortality rate is estimated as 75 deaths per 1,000 live births in 2004 compared to a global rate of 54 deaths per 1,000 live births and a regional rate of 47 deaths per 1,000 live births in Western Asia (Population Reference Bureau, 2005). It is yet unknown how much the practice of khat chewing contributes to deaths during infancy (Khawaja et al., 2008).

KHAT-CHEWING AND CHEMICAL PESTICIDE RESIDUE

Indeed, pesticides are considered as a powerful weapon or magic bullets in the developing countries in order to enhance the agriculture productivity. However, it has been observed that pesticides are causing serious public health hazard and environmental pollution due to haphazard usage of pesticides (Karunamoorthi, Mohammed, and Wassie, 2012; Karunamoorthi, Mohammed, and Jemal, 2011).

Recently chemical pesticides have been incorporated into the cultivation of khat for the purpose of combating common insects and to preserve the freshness of khat leaves. Fresh leaves are normally chewed without any cleaning such as washing, soaking in hot water, or thermal treatments to reduce the concentration of such pesticides, both in the producing and consuming countries.

There is concern that people who do not wash khat before consuming it, will ingest pesticides (Date, Tanida, and Hobara, 2004). Such pesticides contribute to cancers of the digestive system and kidney failure among khat chewers (IRIN, 2007). In addition, it has resulted in adverse health effects such as body weakness, nasal problems too (Date et al., 2004). The exposure of cells to pesticides can lead to cellular oxidative stress, which may have genotoxic effects and may increase cancer risk (Clemens, 1991), as carbamates and organophosphates are the two most common pesticides used by farmers in Yemen (Date et al., 2004),

The use of organochlorine pesticides has been attributed, in part, as contributing to the incidence of oral and oesophageal cancers amongst khat chewers (Al-Habori, 2005; Daba, Hymete, Bekhit, Mohamed, and Bekhit, 2011).

Some patients have been admitted to hospital in Yemen after chewing poisoned khat and within 3 days they have been observed to experience jaundice, coma and sometimes death (Moghram, 2006). The sudden death of some previously healthy young people in Yemen while chewing khat sprayed with insecticide (such as dimethoate) may be explained by the accumulation of acetylcholine from the poison, in the heart and brain involving bradycardia and cardiac arrest (Alhifi, 2006).

Clearly, farmers and their workers applying pesticides to khat and other inter-spaced crops may also be at risk. One example cited is that of a self-inflicted poisoning, where a farmer ingested the pesticide to show others that it was harmless (Al-Hadrani and Thabet, 2000). Parasitic infections, such as fascioliasis, can also be transmitted through the consumption of contaminated khat (Doherty, Price, Moody, Wright, and Glynn, 1995; Cats, Scholten, Meuwissen, and Kuipers, 2000).

Treatment Approaches

The present chapter helps in scrutinizing and exposing a strong freckled conclusion about khat-chewing tradition and practice. Several studies across the globe have reported khat-chewing as a harmful activity on the basis of physio-psycho-socioeconomic consequences. In contrast, few studies suggest that it is an indispensable indigenous tradition for social recreation (Karunamoorthi et al., 2010).

There is no concrete evidence to state whether khat is an addictive drug or a habit-induced drug (Regional Committee for the Eastern Mediterranean, 1961; Kennedy, 1987; Koori Drug Info, 2005). Research has not established whether khat produces withdrawal symptoms when the drug is withheld and whether the user experiences tolerance as they become accustomed to it (Kennedy, 1987).

According to a World Health Organization Expert Group on drug dependence: as stated in (Kalix, 1987, p. 48), ''Khat consumption may induce 'moderate but often persistent psychic dependence', the withdrawal symptoms after prolonged khat use seem to be limited, however, to lethargy, mild depression, slight trembling and recurrent bad dreams''.

A number of khat-chewers believe that khat-sessions preserve their identity as well as help to keep their communities together. Thus, khat-chewing is recognized as a legitimate practice among certain members of these societies.

Apparently, the use of this Flower of paradise, African salad, Tea of the Arabs, (other names for khat) is controversial, and the manner to regulate its continuous use, needs to be debated. The use of khat is interwoven with certain fundamental historic traditional values and religion, which need to be approached very cautiously. This present chapter is in an effort put in perspective for its cultural legitimacy and to obtain a constructive outcome in the near future, it makes the following conclusive recommendations (Karunamoorthi et al., 2010);

- Raising awareness with the general public in terms of the harmful effects of khat-chewing. This can be accomplished via appropriate communication strategies like printed materials and electronic media.
- Since this is a major social issue particularly in East Africa and the Arabian Peninsula, the adverse physico-psycho-socioeconomic impacts of khat-chewing should be included in various academic curricula in particular the primary and secondary schools.
- Posters and billboards portraying the harmful effects of khat should be placed at various strategic locations, including areas adjacent to khat parlors.
- Suitable communication strategies should be developed to educate certain targeted populations about the harmful effects of khat.
- At the village level, special community-based awareness groups should be formed which should include, former khat-chewers, village chiefs, community leaders and religious leaders. It is possible that such an elite village group could unite in an effort to eradicate this khat-chewing debacle.
- Khat parlors should be regulated and closely monitored, by the local administration.
- Special khat rehabilitation programs and units must be developed for avid khat-chewers to provide them timely as well as appropriate counseling and treatment.
- To support and share the scientific research and knowledge on khat in different institutions and universities and to explore the different effects of khat on public health (Hassan et al., 2005).
- Educational programs to prevent khat-chewing habit during pregnancy among the underserved women may be recommended (Khawaja et al., 2008).
- Counseling pregnant women about the health consequences of the habit and effective ways for quitting during the antenatal visits may prove helpful. Further research is needed however before firm recommendations are made (Khawaja et al., 2008).
- The health impact of khat chewing on pregnant women especially necessitates further research in order to help design public health and awareness programs showing the health risks of this habit (Khawaja et al., 2008).
- A cohort study of pregnant women utilizing antenatal health clinics may be recommended in order to assess causality between chewing Khat and various birth outcomes, including low birth weight and neonatal mortality (Khawaja et al., 2008).

ACKNOWLEDGMENTS

I would like to thank Mrs. Melita Prakash for her sincere assistance in editing the manuscript. My last but not least heartfelt thanks go to my colleagues from the Department of Environmental Health Science, College of Public Health and Medical Sciences, Jimma University, Ethiopia, for their kind support and cooperation.

REFERENCES

Abdul Ghani, N., Eriksson, M., Kristiansson. B., and Qirbi, A. (1987). The influence of khat-chewing on birth-weight in full term infants. *Social Science and Medicine,* 24, 625-627.

Abebe, D., Debella, A., Dejene, A., Degefa, A., Abebe, A., Urga, K., and Ketema, K. (2005). Khat chewing habit as a possible risk behaviour for HIV infection: A case-control study. *Ethiopian Journal of Health Development*, (3), 174-181.

Ageely, H.M. (2008). Health and Socioeconomic Hazards associated with Khat consumption. *Journal of Family and Community Medicine*, 15(1), 3-11.

Alem, A., Kebede, D., and Kullgren, G. (1999). The prevalence and socio-demographic correlates of khat chewing in Butajira, Ethiopia. *Acta Psychiatrica Scandinavica Supplementum* , 397, 84-91.

Al-Habori, M. (2005). The potential adverse effects of habitual use of Catha edulis (khat). *Expert Opinion on Drug Safety,* 4, 1145-1154.

Al-Hadrani, A.M., and Thabet, A.M.M. (2000). Acute adverse health effects of pesticides sprayed on khat trees. *Journal of Pesticide Control and Environmental Sciences,* 8(1), 97-106.

Alhifi, M. (2006, 1-3 May). Pesticides: the necessary evil. Yemen Times. Retrieved from www.yementimes. com/article.shtml?i=942andp= healthanda=1.

Al-Motarreb, A., Al-Kebsi, M., Al-Adhi, B., and Broadley, K.J. (2002). Khat chewing and acute myocardial infarction. *Heart,* 87, 279-280.

Al-Motarreb, A., Baker, K., and Broadley, K. J. (2002a). Khat: pharmacological and medical aspects and its social use in Yemen. *Phytotherapy Research*, 16, 403-413.

Al-Motarreb, A., Braincon, S., Al-Jaber, N., Al-Adhi, B., Al-Jailani, F., Salak, M.S., and Broadley, K.J. (2005). Khat chewing is a risk factor for acute myocardial infarction: A case study. *British Journal of Clinical Pharmacology*, 59, 574-581.

Al-Mugahed, L. (2008). Khat chewing in Yemen: turning over a new leaf. *Bulletin of the World Health Organization*, 86(10), 741-742.

Arrafaine, M. (2004). Micro-macro economic analysis of "khat" production in Ethiopia. (Unpublished postgraduate dissertation). Department of Economics, Addis Ababa University, Ethiopia.

Australian Government-Department of Health and Ageing. (2009). Application forms and guidelines: guidance for completing license and import permit applications (khat). Retrieved from http://www.health.gov.au/internet/main/publishing.nsf /Content/ocs-tc-guidance-imp-khat.htm.

Baasher. T. A. (1980). The use of khat: a stimulant with regional distribution. In Drug Problems in the Sociocultural Context - A Basis for Policies and Programme Planning *(ea. G. Edwards and A. Arif), (pp. 86-93). World Health Organization: Geneva.*

Balint, G.A., Ghebrekidan, H., and Balint, E. (1991). Catha edulis an international socio-medical problem with considerable pharmacological implications. *East African Medical Journal*, 68, 555-561.

Baron, D.N. (1999). The qatparty. British Medical Journal, 319, 500.

Bashour, T.T. (1994). Acute myocardial infarction resulting from amphetamine abuse, a spasm-thrombus interplay? *American Heart Journal*, 128, 1237-1239.

Beke, C. (1843). On the countries south of Abyssinia. *Journal of the Royal Geographical Society*, 13.

Belew,M., Kebede, D., Kassaye, M., and Enquoselassie, F. (2000). The magnitude of khat use and its association with health, nutrition and socio-economic status. *Ethiopian Medical Journal*, 38, 11-26.

Bhui, K., Abdi, A., Abdi, M., Pereira, S., Dualeh, M., Robertson, D., Sathyamoorthy, G., and Ismail, H. (2003). Traumatic events, migration characteristics and psychiatric symptoms among Somali refugees-preliminary communication. *Social Psychiatry and Psychiatric Epidemiology,* 38, 35-43.

Bhui, K., and Warfa, N. (2007). Drug consumption in conflict zones in Somalia. *PLoS Medicine*, 4, e354.

Bhui, K., Craig, T., Mohamud, S., Warfa, N., Stansfeld, S.A., Thornicroft, G., Curtis, S., and McCrone, P. (2006). Mental disorders among Somali refugees-developing culturally appropriate measures and assessing socio-cultural risk factors. *Social Psychiatry and Psychiatric Epidemiology*, 41, 400-408.

Bimerew, M.S., Sonn, F.C.T., and Korlenbout, W.P. (2007). Substance abuse and the risk of readmission of people with schizophrenia at Ammanual Psychiatric Hospital, Ethiopia. *Curationis*, 30, 74-81.

Bin Sallam, M. (2004). Qat: 22 million working hours wasted every day. *Yemen Times*, 13(785).

Carrier, N. (2007). A strange drug in a strange land. In: Vanderbroek, A.P. (Ed.), Traveling Cultures and Plants: The Ethnology and Ethnopharmacy of Human Migrations (pp. 186-203). Berghahn Books, New York and Oxford.

Cats, A., Scholten, P., Meuwissen, S.G.M., and Kuipers, E.J. (2000). Acute Fasciola hepatica infection attributed to chewing khat. *Gut*, 47(4), 584-585.

Clemens, M.R. (1991). Free radicals in chemical carcinogenesis. Klinische Wochenschrift, 69, 1123-1134.

Daba, D., Hymete, A., Bekhit, A. A., Mohamed, A.M., and Bekhit, A.E. (2011). Multi residue analysis of pesticides in wheat and khat collected from different regions of Ethiopia. *Bulletin of Environmental Contamination and Toxicology*, 86(3), 336-341.

Dalu, A. (2000). Impact of long-term consumption of khat on public health. *The Sudama Concern*, 5, 15-16.

Date, J., Tanida, N., and Hobara, T. (2004). Qat chewing and pesticides: A study of adverse health effects in people of the mountainous areas of Yemen. *International Journal of Environmental Health Research*, 14, 405-414.

Delay, J., and Deniker, P. (1961). Methods chimiothe´rapiques en psychiatrie: les nouveaux medicaments psychotropes. Paris: Masson et Cie.

Doherty, J.F., Price, N., Moody, A.H., Wright, S.G., and Glynn, M.J. (1995). Fascioliasis due to imported khat. *Lancet*, 143(8947), 462.

Druglink Factsheet Number. 9. (1994). Khat (Qat, Chat). *Institute for the Study of Drug Dependence*, London.

Elmi, A.S. (1983). The chewing of khat in Somalia. *Journal of Ethnopharmacology*, 8, 163-176.

El-Sshoura, S.M., Abdel Aziz Ali, M.E., el-Said, M.M., Ali, K.Z., Keimeir, M.A., Raoof, A.M., Allam, M., and El Malik, E.M. (1995). Deleterious effects of khat addiction on semen parameters and sperm ultrastructure. *Human Reproduction*, 10, 2295-2300.

Eriksson, M., Ghani, N.A., and Kristiansson, B. (1991). Khat-chewing during pregnancy-effect upon the off-spring and some characteristics of the chewers. *East African Medical Journal*, 68, 106-111.

Feyissa, A.M., and Kelly, J.P. (2008). A review of the neuropharmacological properties of khat. *Progress in Neuropsychopharmacology and Biological Psychiatry*, 32, 1147-1166.

Foley, K.F. (2005). Mechanism of Action and Therapeutic Uses of Psychostimulants. Clinical Laboratory Science, 18(2), 107-113.

Gebissa, E. (2004). Leaf of Allah: Khat and Agricultural Transformation in Harerge, Ethiopia (pp. 1875-1991). James Currey, Oxford.

Gebissa, E. (2010). Khat in the Horn of Africa: Historical perspectives and current trends. *Journal of Ethnopharmacology*, 132, 607-614.

Grayson, K. (2008). Chasing Dragons: Security, Identity, and Illicit Drugs in Canada. University of Tronto Press, Toronto.

Griffiths, P., Lopez, D., Sedefov, R., Gallegos, A., Hughes, B., Noor, A., and Royuela, L. (2010). Khat use and monitoring drug use in Europe: The current situation and issues for the future. *Journal of Ethnopharmacology*, 132, 578-583.

Guantai, A., and Maitai, C. (1982). Relative distribution of cathinone and norpseudo-ephedrine in Catha edulis growing in Kenya. *East African Medical Journal,* 59, 394-398.

Gunaid, A.A., Sumairi, A.A., Shidrawi, R.G., al-Hanaki, A., al-Haimi, M., Al-Absi, S., Al-Hureibi, M.A., Qirbi, A.A., Al-Awlagi, S., El-Guneid, A.M. (1995). Oesophageal and gastric carcinoma in the Republic of Yemen. *British Journal of Cancer*, 71, 409-410.

Halbach, H. (1972). Medical aspects of the chewing of khat leaves. *Bulletin of the World Health Organization*, 47, 21–29.

Harris, C.W. (1844). The Highlands of Aethiopia, vol. 3. London, Longman, Brown, Green, and Longmans.

Hassan, N., Gunaid, A., and Murray-Lyon, I. (2005). The Impact of Qat-chewing on Health: A Re-evaluation. Retrieved from http://www.al-bab.com/bys/articles/hassan05.htm.

Hassan, N.A., Gunaid, A.A., Abdo-Rabbo, A.A., Abdel-Kader, Z.Y., al-Mansoob, M.A., Awad, A.Y., and Murray-Lyon, I.M. (2000). The effect of Qat chewing on blood pressure and heart rate in healthy volunteers. *Tropical Doctor*, 30(2), 107-108.

Hassan, N.A.G.M., Gunaid, A.A., Ali, M.S., and Shehab, M.M.I. (2003). The effects of chewing qat leaves on psychotic patients. *The Journal of The Egyptian Society of Pharmacology and Experimental Therapeutics*, 23 (1), 179-190.

Hattab, F.N., and Angmar-MaÊ nsso, B. (2000).Fluoride content in khat (Catha edulis) chewing leaves. *Archives of Oral Biology*, 45, 253-255.

Henry J.A., Jeffries K.J., and Dawling S. (1992). Toxicity and deaths from 3,4-methylene dioxymethamphetamine ("ecstasy"). *Lancet*, 340, 384-386.

Heymann, T.D., Bhupulan, A., Zureikat, N.E., Drinkwater, C., Giles, P., and Murray-Lyon, I.M. (1995). Khat chewing delays gastric emptying of a semi-solid meal. *Alimentary Pharmacology and Therapeutics*, 9(1), 81-83.

Hoffman, R., and Al'absi, M. (2010). Khat use and neurobehavioural functions: suggestions for future studies. *Journal of Ethnopharmacology*, 132, 554-563.

Holligan, A. (2009, March 16). Khat use spreads to British youth. BBC World Service, online news. Retrieved from http://news.bbc.co.uk/2/hi/uk news/7942432.stm.

Hollister, L.E. (1995). Drugs of abuse. In: Katzung, B.G. (Ed.), Basic and Clinical Pharmacology (pp. 482). Prentice-Hall, Englewood Cliffs, New Jersey, United States.

Ihunwo, A.O., Kayanja, F.I., and Amadi-Ihunwo, U.B. (2004). Use and perception of the psychostimulant, khat (Catha edulis) among three occupational groups in south western Uganda. *East African Medical Journal,* 81, 468-473.

*Integrated Regional Information Networks (*IRIN) News. (2007, January 8). Yemen: Illegal pesticides cause cancer. Retrieved from www.irinnews.org/Report.aspx?ReportId=62985.

Islam, M.W., Tariq, M., Ageel, A.M., El-Feraly, F.S., Al-Meshal, I.A., and Ashraf, I. (1990). An evaluation of the male reproductive toxicity of cathinone. *Toxicology*, 60, 223-234.

Kalix, P. (1984). The pharmacology of khat. In international symposium, Addis Ababa, Ethiopia, July 1984 (pp. 69-73).

Kalix, P. (1987). Khat: Scientific knowledge and policy issues. *British Journal of Addiction*, 82, 47-53.

Kalix, P. (1992). Cathinone: a natural amphetamine. *Pharmacological Toxicology*, 70, 79-86.

Kalix, P., and Braenden, O. (1985). Pharmacological aspects of the chewing of khat leaves. *Pharmacological Reviews*, 37, 149-163.

Kandela, P. (2000). Sana'a Women's rights, a tourist boom, and the power of khat in Yemen. *The Lancet*, 355, 1437.

Karunamoorthi, K., Mohammed, A., and Jemal, Z. (2011). Peasant Association Member's Knowledge, Attitudes, and Practices Towards Safe Use of Pesticide Management. *American Journal of Industrial Medicine*, 54, 965-970.

Karunamoorthi, K., Mohammed, M., and Wassie, F. (2012). Knowledge and Practices of Farmers With Reference to Pesticide Management: Implications on Human Health. *Archives of Environmental and Occupational Health*, 67(2), 109-116.

Karunamoorthi, K., Udeani, G., Babu, S.M., Mossie, A. (2010). Psychopharmacosocial Aspects of Catha edulis Forsk (Family: Celastraceae). *African Journal of Pharmaceutical Sciences and Pharmacy*, 1(1), 112-129.

Kassie, F., Darroudi, F., Kundi, M., Schulte-Hermann, R., and Knasmuller, S. (2001). Khat (Catha edulis) consumption causes genotoxic effects in humans. *International Journal of Cancer*, 92, 329-332.

Kassim, S., and Croucher, R. (2006). Khat chewing amongst UK resident male Yemeni adults: An exploratory study. *International Dental Journal*, 56, 97-101.

Kennedy, J.G. (1987). The flower of paradise: The institutionalized use of the drug qat in Northern Yemen. Dordrecht, Holland. D. Reidel Publishing Company.

Khawaja, M., Al-Nsour, M., and Saad G. (2008). Khat (Catha edulis) Chewing during Pregnancy in Yemen: Findings from a National Population Survey. *Maternal and Child Health Journal*, 12, 308-312.

Kimani, S.T., and Nyongesa, A.W. (2008). Effects of single daily khat (Catha edulis) extract on spatial learning and memory in CBA mice. *Behavioural Brain Research*, 195, 192-197.

Koori Drug Information. (2005). Khat. Australian Drug Foundation. Retrieved from http://www.kooridrug info.adf.org.au/fact_sheets/drugfacts/ khat.html.

Krause, K.H., Dresel, S.H., Krauser, J., Kung, H.F., and Tatsch, K. (2000). Increased striatal dopamine transporter in adult patients with attention deficit hyperactive disorder. Effects of methylphenidate as measured by single photon emission computed tomography. *Neuroscience Letters*, 285, 107-110.

Krikorian, A.D. (1984). Kat and its use: an historical perspective. *Journal of Ethnopharmacology*, 12, 115-178.

Kuczkowski, K.M. (2005). Herbal ecstasy: Cardiovascular complications of khat chewing in pregnancy. *Acta Anaesthesiologica Belgica*, 56, 19–21.

Kuczkowski, K.M., and Benumof, J.L. (2003). Amphetamine abuse in pregnancy, anesthetic implications. *Acta Anaesthesiologica Belgica*, 54, 161-163.

Luqman, W., and Danowski, T. (1976). The use of Khat (Catha edulis) in Yemen social and medical observations. *Annals of Internal Medicine*, 85, 246-249.

Makonnen, E. (2000). Constipating and spasmolytic effects of khat (Catha edulis Forsk) in experimental animals. *Phytomedicine*, 74, 309-312.

Mekasha, A. (1983). Clinical aspects of khat (Catha edulis fork): In *Proceedings of the International Symposium on khat* 1983 (pp. 77-83).

Moghram, A. (2006, October 9-11). Pesticide handling in Yemen is uncontrolled. Yemen Times. Retrieved from http://209.85.229.132/ search?q=cache:oyW54ShzOKUJ: yementimes.com/article.shtml%3Fi%3D988%26p%3Dhealth %26a%3D1+qat+poison+deathandcd=8andhl=enandct=clnkandgl=ukandclient=firefox.

Morrish, P.K., Nicolau, N., Brakkenberg, P., and Smith, P.E.M. (1999). Leukoencephalopathy associated with khat misuse. *Journal of Neurology, Neurosurgery and Psychiatry*, 67, 556.

Murad, F. (1983). Social effects of khat. In International Conference On Khat- The Health and Socioeconomic Aspects of Khat Use, in 1983 January 17-21, (pp. 211-214). *International Council on Alcohol and Addictions*, Madagascar.

Mwenda, J.M., Arimi, M.M., Kyama, M.C., and Langat, D.K. (2003). Effect of khat (Catha edulis) consumption on reproductive function: A review. *East African Medical Journal*, 80, 318-323.

Nasr, A.H., and Khatri, M.L. (2000). Head and neck squamous cell carcinoma in Hajjah, Yemen. *Saudi Medical Journal*, 21, 565-568.

Odenwald, M. (2007). Chronic khat use and psychotic disorders: a review of the literature and future prospects. *Sucht*, 53, 9-22.

Odenwald, M., Hinkel, H., Schauer, E., Schauer, M., Elbert, T., Neuner, F., and Rockstroh, B. (2009). Use of khat and Posttraumatic Stress Disorder as risk factors for psychotic symptoms: a study of Somali combatants. *Social Science and Medicine*, 69, 1040-1048.

Odenwald, M., Neuner, F., Schauer, M., Elbert, T., Catani, C., Lingenfelder, B., Hinkel, H., Hafner, H., and Rockstroh, B. (2005). Khat use as risk factor for psychotic disorders: a cross-sectional and case-control study in Somalia. *BMC Medicine*, 3:5. doi:10. 1186 /1741-7015-3-5.

Pantelis, C., Hindler, C.G., and Taylor, J.C. (1989). Use and abuse of khat (Catha edulis). A Review of the distribution, pharmacology, side effects and a description of psychosis attributed to khat chewing. *Journal of Psychology Medicine*, 19, 657-668.

Paris, R. (1958). Abyssinian tea (Catha edulis Forssk, Celastraceae). United Nations Office on Drugs and Crime. *Bulletin on Narcotics*, 2, 29-34.

Population Reference Bureau. (2005). World population data sheet. Population Reference Bureau. Retrieved from http://www.prb.org/pdf05 /05worlddatasheet_eng.pdf

Raja'a, Y.A., Noman, T.A., Al-Warafi, A.K., Al-Mashraki, N.A., and Al-Yosofi, A.M. (2000). Khat chewing is a risk factor of duodenal ulcer. *Saudi Medical Journal*, 21, 887-888.

Raman, R. (1983). Catha edulis Forsk, Geographical Dispersal, Botanical, Ecological and Agronomical Aspects with Special References to Yemen Arab Republic. (Unpublished doctoral dissertation). University of Gottingen, Germany.

Regional Committee for the Eastern Mediterranean. (1961). Khat (Catha edulis Forskal) a preliminary study. Regional Office for the Eastern Mediterranean, World Health Organization.

Safer, D.J., and Krager, J.M. (1998). A survey of medication treatment for hyperactivity/ inattentive students. *Journal of American Medical Association*, 260, 2256-2258.

Schorno, H., Brenneisen, R., and Steinegger, E. (1982). Qualitative and quantitative Untersuchungen uber das Vorkormmen ZNS-aktiver phenylpropylamine in Handels-drogen und uber deren Verteilung in verschidenen Organ van Catha edulis. *Pharmaceutica Acta Helvetica*, 57, 168-176.

Soufi, H.E., Kameswaran, M., and Malatani, T. (1991). Khat and oral cancer. *The Journal of Laryngology and Otology,* 105, 643-645.

Steinberg, M.K. (2004). Introduction. In: Steinberg, M.J. (Ed.), Dangerous Harvest: Drug Plants and the Transformation of Indigenous Landscapes, (pp. 3-8). Oxford University Press, New York, United States of America.

Tesfaye, F., Byass, P., Wall, S., Berhane, Y., and Bonita, R. (2008). Association of smoking and khat (Catha edulis Forsk) use with high blood pressure among adults in Addis Ababa, Ethiopia, 2006. Preventing Chronic Disease, 5, A89.

Toennes, S.W., Harder, S., Schramm, M., Niess, C., and Kauert, G.F. (2003). Pharma-cokinetics of cathinone, cathine and norephedrine after the chewing of khat leaves. *British Journal of Clinical Pharmacology*, 56(1), 125-130.

United Nations Narcotic Laboratory. (1975). Studies on the chemical composition of khat. Investigations on the phenyalkylamine fraction, MNAR/11/75.

US Department of Justice-National Drug Intelligence Center. (2003). Intelligence Bulletin: Khat (Catha edulis). Retrieved from http://www.justice.gov/ndic/pubs3/3920/index.htm.

Warfa, N., Klein, A., Bhui, K., Leavey, G., Craig, T., and Stansfeld, S.A. (2007). Khat use and mental illness: a critical review. *Social Science and Medicine*, 65, 309-318.

WHO Advisory Group. (1980). Review of the Pharmacology of khat. *Bulletin of Narcotics*, 32, 83-93.

WHO Expert Committee on Drug Dependence. (2006). Assessment of khat (Catha edulis Forsk). Retrieved from http://www.who.int/medicines/ areas/quality_safety/4.4 KhatCrit-Review.pdf.

Widler, P., Mathys K., Brenneisen R., *Kalix, P., and Fisch, H.U.* (1994). Pharmacodynamics and pharmacokinetics of khat, a controlled study. *Clinical Pharmacology and Therapeutics*, 55, 556-562.

Yemen Times. (2006, March 9). The qat phenomenon and ideas to stop its use. Yemen Times. Retrieved from http://www.yementimes.com/00/ iss35/health.htm.

Zein, A. (1984). Polydrug abuse among Ethiopian university students with particular reference to khat. In: International symposium on khat in 1984, (pp. 85-89).

In: Drug Use and Abuse
Editor: Marie Claire Van Hout ISBN: 978-1-62618-232-5

Chapter 7

A RESPECTABLE ADDICTION: OVER THE COUNTER CODEINE USE, MISUSE AND DEPENDENCE

*Marie Claire Van Hout**
Department of Health, Sport and Exercise Science.
Waterford Institute of Technology

ABSTRACT

Since 2010, both the European Monitoring Centre for Drugs and Drug Addiction (EMCDDA) and the International Narcotics Control Board (INCB) have highlighted concern about the misuse of over the counter (OTC) medication. Contemporary research has underscored the need for '*increased pharmaco-vigilence*' around OTC codeine dispensing as the most commonly consumed opiate worldwide. Codeine represents an interesting quandary in terms of its regulated status, with individuals varying in their metabolism of codeine, estimation of safe dosages, and dependence potential. Although effects are milder than heroin, abuse potential remains of concern, with physical dependence occurring with regular use over a short period of time. Within user trajectories of codeine use, a variety of sub groups exist in the form of the elderly, youth, parents, recreational, problematic and opiate dependent drug users, and each with their own motives, patterns and outcomes for use. Particular concerns are also evident with regard to problematic drug user extraction of codeine from OTC and web based products, and administered via oral, intranasal, inhalation and injecting routes.

Keywords: Codeine, over the counter, dihydro-codeine

INTRODUCTION

The global emergence of so called *'respectable addiction'* has occurred in recent times, alongside heightened awareness of this issue amongst the general population and health professionals alike (Cooper, 2011a; EMCDDA, 2011). The de-regulation of prescription only

* Corresponding Author. School of Health Sciences, Waterford Institute of Technology. Email: mcvanhout@wit.ie.

medicines to pharmacy status OTC drugs has evolved in order to reduce government drug budgets, general practitioner (GP) workload, and to extend the screening and patient education roles of community pharmacists (MacFadyen MacFadyen, Eadie and McGowan, 2001; Basak, van Mil and Sathyanarayana, 2009; Robinson, Robinson, McCarthy and Cameron, 2010; Cooper, 2011b) According to the EMCDDA Annual Report in 2010, the misuse of prescribed and OTC medication, and the sale of counterfeit medicines sold for therapeutic and non therapeutic use is now under consideration within the European pharmaco-vigilance system, which operates under the responsibility of the European Medicines Agency, and collaborates with the EMCDDA on drug misuse issues. The report underscores the need for timely responses from pharmaceutical and drug control regulatory frameworks (EMCDDA, 2011). Greater efforts to increase user awareness and self monitoring of OTC product use are emphasized in a variety of studies (Frei, Nielsen, Dobbin and Tobin, 2010; Reed, Bond, Witton, Cornish, Hickman and Strang, 2011; Cooper, 2011a;b). Hughes (2003) emphasized how self medication using OTC products is beneficial to all facets of society, but warned of the need to monitor certain key populations and products. Within user trajectories of both intended therapeutic and non therapeutic use of OTC products, a variety of sub groups exist in the form of elderly, youth, parents, recreational and problematic drug users, and each with their own patterns, motives and outcomes for use.

Codeine is the most commonly consumed opiate worldwide. The misuse of codeine products is an emerging public health challenge in many countries around the world, in part because such products are present in a range of OTC medicines regularly dispensed without prescription to the public (Robinson et al., 2010). The greatest proportion of evidence on codeine misuse and dependence is from the United States (US) where codeine based products are not available over the counter, with smaller proportions (but not directly comparable) of studies on OTC codeine use and misuse conducted in the United Kingdom (UK) and Australia. Indeed, research fact sheets provided by the National Institute on Drug Abuse (NIDA) in the US have observed the under prescription of codeine due to the GP overestimation of patient potential for addiction (otherwise known as '*opiophobia*'). A recent review on the changing patterns of codeine based product use was conducted by Reed et al., (2011) and reported on levels of public awareness of misuse potential, and pharmacists' continued concerns for misuse. Reed et al., (2011) observed the need for further investigation, as OTC codeine based drugs become available, either as sold by and under supervision of a pharmacist (P) or sold off the shelf from any outlet (GSL). A clearer understanding of the general public's awareness on the potential risks of codeine use, misuse and dependence, and impact of pharmacy controls of codeine is needed (Agyapong, Sarvage, Sighn, Farren and McLoughlin, 2011; Reed et al., 2011). Research is clearly needed to quantify the extent of OTC codeine use and misuse, whether intentional or non intentional, so as to estimate and create a user profile of use and abuse, evaluate brief interventions, capture individual user perspectives and inform the design of treatment interventions across a variety of regulatory regimes (Cooper, 2011a;b). Moore (2008) observed the increase in problematic use of OTC medicinal products which included codeine based products among older adults. Adolescent related research also points to high rates of teenage abuse of codeine based products with misuse most common among older teens and related to high level dosages, poly drug use and depression, with evident confusion around identification of appropriate products, side effects and product contraindications (Banarij and Anderson, 2001; Acocella, 2005; Steinman, 2006; Ford, 2009; Wilson, Singh, Blumkin, Dallas and Klein, 2010). Allotey, Reidpath and Elisha

(2004) found that children represent a worrying new cohort of codeine mis-users by virtue of parental '*social medication'* to control behaviour, reduce inconvenience of child sickness and due to its potent positive effects on children s mood states.

Indeed, codeine represents an interesting quandary in terms of its pharmacy or GP regulated status, as individuals with different genetic make ups vary in their metabolism of codeine into morphine, and which further underscores scientific concern for estimation of safe dosages, and dependence potential. Codeine or 3-methylmorphine is a short acting weak to mid range acting opiate administered to treat pain or attempt to relieve coughs (*The American Society of Health-System Pharmacists*. http://www.drugs.com/ monograph/codeine. html) and for its analgesic, anti diarrheal or antitussive drug outcomes. The name codeine is derived from the Greek word *kodeia* (κώδεια) for *'poppy head'* and is found in the poppy plant '*Papaver somniferum var. album*'. Dihydrocodeine is a semi-synthetic opioid. OTC codeine based products contain between 5 and 12.5mg of codeine per tablet, and may be marketed as a single ingredient drug or more commonly in combination with non steroidal anti inflammatory drugs such as ibuprofen (i.e. Nurofen Plus), analgesic acetylsalicylic acid or aspirin, co-codprin, acetaminophen or paracetamol (i.e. Solpedeine), co-codamol, paracod, panadeine, paramol, and Tylenol with codeine (i.e. Tylenol 3 and 4 tablets/elixir) and phenacetin (Emprazil with Codeine 1,2,3,and 4) in order to boost the synergistic effect of drug compounds. Codeine products may also be marketed as suppositories, cough syrups, or for sub cutaneous or intramuscular injection. Through oral route of administration of codeine, codeine is effectively absorbed by the GI tract with minimal loss of drug potency (in direct contrast with morphine which loses up to 90% potency) and results in '*opioid analgesia'* which alters perception and emotional responses to pain (euphoric or dreamy feelings), and stimulatory effects by blocking neurotransmitters. Common side effects of opioid analgesics (which include codeine) are less profound than with morphine and include visual disturbances, mood changes, dependence, itching, nausea, vomiting, constipation, drowsiness, pupil constriction, bradycardia, tachycardia, palpitation, oedema, reduced breathing rate, sweating, flushing, clammy skin, postural hypotension, sexual difficulties, tremors, irritation, depression, ureteric spasm, miosis, dry mouth, urinary retention, sleep disturbances, headache, constipation, hallucinations, vertigo, euphoria, dysphoria, confusion, drowsiness, difficulty with micturition, urinary retention, rash, urticaria, pruritus and seizures. The administration of repeated doses contributes to similar effects at lower doses (Reed et al., 2011). There is a risk of respiratory depression, coma and death resulting from codeine toxicity at very high doses, and after oral over-dosage, and in intravenous use by poly drug users using a combination of alcohol or other drugs (Bellville and Seed 1968; Dobbin and Tobin, 2008). Research has also underscored the potential for additional adverse health and life threatening consequences caused by ibuprofen or paracetamol (i.e. GI haemorrhage /perforation or liver damage) in the over consumption and repeated use of combination products (Reed et al., 2011). Codeine is commonly used to manage pain such as headache, but misuse in the form of repetitive daily use has been known to contribute to increased headache called *"Medication Overuse Headache"* (MOH) (Katsarava and Jensen, 2007). Other potential complications associated with long term use include symptoms of anxiety and depression (Romach, Sproule, Sellers, Somer and Busto, 1999; Dobbin and Tobin, 2008).

Conflicting views exist with regard to codeines potential for addiction, particularly when considering combination products and the potential effects of other active ingredients as ibuprofen, paracetamol and caffeine (Wills, 2005; Frei et al., 2010). Misuse according to

Dobbin and Tobin (2008) appears related to the increasing dose of codeine, which increases abuse potential and likelihood of adverse effects, even when combined with safer analgesics such as paracetamol. Despite this, tolerance to codeine develops with regular use over time, with prolonged use additionally strongly associated with depression and dysphoric mood states (Romach et al., 1999). Research shows that awareness of codeine's abuse potential within problematic drug using networks is relatively higher than the general population (Agyapong et al., 2011). Even though effects are milder than heroin, abuse potential remains of concern particularly in the case of regular use over a short period of time, as users become physically dependent. Withdrawals in the case of physical dependency on codeine include classic opiate dependence symptomatologies such as cravings, preoccupation with seeking and taking codeine, lack of control of consumption patterns despite negative side effects, insomnia, restlessness, runny nose, stomach pains, diarrhea and chills. Health outcomes of codeine dependency include perforated gastric ulcers, gastrointestinal bleeding, hepatotoxicity, hypokalaemia, inflammatory bowel conditions, and profound hypokalaemia associated with a severe myopathy, and often in users with no history of substance use disorders and co-morbidity (Chetty, Baoku, Mildner, Bannerjee, Vallance, Haddon and Labib, 2003; Dyer, Martin, Mitchell, Sauven and Gazzard, 2004; Lewis, Kimmel, Localio, Metz, Farrar, Nessel, Brensinger, McGibney and Strom, 2005; Lambert and Close 2005; Dutch, 2008; Robinson et al., 2010; Ernest, Chia and Corallo, 2010; Frei et al., 2010; Nielson, Cameron and Pahoki, 2010).

Individuals with codeine dependency often commence codeine use in an effort to manage pain (Tennant and Rawson. 1982; Frei et al., 2010) with other research describing '*chemical coping*' in the case of codeine use for stress (Nielson et al., 2010). Research has identified two distinct cohorts of dependent user namely; the first cohort who commence codeine use for pain management (either prescribed or via pharmacy sale), initially use appropriately and who intentionally or unintentionally due to lack of awareness or pharmacy/health professional advise increase their dosage or length of time administered in order to ease discomfort (Hughes, McElnay, Hughes and McKenna, 1999; Good and Ford, 2007) and the second cohort who are opiate dependent, may be in methadone maintenance treatment, and using codeine to manage withdrawals when unable to secure either heroin or prescribed methadone (Boekhout van Solinge, 1996; National Council on Patient Information and Education 2002; Roumie and Griffin, 2004; Heard, Sloss, Weber and Dart, 2006; Reed et al., 2011). Recent research on codeine dependence in Australia by Nielson et al., (2010:5) identified three distinct types of codeine user, namely (direct cite);

1. Therapeutic dependence; characterised by not exceeding therapeutic doses but still demonstrating features of codeine dependence and often having a picture of worsening pain. Some cases were consistent with descriptions in the literature of medication overuse headache.
2. Non-medical/recreational users; characterised by use specifically for the euphoric effects of codeine. This group were generally seeking and sharing knowledge to reduce harms.
3. High dose dependence; characterised by the use of high doses (multiple packets per day) and experiencing serious adverse effects from their use. Use almost always stemmed from therapeutic use with participants often having limited insight into

dependence for an extended period of time. In some cases use began for therapeutic use and escalated rapidly once euphoric effects of codeine were experienced.

Recreational codeine use has also been reported and is characterised by consumption of high doses of codeine in *'binge'* episodes and known among users as *'cilly'* due to the generic user reaction to this drug, with nasal, rectal, oral, inhalation and subcutaneous use most common (Leinwand, 2006; Ernest et al., 2010). Online user forums (see www.bluelight.ruu, and www.erowid.com) report users extracting codeine from combination products such as Nurofen Plus by splitting tablets with a sharp blade, discarding the side containing ibuprofen and consuming the tablet side marked N+. Online users of codeine also report *'cold water extraction'* (CWE) processes using multi filtration of the product in order to yield the codeine base. Codeine can also be used to illicitly synthesize morphine (i.e. pyridine or desomorphine). Recent media reports have highlighted this emergent trend of the designer drug '*Krokodil'* in Russia (see http://www.independent.co.uk/news/world/europe/ krokodil-the-drug-that-eats-junkies-2300787.html). Intravenous use is not recommended on such user fora due to lack of first-pass metabolism by the liver inhibiting the drug outcome, difficulties in dissolving the product and also due to potential for pulmonary edema, facial swelling and other life threatening complications, with some users recommending a large dose of anti histamine if choosing this route of administration. Other reported forms of misuse for recreational purposes include consumption along with anti nausea preparations promethazine (i.e. Purple Drink syrup at 60mg of codeine per liquid ounce mixed with Sprite) (Leinwand, 2006), codeine linctus i.e. Nytol (Scottish Specialists in Pharmaceutical Public Health and Trust Chief Pharmacists, 2004), products with higher proportions of codeine, i.e. Nurofen Plus (Matheson, Bond and Pitcairn, 2002) and crushed within caffeine laced drinks (i.e. Red Bull) (Ernest et al., 2010). Indeed, in the US, codeine has been labeled '*Hillbilly Heroin'* with free base smoked on aluminium foil (similar to heroin *'chasing the dragon'*). Poly drug taking represents an additional confounding health consequences and drug outcomes for the recreational misuse of codeine (Reed et al., 2011).

The majority of codeine users use for a short period of time, prescribed or otherwise, with a minority using over longer periods of time and developing tolerance. Reed et al., (2011) comment on the varying uptake of individuals dependent on codeine in drug services due to issues relating to treatment stigma and poor consideration of needs, and underscore concerns around the lack of prevalence data and clear dependent profiles in each cohort. Dr Richard Cooper, University of Sheffield, United Kingdom (UK) has called for the need for further protective mechanisms in the pharmacy profession in order to track and monitor codeine misuse in so called *'respectable addicts'*, in order to provide support and treatment options for those affected. Pates, McBride, Li and Ramadan (2002) have described the potential for *'discrete'* groups of dependent users who fail to seek help due to lack of recognition of their dependence or identification of their codeine use as a problem. The identified '*blurring between therapeutic and problematic use'* serves to compound the individual's problematic codeine use, particularly when opioid withdrawal symptoms are experienced, and individuals consume codeine to self-medicate (Nielson et al., 2010). Research has previously called for the use of standardised criteria to determine client codeine dependence (Tinsley and Watkins, 1998).

The majority of codeine dependent individuals do not view themselves as needing help for their codeine dependence (Nielson et al., 2010). According to the DSM-IV, the characteristics of codeine dependence (American Psychiatric Association, 2000) are (direct cite);

- A strong desire or sense of compulsion to take codeine-containing products;
- Difficulties in controlling codeine-taking behaviour in terms of its onset, termination or levels of use;
- A physiological withdrawal state when codeine use is stopped or reduced, as evidenced by: the characteristic withdrawal syndrome for the substance; or use of the same (or a closely related) substance with the intention of relieving or avoiding withdrawal symptoms;
- Evidence of tolerance, such that increased doses of codeine are required in order to achieve effects originally produced by lower doses;
- Progressive neglect of alternative pleasures or interests because of codeine use, increased amount of time necessary to obtain or take codeine or to recover from its effects;
- Persisting with codeine use despite clear evidence of overtly harmful consequences, such as harm to the liver, depressive mood states or impairment of cognitive functioning.

Despite the use of criteria to establish dependency, recent research has commented on the lack of evidence to guide development of specific treatment and referral pathways for OTC opioid dependence (Thekiso and Farren, 2010; Reed et al., 2011; Cooper, 2011a; b). Increases in treatment uptakes relating to codeine dependency and concerns for appropriate design of treatment protocols have been recorded across a variety of countries (SAMHSA, 2009; Thekiso and Farran, 2010; Bell, 2010; Romelsjo, Engdahl, Stenbacka, Fugelstad, Davstad, Liefman and Thiblin, 2010; Roche, McCabe and Smyth, 2011; Cooper, 2011a;b; EMCDDA Annual Report, 2011). Once accessing treatment, codeine dependent individuals need to taper their use under medical supervision. The primary modes of treatment are similar to that of heroin dependence and focus on a variety of detoxification modalities ranging from no medical support, the prescribing of sedatives, (i.e. benzodiazepines and sedative anti-psychotic medication), the prescribing of Lofexidine (Britoflex) and buprenorphine (i.e. Subutex) or as rapid assisted detoxification under anesthesia (Frei et al., 2010). Rehabilitation involves inpatient and cognitive behavioural therapy. Other options include maintenance therapy in the form of opioid substitution treatment using buprenorphine, naloxone, methadone or dihydrocodeine. Clinical profiles vary but are over represented by females, those in middle to late age, poly substance users and with underlying psychiatric condition (Otto, Crackau, Lohrmann, Zahradnik, Bischof, John and Rumpf, 2009; Thekiso and Farren, 2010; Agyapong et al., 2011). Research in South Africa shows that combination codeine product abuse may also present as secondary problematic substance and ranked second to benzodiazepine dependency, with primary OTC/prescription medication abuse most common in females aged over 40 years, and secondary OTC/prescription medication abuse most common in males over 40 years (Myers, Siegfried and Parry, 2003). However, for those with pain management issues, often stimulating initial misuse of codeine, the re emergence of pain creates a barrier to successful treatment completion (Tennant and Rawson, 1982). Other studies describe poor long term outcomes for codeine dependents at 12 month follow up (Otto et al., 2009; Zahradnik, Otto, Crackau, Lohrmann, Bischof, John and Rumpf, 2009). Reed et al., (2011) conclude their review on OTC codeine based products by highlighting the need to consider the wide variety of clinical profiles and harms incurred for codeine users, misusers and dependents, and the need for timely evidence to guide the development of treatment policy for OTC codeine misuse or dependence.

Much of the research to date has explored perspectives of pharmacy staff and dispensing practices relating to OTC medications. A review of global literature highlights continued pharmacist reporting of concern for codeine misuse (however subjective these perceptions are), despite high levels of public awareness around abuse and dependence potential, mixed views on perceived safety of these products and varying degrees of legislative control and pharmacy consultation (Ball and Wilde 1989; Paxton and Chapple, 1996; Hughes et al., 1999; MacFayden et al., 2001; Matheson et al., 2002; Pates et al., 2002; Roumie et al., 2004; Wazaify, Shields, Hughes and McElnay, 2005; Albsoul-Younes, Wazaify, Yousef and Tahaineh, 2010; Reed et al., 2011). Recent research on codeine dependence in Australia by Nielson et al., (2010:5) identified three distinct types of codeine user, namely:

- Users conscientiously disobeying product instructions so as to experience a drug induced euphoric effect from the codeine present.
- Users who become addicted to codeine based products, are aware of their dependence but continue to use them in response to cravings and to avoid withdrawals.
- Users who are unknowingly misusing codeine based products within the recommended limits but frequently and regularly using to treat drug-induced withdrawal symptoms such as headache.

In France, Orriols, Gaillard, Lapeyre-Mestre and Roussin (2009) conducted a cross sectional pharmaco-epidemiological method using patient data to explore non-medical use, misuse, abuse and dependence on self-medicated drug use. Statistically significant differences in non medical use and misuse, abuse and dependence were present for codeine based products. Hanna and Hughes (2010) conducted research into the pharmacists' decision-making processes regarding product selection and the role of clinical evidence in reaching such decisions, and found that safety and patient demand for certain products influenced the recognition for patient demands. Evidence of effectiveness of the selected product was rarely part of the decision-making process. Research has underscored how the de-regulation of prescription only medications toward pharmacy status medications has moved toward self treatment and the reduction of GP workloads, and reciprocally spotlighted the need for an *'early warning system'*, increased educational, screening, life skills and harm reduction intitiatives within an inter agency community based approach to reduce codeine misuse (Hughes et al., 1999; MacFadyen et al., 2001; McBride, Pates, Ramadan and McGowan, 2003; Fleming, McElnay and Hughes, 2004; Wazaify, Hughes and McElnay, 2006; Basak et al., 2009; Gruenewald, Johnson, Shamblen, Ogilvie and Collins, 2009). Other concerns regarding patient awareness of overuse of OTC codeine and the lack of translation into appropriate codeine consumption by disregarding product packaging or simple lack of patient comprehension that dosage is excessive have been recorded in emergency departments, and have advised clearer product labeling of active ingredients in OTC codeine (Roumie et al., 2004; Heard et al., 2006). Reed et al., (2011) state that this area warrants further investigation and incorporation of improved messaging on brand packaging, information leaflets and public health campaigns.

Conclusion

This chapter has revealed that although the appropriate directed use of codeine based products incurs little risk for the user, excessive or long term use of these products contributes to dependence, associated side effects such as headache, and other adverse and life threatening harms. It remains necessary however codeine is regulated in each respective country, to quantify prevalence of use, misuse and dependence within the broad and '*hidden*' spectrum of therapeutic and non therapeutic patterns of use, and identify sub group characteristics for those most at risk. Additionally, although general treatment for opiate dependency is utilised in the form of detoxification and psychosocial therapy, there is very little rigorous evidence available with which to guide definitive policies, management initiatives and strategies around the provision and development of specific referral and treatment pathways for OTC codeine misuse or dependence (Reed et al., 2011; Cooper, 2011a;b). We are also unclear as to why the misuse of codeine is occurring, and continuing to occur despite varied levels of legislative control, and how best to implement preventative strategies. Also the expansion of web based retailing of legal and new psychoactive drugs worldwide present alternative access routes for those seeking to use and misuse codeine.

References

Acocella, C.M. (2005). Using diaries to assess nonprescription drug use among university students. *Journal of Drug Education, 35*(4), 267-274.

Agyapong, V., Sarvage, M., Sighn, K., Farren, C., and McLoughlin, D. (2011). Use of codeine-containing medicines by patients admitted to an acute psychiatric hospital. *European Psychiatry*, *26*, 1.

Albsoul-Younes A., Wazaify M., Yousef, A.M., and Tahaineh, L. (2010). Abuse and misuse of prescription and nonprescription drugs sold in community pharmacies in Jordan. *Substance Use and Misuse, 45*(9), 1319-1329.

Allotey, P., Reidpath, D.D., and Elisha, D. (2004). "Social medication" and the control of children: a qualitative study of over-the-counter medication among Australian children. *Pediatrics, 114*(3), e378-83.

American Psychiatric Association. (2000). *Diagnostic and Statistical Manual of Mental Disorders* (4th Revised ed.). Washington DC, USA: American Psychiatric Association.

Ball, K., and Wilde, M. (1989). OTC medicines misuse in West Cumbria. *Pharmaceutical Journal, 242*(6516), 40.

Banerji, S., and Anderson, I.B. (2001). Abuse of Coricidin HBP cough and cold tablets: episodes recorded by a poison center. *American Journal of Health System-Pharmacy, 58*(19), 1811-1814.

Basak, S.C., van Mil, J.W., and Sathyanarayana, D. (2009). The changing roles of pharmacists in community pharmacies: perception of reality in India. *Pharmacy World and Science, 31*(6), 612-618.

Bell, J. (2010). The global diversion of pharmaceutical drugs: opiate treatment and the diversion of pharmaceutical opiates: a clinician's perspective, *Addiction, 105*(9), 1531–1537.

Bellville, J.W., and Seed, J.C. (1968). A comparison of the respiratory depressant effects of detropropoxyphene and codeine in man. *Clinical Pharmacology and Therapeutics, 9*(4), 428-434.

Boekhout van Solinge, T. (1996). "7. La politique de soins des années quatre-vingt-dix" (in French). *L'héroïne, la cocaïne et le crack en France. Trafic, usage et politique.* Amsterdam, The Netherlands: CEDRO Centrum voor Drugsonderzoek, Universiteit van Amsterdam.

Chetty, R., Baoku, Y., Mildner, R., Bannerjee, A., Vallance, D., Haddon, A., and Labib, A. (2003). Severe hypokalaemia and weakness due to Nurofen misuse. *Annals of Clinical Biochemistry*; *40* (4), 422-423.

Cohen, D.P., Unoh, E., Barry, H., and O'Connor, J.J. (2009) Codeine misuse among service users on a methadone treatment programme. *Irish Journal of Medical Science, 179*(3), 465.

Cooper, R J (2011b). Over-the-counter medicine abuse – a review of the literature. *Journal of Substance Use,* Early online.1-26.

Cooper, R.J. (2011a). *Respectable Addiction - a Qualitative Study of Over the Counter Medicine Abuse in the UK.* Sheffield, United Kingdom: School of Health and Related Research (ScHARR), University of Sheffield.

Dobbin, M., and Tobin, C. (2008). *Over-the-counter (OTC) Ibuprofen/Codeine Analgesics: Misuse and Harm.* Melbourne, Australia: Drugs Policy and Services Branch, Department of Human Services, Victoria.

Dutch, M.J. (2008). Nurofen Plus misuse: an emerging cause of perforated gastric ulcer. *Medical Journal of Australia, 188*(1), 56-57.

Dyer, B.T., Martin, J.L., Mitchell, J.L., Sauven, N.C., and Gazzard, B. (2004). Hypokalaemia in ibuprofen and codeine phosphate abuse. *International Journal of Clinical Practice; 58*(11), 1061-1062.

EMCDDA Annual Report, 2011. *Annual report on the state of the drugs problem in Europe,* Lisbon, Portugal: European Monitoring Centre of Drugs and Drug Addiction.

Ernest, D., Chia, M., and Corallo, C.E. (2010). Profound hypokalaemia due to Nurofen Plus and Red Bull misuse. *Critical Care and Resuscitation, 12*(2),109-110.

Fleming, G.F., McElnay, J.C., and Hughes, C.M. (2004). Development of a community pharmacy-based model to identify and treat OTC drug abuse/misuse: a pilot study. *Pharmacy World and Science, 26*(5), 282-288.

Ford, J.A. (2009). Misuse of over-the-counter cough or cold medications among adolescents: prevalence and correlates in a national sample. *Journal of Adolescent Health, 44*(5), 505-7.

Frei, M.Y., Nielsen, S., Dobbin, M.D., and Tobin, C.L. (2010). Serious morbidity associated with misuse of over-the-counter codeine-ibuprofen analgesics: a series of 27 cases. *Medical Journal Australia, 193*(5), 294-296.

Good, B., and Ford, C. (2007). Dependence on OTC drugs. *British Medical Journal, 334,* 17-18.

Gruenewald, P.J., Johnson, K., Shamblen, S.R., Ogilvie, K.A., and Collins, D. (2009). Reducing adolescent use of harmful legal products: intermediate effects of a community prevention intervention. *Substance Use and Misuse, 44*(14), 2080 - 2098.

Hanna, L.A., and Hughes, C.M. (2010). 'First, do no harm': factors that influence pharmacists making decisions about over-the-counter medication: a qualitative study in Northern Ireland. *Drug Safety, 33*(3), 245-55.

Hartnoll, R. (1995). A difficult business. *Addiction, 90*(6), 762–763.

Heard, K., Sloss, D., Weber, S., and Dart, R.C. (2006). Overuse of over-the-counter analgesics by emergency department patients. *Annals of Emergency Medicine, 28*(3), 315-318.

Hughes, C.M. (2003). Monitoring self-medication. *Expert Opinion on Drug Safety, 2*(1),1-5.

Hughes, G.F., McElnay, J.C., Hughes, C.M., and McKenna, P. (1999). Abuse/misuse of non-prescription drugs. *Pharmacy World and Science, 21*(6), 251-255.

Katsarava, Z., and Jensen, R. (2007). Medication-overuse headache: Where are we now? *Current Opinion in Neurology, 20*(3), 326-330.

Lambert, AP, and Close, C. (2005). Life-threatening hypokalaemia from abuse of Nurofen Plus. *Journal of the Royal Society of Medicine*; 98(1),21.

Leinwand, D. (2006). DEA warns of soft drink-cough syrup mix. Retrieved from *USA Today:* http://www.usatoday.com/news/nation/2006-10-18-lean_x.htm?csp=34.

Lewis, J.D., Kimmel, S.E., Localio, A.R., Metz, D.C., Farrar, J.T., Nessel, L., Strom, B.L. (2005). Risk of serious upper gastrointestinal toxicity with over-the-counter nonaspirin nonsteroidal anti-inflammatory drugs. *Gastroenterology*; 129(6), 1865-1874.

MacFadyen, L., Eadie, D., and McGowan, T. (2001). Community pharmacists' experience of over-the-counter medicine misuse in Scotland. *The Journal of the Royal Society for the Promotion of Health, 121*(3), 185-192.

Matheson, C., Bond, C., and Pitcairn, J. (2002). Misuse of over-the-counter medicines from community pharmacies: a population survey of Scottish pharmacies. *Pharmaceutical Journal, 269*(7205), 66-68.

McBride, A.J., Pates, R., Ramadan, R., and McGowan, C. (2003). Delphi survey of experts' opinions on strategies used by community pharmacists to reduce over-the-counter drug misuse. *Addiction, 98*(4), 487- 497.

Moore, J. (2008). Drugs in Focus – policy briefing. *Drugnet Ireland, 26*, 29-30.

Myers, B., Siegfried, N., and Parry, C.D. (2003). Over-the-counter and prescription medicine misuse in Cape Town--findings from specialist treatment centres. *South African Medical Journal, 93*(5), 367-370.

NCPIE (National Council on Patient Information and Education). (2002). *Attitudes and beliefs about the use of over-the-counter medications: a dose of reality: a national survey of consumers and health professionals.* Rockville, MD: National Council on Patient Information and Education.

Nielson, S., Cameron, J., and Pahoki, S. (2010). *Over the Counter Codeine Dependence.* Victoria, Australia: Turning Point Drug and Alcohol Centre.

Orriols, L., Gaillard, J., Lapeyre-Mestre, M., and Roussin, A. (2009). Evaluation of abuse and dependence on drugs used for self-medication: a pharmacoepidemiological pilot study based on community pharmacies in France. *Drug Safety, 32*(10), 859-873.

Otto, C., Crackau, B., Lohrmann, I,, Zahradnik, A., Bischof, G., John, U., and Rumpf, H.J. (2009). Brief intervention in general hospital for problematic prescription drug use: 12-month outcome. *Drug and Alcohol Dependence, 105*(3), 221 – 226.

Pates, R., McBride, A.J., Li, S., and Ramadan, R. (2002). Misuse of over-the-counter medicines: a survey of community pharmacies in a South Wales health authority. *Pharmaceutical Journal, 268*(7184), 179-182.

Paxton, R., and Chapple, P. (1996). Misuse of over-the-counter medicines: a survey in one English county. *Pharmaceutical Journal, 256*(6881), 313-315.

Reed, K., Bond, A., Witton, J., Cornish, R., Hickman, M., and Strang, J. (2011). The changing use of prescribed benzodiazepines and z-drugs and of over-the-counter codeine-containing products in England: a structured review of published English and international evidence and available data to inform consideration of the extent of dependence and harm. London and Bristol: The National Addiction Centre, Kings College London and School of Social and Community Medicine, University of Bristol, United Kingdom.

Roberts, R., and Kennington, E. (2010). Pharmacy practice research has an impact on each and every pharmacist. *Pharmaceutical Journal. 284*(7593), 267-268.

Robinson, G., Robinson, S., McCarthy, P., and Cameron, C. (2010). Misuse of over-the-counter codeine-containing analgesics: dependence and other adverse effects. *New Zealand Medical Journal, 123*(1317), 59-64.

Roche, A., McCabe, S., and Smyth, B. (2011). Illicit methadone use and abuse in young people accessing treatment in opiate dependence, *European Addiction Research,* 14(4), 219–225.

Romach, M.K., Sproule, B.A., Sellers, E.M., Somer, G., and Busto, U.E. (1999). Long-term codeine use is associated with depressive symptoms. *Journal of Clinical Psychopharmacology, 19*(4), 373-376.

Romelsjo, A., Engdahl, B., Stenbacka, M., Fugelstad, A., Davstad, I., Liefman, A., and Thiblin, I. (2010). Were the changes to Sweden's maintenance treatment policy 2000–06 related to changes in opiate-related mortality and morbidity?, *Addiction, 105*(9), 1625–1632.

Roumie, C.L., and Griffin, M.R. (2004). Over-the-counter analgesics in older adults, a call for improved labelling and consumer education. *Drugs and Aging, 21*(8), 485-498.

Scottish Specialists in Pharmaceutical Public Health and Trust Chief Pharmacists. (2004). *Drug Misuse and Community Pharmacy: Issues for Pharmaceutical Care.* Scotland: Scottish Specialists in Pharmaceutical Public Health and Trust Chief Pharmacists.

Steinman, K.J. (2006). High school students' misuse of over-the-counter drugs: a population-based study in an urban county. *Journal of Adolescent Health, 38*(4), 445-447.

Stroup, D.F., Berlin, J.A., Morton, S.C., Olkin, I., Williamson, G.D., Rennie, D., Thacker, S.B., for the Meta-analysis of Observational Studies in Epidemiology (MOOSE) Group (2000). Meta-analysis of observational studies in epidemiology: a proposal for reporting. *Journal of the American Medical Association, 283* (15), 2008-2012.

Substance Abuse and Mental Health Services Administration (SAMHSA) (2009). *Trends in nonmedical use of prescription pain relievers: 2002 to 2007*. Rockville, MD: Substance Abuse and Mental Health Services Administration.

Tennant, F.S., and Rawson, R.A. (1982). Outpatient treatment of prescription opioid dependence - comparison of 2 methods. *Archives of Internal Medicine, 142*(10), 1845-1847.

Thekiso, B., and Farren, C. (2010). Over the counter' (OTC) opiate abuse treatment. *Irish Journal of Psychological Medicine, 27* (4), 189-191.

Tinsley, J.A, and Watkins, D.D. (1998). Over-the-counter stimulants: abuse and addiction. *Mayo Clinic Proceedings, 73*(10), 977-82.

Wazaify, M., Hughes, C.M., and McElnay, J,C. (2006). The implementation of a harm minimisation model for the identification and treatment of over-the-counter drug misuse and abuse in community pharmacies in Northern Ireland. *Patient Education and Counselling, 64*(1-3),136-141.

Wazaify, M., Shields, E., Hughes, C.M., and McElnay, J.C. (2005). Societal perspectives on over-the-counter (OTC) medicines. *Family Practitioner, 22*(2), 170-6.

Wills S., (2005), *Drugs of Abuse*, Southhampton: Drug and Medicines Information Centre, Pharmaceutical Press. .

Wilson, K.M., Singh, P., Blumkin, A.K., Dallas, L., Klein, J.D. (2010). Knowledge gaps and misconceptions about over-the-counter analgesics among adolescents attending a hospital-based clinic. *American Academy of Pediatrics, 10*(4), 228-232.

Zahradnik, A., Otto, C., Crackau, B., Lohrmann, I., Bischof, G., John, U., and Rumpf, H.J. (2009). Randomized controlled trial of a brief intervention for problematic prescription drug use in non-treatment-seeking patients. *Addiction, 104*(1), 109 – 117.

In: Drug Use and Abuse
Editor: Marie Claire Van Hout
ISBN: 978-1-62618-232-5

Chapter 8

MARIJUANA MOTIVES AND ASSOCIATED OUTCOMES: RELAXATION AND ENHANCEMENT VERSUS COPING MOTIVATIONS

Andrew D. Hathaway[1]*, Maritt Kirst[2] and Patricia G. Erickson[3]

[1] Department of Sociology and Anthropology, University of Guelph
[2] Ontario Tobacco Research Unit, Dalla Lana School of Public Health, University of Toronto, Ontario, Canada
[3] Department of Sociology, University of Toronto, Ontario, Canada

ABSTRACT

Objective

To better understand how drug use motives are related to the psychosocial consequences of drug use, this chapter takes a closer look at the association between reported motives and effects of marijuana.

Method

A sample of experienced adult users (N=92, 61% male) was recruited to take part in in-depth interviews from a random household survey of the general population of the city of Toronto. Reported motives and effects were factor analyzed and ranked in terms of their importance or relevance to users and compared with findings from a self-selected sample of respondents who used cannabis more heavily and frequently. To determine if effects can be predicted by use motives, the most significant factors from univariate regression analyses were entered into multivariate models with other independent variables of interest.

* Corresponding author: Email - hathawaa@uoguelph.ca; Telephone - 519-824-4120, Ext. 53256; Fax - 519-837-9561.

Results

Nearly every marijuana motive and effect was more frequently reported in the self-selected sample, but the relative importance of each item based on rankings is remarkably consistent between groups. The multivariate model indicates that life enhancement and relaxation motives are linked to positive use outcomes, and that the use of alcohol and number of health problems are significant predictors of more negative effects. Use for coping and transitions in use patterns are also modestly related to experiencing more negative effects; and being female and being married are significant predictors of less positive experiences of use. Conclusion: These results suggest that future research in this area might consider more in-depth examination of the positive and negative effects of marijuana in relation to reported role fulfillment and role conflicts at different stages of the cannabis career.

Keywords: Cannabis, marijuana, drug use motives, drug effects

INTRODUCTION

The use of cannabis (Cannabis sativa/indica and related species, also widely known as 'marijuana') is closer to alcohol in prevalence than other illicit substances in estimated rates of use across the western world (United National Office on Drugs and Crime, 2006). Despite such widespread use, however, its illicit status is a barrier to research on perceptions and experiences of users in the general population. The legal and social acceptability of alcohol has facilitated research across a broad cross-section of drinkers in the general population of adults. A great deal of research effort has, accordingly, been given to the task of gaining a better understanding of alcohol's mood-altering effects. Most people who use alcohol do so for recreation, most often socially, without drinking to excess or showing symptoms of abuse. Some drink to reduce psychological discomfort, particularly feelings of anxiety and stress.

Cross-cultural expectancies of alcohol consumption have long invested drinking with a stress reducing function (Sayette, 1999). Scientific explanation of problem drinking after Conger (1956) has generated a substantial research literature devoted to "reinforcement theory" examining the thesis that individuals use alcohol or drugs to cope with tension (cf. Allan, 1995; Bolton, Robinson, & Sareen, 2008; Kushner, Abrams, & Borchardt, 2000). This expectation is fulfilled for some with mild success (Jung, 2001); however, self-medication for anxiety may worsen the dysfunction and lead to a variety of physical and mental health problems often found with heavy drinking or drug use (Robinson, Sareen, Cox, & Bolton, 2009; Stewart & Zeitlan, 1995). Similar to alcohol, few marijuana users experience adverse effects at moderate use levels, but use for stress or coping could also have the same potential to produce unwanted consequences (Siqueira, Diab, Bodian, & Rolnitzky, 2001).

While generalized and social anxieties relate to tension reduction motives in both youth and adult drinkers (Carruthers, 1993; Kalodner, Delucia, & Ursprung, 1989; Kidorf & Lang, 1999; O'Hare, 1990), this hypothesis has not been as thoroughly examined in studies of illicit substance users (Stewart, Karp, Pihl, & Peterson, 1997). Research has identified two cannabis use motives commonly attributed to alcohol as well. The first is the enhancement of cognitive and social experiences providing 'relaxation.' The second motivation is for 'coping' with distressing affective states or stressful situations. Marijuana use to cope with stress has been reported in a wide variety of studies (cf. Bonn-Miller, Zvolensky, & Bernstein, 2007; Butters, 2004; Green, Kavanagh, & Young, 2004; Osborne & Fogel, 2008; Schafer & Brown, 1991; Siquiera et al., 2001). A study in the UK also found this motivation relates to higher frequency of use (Terry, Wright, & Cochrane, 2007).

There is some debate on whether the same measures used for alcohol can be applied to marijuana users (Lee, Neighbors, & Woods, 2007). The unique 'psychedelic' properties of marijuana in particular led to the development of instruments adapted to account for users' anecdotes of consciousness expansion, gaining valued insights or enhanced awareness (Simons, Correia, Carey, & Borsari, 1998). The different social meanings that are attached to different drugs also shape perceptions and experiences of use. Howard Becker (1963) made the case that, rather than preceding, motivations for drug use develop after the behavior. Motives and actions originate not from within, but from the situation in which individuals find themselves (Mills, 1940). Embedded in the names of motives are the anticipated consequences of specific actions or descriptions of the character of the act.

Motives are thus normative vocabularies by which actors impute meaning onto social interaction and specify the background expectations of the act, or range of explanations that are culturally appropriate (Turner, 1987; Weinstein, 1980). This sociological perspective on use motives is consistent with the development of concepts such as lifestyle, set and setting in research on marijuana and other substance use (Hathaway, 1997; Zinberg, 1984). Experience of benefits and problems widely varies, reflecting expectations and contingencies of lifestyle or specific circumstances in which cannabis is used. Changes in use patterns or role conflicts, for example, are often more important from the standpoint of the user than the amount of marijuana use or frequency per se (Hathaway, 2003; 2004).

Looking past prior emphasis on deviant subcultures or assumptions of pathology corresponding with 'abuse,' more research on cannabis use motives is required to further understanding of use benefits and problems in different populations and socio-cultural contexts. To determine central motives from the user's own perspective, rather than relying on a predetermined scale, Lee et al. (2007) identified self-generated reasons for using marijuana among first-year undergraduates (mean age 18 years). The most important motives they reported were enjoyment, peer pressure or conformity, and experimentation. Other common reasons were relaxation, boredom, enhancement of experiences, and coping (with stress or depression). More use and problematic use were related to such motives as altered consciousness, activity enhancement, and enjoyment; and over and above more use, the coping motivation was associated with more drug-related problems.

Other studies looking at the complex interaction between marijuana motives and use outcomes (cf. Chabrol, Roura, & Kallmeyer, 2004; Hathaway, 2003; Kilmer, Hunt, Lee, & Neighbours, 2007) have also focused mainly on young adults or adolescents, and are primarily derived from samples that were self-selected, not representative of users in the general population. We sought to overcome these limitations in this study involving semi-structured interviews with experienced users (N=92) recruited from a random household survey of adults. This chapter looks at life-enhancement versus coping motivations as predictors of both positive and negative effects. We investigate the links between use motives and use outcomes, and discuss the implications of our findings with respect to informing future avenues of cannabis research.

Method

Participants and Procedures

Unlike most studies of experienced marijuana users that recruit through advertising and snowball sampling techniques (cf. Hathaway, 2004; Osborne & Fogel, 2008; Shukla & Kelley, 2007), the data are derived from in-depth interviews conducted with adults recruited from a population survey. A two-stage mixed method design was employed to recruit and interview eligible respondents living in the city of Toronto, Canada. The protocol for research involving human subjects was reviewed and approved by the Research Ethics Board for the Social Sciences at the University of Toronto. Stage one involved a random 'household' survey of adults, with items focusing on personal experience with cannabis in terms of lifetime prevalence and patterns of consumption. This brief ten-minute survey was administered by telephone (to residential households and individual cell phone numbers in the 416 exchange for metropolitan Toronto) in October and November of 2004 by the University of Toronto's survey research centre. Interviewers asked to speak to the person 18 years of age or older whose birthday was nearest the day of the call.

Of 5000 numbers dialed, 29% of households (1440) were successfully contacted and definitively yielded an eligible respondent. A total of 1081 fully completed the survey, for an overall response rate of 75%. Participants were informed of the confidential nature and purpose of the study, and their anonymity assured. Respondents eligible for follow-up were those who reported that they had used cannabis on 25 or more occasions (N=274). This low use threshold was selected to facilitate recruitment of a sufficient number of "experienced" cannabis consumers, while excluding short-term experimental users (Cohen & Sas, 1998).

The second stage consisted of a comprehensive survey, 1-2 hours in duration, with those verbally agreeing to a follow-up appointment. Ninety-two respondents were successfully contacted and interviewed in person at a downtown research office between October 2004 and July 2005. The interview was focused on use patterns, motivations, and personal experience of cannabis including different disadvantages and benefits of using. A cash incentive ($25) was provided to compensate the interviewees giving of their time and contribution to the study. A comparison of this group with eligible respondents who did not participate in the in-depth interview (N=182) showed no significant group differences on gender, education, income, age, ethnicity, or other demographic characteristics (Table 1). With no apparent bias due to non-response we gain confidence our sample is more fully representative than samples gathered through nonrandom convenience designs.

To augment the analysis, for comparison, included are demographic characteristics and other relevant descriptives (Tables 2-4) from a pilot study of the survey in Toronto that employed nonrandomized recruitment of respondents (see Hathaway, 2003). The earlier self-selected sample, very briefly, was recruited through a local free newspaper advertisement seeking users over 18 with 25 or more times lifetime use. Approximately 200 persons left telephone messages expressing interest in the study. More than half of this group (n=104) were successfully contacted and kept their designated appointments to conduct an in-depth interview at a downtown research office between October 2000 and April 2001. Despite its non-random design limitations, respondent self-selection was considered advantageous as a cost-effective method of attracting more committed, long-term, frequent users to the study.

Table 1. Demographic characteristics of experienced cannabis users

	Eligible respondents who did not take part in interview (N=182)	In-depth inter-view respondents (N=92)
mean age	37 yrs. (SD 12.5)	39 yrs. (SD 12.3)
% male	61	61
% married or common law	48	44
% born in Canada	79	73
% white	89	87
% completed university or college	68	65
% working full-time	74	76
% working part-time	14	10
% Currently in school	13	12
% under $30,000 past-year income*	24	24
% $50,000 or more past-year inc.*	46	40

*2003 personal income before taxes

While many said they came due to their interest in the research, the cash incentive offered ($25) with this method of recruitment evidently influenced the demographic profile. The sample is both skewed in terms of economic status and, compared to random samples drawn from population surveys (see also Borchers-Tempel & Kolt, 2002; Reinarman, Cohen, & Kaal, 2004), used more cannabis more often than those in other studies. Accordingly, the pilot study done in the same city, using the same survey with a self-selected sample, provides an opportunity for meaningful comparison with the present sample of more moderate consumers recruited from the general population of Toronto.

Measures

Marijuana motives are reported based on measures from previous studies of experienced users which include a list of 20 items about reasons to use marijuana (see Cohen & Sas, 1998; Hathaway, 2003). Participants responded on a Likert scale (1=very unimportant to 5=very important) to statements such as "I use marijuana…to relax…to feel better…to cope with depression." Factor analyses were conducted for the purposes of motivation scale development to include as predictors in multivariate analyses. Through this process we identified seven factors that accounted for 64% of total variance explained. These included: relaxation (e.g., to relax, help sleep); enhancement (e.g., to get inspiration, feel less inhibited); mood (to feel good, cope with depression); enjoyment (to see the world with fresh eyes, enjoy music); release (to blow off steam, cure boredom); coping (to get through the day, for medical reasons); and social reasons (to be sociable with friends, as a symbol of defiance). The scales for relaxation, coping, and enhancement had respective Cronbach's alphas of .717, .551, and .583. Those with Chronbach's alphas less than .40 (enjoyment, mood, release, and social reasons) were excluded from the multivariate analyses.

Psychosocial consequences of cannabis were measured using 18 survey items about perceived long-term effects (Cohen & Sas, 1998; Hathaway, 2003). Respondents noted on a Likert scale their level of agreement (1=disagree strongly to 4=agree strongly) with a wide variety of views about the drug—e.g., "as a result of using marijuana…I am happier…more balanced…less ambitious…less productive." Factor analysis revealed two primary factors that amounted to 52% of total variance explained. Items loading on these factors were summed in the creation of scales comprising positive and negative effects. These scales show good reliability, with respective Cronbach's alphas of .874 and .889.

Other independent variables of interest, with particular reference to lifestyles of users, include use patterns, settings (i.e., home alone or out with friends), use of alcohol and/or tobacco, drug dependence and health problems related to the use of marijuana. Health problems due to cannabis reported by respondents (e.g., respiratory problems, insomnia, anxiety) were summed for the creation of a composite scale. And dependence was assessed by summing DSM-IV items specifically designed to measure cannabis misuse (Cohen & Sas, 1998; Hathaway, 2003). These criteria defined respondents as "dependent" if they reported three or more such symptoms of misuse over a 12-month period—i.e., problems cutting down; continued use despite social, psychological, or physical health problems; and neglect of work or family obligations due to use.

Use patterns were established with respect to the duration (length in years since first use), past-year frequency (0=monthly or less; 1=at least weekly), and amount of marijuana used per month over the past year (0=less than 1/8 of an ounce; 1=1/8 of an ounce or more). The effect of life transitions (e.g., work, parenthood, or marriage) on marijuana use was captured with a yes/no question (coded 1 and 0) indicating major changes, disrupted or destabilized use patterns. Control variables included in our multivariate model were defined and coded as follows: gender (0=male; 1=female), age (continuous variable), marital status (0=no partner; 1=partner), birth country (0=Canada; 1=Other), employment (0=unemployed; 1=employed), and monthly income (0=less than $2000; 1=$2000 or more).

Data Analyses

After descriptive statistics were calculated, univariate regression analyses were used to look at the relationships between cannabis use patterns, use settings, demographic characteristics, use motivations, and effects. Variables significantly correlated (up to .10) with either positive or negative long-term use effects were entered into multivariate models. To reduce the problem of multicollinearity, one of each pair of independent variables that were found to be highly correlated with each other (.60 or higher) was omitted from the final model.

Open-ended questions in the questionnaire provided detailed information about marijuana motives that corroborated data from past qualitative studies and the face validity of our more structured items.

Relaxation and enhancement motivations were among the prominent advantages of marijuana mentioned—e.g., it chills me out, calms me down, is a good relaxant. A typical assertion of this variety included: "I view it as a recreational activity…it's fun to share with friends, go to movies, listen to music…go out for a good meal."

Others said it heightened senses, creativity, and gave them "a different sense of consciousness" or more positive perspective. These themes emerged as prominent in quantitative measures we used to study marijuana motives and effects.

RESULTS

Sample Characteristics

As suggested previously, the sample characteristics differ markedly in some respects from the pilot study which employed nonrandom self-selection of respondents. The present sample is on average five years older, more were married; and they reported higher income, higher levels of employment, and greater moderation in their marijuana use.

They used less cannabis, less frequently, and reported fewer problems than respondents in the pilot study (Table 2).

Table 2. Selected demographic and use pattern characteristics

	Random sample (N=92)	**Pilot study (N=104)**
Demographic characteristics		
Mean Age (yrs.)	39 (SD 12.2)	34
% Male	61	62
% Married	36	16
% Working full or part-time	82	68
% Currently in school	8	17
Monthly Take-Home Income (%)	N=65	
Less than $1000	21	36
$1000-$1999	28	46
$2000-$3999	51	11
Marijuana Use Patterns		
Use length – Mean Years	19 (SD 11.4)	18
Frequency of use in last 12 months (%)	N=63	
Less than once a month	36	12
Monthly	16	8
At least weekly	48	80
Amount used in last 12 months (%)	N=62	
Less than 1/8 of an ounce	60	19
1/8 to less than ½ of an ounce	21	30
½ to less than 1 ounce	13	25
1 ounce or more	6	24
Always or often use alone (%)	36	62
% reporting 3 or more symptoms of dependence (lifetime)	19	30

Marijuana Motives and Perceived Long-Term Effects

The most common motivations reported by respondents were to relax and to enjoy music, movies or TV (both 77%), followed by to feel good (66%) and to be sociable with friends (59%). Less than half agreed with any other reason listed; these results are shown in Table 3, with motivations grouped by seven organizing factors, in accordance with the results of the factor analysis.

The most prevalent use outcomes (Table 4) were I know myself better (61%), have more fun in life, take myself less seriously (both 54%), and have more appreciation for beautiful things (50%). Positive assessments were recorded twice as often (mean score 4) as reported negative effects (mean ~ 1.5).

Table 3. Marijuana motives: Stated reason 'important' or 'very important' (%)

Seven factors	Random sample (N=89)	Pilot study (N=104)
Enjoyment		
To enjoy music, movies or TV	77	72
To see the world with fresh eyes	40	55
Relaxation		
To relax	77	89
To feel less anxious	35	55
To help you sleep	30	45
To forget your worries	29	55
Mood		
To feel good	66	81
To cope with depression	19	44
Release		
To blow off steam	43	61
As a cure for boredom	42	64
Social		
To be sociable with friends	59	42
As a symbol of defiance toward authority	13	24
Enhancement		
To get inspiration	40	60
To feel less inhibited	34	33
To enhance sex	30	33
To communicate better	16	16
Coping		
To get through the day	10	36
For medical reasons (e.g., pain, nausea)	10	37
To fight fatigue	4	14

The uniformly lower rates across the listed items, as compared to those found in the self-selected sample, suggest there is consistency at various use levels of the relative importance of use motives and effects.

Put otherwise, regardless of the motive or the outcome (and whether these may be defined as 'positive' or 'negative'), users rank them much the same across the different samples, with the vast majority of items of all types being more frequently reported in the self-selected group.

Table 4. Psychosocial consequences: "As a result of using marijuana…"

	Random sample (N=89)	Pilot study (N=104)
Positive effects (%)		
I have come to know myself better	61	77
I have more fun in life	54	83
I have more appreciation for beautiful things	50	69
I am more open to other people	45	73
I have am more balanced	39	60
I am happier with myself	36	60
I am more open to religious and spiritual matters	33	57
My social life has improved	32	42
My love life is more intense	24	27
I am a better and smarter person	24	43
I go out more often	18	36
Negative effects (%)		
I take myself less seriously	54	50
I am less ambitious	27	30
I am less productive	25	29
I am slower-thinking	24	29
I am less efficient	18	26
I have less interest in normal life	15	23
I have serious problems	6	10

Regression Results: Predicting Positive and Negative Long-Term Use Effects

Univariate regression analyses supported the contention that enhancement and relaxation motivations are related to more positive experiences of use (Table 5). Being female and being married relate to less positive use outcomes, while employment was related to more positive effects. The use of alcohol and number of health problems due to cannabis were associated with more negative use outcomes, as was use for coping, lower age of first use, and changes in use patterns due to major life transitions.

Once adjusted for all control variables, the multivariate model shows that life enhancement ($p<.01$), relaxation ($p<.05$), and employment ($p<.05$) are significantly related to more positive effects. Likewise, being female and married status are related to less positive experiences of use ($p<.05$).While use of cannabis for coping and important life transitions are modestly related to negative experiences ($p<.10$), the use of alcohol and number of health problems were the only significant predictors of adverse consequences related to the use of marijuana ($p<.05$).

Table 5. Regressions of use motives and other characteristics on positive and negative effects

	Positive Effects		Negative Effects	
Independent Variable	**Univariate B (95% CI)**	**Multivariate B (95% CI)**	**Univariate B (95% CI)**	**Multivariate B (95% CI)**
Gender (ref. category Male)				
Female	-1.84 (-3.96, 0.29)$^+$	-2.32 (-4.29, -0.35)*	0.82 (-0.58, 2.22)	
Age (in years)	-0.04 (-0.12, 0.05)		-0.03 (-0.08, 0.03)	
Marital Status (ref. category Single)				
Married/partnered	-2.05 (-4.21, 0.11)$^+$	-2.31 (-4.29, -0.33)*	-0.97 (-2.41, 0.47)	
Employed	2.92 (0.30, 5.55)*	2.98 (0.54, 5.43)*	-0.93 (-2.68, 0.82)	
Income (ref. category <$2000)				
$2000 or more	0.81 (-1.69, 3.31)		0.59 (-1.08, 2.27)	
Age first used marijuana	0.21 (-0.09, 0.50)		-0.16 (-0.35, 0.03)$^+$	-0.08 (-0.28, 0.12)
Use length (in years)	-0.05 (-0.15, 0.05)		-0.02 (-0.08, 0.05)	
Number of health problems	0.34 (-0.30, 1.0)		0.6 (0.2, 1.0)**	0.52 (0.09, 0.96)*
Drank alcohol last 3 months	-0.60 (-4.31, 3.14)		2.74 (0.40, 5.11)*	2.70 (0.20, 5.20)*
Used tobacco last 3 months	-0.18 (-2.36, 2.00)		0.80 (-0.68, 2.27)	
Life transitions affected use	0.93 (-1.45, 3.31)		1.33 (-2.10, 2.86)$^+$	1.43 (-0.07, 2.94)$^+$
Relaxation Motivation	0.27 (-0.04, 0.59)$^+$	0.34 (0.05, 0.63)*	0.16 (-0.05, 0.37)	0.01 (-0.20, 0.22)
Enhancement Motivation	0.43 (0.10, 0.77)*	0.49 (0.18, 0.81)**	0.06 (-0.17, 0.28)	-0.06 (-0.29, 0.20)
Coping Motivation	-0.22 (-0.73, 0.38)	-0.17 (-0.65, 0.31)	0.32 (0.00, 0.65)$^+$	0.30 (-0.03, 0.63)$^+$
R^2		.275		.173

$^+p < .10$; $*p < .05$; $**p < .01$; $***p < .001$

Conclusion

Study Limitations

There are several limitations of this study, so some caution is needed in interpreting results. Our two-stage process of recruitment based on a random household survey arguably improves upon non-random self-selection as a method of recruiting experienced marijuana users from the general population of adults. Sampling from the population through random digit dialling means that a large number of telephone calls are necessary to contact enough respondents who are willing to be surveyed. When the survey includes questions about illegal conduct, a high degree of non-response is typically expected. However, levels of participation in Canadian drug studies are within the standards expected of most surveys (Adlaf, Begin, & Sawka, 2005), and self-reports on drug use have been shown to be quite valid (Harrison, 1995). The trend towards greater acceptance of cannabis may also mitigate to some extent reluctance among users to participate in social scientific research (Reinarman et al., 2004).

We successfully contacted nearly one in three selected households/cell phone subscribers, 75% of which yielded an adult, 18 years or older, who was eligible and willing to complete the survey. Of this group only one-third of those eligible for follow-up were successfully contacted by the research team again to complete an interview in person. Although our findings can be taken as a reasonable reflection of experiences of users in the city of Toronto, our final sample is still small and ultimately self-selected from the larger population of those taking the phone survey. Despite no evident response bias, the final sample gathered is small compared to national drug surveys like the NSDUH (US National Survey on Drug Use and Health, SAMHSA, 2009) and the Canadian Addiction Survey (Adlaf et al., 2005). Accordingly, there is a need for more extensive research on cannabis use motives and psychosocial outcomes in the 'mainstream' general population of adults (Erickson & Hathaway, 2010; Hall & Degenhardt, 2007).

There are further limitations of the anecdotal data produced in self-reports about illicit drug consumption. While findings based on interviews and surveys may be valid (Dennis et al., 2002; Harrison, 1995), especially among non-treatment samples (Cole, Michailidou, Jerome, & Sumnall, 2006), we have no objective measures to corroborate recall of use levels, motivations, or effects. There is substantial overlap among the categories of marijuana motives we included in this study. Enhancement, coping, relaxation, and enjoyment, among others, have multiple dimensions with many nuances or layers, suggesting need for further exploration of these motives. Factor analysis of psychosocial outcomes indicated that a binary division of positive and negative experiences is statistically meaningful or valid. Nonetheless, the most important 'negative' reported ("I take myself less seriously") is commonly perceived as beneficial among users (Hathaway, 1997). Structured survey items of this nature are unlikely to capture the full meaning of the cannabis experience as actually experienced by marijuana users. There is a need for more intensive qualitative research on benefits and problems in relation to use motives, exploring marijuana use as a dynamic process (cf. Hathaway, 1997; Osborne & Fogel, 2008; Shukla & Kelley, 2007; Terry et al., 2007).

Discussion

Despite the limitations of this research, study findings indicate that life enhancement and relaxation motivations are significant predictors of more positive effects. The Lee et al. (2007) finding that both positive (e.g., relaxation, enhancement) and negative motivations (i.e., coping) are related to more problematic use was not corroborated in this study of experienced users recruited from the general population of adults. As compared to younger, experimental users whose motives are more commonly predominantly 'social' (e.g., conformity, rebellion)—but otherwise not far removed from those of older users (Lee et al., 2007)—more 'positive' use motives among this group related to experiencing more benefits of use. Further, in comparison with self-selected samples of the type recruited for the pilot of this study, the 'population' sample is significantly older, more established, and more moderate in their use. Nearly every motive and effect that we considered was observed less frequently among the latter group.

Apart from drinking alcohol and number of health problems, the only independent variables with even moderate predictive power for adverse consequences were use of cannabis for coping and disruptions in use patterns due to the effect of life transitions. Use in adverse circumstances or for coping is avoided by the vast majority of users. Each of the "use for coping" items in this study (i.e., to get through the day, for medical reasons, and to fight fatigue) were reported by one in ten or less of the respondents. Other research indicates avoidance of this pattern may function to alleviate concerns about dependence, negative effects, or problem use (Becker, 1963; Cohen & Sas, 1998; Hathaway, 2003). 'Self-medication' may not always lead to adverse outcomes. Yet some studies indicate that stress is a predictor for cannabis-related problems (Buckner, Schmidt, Bobadilla, & Taylor, 2006; Sinha, 2001) and that coping motivations are related to such problems as fulfilling family obligations (Lee et al., 2007).

Serious negative effects are not reported often by marijuana users in the general population; but the prevalence of use (by youth and other populations who may be more 'at risk' for cannabis-related problems) warrants further research into these associations. With respect to interventions aimed at persons seeking treatment for cannabis dependence or abuse, important insights can be gained from studying consumers who experience few adverse consequences of their use. On the basis of our findings, there is support for future research on influential social roles, role conflicts, and transitions that arise at different junctures of the cannabis career. Perceptions and experience of stigma based on gender, personal relationships, employment, and health status are potential sources of role conflict mediating marijuana use-related benefits and problems.

Whereas 'individual' use motives and effects were found to be statistically related in this study, these associations are inseparable from meanings and societal reactions that are culturally embedded. The corresponding (dis)advantages for users of banned substances differ in important ways from legal drugs like alcohol. Whether motivations follow or precede the drug behavior, understanding social norms and attitudes is central to better understanding the experience of users. Rather than fixed elements in an individual, the imputation and avowal of motives by actors are social phenomena that need to be explained. Along with rules and norms of action for various situations, users learn appropriate vocabularies of motive. As subjective meanings or accepted justifications for present, future, or past acts, motives set out the conditions for certain lines of conduct.

C. Wright Mills' (1940) and other sociological contributions on the role of motives in determining behavior (cf. Scott & Lyman, 1968; Turner, 1987; Weinstein, 1980) remind us these interpretations must be situated socially, historically, and culturally as part of socially distributed knowledge which 'everybody knows.' While words for motives are descriptions of cultural representations or general orientations for interpreting reality, different social groups have different vocabularies reflecting different circumstances and situational experiences. With respect to life enhancement "versus" coping motivations for the use of cannabis among committed users, the task for future research in this area is to further specify the background expectations that determine the range of explanations that are culturally appropriate. The social function of asserted motives in this framework—as opposed to more concern for the sincerity of users, as determined by researchers or clinicians, for example—needs to be more central to the focus of inquiry. Put otherwise, enhancing ecological validity, through in-depth ethnographic research and further qualitative studies on the lived experience of marijuana use, is critical to better understanding the nuances and connections between motives and effects in different settings and at different stages of the cannabis career.

ACKNOWLEDGMENT

This research was funded by an operating grant (#410-2004) from the Social Sciences and Humanities Research Council of Canada (SSHRC).

REFERENCES

Adlaf, E., Begin, P., & Sawka, E. (Eds.). (2005). *Canadian Addiction Survey (CAS): a national survey of Canadians' use of alcohol and other drugs: prevalence of use and related harms: detailed report.* Ottawa: Canadian Centre on Substance Abuse.

Allan, C. A. (1995). Alcohol problems and anxiety disorders—A critical review. *Alcohol & Alcoholism, 30*, 145–151.

Becker, H.S. (1963). *Outsiders: Studies in the Sociology of Deviance.* New York: Free Press.

Bolton, J.M., Robinson, J., & Sareen, J. (2008). Self-medication of mood disorders with alcohol and drugs in the National Epidemiologic Survey on Alcohol and Related Conditions. *Journal of Affective Disorders, 115*, 367-375.

Bonn-Miller, M., Zvolensky, M.J., & Bernstein, A. (2007). Marijuana use motives: Concurrent relations to frequency of past 30-day use and anxiety sensitivity among young adult marijuana smokers. *Addictive Behaviors, 32*, 49-62.

Borchers-Tempel, S., & Kolte, B. (2002). Cannabis consumption in Amsterdam, Bremen and San Francisco: A three-city comparison of longterm cannabis consumption. *Journal of Drug Issues, 32*(2), 395-412.

Buckner, J.D., Schmidt, N.B., Bobadilla, L., & Taylor, J. (2006). Social anxiety and problematic marijuana use: Evaluating the moderating role of stress reactivity and perceived coping. *Behaviour Research and Therapy, 44*, 1007-1015.

Butters, J.E. (2004). The impact of peers and social disapproval on high-risk cannabis use: gender differences and implications for drug education. *Drugs: Education, Prevention & Policy, 11,* 381-390.

Carruthers, C.P. (1993). Leisure and alcohol expectancies. *Journal of Leisure Research.* 25(3), 229-245.

Chabrol, H., Roura, C., & Kallmeyer, A. (2004). Perceptions of cannabis effects: A qualitative study among adolescents. *Encephale, 30*, 259-265.

Cohen, P.D.A., & Sas, A. (1998). *Cannabis Use in Amsterdam.* University of Amsterdam: Centre for Drug Research.

Cole, J.C., Michailidou, K., Jerome, L., & Sumnall, H.R. (2006). The effects of stereotypic threat on cognitive function in ecstasy users. *Journal of Psychopharmacology 20*, 518-525.

Conger, J.J. (1956). Reinforcement theory and the dynamics of alcoholism. *Quarterly Journal of Studies on Alcohol, 17,* 296-305.

Dennis, M., Titus, J., Diamond, G., Donaldson, J. Godley, S.H., Tims, F.M., et al. (2002). The Cannabis Youth Treatment (CYT) experiment. *Addiction, 95,* 1655-1667.

Erickson, P.G., & Hathaway, A.D. (2010). Normalization and harm reduction: Research avenues and policy agendas. *International Journal of Drug Policy, 21*(2), 137-139.

Green, B., Kavanagh, D.J., & Young, R.M.C.D. (2004). Reasons for cannabis use in men with and without psychosis. *Drug and Alcohol Review, 23,* 445-453.

Hall, W., & Degenhardt, L. (2007). Prevalence and correlates of cannabis use in developed and developing countries. *Current Opinion in Psychiatry, 20*, 393-397.

Harrison, L.D. (1995). The validity of self-reported data on drug use. *Journal of Drug Issues, 25,* 91-111.

Hathaway, A.D. (1997). Marijuana and lifestyle: Exploring tolerable deviance. *Deviant Behavior,18,* 213-232.

Hathaway, A.D. (2003). Cannabis effects and dependence concerns in long-term frequent users: A missing piece of the public health puzzle. *Addiction Research and Theory, 11* (6), 441-458.

Hathaway, A.D. (2004). Cannabis careers reconsidered: Transitions and trajectories of committed long-term users. *Contemporary Drug Problems, 31*, 401-423.

Jung, J. (2001). *Psychology of Alcohol and Other Drugs: A Research Perspective.* Sage Publications, Inc.

Kalodner, C.R., Delucia, J.L., & Ursprung, A.W. (1989). An examination of the tension reduction hypothesis: The relationship between anxiety and alcohol in college students. *Addictive Behaviors, 14*, 649-654.

Kidorf, M., & Lang, A.R. (1999). Effects of social anxiety an alcohol expectancies on stress-induced drinking. *Psychology of Addictive Behaviors, 13*(2), 134-142.

Kilmer, J.R., Hunt, S.B., Lee, C.M., & Neighbors, C. (2007). Marijuana use, risk perception and consequences: Is perceived risk congruent with reality? *Addictive Behaviors, 32*, 3026-3033.

Kushner, M. G., Abrams, K., & Borchardt, C. (2000). The relationship between anxiety disorders and alcohol use disorders: A review of major perspectives and findings. *Clinical Psychology Review, 20*(2), 149–171.

Lee, C.M., Neighbors, C., & Woods, B.A. (2007). Marijuana motives: Young adults' reasons for using marijuana. *Addictive Behaviors, 32*(7), 1384-1394.

Mills, C.W. (1940). Situated actions and vocabularies of motive. *American Sociological Review, 5*(6), 904-913.

O'Hare, T.M. (1990). Alcohol expectancies and social anxiety in male and female undergraduates. *Addictive Behaviors, 15*, 561-566.

Osborne, G.B., & Fogel, C. (2008). Understanding the motivations for recreational marijuana use among adult Canadians. *Substance Use & Misuse, 43*, 539-572.

Reinarman C., Cohen, P.D.A., & Kaal, H.L. (2004). The limited relevance of drug policy: Cannabis in Amsterdam and San Francisco. *American Journal of Public Health, 94*(5), 836-842.

Robinson, J., Sareen, J., Cox, B.J., & Bolton, J. (2009). Self-medication of anxiety disorders with alcohol and drugs: Results from a nationally representative sample. *Journal of Anxiety Disorders,* **23(1)**, 38-45.

Sayette, M.A. (1999). Does drinking reduce stress? *Alcohol Research & Health, 23*(4), 250-255.

Schafer, J., & Brown, S.A. (1991). Marijuana and cocaine effect expectancies and drug use patterns. *Journal of Consulting and Clinical Psychology, 59* (4), 558-565.

Scott, MB., & Lyman, S.M. (1968). Accounts. *American Sociological Review, 33*(1), 46-62.

Shukla, R., & Kelley, M. (2007). Investigating how decisions to use marijuana change over time. *Substance Use & Misuse, 42*, 1401-1425.

Simons, J, Correia, C.J., Carey, K.B., & Borsari, B.E. (1998). Validating a five-factor marijuana motives measure: Relations with use, problems, and alcohol motives. *Journal of Counseling Psychology, 45* (3), 265-273.

Sinha, R. (2001). How does stress increase risk of drug abuse and relapse? *Psychopharmacology, 158*, 343-359.

Siqueira, L., Diab, M., Bodian, C., & Rolnitzky, L. (2001). The relationships of stress and coping methods to adolescent marijuana use. *Substance Abuse, 22*(3), 157-166.

Stewart, S.H., & Zeitlin, S.B. (1995). Anxiety sensitivity and alcohol use motives. *Journal of Anxiety Disorders, 9*(3), 229-240.

Stewart, S.H., Karp, J., Pihl, R.O. & Peterson, R.A. (1997). Anxiety sensitivity and self-reported reasons for drug use. *Journal of Substance Abuse, 9,* 223-240.

Substance Abuse and Mental Health Services Administration. (2009*). Results from the 2008 National Survey on Drug Use and Health:* National Findings (Office of Applied Studies, NSDUH Series H-36, HHS Publication No. SMA 09-4434). Rockville, MD.

Terry, P., Wright, K.A., & Cochrane, R. (2007). Factors contributing to changes in frequency of cannabis consumption by cannabis users in England: A structured interview study. *Addiction Research & Theory, 15*(1), 113-119

Turner, J.H. (1987). Toward a sociological theory of motivation. *American Sociological Review, 52*(1), 15-27.

United National Office on Drugs and Crime. (2006). *World Drug Report.* Vienna: UNODC.

Weinstein, R.M. (1980). Vocabularies of motive for illicit drug use: An application of the accounts framework. *The Sociological Quarterly, 219*(4), 577-593.

Zinberg, N. (1984). *Drug, set, and setting: The basis for controlled intoxicant use.* Yale University Press.

In: Drug Use and Abuse
Editor: Marie Claire Van Hout

ISBN: 978-1-62618-232-5

Chapter 9

MOLECULAR GENETIC MECHANISMS OF ADDICTION INVOLVING THE ΔFOSB PATHWAYS

John Grandy
North Country Urgent Care and Whitestone Consulting LLC

ABSTRACT

The prolonged presence of behavioral abnormalities that are associated with drug addiction can persist months after cessation of drug use. This strongly suggests that the regulation of genetic expression is involved in the mechanisms by which recreational drug use translates into the chronic state of addiction. Gene expression is tightly regulated by transcription factors.

A major mechanism by which drugs of abuse are proposed to affect the regulation of gene expression is by their effect on the expression of certain transcription factors. Many transcription factors have been identified and an overwhelming amount of evidence suggests that ΔFosB pathways represent one of the genetic mechanisms in where drugs of abuse can produce stable genetic states of expression in the brain that directly contribute to addiction. In this chapter the primary focus will be on what is known about the effects of amphetamines, cocaine, nicotine, and opioids on ΔFosB pathways and the effect these pathways have on the brain.

Keywords: deltaFosB transcription factor; Fos family transcription factors; dynorphin gene; cdk5 gene; NF-kappaB gene; GluR2 gene; nucleus accumbens

GLOSSARY

Alternative splicing- is a regulatory mechanism that incorporates variations in the exon (the coding region) from the DNA into the mRNA, which ultimately results in different forms of the same protein. This allows one gene to produce many isoforms of the same protein.

Behavioral phenotype- is a characteristic pattern of abnormalities that is consistent with a biological disorder. These abnormalities can be seen in motor, cognitive, linguistic, and/or social skills.

Consensus sequencing- is a short sequence of nucleotides that represents a binding site on a protein. This type of notation can be used to show which protein residues are conserved.

Degron- is a specific amino acid sequence on a protein (or transcriptional factor) that serves as a biological target to initiate protein degradation. Some degrons can be temperature sensitive or ligand controlled.

DNase I analysis- this is a technique utilized to locate specific binding sites of proteins (in this case DNase I) on the DNA. This strategy takes advantage of the fact that DNA-protein interactions exist to protect the DNA from enzymatic cleavage.

Epigenetics- are changes in the phenotype caused by mechanisms other than changes in the actual DNA sequence. Examples of these types of mechanisms include histone tail modification, DNA methylation, and microRNAs.

Footprinting analysis- this is a laboratory technique in where DNA fragments are typically labeled with radioactivity in order to indentify the binding sites on the DNA being studied.

Functional activator protein- is a protein in a particular pathway that is required for transcriptional activity. This performs the opposite function of a repressor protein/element.

Hyperalgesia- is a clinical syndrome in where there is an increased sensitivity to pain or the presence of pain levels that are not proportionate to the injury or stage of recovery.

Hyperkatifeia- is a clinical syndrome in where a patients using opioids displays hypersensitivity to negative emotional states and/or increased intensity of emotional distress.

Medium spiny neurons- are GABAergic projection neurons from the ventral and dorsal striatum, and the nucleus accumbens.

Microarray analysis- is a research technique used to measure the expression levels of genes. This method can genotype multiple regions of the total genetic content contained in a haploid set of chromosomes.

Opioid-induced hyperalgesia- is hyperalgesia that is caused from the administration of opioids.

Promoter region- this is the region of the DNA molecule that proceeds the coding region. The promoter region controls the expression of the coding region.

Sensitization- is the enhanced drug responsiveness with repeated exposure to that drug at the same constant dose.

Transcription factor- is a sequence-specific DNA-binding factor. This is a protein that binds only to a specific DNA sequence or response element on the promoter region of a target gene. This allows the transcription factor to regulate the target gene's expression.

Transgenic mice- are genetically modified for the purpose of genetic research. In most of the studies mentioned in this chapter, the mice were genetically modified to overexpress ΔFosB.

Truncation- this is a biological process in where a protein is shortened. This is often a result of mutations that effect the translation of the mRNA.

Western blot- is a molecular biology technique to detect the presence of certain proteins. This is typically achieved using an antibody specific to the protein, which is put through a gel electrophoresis.

INTRODUCTION

It has long been observed, at least in a clinical sense, that recreational drug use often leads to continued or prolonged use and this somehow translates into a chronic state of addiction (see Figure 1). It is usually the chronic state of addiction in where the patient encounters difficulties in functioning cognitively, socially, occupationally, or psychologically. Physiological deterioration, which can manifest as medical problems, often accompanies chronic addiction as well.

Addictive behavior can be compulsive in nature and the addict continues to pursue drug consumption despite these harmful outcomes. Can these profound changes in behavior that are self-destructive in nature be accounted for on a genetic level?

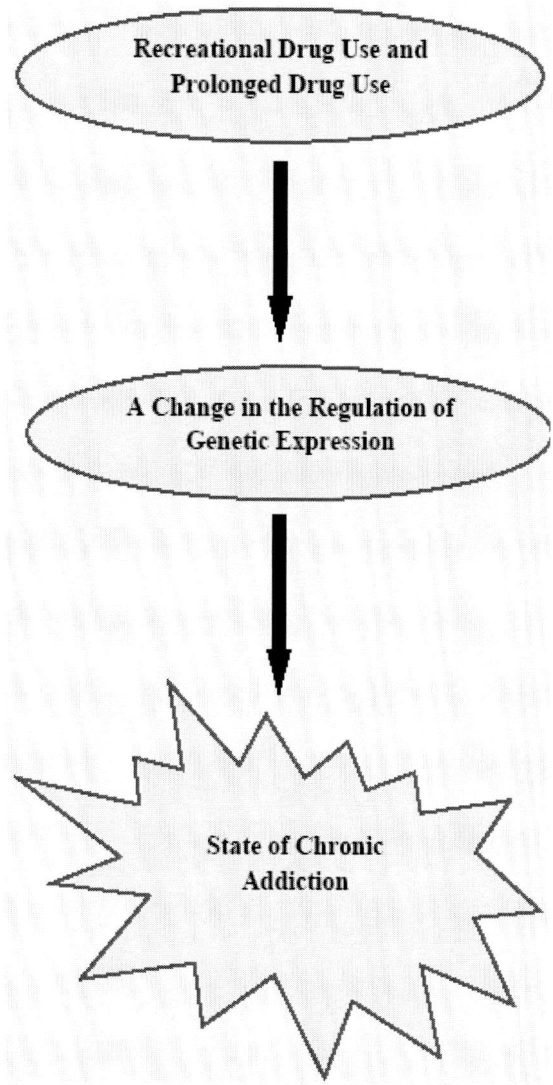

Figure 1. This demonstrates a visualization of the transition from recreational drug use to the state of chronic addiction.

ΔFosB pathways are strongly indicated in the production of stable genetic states of expression. These genetic changes have consequent effects which are proposed to underlay changes in the brain that ultimately affect human behavior. Drugs of abuse, in particular amphetamines, cocaine, and opioids can induce these genetic changes in gene expression. A large amount of research has been completed that characterizes the response of ΔFosB pathways to exposure to drugs of abuse. In addition, research has also been completed on ΔFosB expression and the ensuing effects on neurophysiology that may account for addiction behavior. In this chapter I will discuss the transcription factor ΔFosB, proposals for the genetic model of addiction involving ΔFosB pathways, drugs of abuse that induce ΔFosB expression, target genes that are influences by ΔFosB overexpression, some of the complex effects that these genes have on the brain and the response to drugs of abuse, and ultimately addiction behavior.

THE ΔFOSB TRANSCRIPTION FACTOR

The FosB gene codes for FosB protein. ΔFosB is a truncated slice variant of FosB that contains the dimerization and DNA-binding domain, but it lacks the C-terminal transactivating domain (Nestler 2008). Research in 1991 demonstrated that the FosB gene, through a process known as alternative splicing, produced both mRNA products that result in FosB and ΔFosB proteins (Dobrzanski et al. 1991). Although, at that time ΔFosB was referred to as FosB/SF (short form) as it is a truncated version of the FosB protein.

The Fos family transcription factors (ΔFosB, c-Fos, FosB, Fra1, and Fra2) chemically bind with Jun family proteins (c-Jun, JunB, or JunD) that in turn form a functional activator protein-1 (AP-1) complex (McClung and Nestler 2004). These active AP-1 transcription factors bind to AP-1 sites (consensus sequence: TGAC/GTCA) that are present on the promoter region on certain genes, which in turn regulates the transcription of those genes (see Figure 2). The AP-1 transcription factor was defined in 1987 in human cells as an activity that binds selectively to enhancer elements in the promoter region of certain vertebrate genes, which was confirmed with footprinting analysis (Angel et al. 1987) and utilizing DNase I protection analysis (Lee et al. 1987). ΔFosB has been shown to predominantly dimerize with JunD to form an active AP-1 complex that demonstrates long-lasting sustainment in neurons in specific brain regions.

ΔFosB has been proposed to be involved in many molecular and genetic pathways that are implicated in the transition from recreational drug use to the chronically addicted state. There are four main reasons for this. First, ΔFosB expression can be affected by drugs of abuse of. These various effects will be discussed in later sections of this chapter. Secondly, ΔFosB expression is long-acting and it can act as a sustained molecular switch for addictive behavior (Nester et al. 2001). Third, ΔFosB is known to control the expression of target genes i.e. it functions primarily as a transcriptional activator and also as a repressor on a smaller subset of genes (McClung and Nestler 2003). Examples of target genes that are activated and deactivated by ΔFosB will also be discussed in a later section of this chapter. The ability of ΔFosB to both turn on and turn off other genes is what makes studying these pathways so difficult.

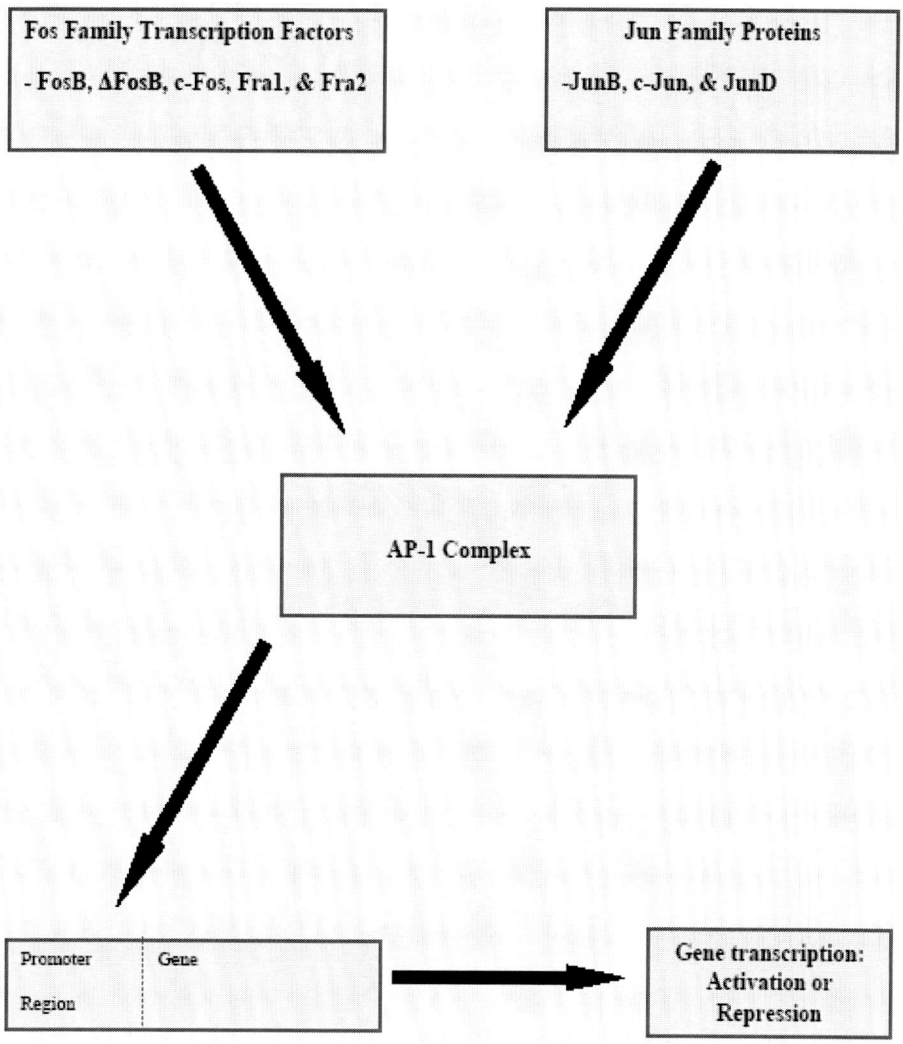

Figure 2. The AP-1 complex is formed from the combination of any one of the Fos family transcription factors and any one of the Jun family proteins. This complex attaches to the promoter region of the gene and regulates the transcription of that gene.

Fourth, ΔFosB produces complex effects on neuronal plasticity and ultimately complex behaviors. This phenomenon plays an essential role in long-term adaptive changes in the brain. This can also be seen in neuroplastic changes in other disorders e.g. Parkinson's disease and depression; as well as drug addiction (McClung et al. 2004). When these four reasons are taken collectively they converge into a main paradigm. For a conceptualization of this paradigm see Figure 3.

In the next sections of this chapter we will discuss early and modern discovers that fortify the significance of ΔFosB pathways and their involvement in the development of the prolonged presence of behavioral abnormalities that are associated with drug use and proposed mechanisms of addictions. In addition, we will also discuss some of the molecular genetics (and epigenetics) involved and how this results in changes in specific brain regions and ultimately the correlation to behavior.

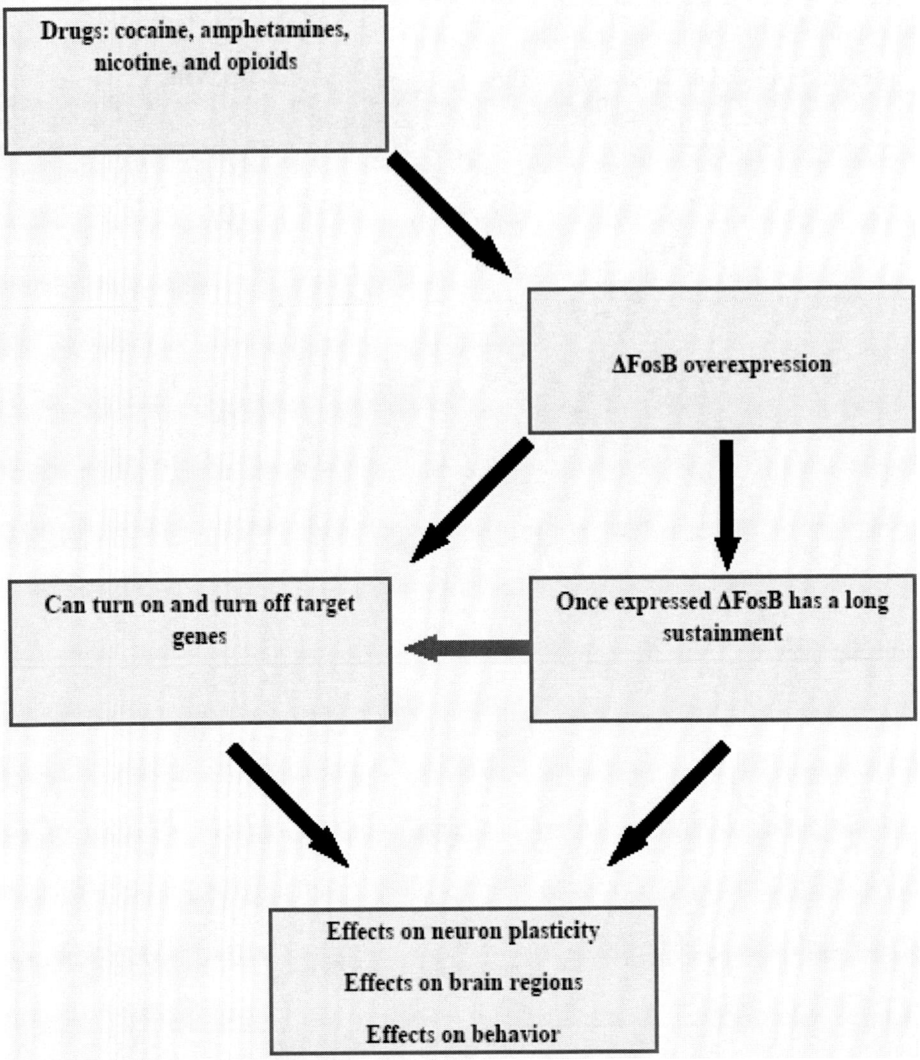

Figure 3. This diagram demonstrates conceptually that drugs affect ΔFosB expression, which can in turn induce or repress the expression of other target genes. Once activated, ΔFosB expression has a long half-life in the neuron, which continues to affect the target genes (red arrow). The long-term sustainment of the genes being expressed has complex effects on neuron plasticity. The changes at the level of the neurons can collectively affect specific brain regions, which can ultimately affect behavior.

PROPOSALS FOR ADDICTIVE BEHAVIOR INVOLVING ΔFOSB

The objective behavioral abnormalities observed in patients in the chronic state of addiction e.g. excessive or obsessive drug consumption despite harmful consequences has given rise to the proposal that these behaviors may be mediated, to some degree, by changes in gene expression. This is an attempt to explain how the drug "takes hold" of the drug addict. There are early observations that support this genetic proposal based on the consequences of drug-enhanced dopamine in the brain, particularly in the striatum (Berke and Hyman 2000).

The striatum is composed of the caudate nucleus and the putamen, which is where responses to psychomotor stimulants e.g. cocaine and amphetamines can occur. After exposure to these drugs they can cause what are known as neuronal adaptive changes due to the release of excessive dopamine. Adaptive changes such as these can be either homeostatic responses or synaptic plasticity responses.

Homeostatic responses are physiologic tendencies of a biological system to maintain equilibrium, which is also known as compensatory adaptation. This response to drug administration may underlie aspects of drug dependence and withdrawal symptoms when the administration of the drug is stopped. This is because neurons in the brain undergo biologic changes in an attempt to counter the effects of repeated drug exposure and when unmasked by cessation of the drug can cause dysfunctioning of the central nervous system, which is manifested clinically as withdrawal.

It is debatable that these homeostatic responses to drug administration cannot account for the compulsive nature of chronic drug abuse. However, synaptic plasticity seems to provide a mechanism which allows for the association of drug-related stimulus with specific learned behaviors. As the addict continues to use the drug the neurons make new connections to other neurons while losing connections to others. These neuroadaptive changes essentially "rewire" the brain to be more motivated toward drug seeking behavior.

There is evidence to support this proposal of synaptic plastic changes underlying brain changes. It has been demonstrated that addictive drugs can engage molecular mechanisms involved in associative learning, specifically the stimulation of dopamine D1 receptors, the activation of the cAMP/PKA/CREB signal transduction pathways, and transient burst of altered gene expression (Berke and Hyman 2000). These three mechanisms can result in rearrangements in synaptic morphology of the neurons. The main paradigm mentioned earlier suggests that these synaptic changes i.e. neuron plasticity underlay the changes in specific brain regions that ultimately has an effect on behavior (see Figure 3).

Interestingly, similar changes in synaptic connectivity occur during memory formation. It is this synaptic plasticity in multiple neuronal systems may more accurately account for distinct phases of addiction and the shift from controlled recreational drug use to the transition of compulsive drug use that involves normal habit learning pathways. As the drug-reward cycle and/or the pleasure response persist so do the habit memories involving drug use. This cycle would ultimately involve changes in synaptic connectivity that would cultivate and later cement addictive behaviors.

ΔFosB pathways are known to be involved in synaptic plasticity. Drugs of abuse can induce these ΔFosB pathways. Therefore drugs of abuse can initiate changes in ΔFosB expression that consequently affects synaptic plasticity. Let us look at how certain drugs affect ΔFosB.

ΔFosB Induction

The involvement of ΔFosB induction in the development of addiction has been proposed because it has long been established that drug exposure results in ΔFosB accumulation that can persist for several weeks after cessation of drug administration. Early studies have proven that ΔFosB induction can be facilitated by drugs of abuse e.g. cocaine (Nye et al. 1995), morphine (Nye et al. 1996), and nicotine (Pich et al. 1997).

The induction of ΔFosB, along with other biochemically modified isoforms of ΔFosB, has been shown to happen in response to all drugs of abuse: opiates, cocaine, amphetamine, methamphetamine, nicotine, ethanol, phencyclidine (PCP), and cannibiniods- the magnitude of the induction is known to vary from drug to drug. Conversely, the other Fos family transcription factors show reduced induction when compared to initial responses of the drug. Next, we will look at how ΔFosB is able to sustain its expression for remarkably long periods of time.

The Sustained Expression of ΔFosB

The extraordinary half-life of ΔFosB was demonstrated in 1997 using one and two-dimensional Western blots (Chen et al. 1997). The gradual accumulation of ΔFosB has been reviewed and compared to the transient induction of other Fos family proteins (c-fos, FosB, Fra1, and Fra2) in response to the administration of drugs of abuse (Nestler et al. 2001). It has been demonstrated that ΔFosB accumulations persist for several weeks with repeated stimuli, which is much longer than the other Fos family proteins comparatively. The other Fos Family proteins return to basal levels hours after drug administration.

Due to the extraordinary half-live of ΔFosB it is able to accumulate in the neurons after drug exposure. This accumulation can persist for several weeks after the drug of abuse is discontinued. This allows the effects of ΔFosB on other target gene pathways to perpetuate.

There are two molecular reasons that account for the unusual stability of ΔFosB (Nestler 2008). First, ΔFosB lacks the two degron domains that are present on all of the other Fos family transcription factors including FosB. Degron domains are molecular targets for the initiation of rapid protein degradation. Lacking the degron domains allows ΔFosB to avoid the rapid degradation or inactivation that the other Fos transcription factors are subjected to. Secondly, ΔFosB is further stabilized by phosphorylation by protein kinases, most notably casein kinase 2 (ck2). This additional stability that cd2 phosphorylation provides allows ΔFosB to continue functioning for prolonged durations. These two molecular properties of ΔFosB explain how it is able to attain sustained levels that can gradually accumulate in response to drug exposure in comparison to the rapid and transient induction of the other Fos family transcription factors.

The robust temporal expression of ΔFosB has demonstrated various properties on the rewarding effects of certain drugs. This appears to be a function of duration and degree of ΔFosB expression. For example, the short-term expression of ΔFosB reduces the rewarding effects of cocaine, but prolonged expression increase the drug rewarding effects of cocaine (McClung and Nestler 2003). It is now known that the various responses to drugs of abuse are due to the target genes of ΔFosB. Next, we will survey some these target genes of ΔFosB.

Targets Genes Affected by ΔFosB

ΔFosB transcription factor may be able to influence changes in behavioral plasticity by altering the expression of other target genes. It effects the expression of other target genes by acting as both an inducer and repressor of AP-1-mediated transcription, which is dependent on the particular AP-1 site on the promoter region of the target gene (see Figure 2). Several target genes have been discovered and others are currently under investigation. First we will discuss three genes that are activated by ΔFosB drug-induction.

GluR2 Gene

The α-amino-3-hydroxy-5-methyl-4-isoxozolepropionic glutamate receptor two (AMPA-GluR2) is an excitatory receptor that responds to the neurotransmitter glutamate. The GluR2 gene codes for the GluR2 sub-receptor portion of the AMPA-GluR2 receptor complex. GluR2 gene is induced (but not the AMPA gene) in the neurons of the nucleus accumbens when ΔFosB is overexpressed, as the GluR2 promoter region contains an AP-1 site. GluR2 induction in response to ΔFosB was demonstrated in studies using transgenic mice that specifically induce ΔFosB in neurons in the nucleus accumbens (Klez and Chen 1999).

Sensitivity to drugs like cocaine and amphetamines is mediated in part by increases in GluR2. This is mainly due to the increases in the responsiveness to the rewarding and locomotor-activating effects of these two drugs. GluR2 induction reduces the overall conductivity (or excitation) of the AMPA receptor in nucleus accumbens neurons. The reduction in the responsiveness to the glutamate excitatory inputs is believed to augment the response to cocaine and amphetamines.

This was validated in earlier current-response studies involving cocaine and amphetamines, which showed that nucleus accumbens neurons treated with these two drugs, became less sensitive to the rate-enhancing effects of glutamate i.e. reduced glutamatergic responses (White et al. 1995).

Cdk5 Gene

Cyclin-dependent kinase-5 (cdk5) gene is induced by ΔFosB in both the nucleus accumbens and the dorsal striatum. This has been validated in earlier studies involving the use of microarray analysis after chronic cocaine administration (Bibb et al. 2001). ΔFosB activates the cdk5 gene by binding to the AP-1 site on the promoter region (Chen et al., 2000). Cdk5 expression is important because it regulates proteins involved in dopamine signaling and glutamate transmission, mostly in the striatum.

Cdk5 levels increase in a ΔFosB-dependent process with chronic exposure to cocaine. This was confirmed in research using cdk5-inhibitors roscovitine and olomoucine (Taylor et al. 2007).

In this study subsequent cocaine injections in mice pretreated with the cdk5-inhibitors demonstrated an augmented sensitivity to the effects of cocaine. An enhancement was also seen in locomotor responses to additional cocaine administration. This supports to notation that cdk5 inhibition is strongly associated with locomotor sensitization and incentive-motivational behaviors in response to chronic cocaine exposure, which also suggests that cdk5 negatively regulates biochemical and behavioral effects that are associated with cocaine exposure. Therefore, cocaine-induced increases in ΔFosB expression cause increases in cdk5 expression, which decreases sensitivity and locomotor responses to cocaine.

NFκB Gene

Nuclear factor κB (NFκB) is a transcriptional factor that is known for its role in inflammation and immune response; as well as being involved in the maintenance of cellular structure. NFκB is also increased in the nucleus accumbens by ΔFosB over-expression. This was established by studies using mircroarry analysis (Ang et al. 2001).

NFκB activation increases the number of dendritic spines on neurons in the nucleus accumbens and inhibition of NFκB decreases the number of these dendritic spines. This was confirmed in a study involving viral-mediated gene transfer (Russo et al. 2009). The structural changes of the dendritic spine density of the medium spiny neurons is correlated with the sensitization of behavioral responses to cocaine i.e. inhibition of NFκB decreases the rewarding effects and induction of NFκB increases the rewarding effects. Therefore, cocaine induces ΔFosB expression that induces NFκB expression, which increases the reward response to cocaine.

We have now discussed three target genes that are activated by drug-induced ΔFosB expression. Interestingly, the ΔFosB-dependent increases of cdk5 decrease cocaine sensitivity while GluR2 increases augment the sensitivity to cocaine, and NFκB increases augment the reward response to cocaine. Next I will discuss a gene that is repressed by ΔFosB-induction.

Dynorphin Gene

Dynorphin gene is expressed by a subset of neurons in the nucleus accumbens- the medium spiny neurons, which were mentioned previously. Medium spiny neurons are important because they innervate the dopamine-containing terminals of other neurons e.g. the ventral tegmental area. ΔFosB decreases the expression of dynorphin (Nestler 2001). Dynorphin inhibits the dopaminergic neurons that innervate the nucleus accumbens medium spiny neurons by κ-opioid receptors. Furthermore, while the ΔFosB repression of the dynorphin gene decreases the expression of dynorphin there are subconsequent decreases in the inhibition of dopamine, which results in an increase in dopamine release. The release of dopamine contributes to the enhancement of drug reward mechanisms. This has been verified in bitransgenic mice that selectively express ΔFosB in dynorphin-containing medium spiny neurons (Klez and Chen 1999).

Similar findings were substantiated in bitransgenic mice in where the repression of dynorphin caused by ΔFosB overexpression increased the sensitivity of the awarding effects to morphine and appeared to intensify the physical dependence to the drug (Zachariou et al. 2006).

A more recent study utilizing intracranial self-stimulation of cocaine effects in ΔFosB overexpressing mice also demonstrated an increase to drug reward (Muschamp et al. 2012). This study also demonstrated that these test subjects were less sensitive to the pro-depressive threshold-elevating effects of κ-opioid receptor agonist U50488, which resulted in a reduced sensitivity to aversion.

This suggests that this type of genetic expression or phenotype has a propensity toward addiction and resistance to stress. Collectively, all of these findings help solidify that ΔFosB-induced dynorphin gene repression is involved in the ΔFosB behavioral phenotypes induced by drugs of abuse.

In this section four different target genes were examined. ΔFosB demonstrated various effects on these target genes. The effect of ΔFosB overexpression on the functioning of the individual target genes is summarized in Figure 4. It should also be obvious that sensitization to drug effects and increases in the reward response are in all likelihood associated with drug craving, compulsive drug use, and relapse.

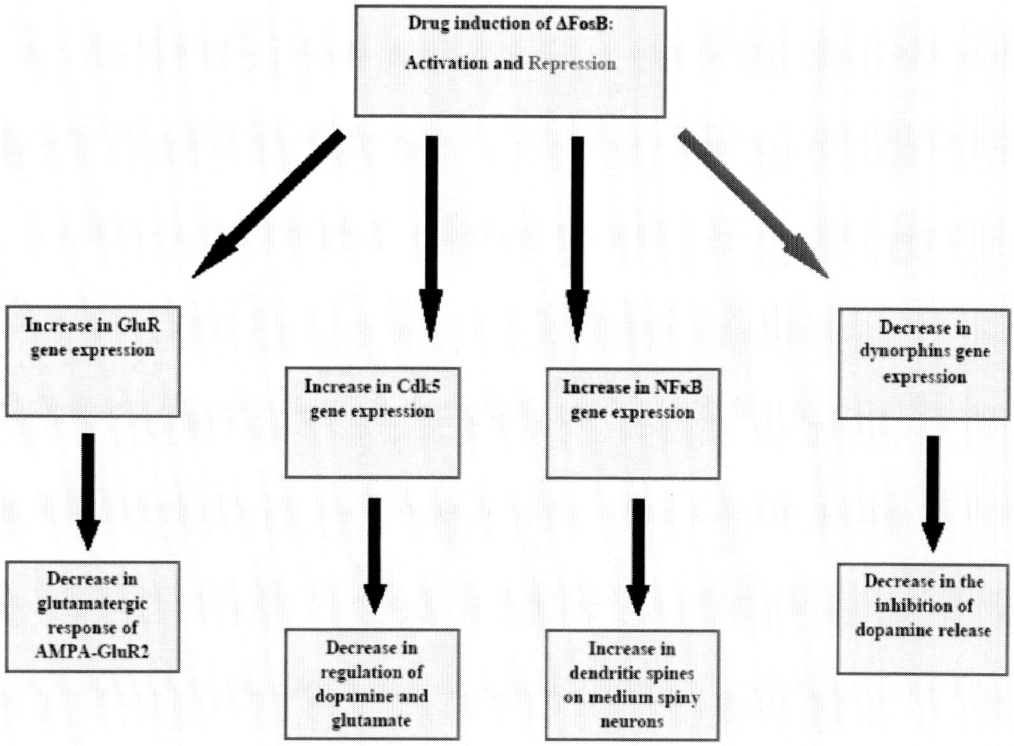

Figure 4. This demonstrates the biological effects of drug-induced ΔFosB induction on target genes.

ΔFosB Neuron Plasticity and Affects on Specific Brain Regions

The sustained levels of ΔFosB can provide the mechanism required for the long-term behavioral plasticity in specific regions of the brain caused by drug administration. Early evidence of this was suggested in experiments using transgenic mice, which demonstrated the selective transduction of ΔFosB in the striatum (Chen et al. 1998) and in the nucleus accumbens (Kelz and Chen 1999). These two regions are significant due to their established role in behavioral response to drugs of abuse and addiction. Therefore, the sustained accumulation of ΔFosB in these brain regions can act as a molecular switch. This is significant as it is an indicator that ΔFosB pathways mediate some elements of persistent neural and behavioral plasticity that results from drug administration.

In discussing ΔFosB target genes and their functions, the importance of the medium spiny neurons in the nucleus accumbens became obvious. There is early evidence that the ΔFosB induction is selective for the dynorphin/substance P-containing subset of medium spiny neurons located in the striatum and nucleus accumbens (Nye 1995; Moratalla 1996). In these studies it was discovered that the selective overexpression of ΔFosB was localized to dynorphin/substance P-containing medium spiny neurons.

The effects of ΔFosB overexpression in the nucleus accumbens is the most studied. However, ΔFosB accumulation secondary to drug induction was noted in other brain regions e.g. amygdala and the medial prefrontal cortex (Nye et al. 1995); as well as the hippocampus, the bed nucleus of the stria terminalis (this innervates the amygdala to the brainstem), interstitial nucleus of the posterior limb of the anterior commissure, the lateral septum, periaqueductal grey, and the GABA-cells in the posterior ventral tegmental area (Nestler 2008). In addition, a recent study examining the effects of morphine on Fos/ΔFosB levels utilizing quantitative immunohistochemistry recognized Fos/ΔFosB plasticity in the motivational pathways of the nucleus accumbens core as well as motor outputs of the dorsomedial caudate-putamen, the basolateral subdivision of the amygdala, and the central nucleus of the amygdala (Kaplan et al. 2011).

In several of the experiments discussed in this chapter it was demonstrated that transgenic expression of ΔFosB in the striatum results in an enhancement of the rewarding properties of cocaine and opiates. However, not much was mentioned about the effects of tetrahydrocannabinol (THC). In a recent study using bitransgenic mice with inducible expression of ΔFosB, specifically in dopamine D1 receptor/dynorphins-containing striatal neurons, some contrast was seen between opioid and cannabinoid exposure (Sim-Selley et al. 2011). The results showed that opioid-mediated receptor signaling was enhanced by ΔFosB expression; whereas cannabinoid-mediated receptor signaling did not demonstrate any appreciable difference in response to ΔFosB expression. This suggests that receptor signaling of opioids and cannabinoids are modulated differently by ΔFosB expression, which may be brain region specific. This may also be supported by the observation that THC-induction of ΔFosB expression seems to increase Zif268 and c-Fos (other target genes of ΔFosB) transcription factors in the forebrain (Lazenka et al. 2012). This represents the differential regional expression of target genes and the effects of cannabinoid receptor signaling that may account for the behavioral effects of THC when compared to other drugs.

Newer subcompartments of the brain continue to be defined. The tail of the ventral tegmental area (tVTA), which is also referred to as the rostromental nucleus, also demonstrates ΔFosB induction in response to drugs of abuse. This was validated in immunohistochemistry studies following drug administration (Kaufling et al. 2010). This study showed that induction of FosB/ΔFosB expression was seen in the tVTA GABAergic cells in response to the administration of cocaine, MDMA, methylphenidate, and caffeine; but no induction was seen with the administration of ethanol, diazepam, GBH, morphine, ketamine, PCP, THC, sodium valproic acid, or gabapentin. In addition, tVTA GABAergic cells showed induction of FosB/ΔFosB to dopamine transport inhibitor GBR12909, but not to antidepressants- reboxetine, nortriptyline, fluoxetine, or velafaxine. This further demonstrates the variance of ΔFosB expression to different types of drugs and the significance of dopamine mediation in the tVTA.

We have discussed several different brain regions that show ΔFosB expression secondary to drug exposure and discussed some of the biological consequences and changes in neuron plasticity. However, we have not discussed how this results in changes in behavior.

Mephedrone is a synthetic designer drug that is structurally related to MDMA and methamphetamine. This compound is found in several products referred to as "Bath Salts". One study demonstrated that intravenous use of mephedrone-containing products resulted in compulsive re-injection with excessive binge use over long periods, intense paranoia, violent behavior, aggression, and the emergence of Parkinson-type symptoms (Van Hout and Bingham 2012). The effects of mephedrone on ΔFosB expression have not yet been clarified at this point, but it would be reasonable to propose that its activity is similar to the structurally related parent drug methamphetamine. This could account for the development of the compulsive behavior seen in this cohort of addicts. However, major differences have been observed in the manner in which mephedrone interacts with the body that is very different from how structurally similar drugs act. This was seen in a case study involving kidney and heart failure following the use of mephedrone-containing products (Grandy 2012a).

Changes in brain regions secondary to the use of prescription opioids have been correlated with the manifestation of clinical syndromes e.g. opioid-induced hyperalgesia and hyperkatifeia (Grandy 2012b). In these two syndromes the patient becomes more sensitive to physical pain and emotional distress due to chronic administration of prescription and non-prescription opioids. This correlation was made with the observation of gross brain atrophy in the amygdala and three of the white matter tracts that innervate it to other brain regions: the uncinate fasciculus, the stria terminalis, and the ventral amygdalofugal white matter tracts which were due to long-term prescription opioid use (Upadhyay et al. 2010).

Other ΔFosB Inducing Agents: Stress and Sex

In this chapter many different drugs were mentioned and their effect on ΔFosB expression. However, other natural responses can cause ΔFosB induction. We will briefly mention how stress and sex affect ΔFosB induction in certain regions of the brain.

ΔFosB expression in response to chronic social stress was studied in a small study involving 24 patients (Teyssier et al. 2011). It is known that ΔFosB expression is increased in the nucleus accumbens in response to chronic social stress but it is down-regulated in patients with major depressive disorder. A different study using transgenic mice with reduced expression of FosB and enhanced expression of ΔFosB demonstrated that ΔFosB is essential for stress tolerance (Ohnishi et al. 2011). The Teyssier et al. study utilized real-time quantitative PCR and demonstrated that ΔFosB (and GluR2 gene) expression was increased in Brodmann area 46 in patients with major depressive disorder.

It appears that ΔFosB-mediated transcription in the nucleus accumbens is the opposite of that in Brodmann area 46 in these test subjects with major depressive disorder, which could in part be due to a shift in the excitability of glutamatergic synapses; possibly due to GluR2 induction.

Sex can also elicit an induction of ΔFosB expression. This was demonstrated in a study manipulating ΔFosB activity in ΔFosB overexpressing mice and in mice expressing a dominant negative-binding partner, ΔJunD (Pitchers et al. 2010). The study showed that sexual experiences resulted in ΔFosB accumulations in the nucleus accumbens, medial prefrontal cortex, ventral tegmental area, and the caudate putamen. This supports that ΔFosB expression plays a critical role for reinforcing the effects of sexual behavior as well as the sexual experience-induced facilitation of sexual performance. Interestingly, as with other drugs of abuse, orgasm is also associated with dopamine release.

Epigenetic Mechanisms to Understand ΔFosB Pathways

In most of the studies mentioned in this chapter the focus regarding transcriptional regulation has relied solely on the steady-state expression of mRNA levels. However, mechanisms of transcriptional regulation can show variation from one cell type to another.

This leaves much gray area in how drugs of abuse and ΔFosB overexpression affect specific genes *in vivo*. A recent attempt to overcome this issue has involved studying epigenetic mechanisms.

Epigenetics has been utilized to observe structural adaption in the regions of the chromosomes and the resulting altered state of activity. ΔFosB epigenetic mechanisms may also help explain the different consequences that ΔFosB overexpression can have on the target genes i.e. that activation or repression of that gene. I will briefly explain some mechanisms of epigenetic regulation that have been proposed to be involved in addiction (Robinson and Nestler 2012).

Histone Tail Modification

Histone acetylation is induced by drugs of abuse and is associated with the activation of gene transcription. This process changes the protein residue on the histone tail. Histone tail modifications utilize histone acetyltransferases and histone deacetylases, but also utilize phosphorylation, ubiquitination, sumoylation, and ADP-ribosylation.

DNA Methylation

DNA methylation is process that typically represses gene transcription using corepressor complexes. Recently multiple new links have been found between DNA methylation and addiction mechanisms involving MeCP2 expression in the nucleus accumbens and the dorsal striatum.

Gene Priming and Desensitization

Chromatin regulation in addiction models have demonstrated epigenetic modification in individual genes that alter the inducibility of other genes and desensitize them. The primed genes are genes that were not affected by the initial drug exposure but became induced after chronic exposure. The gene priming and desensitization of these genes have been seen in microarray studies.

MicroRNAs

The microRNAs are non-coding RNA species that are post-translational regulators that bind to complementary sequences on the target mRNA. When this takes place the target mRNA translation is repressed and in essence silenced.

These mechanisms can alter the transcription of a gene with out making any alterations to the actual DNA sequence. In this way they are acting epigenetically or outside the genome.

Conclusion

The sustainment of behavioral abnormalities that define the chronic state of addiction can be explained in part by the regulation of gene expression, which is controlled by transcription factors. A large acumen of research supports the highly stable protein ΔFosB as a mechanism that can produce and sustain these lasting changes in gene expression.

The majority of the genetic changes are seen in specific parts of the brain e.g. the nucleus accumbens and the dorsal striatum. These two regions are significant to the drug rewarding responses and to the locomotor actions of the drugs of abuse. However, many other regions of the brain have been shown to be affected. This supports the proposal of the involvement of synaptic plasticity in multiple neuronal systems.

Based on the known molecular properties of ΔFosB it appears that ΔFosB pathways function to sustain a molecular switch. This is seen initially when increases in ΔFosB expression and accumulation reinforces neural circuits involved in habit memories and compulsive behaviors, and then later in qualitative changes; and perhaps clinical syndromes that promote drug seeking behavior.

It is also interesting to propose that because a robust amount of the propensity towards addiction is based on gene-gene interactions via transcription factors that perhaps a cure may lay in gene therapy or what has been referred to in other works as selected genetic destination (Grandy 2010). The fact that a substance or drug can affect gene expression and that gene expression can affect molecular cascades that ultimately influence human behavior and perhaps consciousness is also a topic of interest. The proposal that DNA can give rise to human consciousness and then provide a continuum of consciousness is knows as DNA consciousness (Grandy 2011). Obviously more needs to be learned about ΔFosB pathways and epigenetics in order to explain addiction and possibly someday human consciousness.

REFERENCES

Ang, Eugnius, Chen J., Zagouras P., Magna H., Holland J., Schaeffer E., and Nestler E. J. (2001). Induction of nuclear factor-κB in nucleus accumbens by chronic cocaine administration. *Journal of Neurochemistry,* 79, 221-224.

Angel P., Imagawa M., Chiu R., Stein B, Imbra R.J., Rahmsdorf H.J., Jonat C., Herrlich P., and Karin M. (1987). Phorbol ester-inducible genes contain a common cis element recognized by a TPA-modulated trans-acting factor. *Cell* 49 (6), 729-739.

Berke, J.D. and Hyman S.E. (2000). Addiction, Dopamine, and the Molecular Mechanisms of Memory. *Neuron,* 25, 515-532.

Bibb J. A., Taylor J. R., Svenningsson P., Nishi, A., Snyder G. L., Yan Z., Sagawa Z. K., Ouimet C. C., Naim A. C., Nestler E. J., and Greengard P. (2001). Effects of chronic exposure to cocaine are regulated by the neuronal protein Cdk5. *Nature 410* (6826), 376-380.

Chen, J., Kelz M. B., Hope, B. T., Nakabeppu, Y., and Nestler, E. J. (1997). Chronic Fos-Related Antigens: Stable Variants of ΔFosB Induced in Brain by Chronic Treatments. *Journal of Neuroscience,* 17 (13), 4933-4941.

Chen, J., Kelz, M. B., Zeng, G., Sakai, N., Steffen, C., Shockett, P. E., Picciotto, M. R., Duman, R. S., and Nestler, E. J. (1998). Transgenic Animals with Inducible, Targeted Gene Expression in Brain. *Molecular Pharmacology,* 54, 495-503.

Chen, Jingshan, Zhang Y., Kelz M. B., Steffen C., Ang E. S., Zeng L., and Nestler E. J. (2000). Induction of Cyclin-Dependent Kinase 5 in the Hippocampus by Chronic Electroconvulsive Seizures: Role of ΔFosB. *The Journal of Neuroscience 20* (24), 8965-8971.

Dobrzanski, P., Noguchi T., Kovary K., Rizzo C.A., Lazo P.S., and Bravo R. (1991). Both Products of the *fos*B Gene, FosB and Its Short Form, FosB/SF, Are Transcriptional Activators in Fibroblast. *Molecular and Cellular Biology, 11* (11), 5470-5478.

Grandy, J. K. (2010). Selected Genetic Destination and the Rise of *Homo Sapiens Genomicus.* The International Journal of Arts and Sciences 3(9): 166-190. Also discussed in: (2010). DNA and Genetic Engineering. *21st Century Anthropology.* Sage Publications, Inc. Thousand Oaks, California. Vol. 1 (pp. 76-90).

Grandy, J. K. (2011). The DNA molecule is autopoietic, dynamic, evolving, and a form of consciousness. *The International Journal of Arts and Sciences, 4*(20), 7-28.

Grandy, J. K. (2012a). Case Report: Drug Toxicity Following Trip to the Local Head Shop. *The Journal of Urgent Care Medicine, 6* (9), 22-25.

Grandy, J. K. (2012b). A Clinical Correlation Made Between Opioid-induced Hyperalgesia and Hyperkatifeia with Brain Alterations Induced by Long-term Prescription Opioid Use. *Research and Reviews: A Journal of Neuroscience* 2 (2), 1-11.

Kaplan, G. B., Leite-Morris K. A., Fan W. Y., Young A. J., and Guy M. D. (2011). Opiate Sensitization Induces FosB/ΔFosB Expression in Prefrontal Cortical, Striatal and Amygdala Brain Regions. *PLoS ONE* 6(8): e23574.

Kaufling, J., Waltisperger E., Bourdy R., Valera A., Veinante P., Freund-Mercier M. J., and Barrot M. (2010). Pharmacological recruitment of the GABAergic tail of the ventral tegmental area by acute drug exposure. *British Journal of Pharmacology, 161,* 1677-1691.

Kelz, M.B. and Chen, J. (1999). Expression of the transcription factor deltaFosB in the brain controls sensitivity to cocaine. *Nature, 401* (6750): 272-276.

Lazenka M. F., Selley D. E., and Sim-Selley L. J. (2012). Brain regional differences in CB1 receptor adaptation and regulation of transcription. *Life Sciences* [Epub ahead of print].

Lee, W., Mitchell P., and Tjian R. (1987). Purified transcription factor AP-1 interacts with TPA-inducible enhancer elements. *Cell 49* (6): 741-752.

McClung, C.A. and Nestler, E.J. (2003). Regulation of gene expression and cocaine reward by CREB and DeltaFosB. *Nature Neuroscience, 6* (11), 1208-1215.

McClung, C.A., Ulery P.G., Perrotti L.I., Zachariou V., Berton O., and Nestler E.J. (2004). DeltaFosB: a molecular switch for long-term adaptation in the brain. *Brain Research and Molecular Brain Research, 132* (2), 146-154.

Muschamp J. W., Nemeth C. L., Robison A. J., Nestler E. J., and Carlezon W. A. (2012). ΔFosB enhances the rewarding effects of cocaine while reducing the pro-depressive effects of the kappa-opioid receptor agonist U50488. *Biological Psychiatry 71*(1), 44-50.

Nestler, E. J. (2008). Transcriptional mechanisms of addiction: role of ΔFosB. *Philosophical Transactions of the Royal Society. B* 363: 3245-3255.

Nestler, E. J., Barrot M., and Self, D. W. (2001). ΔFosB: A sustained molecular switch for addiction. *PNAS,* 98 (20): 11042-11046.

Nye, H. E., and Nestler, E. J. (1996). Induction of chronic Fos-related antigens in rat brain by chronic morphine administration. *Molecular Pharmacology. 49* (4), 636-645.

Nye, H. E., Hope B. T., Keiz M. B., Ladarola M., and Nestler E. J. (1995). Pharmacological studies of the regulation of chronic FOS-related antigen induction by cocaine in the striatum and nucleus accumbens. *Journal of Pharmacological Experimental Therapeutics* 275 (3), 1671-1680.

Ohnishi, Y. N. et al. (2011). FosB is essential for the enhancement of stress tolerance, and antagonizes locomotor sensitization by ΔFosB. *Biol Psychiatry* 70(5), 487-495.

Pich, E. M., Pagliusi S. R., Tessari-Ayer D., Hooft van Huijsduijnen R., and Chiamulera C. (1997). Common neural substrates of the addictive properties of nicotine and cocaine. *Science.* 275 (5296), 83-86.

Pitchers, K. K., Frohmader K. S., Vialou V., Mouzon E., Nestler E. J., Lehman M. N., and Coolen L. M. (2010). DeltaFosB in the nucleus accumbens is critical for reinforcing effects of sexual reward. *Genes and Brain Behavior. 9* (7), 831-840.

Robinson A. J., and Nestler E. J. (2012). Transcriptional and Epigenetic Mechanisms of Addiction. *Nature Review of Neuroscience 12* (11), 623-637.

Russo, S. J. et al. (2009). Nuclear Factor κB Signaling Regulates Neuronal Morphology and Cocaine Reward. *Journal of Neuroscience.* 29 (11), 3529-3537.

Sim-Selley L. J., Cassidy M. P., Sparta A., Zachariou V., Nestler E. J., and Selley D. E. (2011). Effect of ΔFosB overexpression on opioid and cannabinoid receptor-mediated signaling in the nucleus accumbens. *Neuropharmacology 61*(8), 1470-1476.

Taylor, J. R., Lynch W. J., Sanchez H., Olausson P., Nestler E. J., and Bibb J. A. (2007). Inhibition of Cdk5 in the nucleus accumbens enhances the locomotor-activating and incentive-motivational effects of cocaine. *PNAS* (104) 10, 4147-4152.

Teyssier J. R., Ragot S., Chauvet-Gelinier J. C., Trojak B., and Bonin B. (2011). Activation of a ΔFosB dependent gene expression pattern in the dorsolateral prefrontal cortex of patients with major depressive disorder. *Journal of Affective Disorder 133*(1-2), 174-178.

Upadhyay, Jaymin et al. (2010). Alterations in Brain Structure and Functional Connectivity in Prescription Opioid-Dependent Patients. *Brain 133* (7), 2098-2114.

Van Hout M. C. and Bingham T. (2012). "A Costly Turn On": Patterns of Use and Perceived Consequences of Mephedrone Based Head Shop Products Amongst Irish Injectors. *International Journal of Drug Policy 23* (3), 188-197.

White, F. J., Hu, X. T., Zhang, X. F., and Wolf, M. E. (1995). Repeated administration of cocaine or amphetamine alters neuronal responses to glutamate in the mesoaccumbens dopamine system. *Journal of Pharmacological Experimental Therapeutics. 273* (1): 445-454.

Zachariou, V. et al. (2006). An essential role for ΔFosB in the nucleus accumbens in morphin action. *Nature Neuroscience 9:* 205-211.

In: Drug Use and Abuse
Editor: Marie Claire Van Hout

ISBN: 978-1-62618-232-5

Chapter 10

THE ROLE OF STRESS IN PSYCHOSTIMULANT ADDICTION: TREATMENT APPROACHES BASED ON ANIMAL MODELS

Marta Rodríguez-Arias, Maria Pilar García-Pardo, Sandra Montagud-Romero, Jose Miñarro and Maria Asunción Aguilar*

Department of Psychobiology, Faculty of Psychology,
University of Valencia

ABSTRACT

Drug addiction is a chronic relapsing multifactorial disorder arising as a result of the interaction between biological and environmental factors and characterized by a loss of control over use of the drug. It has been repeatedly demonstrated that stress is a risk factor for the initiation and maintenance of drug consumption and for relapse after detoxification periods. Several animal models have been developed to study the neurobiology of drug addiction, among which the self-administration (SA) and conditioned place preference (CPP) paradigms are the most used. The extinction /reinstatement procedures of SA and CPP allow a situation similar to relapse - the main problem in the treatment of drug addiction - to be modeled. Stressful experiences can increase drug-seeking, compulsive drug-taking and reinstatement after long-term withdrawal in rodents. The objective of this chapter is to provide an up-to-date review of studies regarding the role of stress in the development of addiction to psychostimulant drugs in these animal models. First, we describe the physiological response to stress and the relationship between the brain systems involved in addiction and stress. Next, we describe SA and CPP animal models of addiction and the different kind of stressors used in experiments in these models, with special reference to social defeat stress. Later we discuss the results of studies showing how different stressors modify the acquisition and reinstatement of SA and CPP. Finally, we focus on studies that have evaluated the capacity of different drugs to reduce the effects of stress on the acquisition and

* Email: asuncion.aguilar@uv.es.

reinstatement of SA and CPP, such as NA, CRF, kappa, DA and hypocretin antagonists. We hope to offer a perspective of potential treatment approaches based on the data obtained in studies with these animal models and propose new priorities for future work in the field.

Keywords: Amphetamine, cocaine, conditioned place preference, corticotropin-releasing factor, crowding, dopamine, environmental enrichment, food restriction, footshock, forced swim, isolation, kappa opioid receptors, maternal separation, methamphetamine, noradrenaline, reinstatement, restraint, rodents, self-administration, social defeat, social interaction, stress, tail pinch, yohimbine

ABBREVIATIONS

α2AR: alpha 2 adrenergic receptor
ACTH: adrenocorticotropin hormone
AMPH: amphetamine
β 1AR: beta 1 adrenergic receptor
β 2AR: beta 2 adrenergic receptor
BLA: basolateral nucleus of amygdala
BNST: bed nucleus of stria terminalis
CB: cannabinoid
CeA: central nucleus of amygdala
COC: cocaine
CPP: conditioned place preference
CRF: corticotropin-releasing factor
DA: dopamine
EE: environmental enrichment
HPA: Hypothalamus-Pituitary-Adrenal
KOR: kappa opioid receptor
LC: locus coeruleus
MDMA: 3,4-methylenedioxymethamphetamine
METH: methamphetamine
NA: noradrenaline
NAcc: nucleus accumbens
PFC: prefrontal cortex
POMC: proopiomelanocortin
SA: self-administration
VTA: ventral tegmental area

INTRODUCTION

Drug addiction is a chronic multifactorial relapsing disorder that is a result of the interaction between biological and environmental factors (Ellenbroek, van der Kam, van der Elst, and Cools, 2005; Enoch, 2006). It is a chronic and recurrent illness characterized by a loss of control over use of the drug and by relapse (Koob, 2010; Koob and Volkow, 2010). Even following a successful detoxification process and after long-term abstinence, relapse can appear when individuals are exposed to stimuli such as the drug of abuse, stress, or cues associated with drug consumption (Koob, 2009; Sinha, 2011). Thus, relapse to compulsive drug-taking is the main problem in the treatment of drug addiction. This trend towards relapse in addiction suggests that drugs of abuse produce permanent alterations in the brain (Nestler, 2004; Sun, 2011; Van den Oever, Spijker, Smit, and De Vries, 2010).

Several animal models have been developed to study the neurobiology of addiction, among which the self-administration (SA) and conditioned place preference (CPP) paradigms are the most used. These models allow the rewarding effects of drugs of abuse to be evaluated and have been designed to accurately reflect the characteristics of drug addiction. The extinction/reinstatement procedures of SA and CPP reproduce a situation similar to relapse. Reinstatement is an operant event that can be measured directly when a laboratory animal reinitiates a particular behaviour after extinction (Aguilar, Rodríguez-Arias, and Miñarro, 2009; Shaham, Shalev, Lu, De Wit, and Stewart, 2003).

It has been repeatedly demonstrated that stress is a risk factor for the initiation, maintenance and escalation of drug consumption and for relapse after periods of detoxification (Koob, 2010; Logrip, Koob, and Zorrilla, 2011; Logrip, Zorrilla, and Koob, 2012; Sinha, 2008; Sinha, Shaham and Heilig, 2011). There is a narrow relationship between stress and addiction brain systems, and stressful experiences modify the activity of brain areas involved in the rewarding effects of psychostimulants (Belujon and Grace, 2011; Koob, 2009; Sinha, 2008). There is a positive association between stress and increased drug intake and relapse to drug use (for a review see Sinha et al., 2011). In rodents, exposure to stressors (e.g., footshock, immobilization, forced swim, maternal separation, social isolation, social defeat stress) and activation of neural and hormonal stress mechanisms can produce behavioral and neurochemical adaptations that render individuals more prone to drug-seeking and drug-taking behaviours (Goeders, 2002a; Koob and Kreek 2007; Logrip et al., 2012; Marinelli and Piazza 2002; Miczek et al. 2008; Moffett et al., 2007).

The relationship between stress and psychostimulant addiction has been evaluated mainly using the SA paradigm and somewhat less so using the CPP paradigm. Many studies have focused on acquisition, but fewer on reinstatement. Most previous studies have employed morphine or COC (COC) to evaluate the effects of stress on acquisition and reinstatement of drug-taking, although a few have employed other psychostimulants. Similarly, social stressors have seldom been used, even though it is more relevant to humans. Finally, studies of which drugs mitigate the effects of stress on drug consumption and reinstatement have only recently appeared.

The main objective of this chapter is to provide an up-to-date review of published studies regarding the role of stress in the development of addiction to psychostimulant drugs in animal models. First, we describe the physiological response to stress and the relationship between the brain systems involved in addiction and stress, particularly the circuit of extended amygdala. Next, we describe SA and CPP animal models of addiction and the different stressors used in the experiments performed with these models, with special reference to social stress. Later we discuss the results of studies showing how different stressors modify the acquisition and reinstatement of psychostimulant SA and CPP. We then focus on studies that have evaluated the capacity of different drugs to reduce the effects of stress on the acquisition and reinstatement of SA and CPP, such as noradrenaline (NA), corticotropin-releasing factor (CRF), kappa opioid and dopamine (DA) antagonists. We aim to offer a perspective of potential treatment approaches to drug addiction based on the data obtained in studies with these animal models, primarily with the drugs that have proven effective in reducing the effects of stress on reinstatement. Finally, we explain the protective factors that can reduce the effects of stress on addiction. To end the review we will propose new priorities for future work in the field.

Neurobiology of Stress Response

Organisms work for the body's welfare throughout life and are biologically prepared to compensate for deficits that may disrupt our natural homeostasis. When we are hungry, our body prepares to hunt for food, as if we have no other biological necessity. The imbalance created in our bodies by both internal and external stimuli can be compensated biologically or through our behavior.

Stress is one of the conditions that can alter the biology of organisms. Faced with a stressful situation, there is a break in the homeostasis of individuals that needs to be compensated. Therefore, different neurobiological, chemical and behavioural actions are initiated to resolve this situation. In this way, stress is an essential condition of life and is an important factor in the maintenance of health and development of illness.

The physician Hans Selye defined theterm "stress"for the first time as a non-specific response of the body to any demand characterized by the action of neurobiological systems such as glucocorticoids (Selye, 1975). Selye developed a new concept in this area - "the general adaptation syndrome" - which encompasses an alarm reaction, a stage of resistance, and finally a stage of exhaustion. Many have attempted to describe the stress concept and it has been difficult to establish a consensus, as each investigator has emphasized different aspects of stress, whether it be cognition, motivation, emotion, behavior or biological aspects. However, the different definitions are in agreement with respect about the response to stress; different regulatory systems of the body are activated to adapt the organism to internal or external challenges, such as the Hypothalamus-Pituitary-Adrenal (HPA) system, a central control and regulatory system of the organism that is involved in the stress response with hormones such as corticotropin-releasing factor (CRF), adrenocorticotropin hormone (ACTH) and glucocorticoids; or the symphatic-adrenal system, with catecholamines (adrenaline and NA) (Kupfermann, 1991). There are other important systems involved in the stress response, such as the immune system (for a review see Capuron and Miller, 2011; Costa-Pinto and Palermo-Neto, 2010). Different brain areas are activated depending on the type of stress invoked: physical or social. For example, stimuli of social stress do not present an immediate threat for the organism and needs to be processed by the prefrontal cortex (PFC). Although stressors can elicit different responses in different individuals depending on "conditioning" or interaction with the environment, it is the sympathetic nervous system and the HPA system that are usually activated (Stratakis and Chrousos, 1995). As can be seen in Figure 1, in a situation of stress, the HPA axis is activated by the secretion of CRF from the hypothalamus (Goeders, 2002b; Sarnyai, Shaham, and Heinrichs, 2001; Turnbull and Rivier, 1997). CRF-containing neurons projecting from the paraventricular nucleus to the median eminence release the peptide into the adenohypophyseal portal circulation. The binding of CRF to receptors located in the anterior hypophysis results in the synthesis of proopiomelanocortin (POMC), a large precursor protein that produces several smaller peptides, including ACTH and β-endorphin. ACTH diffuses through the general circulation until it reaches the adrenal glands, where it stimulates the biosynthesis and secretion of adrenocorticosteroids (e.g. cortisol in humans or corticosterone in rats), which act at diffuse body sites to assure the overall response to stress (Goeders, 2003). Under stress, cortisol redirects energy utilization to the various organs, simultaneously amplifying energy-mobilizing mechanisms and inhibiting less relevant organ functions (Chrousos and Gold, 1992; McEwen, 2003). The general function of the HPA axis is controlled by several negative feedback loops (Herman, McKlveen, Solomon, Carvalho-Netto, and Myers, 2012) regulated by mineralocorticoid and glucocorticoid receptors (Harris, Holmes, de Kloet, Chapman, and Seckl, 2012). Glucocorticoids act in a negative feedback mode by decreasing production and release of CRF in the hypothalamus and of POMC and its neuropeptides in the anterior pituitary (Zhou et al., 2006). The sympathetic nervous system activated the adrenal medulla by inducing adrenaline and NA release (see Figure 1), which leads to a variety of physiological processes that prepare the organism for flight or fight, or in other words to face the stressor or to escape it: increase in heart rate, a rise in blood pressure, a shift in blood flow to the skeletal muscles, an increase in blood glucose, dilation of the pupils and stimulation of respiration (Goeders, 2003).

Drug addiction is often characterized as a chronic cycle of drug intoxication, withdrawal and relapse (Koob, 2010). The mesocorticolimbic DA system, originating in the ventral tegmental area (VTA) and projecting to the nucleus accumbens (NAcc) and PFC (see Figure 2), is known to play a major role in appetitive behaviors (Carlezon and Thomas, 2009; Dalley and Everitt, 2009; Kelley and Berridge, 2002; Wise, 2008) and is the main neural substrate of the rewarding effects produced by drugs (McBride, Murphy, and Ikemoto, 1999; Wise et al., 1998).

There is a positive relation between psychostimulant SA behaviour and the level of activation of the mesolimbic DA brain system (Cadoni et al., 2005; Calipari et al., 2012; Chevrette, Stellar, Hesse, and Markou, 2002; Di Chiara et al., 2004; Everitt and Wolf, 2002; Franken, Booij and van den Brink, 2005; Wise, 2005), with animals with heightened DA transmission being more likely to develop psychostimulant SA behaviour (Hooks, Jones, Smith, Neill, and Justice, 1991; Hooks, Colvin, Juncos, and Justice, 1992; Marinelli and White, 2000; Rouge-Pont, Piazza, Kharouby, Le Moal, and Simon, 1993). Moreover, reductions in DA function have been implicated in the reduced reward function reflected in increases in the threshold for intracranial self-stimulation that accompanies withdrawal from COC use (Antkiewicz-Michaluk, 2006; Markou and Koob, 1992).

Manipulation of the main afferents to the mesolimbic DA system also modifies the rewarding effects of psychostimulants. The systemic administration of the γ-aminobutyric acid $(GABA)_B$ receptor agonists, such as baclofen, at doses that inhibit DA release reduces SA of psychostimulants under different schedules of reinforcement (Brebner, Phelan, and Roberts, 2000; Brebner, Froestl, and Roberts, 2002; Di Ciano and Everitt, 2003; Roberts, Andrews, and Vickers, 1996; Shoaib, Swanner, Beyer, Goldberg, and Schindler, 1998; Xi and Stein, 1999, 2000) and psychostimulant-induced CPP (Halbout, Quarta, Valerio, Heidbreder, and Hutcheson, 2011). Glutamate antagonists also reduce the rewarding effects of psychostimulants in SA and CPP (Hyytia, Bäckström, and Liljequist, 1999; Maldonado,

Rodríguez-Arias, M., Castillo, A., Aguilar, M.A., and Miñarro, 2007; Osborne and Olive, 2008) paradigms.

Activation of brain stress systems seems to be a key element of the negative emotional state produced by dependence and which drives drug-seeking through negative reinforcement mechanisms (Koob, 2009).

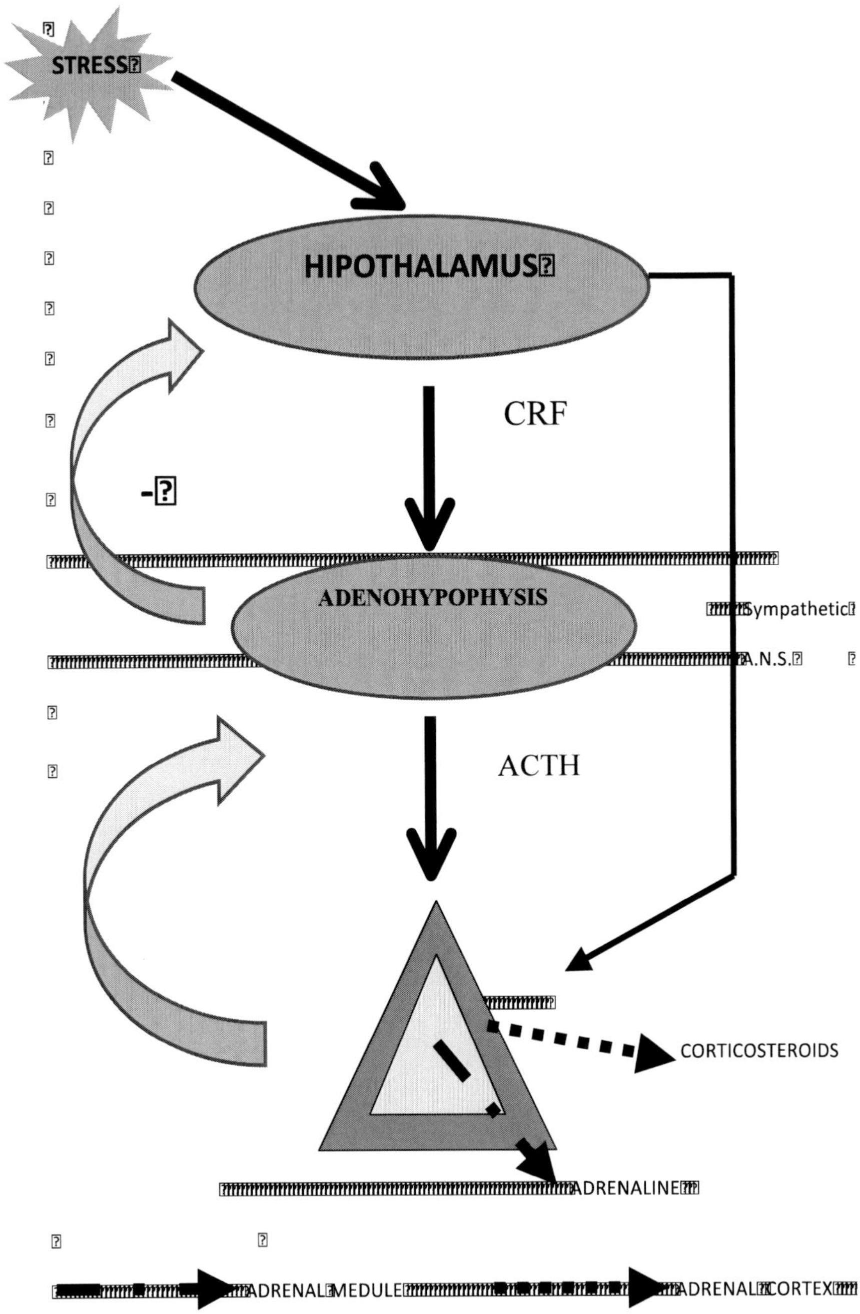

Figure 1. Physiology of the response to stress.

RELATIONSHIP BETWEEN BRAIN SYSTEMS INVOLVED IN STRESS AND DRUG ADDICTION

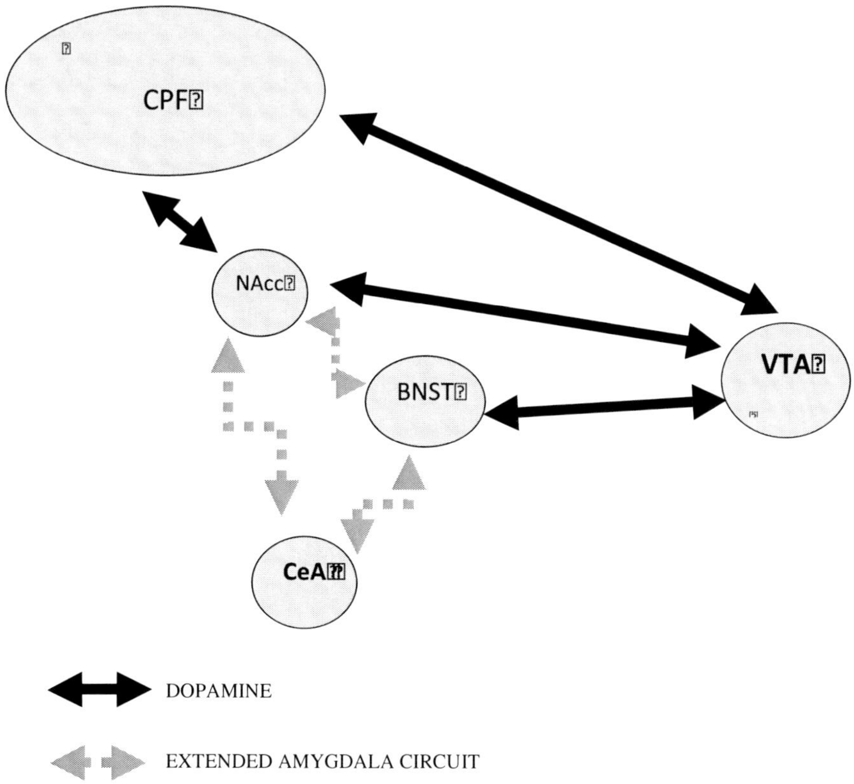

Figure 2. The mesocorticolimbic DA system and the extended amygdala circuit.

Many of the motivational effects of drugs may involve a common neural circuitry that forms a separate entity within the basal forebrain, termed the "extended amygdala" (Alheid and Heimer, 1988). The extended amygdala circuitry extends from the shell of the NAcc to the bed nucleus of the stria terminalis (BNST) and central nucleus of the amygdala (CeA) (Alheid and Heimer, 1988; de Olmos and Heimer, 1999; Koob, 2009), where neuro-transmitters such as CRF, NA, and DA interact (see Figure 2).

The extended amygdala is innervated by the dorsal and ventral NA pathway originating in the locus coeruleus (LC) (Aston-Jones, Rajkowski, Kubiak, Valentino, and Shipley, 1996; Moore and Bloom, 1979), The CeA and BNST are also innervated by DA neurons originating from regions of the midbrain, including the VTA (Hasue and Shammah-Lagnado, 2002). Both NA and DA neurons synapse with, or in close proximity to, CRF neurons in the CeA and BNST (Eliava, Yilmazer-Hanke, and Asan, 2003; Phelix, Liposits, and Paull, 1994). CRF neurons in the CeA project to the BNST (Sakanaka, Shibasaki, and Lederis, 1986) and VTA (Rodaros, Caruana, Amir, and Stewart, 2007) and CRF neurons in the BNST provide a local source of CRF and also project to the VTA (Rodaros et al., 2007). CRF in the VTA has an excitatory effect on DA and glutamate transmission in the region (Wang et al., 2005).

DA has been found to play an important role in the neurobiology of fear and anxiety (de Oliveira, Reimer, and Brandão, 2006; Macedo, Martinez, Albrechet-Souza, Molina, and

Brandão, 2007; Pezze andFeldon, 2004; Reis, Masson, de Oliveira, and Brandão, 2004). Moreover, the PFC has been shown to be a potent regulator of the stress response, in part via attenuation of responses in the amygdala (Rosenkranz and Grace, 2002a, b; Rosenkranz, Moore, and Grace, 2003), which is the brain region in which fear and anxiety are expressed (LeDoux, 2000). Another brain region that has been shown to be particularly susceptible to the deleterious effects of maintained stress is the hippocampus (Sapolsky, Uno, Rebert, and Finch, 1990; Sapolsky, 2000; Lee, Ogle, and Sapolsky, 2002).

Similarly to repeated administration of psychostimulants and other drugs of abuse, repeated exposure to stress can heighten sensitivity to drug-induced psychomotor stimulation. In some cases, this sensitized behavioral response is correlated with enhanced drug-induced DA and glutamate responses in the NAcc and increased cellular activation of reward-associated brain regions (Deroche et al., 1995; Miczek, Covington, Nikulina, and Hammer, 2004; Nikulina, Covington, Ganschow, Hammer, and Miczek, 2004; Pacchioni, Gioino, Assis, and Cancela, 2002; Rouge-Pont, Marinelli, Le Moal, Simon, and Piazza, 1995). For example, the exposure to a brief, intermittent episode of social defeat stress activates mesolimbic DA pathways that project from the VTA to the NAcc and medial PFC (Anstrom, Miczek, and Budygin, 2009; Di Chiara and Imperato, 1988; Tidey and Mizek, 1997). Single or repeated exposure to stress or drugs can also induce neurochemical sensitization, as demonstrated by augmented drug-induced DA responses in the NAcc (del Rosario, Pacchioni, and Cancela, 2002; Grimm et al., 2003; Miczek, Mutschler, van Erp, Blank, and McInerney, 1999a; Rouge-Pont et al., 1995), which are often accompanied by enhanced drug-induced psychomotor responses (del Rosario et al., 2002; Deroche et al., 1992; Deroche et al., 1995; Leyton and Stewart, 1990; Nikulina, Miczek, and Hammer, 2005; Stohr et al., 1999). These results suggest that environmental stressors can activate long-term changes in the function of brain reward pathways, just as drugs of abuse do (Quadros and Miczek, 2009). Different stressors increase DA activity in the VTA via potentiation of the ventral subiculum-NAcc pathway, which underlies the increase in the behavioral response to psychostimulants. This pathway can be activated by the LC-NA system and/or the basolateral amygdala (BLA) (Belujon and Grace, 2011).

Brain stress systems, CRF and NA in the extended amygdala also play a key role in the transition to and maintenance of dependence (Koob et al., 2009). Both the mesocorticolimbic DA system and the extended amygdala circuit have been implicated in stress-induced reinstatement of COC seeking (Koob, 2010: McFarland, Davidge, Lapish, and Kalivas, 2004; Shaham et al., 2003). The ventral NA pathway projecting to the extended amygdala has been specifically related to the effects of NA on stress-induced reinstatement of drug seeking (Shaham, Erb and Stewart, 2000; Wang, Cen, and Lu, 2001). Footshock stress causes initial activation of lateral tegmental NA neurons, which in turn activates CRF projection neurons from CeA to BNST, and local CRF interneurons in the BNST (Erb, Salmaso, Rodaros, and Stewart, 2001; Shaham et al., 2000; Wang et al., 2001). Thus, stress-induced reinstatement appears to involve the lateral tegmental NA nuclei (Highfield et al., 2000; Shaham et al., 2000) and their NA projections through the ventral NA bundle (Moore and Bloom, 1979) to the CeA, BNST, hypothalamus, medial septum and NAcc (Shaham et al., 2003). In addition to the CRF-containing pathway from the CeA to the BNST (Erb et al., 2001), VTA glutamate (Wise, 2009) plays an important role in stress-induced reinstatement of COC seeking in rats. It has been proposed that footshock activates limbic circuitry in the CeA, which in turn activates a VTA DA projection to the dorsal PFC, with the subsequent rise in DA producing reinstatement via a glutamatergic projection to the NAcc core (McFarland et al., 2004). The administration of the nonselective CRF receptor antagonist into the VTA blocks footshock-induced VTA glutamate release, DA activation and reinstatement, suggesting that footshock reinstates COC seeking by inducing CRF and glutamate release in the VTA and activating VTA DA neurons as a result (Wang, You, Rice, and Wise, 2007). More recent studies have demonstrated the involvement of CRF2 receptors in the VTA and the CRF1 receptors in the BNST in stress-induced reinstatement (Gysling, 2012; Wang, You, and Wise, 2009). Activation of the BNST is necessary for reinstatement of COC seeking, since its inactivation with lidocaine blocks forced swim-induced reinstatement of COC CPP (Briand, Vassoler, Pierce, Valentino, and Blendy, 2010). The study in question also demonstrated that CREB is required for the activation of the circuit that converges on the DA reward pathway in order to elicit reinstatement of drug reward, with the BNST constituting a key intersection between stress and reward circuits (Briand et al., 2010).

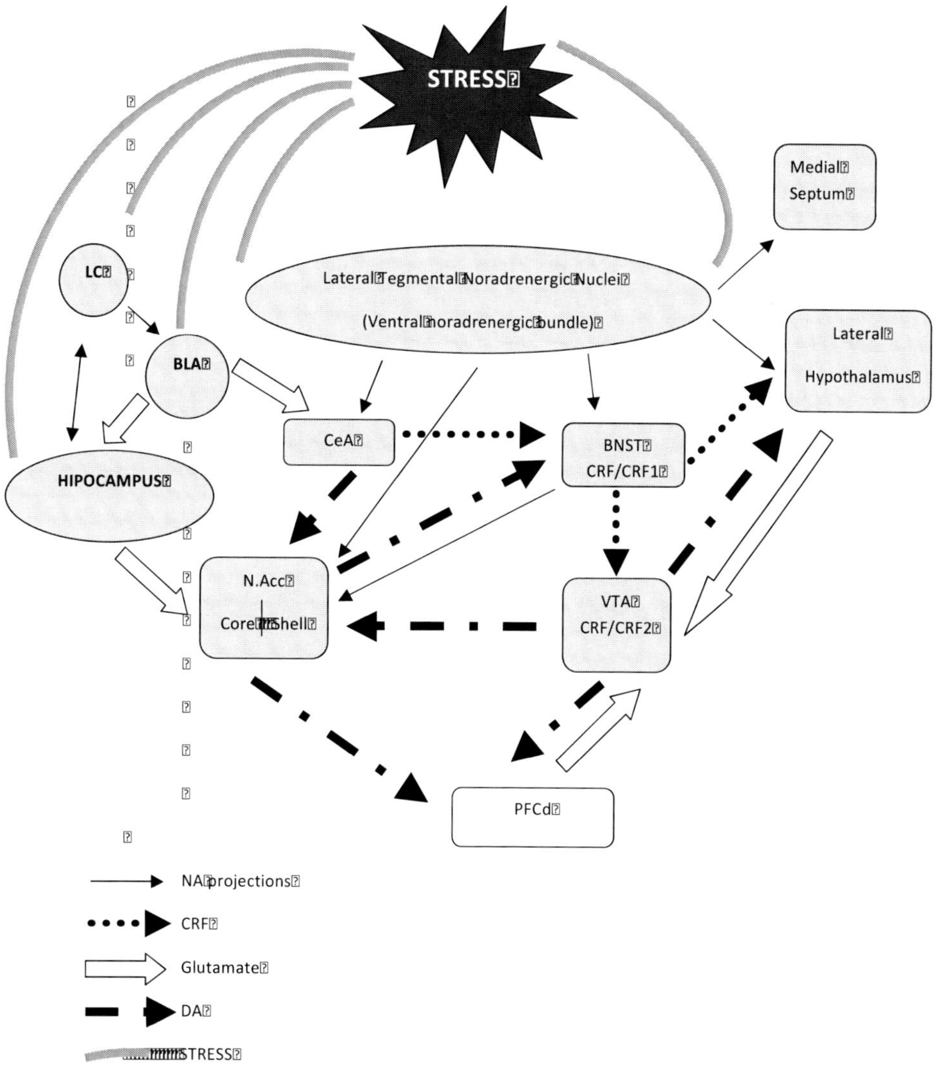

Figure 3. Neural substrates of stress induced reinstatement.

The NAcc is also involved in COC-seeking behavior triggered by footshock stress or by COC priming and drug-associated conditioned stimuli (Fuchs, Ramirez, and Bell, 2008). Similarly, NA transmission in the extended amygdala plays an important role in increased drug seeking and stress-induced reinstatement (Smith and Aston-Jones, 2008). Experience with COC induces an alteration of the complex interaction of CRF, glutamate and the mesocorticolimbic DA system, which appears to contribute to the transition from casual to compulsive COC-seeking (Wise and Morales, 2010).

Adrenal activity during repeated long-access COC SA is also required for stressor-induced reinstatement (Graf et al., 2011), and the existence of a CRF/kappa opioid receptor (KOR) connection that mediates stress-induced reinstatement has been proposed (Bruchas, Land, and Chavkin, 2010).

Two main afferents to the NAc, the BLA and the ventral subiculum of the hippocampus, and their interactions with the LC-NA system have also been associated with stress-induced reinstatement (Belujon and Grace, 2010). Increases in NA release in the BLA and PFC have also been related with the potentiation of cue-induced reinstatement induced by yohimbine, which seems to enhance the motivational salience of conditioned cues (Buffalari and Grace, 2009). Increases in CRF in the amygdala are also responsible for reinstatement of methamphetamine (METH) seeking behavior induced by shock (Nawata, Kitaichi, and Yamamoto, 2012).

Therefore, in addition to the activation of the mesolimbic DA system, aversive events and triggering of stress systems play key roles in modulating addictive behavior (Sinha, 2008). A key element of the addiction process involves the activation of brain stress systems that are localized in the circuitry of the extended amygdala and which produce a negative emotional state that becomes a powerful motivation for the drug-seeking associated with compulsive use.

The CRF and NA have an important role in addiction as central elements of a complex system that maintains emotional homeostasis (Koob, 2010). COC and stress interact directly with DA neurons in the VTA, with these interactions having an impact on stress-induced relapse (Ungless, Argilli, and Bonci, 2010).

Most Used Animal Models of Addiction

Most of the recent progress gained regarding knowledge of the underlying mechanisms of addiction and relapse has been a result of studies with animal models. The use of animal models has the advantage of greater control of experimental variables (age of initial exposure, drug, dose, duration, timing of exposure, etc.) and has provided much valuable information. The main drawback to animal studies is that any model reproduces all the stages in the development of drug addiction. Results obtained with multiple behavioural and neurobiological models are necessary to achieve a deeper understanding of this disorder (Ahmed, 2010; Sanchis-Segura and Spanagel, 2006; Schramm-Sapyta, Walker, Caster, Levin, and Kuhn, 2009; Shippenberg and Koob, 2002; Weiss, 2010). Although several animal models have a high predictive value, most studies have been performed with the SA or the CPP paradigms.

Drug Self-Administration (SA)

The technique of SA is essential in drug addiction research, as nearly all drugs that are addictive in humans are self-administered by laboratory animals, which show patterns of drug intake that mimic those of human users (Caine and Koob, 1993; Collins, Weeks, Cooper, Good, and Russell, 1984; Deroche-Gamonet, Belin, and Piazza, 2004; Yap and Miczek, 2008). SA models human drug-taking behavior and is the most straightforward procedure for evaluating the intrinsic primary reinforcing properties of a substance (by testing whether animals will work to obtain the substance) (Yahyavi-Firouz-Abadi and See, 2009; Moser, Wolinsky, Duxon, and Porsolt, 2010). In this procedure, laboratory animals are trained to emit a response, such as pressing a lever or performing a nose-poke, to self-administer a drug. If the animal responds, it is rewarded with the drug. As a consequence, the animal acquires the new operant behavior (Yahyavi-Firouz-Abadi, 2009). As SA measures the animal's behavior according to its search for the drug, this technique can be used to study the neurobiological mechanisms involved in drug taking and drug seeking (Fuchs, Feltenstein, and See, 2006a; See, 2005; Stewart, 2000). Compared to other models of addiction, SA models the abuse of drugs by humans more closely in both the route of drug administration (iv) and the response-contingent mode of administration (O´Connor, Chapman, Butler, and Mead, 2011).

The main shortcoming of the SA paradigm is the complexity of the technique, as it involves surgery to implant an iv or intracerebral catheter that allows the animal to self-administer the drug freely (Graf et al., 2011). Another disadvantage of SA is the lack of a standardized procedure for evaluating substances with different potencies, reinforcement properties and pharmacokinetics. The choice of training substance, species and procedural parameters can radically affect the results obtained (Moser et al., 2011). Animals that acquire drug-taking behaviour more quickly or indulge in it more frequently can be considered to resemble human drug addicts. However, drug taking, even when acquired quickly, is not equivalent to drug dependence (Ahmed, 2010).

As rodents learn to self-administer drugs, there are time- and experience-dependent changes in the frequency and intensity of their behavior (Yap and Miczek, 2008). Thus, acquisition is a process whose defining feature is an increase in drug use over time. Indeed, acquisition is just one example of SA behavior in transition (Yap and Miczek, 2008); others include the escalation of drug use during extended access or "binge" conditions as physical dependence develops (Dai, Corrigall, Coen, and Kalant, 1989) or as brain reward systems are altered (Ahmed and Koob, 1998; Ahmed, Kenny, Koob, and Markou, 2002; Covington and Miczek, 2001; Covington, Tropea, Rajadhyaksha, Kosofsky, and Miczek, 2008; Paterson and Markou, 2003, 2004; Tornatzky and Miczek, 2000).

There are many pharmacological and environmental factors to be considered when evaluating SA of substances and acquisition (Ator and Griffiths, 2003), including dose (Campbell Thompson, and Carroll, 1998; Carroll and Lac, 1997), availability of alternative reinforcement (Carroll et al, 1996), sex (Donny et al., 2000; Lynch, Kushner, Rawleigh, Fiszdon, and Carroll, 1999), animal strain (Shoaib, Schindler, and Goldberg, 1997), developmental stage (Adriani, Macrì, Pacifici, and Laviola, 2002) and the presence of drug-paired sensory stimuli (Caggiula et al., 2002). However, these elements are not all equally important. Indeed, available data suggest that the choice of training substance may not be the most important variable in a SA study, but rather that other factors, such as session length or the response requirement for drug infusion, are more important determinants (Moser et al., 2010). Most operant SA procedures employ a FR schedule of reinforcement whereby the animal must perform a fixed number of responses to receive an intravenous drug infusion. The number of responses an animal will emit to obtain an infusion generally increases for substances possessing markedly positive reinforcing properties (Moser et al., 2010).

Variations of the SA model have been developed to study the main features of addiction. Time-out and punished responding both model compulsive use (Deroche-Gamonet et al., 2004; Vanderschuren and Everitt, 2004), and long-access training schedules model high-level use (Knackstedt and Kalivas, 2007). Additionally, models of habitual drug-seeking have also been developed (Everitt et al., 2008). On the other hand, studies using SA sessions of continuous access to the drug for an extended period of time or the progressive ratio schedule highlight different aspects of drug taking behavior (Yap and Miczek, 2008). Specifically, rodent models of prolonged access to COC indicate an apparent shift from controlled, regulated drug intake to out-of-control or dysregulated intake (Tornatzky and Miczek, 2000). SA models of continuous access "binges" allow the animal to control the rate of consumption (Markou et al., 1993).

One commonly used schedule employed to investigate the effects of stress on motivation to consume a drug is the progressive ratio schedule, designed by Hodos (1961), who varied the sweetness and volume of milk in order to measure reward strength. With the progressive ratio method, motivational (desire/wanting) rather than consummatory (taking) components of SA behavior can be measured (Tabakoff and Hoffman, 2000), since rates of response to the drug provide an index of the animal's motivation to obtain it (Depoortere, Li, Lane, Emmett-Oglesby, 1993). In the progressive ratio paradigm the instrumental response requirement to obtain a drug reinforcer progressively increases until the animal ceases to respond (Brown, Jackson, and Stephens, 1998; Moser et al., 2010). The last response that the animal performs to obtain the drug is known as the "break point" (Yap and Miczek, 2008). By varying the schedule of reinforcement, it is possible to measure different aspects of motivation (Ripley and Stephens, 2011) other than the initial motivation of the animal to self-administer the drug (Oleson and Roberts, 2009).

A major clinical problem in treating drug abusers or addicts is the high rate of relapse to abuse, even long after abstinence (Hunt, Barnett, and Branch, 1971; Kalivas, Volkow, and Seamans, 2005; O'Brien et al., 1997). A variation of the SA paradigm, including the extinction and reinstatement of the instrumental response after acquisition of SA, has been developed to model relapse. The extinction-reinstatement model of the iv SA paradigm is the most widely used animal model in the study of relapse to drug-seeking (Epstein, Preston, Stewart, and Shaham, 2006; Shaham et al., 2003) and for a long time was practically the only paradigm employed to study relapse (Carroll et al. 1996). Relapse to a prior behavioural response following extinction is known as reinstatement, and the stimuli that induce it are called "primers" (Self, 1998). The most powerful "primers" are injection of the self-administered drug, drug-associated stimuli or cues, and exposure to stress (De Vries, Schoffelmeer, Binnekade, Mulder, and Vanderschuren, 1998; Ettenberg, MacConell, and Geist, 1996; McFarland and Ettenberg, 1997; Shaham, Rajabi, and Stewart 1996; Shaham, Erb, Leung, Buczek, and Stewart, 1998). Therefore, reinstatement of drug-seeking after extinction, which implies the restoration of a concrete operant response (Yahyavi-Firouz-Abadi and See, 2009), is an animal model of the propensity to relapse to drug taking (Goeders, 2003; Epstein et al., 2006; Shaham et al., 2003).

Drug SA studies about the effects of stress on drug addiction are typically divided into four temporally distinct phases: acquisition, maintenance, extinction and reinstatement. The acquisition phase is defined as the period of time required to attain a stable rate of drug SA. This phase is followed by a maintenance phase of days or weeks. Extinction training is usually introduced prior to reinstatement tests, and is carried out to achieve an operationally defined criterion that can involve within-session parameters on a single test trial, or multiple daily sessions where no drug reinforcement is available. Extinction refers to a progressive decrease in drug-associated operant responding when the drug is no longer available (Epstein et al., 2006; Shaham et al., 2003; Stewart, 2000). In the reinstatement phase, after extinction of SA behaviour, the ability of several stimuli to reinstate the response is determined. Alternatively, subjects may be tested after a period of withdrawal in the absence of explicit extinction trials (abstinence) when returned to the environment where drug was previously available (Fuchs, Branham, and See, 2006b). Relapse is an operant event that can be measured directly when a laboratory animal reinitiates a particular behavioural response, such as the lever-press (Shaham et al., 2003; Stewart, 2000). The reinstatement phase occurs when the persistence of drug-seeking behavior is measured by responding to an operandum (usually a lever or a poke) where the drug was previously available (See et al., 2011). The drug SA version of the extinction-reinstatement procedure is based on the similarities in the development of drug dependence/addiction between humans and laboratory animals (Yan and Nabeshima, 2008). Clinical and epidemiological evidence documents the relapsing nature of drug addiction, thus, adequate experimental models are required to gain further insight into the factors that promote and trigger relapse (Yap and Miczek, 2008).

Conditioned Place Preference (CPP)

The CPP paradigm offers a simple method of assessing the conditioned reward induced by different stimuli (Bardo and Bevins, 2000; Tzschentke, 1998, 2007) and has been widely used to study the conditioned rewarding effects of addictive drugs (Aguilar et al., 2009). It is a simple and fast procedure, and was the first to assess positive rewarding properties of stimuli (Moser et al., 2010). In this paradigm, contextual or environmental stimuli acquire secondary appetitive properties (conditioned rewarding effects) when paired with a primary reinforcer (Tzschentke, 1998, 2007). For example, an initial neutral environment (such as the colour of one compartment in the CPP box) is associated with the specific effects of a drug of abuse during several conditioning sessions (Manzanedo et al., 2001), while another compartment is associated with the injection of a vehicle. Following conditioning, if the animal spends more time in the compartment previously associated with the drug, it is assumed that CPP has developed (Aguilar et. al., 2009). Conditioned reward implies that the animal attributes positive incentive value to the cues associated with the primary reinforcer, and will thus perform flexible or voluntary responses to obtain access to such cues (Robbins, 1978). Under appropriate conditions, CPP can be sensitive to a wide range of substances, including psychostimulants (Moser et al., 2010).

In this paradigm itis considered that animals have acquired CPP when there is a difference between the neutral preference of animals for each of the CPP compartments in the pre-conditioning test and the time animals spend in each CPP compartment after the conditioning phase (Parker and McDonald, 2000; Wang, Luo, Zhang, and Han, 2000; Wang,

Luo, Ge, Fu, and Han, 2002). Generally, the CPP paradigm consisted of three phases. The first phase, known as "preconditioning", confirms the lack of an innate preference for a given compartment of the CPP box. In the second phase, called "acquisition", conditioning itself takes place. The main objective of this phase is that the animal associates the reinforcing effect of the drug with a specific compartment and the lack of effects of a vehicle injection with the other compartment. This association is developed during several conditioning sessions (generally four with the drug and four with saline) that animals undergo daily (both drug and vehicle conditioning sessions every day, separated by an interval of several hours), or every two days (drug and vehicle administered on alternate days). In the last stage of the procedure, the "post-conditioning" phase, the presence of CPP is evaluated. If the animal spends more time in the compartment where the drug was administered than during the pre-conditioning phase or than that spent in the vehicle-paired compartment, the animal is considered to have acquired CPP.

As with the SA model, the CPP paradigm has been adapted to study the main features of addiction. For example, the number of conditioning training sessions can be increased in order to augment exposure to contextual cues associated with the effects of COC in order to model human conditions of extended access to the drug (Rodriguez-Arias, Castillo, Daza-Losada, Aguilar, and Miñarro, 2009). Another variation of the CPP including extinction /reinstatement has been developed as an animal model to study relapse (Aguilar et al., 2009). In this model, the animals are first trained to acquire a CPP (as explained before) and later undergo a process of extinction of the CPP. Extinction is defined as the decrease in the frequency or intensity of learned responses after removal of the unconditioned stimulus (i.e. a drug) that has reinforced the learning (Pavlov, 1927). During an extinction phase, the acquired preference for the drug-paired context is extinguished by pairing injections of the vehicle with both compartments (drug-associated and vehicle-associated), or by allowing subjects to explore the drug- and vehicle-associated compartments during daily sessions in the absence of the drug. Either procedure will produce extinction of the original drug-induced CPP (Yahyavi-Firouz-Abadi and See, 2009).

After extinction, re-exposure to a low dose of the conditioning drug (known as priming) and exposure to a stressful event induce reinstatement of the CPP (Shaham et al., 2003; Shalev, Grimm, and Shaham, 2002; Tzschentke, 2007; Weiss, 2005). For example, amphetamine (AMPH) (Cruz, Marin, and Planeta, 2008; Li, Ren, and Zheng, 2002) and 3,4-methylenedioxymethamphetamine (MDMA) (Daza-Losada et al., 2007) priming induces the reinstatement of AMPH or MDMA CPP, respectively. Similarly, COC CPP is reinstated by intermittent footshock (Lu, Zhang, Liu, and Zhang, 2002), restraint stress (Sanchez, Bailie, Wu, Li, and Sorg, 2003), conditioned fear stimuli, such as a tone or an odor previously associated with footshock (Sanchez and Sorg, 2001), among other stressful events.

Kinds of Stressors Used in Experimental Models

As discussed previously, stress is a well-known risk factor in the development of addiction and in vulnerability to relapse in drug addiction (Sinha, 2008). Studies with laboratory animals reported a significant association between acute and chronic stress and an increase in motivation to initiate use and augment the consumption of addictive substances

(Sinha, 2001; Sinha, Garcia, Paliwal, Kreek, and Rounsaville, 2006; Koob and Kreek, 2007; Miczek, Yap, and Covington, 2008). Relapse during abstinence, which constitutes the main problem in drug addiction treatment, is often associated with stress exposure, which can provoke a subjective state of drug craving. Stress-induced relapse and craving in humans can be modeled in mice, rats and monkeys using the reinstatement model, in which drug-taking behaviors are extinguished and then reinstated by acute exposure to certain stressors (Sinha et al., 2011).

In animal models, drug craving and reinstatement following extended periods of abstinence are reliably triggered by exposure to stressful events (Shaham et al., 2000; Sinha, 2001; Sinha 2005; Yahyavi-Firouz-Abadi and See, 2009).

Stress is a complex construct (Cannon, 1935; Selye, 1956) that is not yet well defined operationally (Chrousos and Gold, 1992). However, different authors have defined the term "stress" as forced exposure to events or conditions that are normally avoided by an animal (Piazza and LeMoal, 1998). Different types of stressors have been used in studies about the role of stress in drug addiction in animal models (Lu, Shepard, Hall, and Shaham, 2003; Aguilar et al., 2009). We have classified these stressors in four categories: pharmacological, physical, emotional and social stressors.

Pharmacological Stressors

Various pharmacological agents are able to induce a stress response and subsequent craving or drug-seeking for psychostimulants. The advantages of employing a pharmacological stressor are that the same stressor can be used in different species, the level of stress can be varied by modifying the dose of compound, and the pathways it activates are well identified. The most used pharmacological stressors are noradrenergic compounds and CRF, but there are other agents, such as neuroactive peptides related to central stress responses (vasopressin and substance P) and inverse benzodiazepine agonists, can also be employed (See and Waters, 2010).

Yohimbine

Some studies have used the pharmacological stressor yohimbine (YOH) to induce stress in animals (Buffalari and See, 2011; See and Waters, 2010). YOH enhances anxiety-like behaviors in several paradigms in experimental animals (File, 1986; Johnston and File, 1989; Bijlsma, de Jongh, Olivier, and Groenink, 2010), increases levels of cortisol (Banihashemi and Rinaman, 2006) and has well-characterized stress and anxiety effects in humans (Southwick, Morgan, Charney, and High, 1999).

The use of YOH as a stressor in animal models of drug addiction offers two main experimental and translational advantages. Firstly, it is a homologous method of stress activation across species. Secondly, it has a relatively long half-life of several hours (Hubbard, Pfister, Biediger, Herzig, and Keeton, 1988), allowing the stress to be maintained across the duration of other experimental procedures, such as a session of SA or CPP, as well as during a reinstatement test (Buffalari and See, 2011).

Several studies have successfully used systemic injections of YOH to trigger stress-induced reinstatement of COC and METH seeking in rats (Bongiovanni and See, 2008; Lee et al., 2004; Le, Harding, Juzytsch, Funk, and Shaham, 2005; Shepard, Bossert, Liu, and

Shaham, 2004). Moreover, YOH potentiates conditioned cue-induced reinstatement of COC seeking (Feltenstein and See, 2006; Buffalari and See, 2009a; Buffalari and See, 2011), and increases NA in the amygdala and BNST through the antagonism of α-2 NA receptors (Buffalari and Grace, 2009; Forray, Bustos, and Gysling, 1997; Galvez,Mesches, McGaugh, 1996; Khoshbouei, Cecchi, Dove, Javors, and Morilak, 2002; Tjurmina, Goldstein, Palkovits, and Kopin, 1999). It has been suggested that stress activation via YOH may rely on intact BNST function, since NE receptor blockade in the BNST disrupts COC seeking caused by stress (Leri, Flores, Rodaros, and Stewart, 2002). Alternative mechanisms in the BNST and other brain regions may contribute to the effects of YOH on reinstatement of drug seeking, since it has been shown to have affinity for serotonin (Millan et al., 2000) and DA (Scatton, Zivkovic, and Dedek, 1980) receptors and increases prefrontal NA tone (Garcia et al., 2004). Moreover, the administration of NA in the BNST and CeA also induces the reinstatement of COC SA in rats (Brown, Tribe, D'souza, and Erb, 2009; Brown, Nobrega, and Erb,2010).

Corticotropin-Releasing Factor (CRF)

As explained previously, in the anterior pituitary CRF is the primary neurohormone from which ACTH is released in response to stress, while CRF-containing axon terminals and receptors are present outside the pituitary. Administration of CRF mimics many of the autonomic and behavioral aspects of the stress response (Bale and Vale, 2004; Owens and Nemeroff, 1991). Similarly, centrally-administered CRF (icv or into the VTA) has been reported to induce reinstatement of COC SA (Blacktop et al., 2011; Brown et al., 2009; Brown, Kupferschmidt, and Erb, 2012; Buffalari, Baldwin, Feltenstein, and See, 2012; Erb, Kayyali, and Romero, 2006; Graf et al., 2011; Mantsch et al., 2008; Wang et al., 2005), though not when administered in the CeA (Erb and Stewart, 1999). The CRF2 receptor agonist urocortin II located in the VTA also induces reinstatement of COC SA (Wang et al., 2007).

Other Drugs

The reinstatement of COC SA is achieved by administration of other drugs such as hypocretin (orexin) 1 (Boutrel et al., 2005; Wang et al., 2009), KOR agonists such as U50,488 (Redila and Chavkin, 2008) or spiradoline and enadoline (Valdez, Platt, Rowlett, Rüedi-Bettschen, and Spealman, 2007), and neuropeptide S (Pañeda et al., 2009).

Physical Stressors

Experimental manipulations that consist of exposing the subject to an aversive environmental event, such as footshock, restraint or tail pinch, are considered physical stressors.

Intermittent Shock

Footshock is one of the most commonly used methods of inducing stress (Lu et. al., 2003) and is the primary stimulus for aversive Pavlovian conditioning in rodents (Logrip et al., 2012). The main advantage of this type of stressor is that it is discretely manipulable, since the experimenter can regulate its duration, frequency, intensity, predictability and controllability (Logrip et al., 2012). Different authors have used intermittent, inescapable footshock in rats and mice to study the effects of stress exposure on the rewarding properties of psychostimulants in the SA and CPP paradigms (for a review see Lu et al., 2003; Shalev, Highfield, Yap, and Shaham, 2000; Shalev, Erb, and Shaham, 2010). The intensity and duration of footshock are variable, although values are generally between 0.1 and 1 mA and 0.1-0.5s, respectively. Frequency of footshock delivery is the total number of shocks or the total time during which shocks are administered (for example 15 min). Exposure to footshock prior to SA and CPP sessions can enhance acquisition, maintenance and reinstatement of psychostimulant intake (Logrip et al., 2012; Lu et al., 2003; Shalev et al., 2010).

It has been suggested that footshock-induced corticosterone secretion mediates the effect of this stressor on psychostimulant SA (Piazza and LeMoal, 1998). Acquisition of COC SA is enhanced in rats exposed to shocks (Goeders and Guerin, 1994) and plasma levels of the corticosterone prior to the test correlate with the initiation of COC SA behavior (Goeders and Guerin, 1996). Moreover, manipulations that reduce or eliminate corticosterone have been shown to decrease COC SA, which can be interpreted as an undermining of the reinforcing efficacy of this drug (Goeders and Guerin, 1996; Marinelli and Piazza, 2002; Piazza and Le Moal, 1997). Similar manipulations of corticosterone secretion decrease psychostimulant-induced locomotor activity and extracellular DA levels in the NAc (Marinelli and Piazza, 2002; Piazza and LeMoal, 1998). In addition, exposure to chronic stressors may involve long-term adaptations in neural mechanisms outside the HPA axis, such as the mesolimbic DA system and extended amygdala (Lu et al., 2003; Shalev et al., 2010).

Restraint or Immobilization

Different studies have employed immobilization or restraint to evaluate the effects of stress on the rewarding properties of psychostimulants and reinstatement after extinction (Lu et al., 2003; Shalev et al., 2000, 2010). In these studies, rats or mice are restrained for several minutes or hours for either 1 day (acute) or several days (repeated daily) in a glass or Plexiglas restraining device.

It has been observed that acute, but not repeated (7 days), restraint one day before CPP training with AMPH enhances the CPP produced by a medium dose (1.5 mg/kg) but not that produced by high or low doses (Capriles and Cancela, 1999, 2002). This enhancement of AMPH CPP by acute restraint is blocked when D2 receptor antagonists are administered prior to exposure to restraint (Capriles and Cancela, 1999). Cancela and colleagues showed that acute restraint enhances AMPH-induced increases in motor activity and extracellular DA levels in the striatum, and that NMDA glutamatergic receptors are involved in these effects (Pacchioni et. al., 2002). Acute exposure to restraint before the reinstatement test also induces the reinstatement of COC (Sanchez et al., 2003) and METH (Qi et al., 2009) CPP.

Restraint of pregnant female rats has been used to study the effects of prenatal stress on the subsequent response of adult offspring to psychostimulants. For example, in one study, restraint stress exposure three times per day for the last 7 days of gestation induced an enhancement in the effects of COC in offspring of 10 weeks of age. Prenatal stressed rats exhibited elevated locomotor activity, enhanced DA levels in the NAcc and PFC, and higher levels of glutamate in the NAcc in response to COC administration. Moreover, although no effects were observed on COC SA, a greater lever response was observed during extinction and COC-primed reinstatement (Kippin, Szumlinski, Kapasova, Rezner, and See, 2008).

Tail Pinch

Although the term "tail pinch" originally referred to a momentary application of pressure (Antelman, Szechtman, Chin, and Fisher, 1975), it now refers to continuous pressure for a period of several minutes (generally between 10 and 20 min) that induces a stress response in rats (Brake, Zhang, Diorio, Meaney, and Gratton, 2004; Marinelli, Quirion, and Gianoulakis, 2004) and mice (Ribeiro Do Couto et al., 2006). Typically animals receive a single session of tail pinch, although the intensity and frequency can vary. For example, in one study in our laboratory mice were individually placed in a transparent plastic cage (23 × 13.5 ×13 cm) and a plastic clothespeg (creating a pressure of 800 g) was fastened to their tails (at 1–1.5 cm from the body) for 15 min (Ribeiro Do Couto et al., 2006).

Tail pinch is considered a mild stressor, and although animals occasionally attempt (without success) to remove the peg, no tissue damage is produced. Stress induced by tail pinch has been found to enhance the initiation of psychostimulant SA (Lu et al., 2003; Piazza, Deminiere, Le Moal, and Simon, 1990; Rougé-Pont et al., 1993).

Tail pinch induces cortisol release (Ribeiro Do Couto et al., 2006) and can also increase DA levels (Keller, Maisonneuve, Nuccio, Carlson, and Glick, 1994; Rougé-Pont et al., 1993). Moreover, it has been reported that COC administration enhances the increase in DA evoked by tailpinch (Kiyatkin, 1993).

Emotional Stressors

This category includes discrete stressors, such as food restriction/deprivation and forced swim, or a combination of multiple stressors known as the chronic unpredictable stress paradigm. These events have been used to study how exposure to stress affects rodent behavioral responses in the CPP and SA paradigms (Aguilar et al., 2009; Lu et al., 2003).

Food Deprivation/Restriction

To induce stress with this procedure, animals are exposed to a regimen that reduces their body weight to an average of 90-80% of free-feeding weight by the beginning of experimental manipulations and maintains it at that level throughout the experiment. This paradigm works by applying acute food deprivation/restriction (typically 24 h of either deprivation or restriction by providing a small 5–8 g ration) or chronic food restriction (several days or weeks of limited access to food) (Lu et al., 2003).

Acute or chronic food restriction significantly increases the initiation and maintenance of psychostimulant SA (Carroll, 1984, 1985; Carroll and Meisch, 1981; Carroll, France, and Meisch, 1981; Carroll, Lac, Walker, Kragh, and Newman, 1986; Glick, Hinds, and Carlson, 1987; Lu et al., 2003; Takahashi et al.. 1978) and enhances COC and AMPH CPP (Bell, Stewart, Thompson, and Meisch, 1997; Stuber, Evans, Higgins, Pu, and Figlewicz, 2002). Acute food deprivation also induces the reinstatement of psychostimulant seeking (Carroll, 1985; Comer, Lac, Wyvell, Curtis, and Carroll, 1995; Shalev, Marinelli, Baumann, Piazza, and Shaham, 2003).

Forced Swim

In this procedure animals are placed in a deep cylindrical container (made of polypropylene, glass, etc.) filled with water (at 20-25° C) and are forced to swim during a period of several minutes (5-10). In some studies the procedure consists of a single exposure to forced swim (Kreibich et al., 2009; Mantsch et al., 2010), while others submit subjects to chronic exposure prior to the SA or CPP sessions (Kreibich et al., 2009). Chronic forced swim stress enhances acquisition of the CPP induced by COC and a single exposure to forced swim reinstates the extinguished CPP (Kreibich et al., 2009).

The Chronic Unpredictable Stress Paradigm

One model of emotional behavior is the chronic unpredictable stress (CUS) paradigm, which involves exposing mice to a variety of mild stressors in an unpredictable manner.

Following habituation to individual housing, mice undergo two weeks of exposure to different stressors: 1h in a restraint tube, inversion of the light/dark cycle, 2h of access to an empty water bottle, 15h of food restriction, 30 min forced swim 32+/-2°C water, and 10 min paired housing with damp bedding. During the two weeks of CUS, mice are exposed to 1-3 stressors per day, and are never exposed to the same stressor more than once on the same day (Miller, Ward, and Dykstra, 2008).

Varying results have been reported with the CUS paradigm, including a decrease in the consumption of/preference for sweet foods, disruption of grooming, increase of aggression, more immobility in the forced swim test and increased learned helplessness (reviewed in Willner, 2005). In light of these results, the CUS paradigm is often used as a model of depression, as these effects are reversible by antidepressant treatment (Willner, Towell, Sampson, Sophokleous, and Muscat, 1987). In addition, it has been reported that exposure to CUS may alter the rewarding effects of COC in the CPP paradigm (Miller et al., 2008).

Social Stressors

Considerable evidence points to different kinds of social stress as risk factors for initiation, escalating and relapse to drug abuse (Brady and Sinha, 2005; Brady, Dansky, Sonne, and Saladin, 1998; Shaham et al., 2000; Sinha et al., 2006).

There are different social experiences and conditions which induce social stress in animals, such as maternal deprivation, acute (brief) social stress, intermittent repeated social stress, subordination, crowding and isolation (Lu et al., 2003; Miczek et al., 2008; Ribeiro Do Couto, Aguilar, Lluch, Rodríguez-Arias, and Miñarro, 2009; Shaham et al., 2003). These manipulations can be performed at different ages (adolescence or adulthood) and at different phases of experimental procedures of SA and CPP (acquisition, maintenance, extinction and reinstatement).

Maternal Separation

Early life stress can profoundly affect adult behavior, and childhood trauma is closely associated with the severity of drug dependence (Enoch et al., 2010; Triffleman, Marmar, Delucchi, and Ronfeldt, 1995). Maternal separation/deprivation provides a good model with which to study the protracted effects of childhood trauma in rodents and to observe later responses to addictive drugs in the SA and CPP paradigms (Logrip et al., 2012; Lu et al., 2003). There are different models of maternal separation/deprivation, and studies vary in the way they enforce separation. One common model involves repeated separation of pre-weaning pups from their mothers for varying periods of minutes (15-180 min) or hours (for example 6h) every day on several consecutive postnatal days (PND), generally on PND 1-2 and PND12-15 (Campbell and Spear, 1999; Faure, Stein, and Daniels, 2009; Kosten, Miserendino, and Kehoe, 2000; Matthews, Robbins, Everitt, and Caine, 1999; Moffett et al., 2006). Other studies have employed a single 24 h period of maternal deprivation on PND9-10 (Llorente-Berzal et al., in press; Martini and Valverde, 2012).

Different studies have been performed to study the effects of maternal separation on acquisition of COC (Kosten et al., 2000; Martini and Valverde, 2012; Matthews et al. 1999; Moffett et al., 2006) and AMPH (Der-Avakian and Markou, 2010) SA and the CPP induced by AMPH (Campbell and Spear, 1999), methamphetamine (Faure et al., 2009) and MDMA (Llorente-Berzal et al., in press). Reinstatement of psychostimulant-seeking may also be modulated by a history of maternal separation (Lynch, Mangini, and Taylor, 2005).

Social Isolation

Some authors use social isolation to induce stress and then compare the effects of this manipulation on behavioural responses to drugs of abuse with those in animals living in groups and interacting socially. The effect of chronic isolation is highly dependent on the age of onset and length of exposure. Social housing at different stages of the SA and CPP procedures can influence the response to drugs of abuse (Ribeiro Do Couto et al., 2009; Schenk, Lacelle, Gorman, and Amit, 1987), with isolated rats showing a greater propensity to self-administered COC (Ding et al, 2005; Kosten et al., 2000; Schenk et al., 1987) and more sensitivity to the reinforcing properties of this drug (Smith, Neill, and Costall, 1997). Neonatal isolation increases the acquisition, maintenance (Lynch et al., 2005; Zhang, Sanchez, Kehoe, and Kosten, 2005), and cue-induced reinstatement of COC SA in adults rats (Lynch et al., 2005). Similarly, isolation during the period just after weaning (termed 'isolation rearing') potentiates DA-dependent behaviours, such as locomotor activity induced by psychostimulant drugs (Hall et al., 1998), and reinstatement of CPP induced by COC priming (Ribeiro Do Couto et al., 2009).

Crowding

Another condition that can induce stress in adult animals is crowding. In one study carried out in our laboratory we induced stress in animals by housing eight mice together in small plastic cages (25x25x14cm). On PND 21, male mice were housed in groups of four (experimental animals), and from PND 60 onwards, a new mouse was introduced into the cage every 2 days until each cage housed a total of eight mice (including four that were not used in the subsequent experimental procedures). We observed that crowding increased the reinstating effects of COC priming on the CPP induced by COC (Ribeiro Do Couto et al., 2009). It is important to note that crowding is not experienced as a stressful experience in adolescent mice (Ribeiro Do Couto et al., 2009).

Acute/Brief Social Defeat

A rodent model of social stress is the paradigm of social defeat. In this model, the effects of suffering a social defeat on the subsequent response of the defeated animal to drugs of abuse are evaluated. There are two main variations of this model according to the paradigm of aggression used: resident/intruder or agonistic encounter in a neutral environment.

In the first, which is more common, a territorial resident rat or mouse confronts and dominates an intruder, which is generally the experimental animal (Miczek et al., 2008). To study the effects of a brief episode of social defeat, an "intruder" is introduced into the home cage of an experienced aggressive male resident, where it is threatened and attacked by the resident until it shows clear signs of submission, usually after a few minutes of confrontation. In other studies, repeated, intermittent agonistic encounters ending in social defeat for the experimental animal are staged. In this case, each brief episode of social defeat consists of three phases. During the initial phase, the intruder's (smaller) home cage is placed inside the resident's cage. The cage protects the intruder from attacks bythe resident but allows social contactand species-typical threats from the male aggressive resident, thus instigating provocation (Covington and Miczek, 2001; Fish, Faccidomo, and Miczek, 1999). In the second phase, the protective cage is removed and the intruder is placed directly into the resident´s chamber for the confrontation, which should last no more than 5 min. A defeat is defined when the intruder displays a supine posture for five consecutive seconds, a response that typically occurs after three to five biting attacks from the resident, at which point the confrontation is terminated. In the third and final phase, the intruder is immediately returned to its protective home cage, which is once more placed inside the larger resident's cage for another 10 min to allow social threats from the resident. Socially defeat-stressed animal are exposed to four episodes of social defeat separated by intervals of 2 days (for example on days 1, 4, 7 and 10) (Torntzky and Miczek, 1993; Quadros and Miczek, 2009). Repeated, intermittent exposure to brief episodes of social defeat stress can produce persistent long-term consequences in rats and mice, including faster acquisition of drug SA (Kabbaj, Isgor, Watson, and Akil, 2001; Tidey and Miczek, 1997).

Although both resident and intruder usually exhibit increased corticosterone secretion, only stressed intruders engage in escalated patterns of psychostimulant SA; for example, with COC (Covington and Miczek 2001, 2005; Covington et al., 2005; Kabbaj et al., 2001; Miczek and Mutschler, 1996; Nikulina, Marchand, Kream, and Miczek, 1998) and AMPH (Miczek et al., 1999a; Yap and Miczek, 2007). On the other hand, it has been demonstrated that brief episodes of social defeat engender neural, physiological and behavioral effects which contrast with those caused by continuous subordination stress (Covington and Miczek, 2005; Fuchs, Czéh, and Flügge, 2004; Kozorovitskiy and Gould, 2004; Miczek, Nikulina, Kream, Carter, and Espejo, 1999b; Sgoifo, Koolhaas, Alleva, Musso, and Parmigiani, 2001; Razzoli, Carboni, Guidi, Gerrard, and Arban, 2007; Tornatzky and Miczek, 1993, 2001). Besides the increase in plasma corticosterone levels (Hucklebridge and Nowell, 1974; Miczek et al., 1999b), brief episodes of social defeat stress produce long-lasting sensitized neural responses to psychomotor stimulant challenge, particularly in the VTA, and decrease activation in the medial PFC (Covington et al., 2005; Nikulina et al., 2004).

In the second paradigm the experimental animal suffers social defeat in an aggressive social encounter with a conspecific of equal age and body weight (Ribeiro Do Couto et al., 2006). Aggressive opponents are housed individually for a month prior to encounter, since this isolation schedule heightens aggression in mice (Rodriguez-Arias, Miñarro, Aguilar,

Pinazo, and Simón, 1998). An agonistic encounter of 15 min takes place in a neutral transparent plastic cage. Experimental mice exhibit avoidance/flee and defensive/submissive behaviours after suffering the aggressive behaviours (threat and attack) of the opponent, which has been individually housed, has had previous fighting experience, and has been screened for a high level of aggression. The criterion used to define an animal as defeated is the adoption of a specific posture of defeat, characterized by an upright position, limp forepaws, upwardly angled head, and retracted ears (Miczek, Thompson, and Shuster, 1982). Defeated mice always exhibit this extreme form of "upright submissive" behaviour (Rodríguez-Arias et al., 1998). This type of social defeat produces an increase in corticosterone levels and enhanced priming-induced reinstatement of the CPP induced by COC (Ribeiro Do Couto et al., 2009).

Effects of Stress on the Acquisition and Reinstatement of Psychostimulant Self-Administration

In experimental models, acute exposure to different stressful experiences can promote psychostimulant use and increase the escalation of consumption (Covington and Miczek 2001, 2005: Goeders and Guerin 1994; Haney, Maccari, Le Moal, Simon, and Piazza, 1995; Kosten et al., 2000; Miczek and Mutschler, 1996; Piazza et al., 1990; Ramsey and van Ree, 1993; Shaham and Stewart, 1994). Moreover, chronic stress exposure increases drug craving (Shaham et al., 2000, 2003; Sanchez et al., 2003). Animal models of stress-induced reinstatement of drug-seeking also allow the neuropharmacological and neurobiological features of stress-induced relapse to be determined (See and Waters, 2011). As discussed previously, these stressful experiences can enhance SA of COC and AMPH and induce reinstatement of psychostimulant seeking by acting on the VTA-NAcc-medial PFC-extended amygdala circuit (Yap and Miczek, 2008; Koob, 2010).

Effects of Stress on Acquisition of Psychostimulant Self-Administration

The ability of stressors to alter the acquisition of psychostimulant SA in rats has received considerable attention (Goeders, 2003; Lu et al., 2003; Piazza and Le Moal, 1998). In the present chapter, we summarize the data obtained by studies of the effects of environmental stressors on acquisition of psychostimulant SA conducted during the last ten years (see Table 1).

Intermittent *footshock* can increase COC SA behavior in adult rats subjected to different training procedures (Ramsey and Van Ree, 1993; Sanchez and Sorg, 2001). One study reported enhanced acquisition of COC SA in rats administered footshock during sessions of food SA immediately prior to sessions of COC SA (Goeders and Guerin, 1994). Ramsey and Van Ree (1998) found that when rats observed another rat receiving a footshock just before acquisition sessions initiated COC SA with a very low dose (0.031 mg/kg/infusion). Thus, footshock stress itself or the psychosocial experience of witnessing a conspecific receive footshock appears to enhance acquisition of COC SA.

Table 1. Effect of stress on psychostimulant self-administration

Authors	Year	Drug	Stressor	Process	Animal	Effects
Anker & Carroll	2010	COC	YOH	reinstatement	rat	Reinstatement of drug seeking
Beardsley et al.	2010	COC	footshock	reinstatement	rat	Reinstatement of drug seeking (RTI-194 blocks reinstatement).
Beardsley et al.	2005	COC	footshock	reinstatement	rat	Reinstatement of drug seeking (JDTic reduces reinstatement)
Blacktop et al.	2011	COC	footshock	reinstatement	rat	Reinstatement of drug seeking (Bilateral intra-VTA CRF produced reinstatement in long-acces)
Bongiovanni & See	2008	COC	YOH	reinstatement	rat	Reinstatement of drug seeking (YOH increases cue-induced reintatement)
Boutrel et al.	2005	COC	hypocretin	reinstatement	rat	Reinstatement of drug seeking (blockade of NA and CRF blocks reinstatement)
Brown & Erb	2007	COC	footshock	reinstatement	rat	Reinstatement of drug seeking
Brown et al.	2012	COC	YOH	reinstatement	rat	Reinstatement of drug seeking (SCH23390 and SCH31966, but not raclopride, blocked reinstatement)
Buffalari & See	2009	COC	footshock	reinstatement	rat	Reinstatement of drug seeking
Buffalari & See	2011	COC	YOH	reinstatement	rat	Reinstatement of drug seeking (YOH increases cue-induced reintatement)
Campbell & Carroll	2001	COC	food restriction	acquisition	rat	Speed up acquisition of SA
Capriles et al.	2003	COC	footshock	reinstatement	rat	Reinstatement of drug seeking (SCH 23390 prevents reinstatement)
Carroll	1985	COC	food restriction	acquisition	rat	Increase the maintenance of cocaine SA
				reinstatement		Reinstatement of drug seeking
Carroll et al.	1981	COC	food restriction	acquisition	rat	Increases SA
Carroll et. al.	1986	COC	food restriction	acquistion	rat	Increases SA
Conrad et al.	2010	COC	forced swim	reinstatement	rat	Reinstatement of drug seeking
Covington & Miczek	2001	COC	social defeat	acquisition	rats	Increased SA and breaking point.
Covington et al.	2005	COC	social defeat	acquisition	rat	Escalated pattern of SA
Cruz et al.	2011	COC	social defeat	acquisition	rat	Escalated pattern of SA
de Guglielmo et al.	2012	COC	YOH	reinstatement	rat	Reinstatement of drug seeking (pregabalin abolishes reinstatement)
De Vry et al.	1989	COC	food restriction	acquisition	rat	Speed up acquisition of SA
Ding et al.	2005	COC	isolation	acquisition	rat	Increases SA
Erb et al.	1996	COC	footshock	reinstatement	rat	Increases SA
Erb et al.,	2000	COC	footshock	reinstatement	rat	Reinstatement of drug seeking (Clonidine and lofexidine attenuate reinstatement)
Erb et al.,	2001	COC	footshock	reinstatement	rat	Reinstatement of drug seeking
Erb et. al.,	2004	COC	footshock	reinstatement	rat	Reinstatement of drug seeking
Feltenstein & See	2006	COC	YOH	reinstatement	rat	Reinstatement of drug seeking (exposure to drug-paired cues potentiates reinstatement)
Feltenstein et al.	2011	COC	YOH	reinstatement	rat	Reinstatement of drug seeking (females demostrated higher reinstatement)
Figueroa-Guzman et al.	2011	COC	footshock	reinstatement	rat	Reinstatement of drug seeking (l-THP attenuates reinstatement)
Fuchs et al.	2008	COC	footshock	reinstatement	rat	Reinstatement of drug seeking (inactivation of NAC attenuated reinstatement)
Glick et al.	1987	COC	food restriction	acquisition	rat	Increases SA
		AMPH				Increases SA
Goddard & Leri	2006	COC	footshock	reinstatement	rat	Reinstatement of drug seeking
Goeders & Guerin	1994	COC	footshock	acquisition	rat	Increases SA
Graf et al.,	2011	COC	footshock	reinstatement	rat	Reinstatement of drug seeking (Alpha-helical CRF9-41 blocks reinstatement)
			CRF			
Haney et al.,	1995	COC	social defeat	acquisition	rat	Increases SA
Highfield et al.	2002	COC	food restriction	reinstatement	rat	Reinstatement of drug seeking
Howes et al.	2000	COC	isolation	acquisition	rat	Increases SA at low doses but slows it at high dose
Kabbaj et al.	2001	COC	social defeat	acquisition	rat	Increases SA
Kippin et al.	2008	COC	prenatal stress	acquisition	rat	No effects
				reinstatement		Increase reinstatement of drug seeking
Kosten et al.	2000	COC	neonatal isolation	acquisition	rat	No effects
Kupferschmidt et al.	2012	COC	footshock	reinstatement	rat	Reinstatement of drug seeking (AM251 does not block reinstatement)
			CRF			Reinstatement of drug seeking (AM251 prevents reinstatement)
Kupferschmidt et al. (a)	2011	COC	footshock	reinstatement	rat	Reinstatement of drug seeking (influence of the intensity and duration of footschock)
Kupferschmidt et al. (b)	2011	COC	footshock	reinstatement	rat	Reinstatement of drug seeking (TCAP-1 does not block reinstatement)
			CRF			Reinstatement of drug seeking (TCAP-1 blocks reinstatement)
Kupferschmidt et al.	2009	COC	YOH and footshock	reinstatement	rat	Reinstatement of drug seeking (influence of exposure to stress during extinction)
Land et al.	2009	COC	social defeat	reinstatement	mice	Reinstatement of drug seeking
Leri et al.	2002	COC	footshock	reinstatement	rat	Reinstatement of drug seeking (B1/B2 antagonists attenuates reinstatement)
Lynch et al.	2005	COC	neonatal isolation	acquisition	rats	Increases SA
				reinstatement		Reinstatement of drug seeking
Mahler et al.	2012	METH	YOH	reinstatement	rat	Reinstatement of drug seeking
Mantsch & Katz	2007	COC	footshock	acquisition	rat	Escalated pattern of SA
Mantsch et al.	2008	COC	footshock and CRF	reinstatement	rat	Reinstatement of drug seeking (greater in long-access)
Martin-Fardor & Weiss	2012	COC	footshock	reinstatement	rat	Reinstatement of drug seeking (LY379268 and MTEP prevent reinstatement)
Martini & Valverde	2012	COC	maternal separation	acquisition	mice	Increases SA
Matthews et al.	1999	COC	maternal separation	acquisition	rat	Increases SA in male and decreases in female rats
Miczek et. al.	2011	COC	social defeat	acquisition	rat	Increases SA
Moffett & Goeders	2005	METH	footshock	acqusition	rat	Decreases SA
Moffett et al.	2006	COC	maternal separation	acquisition	rat	Increaes SA (low doses)
Nawata et al.	2012	METH	footshock	reinstatement	rat	Reinstatement of drug seeking (CRF receptor antagonist block reintatement)
Papasava & Singer	1985	COC	food restriction	acquisition	rat	Increases SA
Piazza et al.	1990	AMPH	tail pinch	acquisition	rat	Increases SA
Piazza et al.	1989	AMPH	prenatal stress	acquisition	rat	Increases SA
Quadros & Mizcek	2009	COC	social defeat	acquisition	rat	Escalated pattern of SA, increased break points
Ramsey & van Ree	1993	COC	footshock	acquisition	rat	Increases SA
Ribeiro Do Couto et al.	2009	COC	social defeat	reinstatement	mice	Increases reinstatement induced by priming
Rougé-Pont et al.	1993	AMPH	tail pinch	acquisition	rat	Increases SA
Sanchez & Sorg	2001	COC	footshock	reinstatement	rat	Reinstatement of drug seeking
Shaham et al.	1998	COC	footshock	reinstatement	rat	Reinstatement of drug seeking
Shalev et al.	2003	COC	food restriction	reinstatement	rat	Reinstatement of drug seeking (CP-154,526 attenuates reinstatement)
Shepard et al.	2004	METH	YOH and footschock	reinstatement	rat	Reinstatement of drug seeking
Sorge et al.	2005	COC	footshock	reinstatement	rat	Reinstatement of drug seeking (buprenorphine does not affect reinstatement)
Soria et al.	2008	COC	footshock	reinstatement	mice	Reinstatement of drug seeking
Tidey & Miczek	1997	COC	social defeat	acquisition	rat	Increases SA
Wang et al.	2009	COC	hypocretin	reinstatement	rat	Reinstatement of drug seeking
Wang et al.	2007	COC	footshock	reinstatement	rat	Reinstatement of drug seeking (CRF2 antagonists prevent reinstatement)
Wang et al	2005	COC	footshock	reinstatement	rat	Reinstatement of drug seeking (CRF is necessary)
Xi et al.	2004	COC	footshock	reinstatement	rat	Reinstatement of drug seeking (SB-277011A attenuates reinstatement)
Yap & Miczek	2008	COC	different stressors	acquisition	rat	Increases SA
		AMPH				
				reinstatement		Reinstatement of drug seeking
Yoon et al.	2012	COC	footshock	reinstatement	rat	Reinstatement of drug seeking (acupuncture reduces reinstatement)
Zhang et al.	2005	COC	neonatal isolation	acquisition	rat	Enhances maintenance of SA
Zhou et al.	2012	COC	YOH	reinstatement	rat	Reinstatement of drug seeking (orexin antagonists block reinstatement)

The capacity of repeated daily exposure to electric footshocks to escalate COC SA has been also investigated. Male Sprague-Dawley rats were trained to self-administer COC during 2-h sessions comprised of four 30-min SA components. Repeated daily footshock was delivered 5 min before each of the four SA components over 14 days of SA testing. Daily exposure to 4 alternating blocks of 5-min footshock / 30-min COCSA triggered a significant escalation in COC SA that lasted for the whole 14-day experimental period (Mantsch and Katz, 2007). In the study in question, it was also observed that adrenalectomy plus corticosterone replacement prevented footshock-induced escalation of COC SA, indicating that the escalating effects of footshock were dependent on increases in circulating levels of glucocorticoids.

Elevation of corticosterone through repeated daily injections failed to reproduce the effects of repeated daily footshock on SA, but restored the effects of footshock on escalated COC SA in adrenalectomized rats receiving corticosterone replacement, suggesting that a rise in glucocorticoid levels was necessary but not enoughon its own to produce said escalation (Mantsch and Katz, 2007). These studies indicate that exposure to footshock can increase both acquisition and maintenance of COC intake, although further investigation is required to differentiate between the short- and long-term effects of this stressor on psychostimulant SA. In contrast with that observed with COC, electric footshock exposure does not increase METH SA in adult male Wistar rats (Moffett and Goeders, 2005). Following initial food training, rats were allowed to self-administer METH at doses that were doubled weekly. Neither non-contingent electric footshock nor treatment with corticosterone altered the lowest dose at which the rats first acquired METH SA. These results suggest that the HPA axis does not have a major role in the acquisition of METH SA.

In addition, several studies have shown that acute food deprivation or restriction (24-hr deprivation of food or restriction of food supply to 5–8 g per day in rats) or chronic food restriction (i.e., multiple days or weeks of limited access to food) significantly increases the initiation and maintenance of psychostimulant SA (Yap and Miczek, 2008). Takahashi et al. (1978) reported that chronic restricted feeding to 80% of free feeding body weight brought forward AMPH SA over a range of unit doses (0.05–0.8 mg/kg). These findings have been extended to the initiation and maintenance of COC SA (De Vry, Donselaar, and Van Ree, 1989; Papasava and Singer, 1985), and it has been reported that the effect of food deprivation is much more pronounced on COC than on AMPH SA (Glick et al., 1987). Carroll and colleagues reported that acute food restriction (8 g of food every third day) increased COC SA during the maintenance phase (Carroll, 1985; Carroll et. al., 1981, 1986). Moreover, mild chronic deprivation (20 g/day) also speeded up COC SA (Campbell and Carroll, 2001).

Stress induced by tail pinch also enhances AMPH SA in rats (Piazza et al., 1990). Rougé-Pont et al. (1993) observed that this stressor induced an increase in DA levels and suggested that this biochemical modification was related with the enhanced predisposition to acquire psychostimulant SA in animals with higher DA activity in the NAcc (Rougé-Pont et al., 1993). In another study tail pinch produced a significant increase in DA in rats that had been exposed prenatally to COC (Keller et al., 1994).

Prenatal and neonatal stress also increases psychostimulant SA. The group of Piazza et al. performed a study in which female dams were restrained during the last week of pregnancy (45 min per day, for 3 days). Subsequently, adult offspring were trained to self-administer a low dose of AMPH (0.03 mg/kg/infusion) in five daily sessions. The authors observed drug SA only in rats in the prenatal stress group, and not in control animals (Piazza, Deminière, Le Moal, and Simon, 1989; Piazza and LeMoal, 1998). On the other hand, Kippin et al. (2008) assessed the influence of maternal stress during gestation (restraint stress three times per day for the last 7 days of gestation) on COC SA behavior in offspring at 10 weeks of age. Prenatal stress did not increase active lever pressing or alter intake of COC during SA, though it did enhance motivational responsiveness to COC during extinction and reinstatement (Kipping et al., 2008).

Neonatal isolation increases the acquisition and maintenance of COC SA in adult rats (Lynch et al., 2005; Zhang et al., 2005). Maternal separation also differentially modulates adult responses to psychostimulants in accordance of the severity of said separation. Neonatal handling blunts male rats' locomotor responses to acute doses of COC (Brake et al., 2004), while mice with a history of extended maternal separation display higher locomotor sensitization to COC (Kikusui, Faccidomo, and Miczek, 2005), an effect not observed in the case of AMPH, strangely enough (Weiss, Domeney, Heidbreder, Moreau, and Feldon, 2001). Matthews et al. studied the effect of maternal separation (3-6 h/day for 10 days, between PND 5 and 20) on the initiation of COC SA in male and female rats. Maternally deprived male rats showed a downward shift in the dose–response curve for the rate of intravenous COC self-administration in adulthood, while their female counterparts self-administered more COC than their respective controls (Matthews et al., 1999). In a similar line, Kosten et al. (2000) reported that maternal separation (for 1 h/day between the age of 2 and 9 days) increased the acquisition of COC SA. Longer periods of maternal separation (180 min, PND2-15) increase the rewarding effects of COC, while shorter periods of maternal separation (15 min, PND2-15) blunts the reinforcing effects of this drug, which suggests that extended maternal separation heightens sensitivity to the reinforcing effects of low doses of COC (Moffett et al., 2006). Recently, Martini and Valverde (2012) observed that 24h of MD on PND9 increased the time required for meeting the acquisition criteria of COC SA and reduced breaking point values in a progressive schedule in maternally deprived adolescent mice, pointing to an impairment of rewarding functions. Behavioural tests have also confirmed an increase in anxiety- and depression-related behaviours in these animals, which exhibit a decrease in BDNF levels in the amygdala and hippocampus (Martini and Valverde, 2012).Research also indicates an enhancement of the facilitatory effect of psychostimulants on brain reward function following a history of extended maternal separation. AMPH treatment reduces threshold currents for intracranial self-stimulation of the lateral hypothalamus to a greater degree in rats with a history of maternal separation than in controls (Der-Avakian and Markou, 2010).

Since the main source of stress in humans is social interaction, stress induced in rodents by *social defeat* in an agonistic encounter may represent a stressor of ecological and ethological validity (Tornatzky and Miczek, 1993) that increases vulnerability to acquiring and maintaining COC SA and reinstatement of drug-seeking behaviours in these animals (Miczek et al., 2008). Social defeat promotes and intensifies COC SA when assessed by performance in a progressive ratio schedule and in conditions of extended binge-like access (Boyson, Miguel, Quadros, Debold, and Miczek, 2011; Covington and Miczek, 2001, 2005; Covington et al., 2008; Cruz, Quadros, Hogenelst, Planeta, and Miczek, 2011; Haney et al., 1995; Kabbaj et al., 2001; Miczek and Mutschler, 1996; Miczek et al., 2008; Nikulina et al. 1998; Tidey and Miczek, 1997). Four brief episodes of social defeat stress over the course of one week increase the acquisition of a low dose of COC iv SA in both male (Haney et al., 1995, Tidey and Miczek, 1997) and female rats (Haney et al., 1995). Under conditions of unlimited access to COC for 24 h (binge), socially defeated rats self-administer COC with shorter inter-infusion intervals, thus consuming higher quantities (Covington and Miczek, 2005). Once COC SA is established, brief episodes of social defeat stress prior to each experimental session can increase the rate of drug intake significantly, particularly at lower doses (Miczek and Mutschler, 1996). While defeat immediately prior to operant sessions increases COC SA, progressively longer delays between social defeat exposure and COC SA training dissipates the effects of stress on acquisition (Covington and Miczek, 2001; Covington et al., 2005). More recently, it has been demonstrated that intermittent defeats increase COC consumption and rates of response during binges (Covington et al., 2008). Moreover, it has been reported that previous exposure to brief episodes of social defeat stress intensifies the escalation of COC SA associated with extended access conditions in rats. In one study, four episodes of social defeat stress induced cross-sensitization to a COC challenge, increased breaking points for COC SA, and produced persistent, escalated COC taking during a 24-h binge (Quadros and Miczek, 2009).

The capacity of social defeat to heighten sensitivity to a drug's stimulant effects and escalation of drug intake has been associated with stress-induced neuroadaptations in brain reward pathways (Miczek et al., 2008; Shalev et al., 2002). Brief social stress can produce enduring neural sensitization expressed through immediate early gene activation in the mesocorticolimbic circuit, and this defeat stress-induced sensitization can be responsible for increased COC SA (Covington and Miczek, 2001). Cross-sensitization between these brief stressors and stimulant drugs suggests shared neural mechanisms in rodents (Covington and Miczek, 2001; Pacchioni, Cador, Bregonzio, and Cancela, 2007; Yap and Miczek, 2007). In one study, the relationship between behavioral sensitization, induced by either social defeat or an AMPH, and intravenous COCSA was explored in mice. Male mice were exposed to a defeat experience, an AMPH or saline injection every day for 10 days. Ten days after the last defeat or injection, mice were challenged with AMPH and then trained to nose poke for iv COC. Repeated social defeat produced a sensitized motor response to AMPH challenge. AMPH-pretreated mice exhibited increased COC SA during acquisition and elevated breaking points during their performance in a progressive ratio schedule of reinforcement when compared to stress-sensitized and control animals. Thus, contrary to that seen in rats, increased levels of COC SA are seen in AMPH-pretreated mice but not after repeated defeat stress (Yap and Miczek, 2008). On the other hand, in spite of strong evidence suggesting that social defeat promotes escalated COC SA, it remains to be determined whether or not the consequences of social defeat are generalized in escalated patterns of intake of psychostimulants besides COC (Cruz et al., 2011).

Subordination, an alternative type of social stress, induces the opposite effects to episodic social defeat (Miczek, Nikulina, Shimamoto, and Covington, 2011). The latter stress consists of four brief confrontations between the experimental rat and an aggressive resident rat over the course of 10 days. The former stress involves continuous exposure to an aggressive resident for five weeks while living in a protective cage within the resident's home cage, with the brief daily confrontations that this provokes. While episodically defeated intruder rats exhibit increased iv COC SA under a fixed ratio schedule with prolonged binge-like access, subordination stress suppresses COC intake. Moreover, a sensitized DA response in the NAcc and increased tegmental BDNF has been observed in episodically defeated rats, whereas the DA and BDNF responses of continuously subordinated rats were inhibited (Miczek et al., 2011). It is likely that intermittency and controllability of social stress experience contributes to the effects observed.

An important factor that can influence the effects of stress on psychostimulant SA is the age of the animal, since the impact of social stressors during adolescence can dramatically influence neural development. In adult rodents, repeated intermittent exposures to a psychomotor stimulant progressively augment behavioral effects (i.e. behavioral sensitization), whereas adolescents are far less sensitive to the effects of repeated COC or

AMPH administration (Bolanos, Glatt, and Jackson, 1998; Collins and Izenwasser, 2002; Lanier and Isaacson, 1977). Social isolation during adolescence enhances the acquisition of iv COC SA at low unit doses but decreases the acquisition of high unit doses, which points to a leftward shift in the dose–response curve for COC response (Howes, Dalley, Morrison, Robbins, and Everitt, 2000). Using a fixed ratio schedule of reinforcements, it has been observed that adolescent rats deprived of social interactions self-administered more COC than non-isolated rats (Ding, Belin, and Piazza, 2005). The effects of social defeat can also differ between adolescent and adult animals. Social defeat stress attenuates the induction of behavioral sensitization to a subsequent COC challenge in adolescent hamsters (Trzcinska, Bergh, DeLeon, Stellar, and Melloni, 2002). Moreover, the induction of behavioral sensitization to AMPH in adult rats is attenuated by repeated experience of social defeat at the hands of an older and larger aggressor during adolescence (Kabbaj et al., 2002).

Effects of Stress on the Reinstatement of Pyschostimulant Self-Administration

Stressful life experiences, as well as promoting drug abuse, can trigger relapse after long-term periods of abstinence (Brady and Sinha, 2005; Shaham et al., 2000). Reinstatement of drug seeking after extinction of SA is the most used animal model of the propensity to relapse to drug taking after prolonged drug use and discontinuation (Lu et al., 2003; See, Fuchs, Ledford, and McLaughlin, 2003; Shaham et al., 2000; Shaham et al., 2003) and involves mechanisms related to the development and expression of craving (Gerber and Stretch, 1975; Stewart and Wit, 1987).

Many studies have employed the reinstatement procedure of the SA paradigm to explore the relationship between stress and relapse, demonstrating that stress is clearly associated with increased reinstatement of psychostimulant seeking (Yap and Miczek, 2008; Anker and Carroll, 2010a). In this procedure, mice and rats are trained to respond in order to access drug infusions, typically by pressing a lever. Subsequently, following extinction of the drug-reinforced response, the ability of certain stressors to induce non-reinforced pressing of the drug-associated lever (reinstatement) is determined. A number of excellent reviews on the reinstatement of extinguished drug seeking have been published (Goeders, 2002a; Goeders, 2003; Shaham et al., 2003; Lu et al., 2003; Shalev et al., 2002), and so we wish to merely summarize the data obtained by studies of the effects of environmental stressors on reinstatement of drug seeking previously reinforced by psychostimulant drugs conducted during the last ten years (see Table 1).

Previously published studies have tended to employ intermittent *footshock* to induce reinstatement of psychostimulant-seeking behavior (Ahmed and Koob, 1997; Beardsley, Howard, Shelton, and Carroll, 2005; Beardsley, Shelton, Hendrick, and Johnson, 2010; Blacktop et al., 2011; Boutrel et al., 2005; Erb, Shaham, and Stewart, 1996; Erb, Lopak, and Smith, 2004; Figueroa-Guzman et al., 2011; Graf et al., 2011; Kupferschmidt, Klas, and Erb, 2012; Martin-Fardor and Weiss, 2012; Nawata et al., 2012; Shaham et al., 2000; Stewart, 2000; Wang et al., 2007; Xi et al., 2004; Yoon et al., 2012) and to study the neural substrates of stress-induced reinstatement (Erb et al., 2001; McFarland et al., 2004).

In fact, footshock stress has been was found to be as effective as priming injections of drugs in inducing high response levels in reinstatement tests employing different psychostimulants, doses, schedule requirements, footshock parameters, and strains of rats (Lu et al., 2003; Shaham et al., 2000, 2003). Footshock has also been shown to induce reinstatement of COC SA in mice (Soria, Barbano, Maldonado, and Valverde, 2008).

Although footshock-induced reinstatement of psychostimulant seeking can be achieved reliably and robustly, it can be sensitive to certain procedural variables, such as the procedure of extinction and reinstatement test sessions, the intensity and duration of the footshock stress, and the presence of drug-associated cues during extinction and reinstatement (Kupferschmidt, Brown, and Erb, 2011).

For example, footshock stress-induced reinstatement of COC may be affected by the history of drug use, the time since drug taking ceased and the interval between stress exposure and reinstatement test.

Exposure to 15 min of intermittent, inescapable, footshock stress induces suppression of response at early time points (after 1 day of extinction) but enhances reinstatement progressively over time in rats with more exposure to COC, in whom reinstatement is stronger 60 days after extinction (Sorge and Stewart, 2005).

The reinstating effects of acute footshock have been shown to persist for up to 40 min (but not 60 min) after a single session of intermittent footshock (Brown and Erb, 2007). Rats self-administered COC under long-access (6h daily) conditions for 14 days are more susceptible to footshock induced reinstatement than those exposed to short-access conditions (2h daily) (Mantsch et al., 2008).

Footshock stress can induce reinstatement by reactivating the motivational value of COC-conditioned cues. In this sense, Goddard and Leri (2006) reported that footshock stress can induce the reinstatement of operant responding maintained by a COC-conditioned stimulus in rats never trained to actively self-administer COC.

More recently, Buffalari and See (2009) examined whether three different levels of intermittent footshock would trigger reinstatement or potentiate reinstatement of COC-seeking caused by conditioned cues.

In their study, male rats underwent daily i.v. COC SA, followed by extinction of lever responding in the absence of previously COC-paired cues. Reinstatement of COC-seeking was measured during presentation of COC-paired cues, following pretreatment with three levels of intermittent footshock (0.25, 0.5, and 0.75 mA) or footshock plus cues.

Footshock at the 0.5 and 0.75 mA levels (without cues) led to significant reinstatement and also potentiated the reinstatement triggered by the presentation of conditioned cues. These results demonstrate that stress and drug-paired cues interaction leads to stronger reinstatement (Buffalari and See, 2009).

YOH induces reinstatement of COC SA in rats (Anker and Carroll, 2010b; Brown et al., 2012; de Guglielmo et al., 2012; Zhou et al., 2012) and markedly increases cue-induced reintatement of COC seeking in rats (Bongiovanni and See, 2008; Feltenstein and See, 2006; Feltenstein, Henderson, and See, 2011; Lee et al., 2004), with a greater increase being noted in females (Feltenstein et al., 2011).

In addition, it reinstates METH SA (Shepard et al., 2004; Mahler et al., 2012). Different studies have shown that YOH potentiates conditioned cue-induced reinstatement of COC seeking (Feltenstein and See, 2006; Buffalari and See 2009a; Buffalari and See, 2011).

In another study, Kupferschmidt et al. (2009) investigated whether repeated exposure to YOH during extinction training affects the time-course of extinction and the magnitude of subsequent YOH- or footshock-induced reinstatement of COC seeking. Rats trained to self-administer COC were given five days of extinction training, during which they were injected with YOH. Following additional extinction training in the absence of YOH, animals were tested for YOH- or footshock- induced reinstatement Animals injected with YOH during extinction showed an attenuated rate of extinction, and, following additional extinction training in the absence of YOH, a marked attenuation of YOH-induced reinstatement of COC seeking.

YOH treatment during extinction did not, however, affect the magnitude of reinstatement induced by footshock. These findings demonstrate that repeated exposure to a stressor during extinction training can modulate extinction learning and the subsequent reinstatement of drug seeking induced by that stressor (Kupferschmidt, Tribe, and Erb, 2009).

Dietary restriction is another method used to promote appetitive drug-seeking in the operant context.

Acute (1 day) food restriction and/or deprivation (no food) can act as a stressor to facilitate the reinstatement of COC seeking behavior (Bongiovanni and See, 2008; Carroll, 1985; Highfield, Mead, Grimm, Rocha, and Shaham, 2002; Shaham et al., 2003; Shalev et al., 2003).

Cold swim stress also induces the reinstatement of COC-seeking behavior in rats trained to self-administer COC after 16 days of extinction. Indeed, the reinstating effects of stress are evident even 3 days after stress exposure (Conrad et al., 2010). A previous study has reported that a history of COC consumption and prolonged (14 days) abstinence can increase the endocrine response to stress (enhanced corticosterone levels after cold swim in COC vs. saline treated rats), which may facilitate the reinstatement of drug-seeking behavior (Cleck, Ecke, and Blendy, 2008).

Maternal stress during gestation (restraint stress three times per day for the last 7 days of gestation) also can affect the reinstatement of COC SA. In offspring of 10 weeks of age, prenatal stress promotes active lever responding both during extinction and COC-primed reinstatement, but not during conditioned-cued reinstatement (Kippin et al., 2008). A history of *maternal separation* can also modulate the reinstatement of psychostimulant-seeking. Zhang and colleagues (2005) found no significant alteration of COC-induced reinstatement in adult rats that had experienced 1-h maternal isolation, a paradigm involving not only maternal separation but also isolation from littermates.

However, the same isolation paradigm has been shown to yield increased cue-induced reinstatement (Lynch et al., 2005). Additional studies employing maternal separation and brief handling are required to fully understand the impact of neonatal handling on reinstatement and the magnitude of relapse to drug-seeking after periods of abstinence.

To date, no studies have employed stressful events of a more ethological relevance, such as social defeat, to evaluate the effect of stress on reinstatement of psychostimulant SA. Only two studies have used social defeat stress as a trigger for reinstatement of the CPP induced by morphine (Ribeiro Do Couto et al., 2006) or COC (Land et al., 2009).

Similarly, only one study in the CPP paradigm has evaluated the effects of social stressors such as isolation, crowding and social defeat to modulate the priming-induced reinstatement of COC CPP (Ribeiro Do Couto et al., 2009). These studies are described in the following section. In this way, the capacity of social stressors to reinstate psychostimulant SA has yet to be determined.

EFFECTS OF STRESS ON THE ACQUISITION AND REINSTATEMENT OF PSYCHOSTIMULANT CONDITIONED PLACE PREFERENCE

Effects of Stress on the Acquisition of the Conditioned Place Preference Induced by Psychostimulants

Several studies have found that exposure to different stressors (forced swim, maternal deprivation, social defeat, etc.) can modify the rewarding effects of psychostimulants in the CPP paradigm (see Table 2). However, in contrast to the results observed with the SA paradigm, stress induced by tail or foot shock does not modify the rewarding effects of COC or AMPH in the CPP paradigm. For example, a single session of an uncontrollable, inescapable tailshock prior to CPP has been shown to have no effect on the CPP responses to COC in male rats (Der-Avakian et al., 2007). In a similar way, footshock stress in adolescence does not alter adult AMPH CPP (Burke, Watt, and Forster, 2011), while exposure to restraint stress (during 2h) in adolescence (PND 35) undermines the subsequent acquisition of CPP induced by a low dose of AMPH (0.5 mg/kg), in adulthood (Richtand et al., 2012). These results suggest that emotional or social stressors may have a greater impact than footshock on the response to drugs in the CPP paradigm.

Using the chronic unpredictable stress (CUS) paradigm, a model of emotional behavior, it has been reported that mice exposed to a variety of mild stressors (restraining, inversion of the light/dark cycle, access to an empty water bottle, food restriction, forced swim and housing with damp bedding) in an unpredictable manner can modify the rewarding effects of COC in the CPP paradigm. Exposure to CUS significantly increases COC CPP in CB1-KO mice, but tends to decrease it in wild-type mice with respect to untreated mice (Miller et al., 2008).

Chronic food restriction also increases the acquisition of psychostimulant CPP, although the effects seem to be in function of the dose used. Food restriction to 80% of free-feeding body weight modestly increases COC CPP for a medium dose (5 mg/kg), but not for lower (2.5 mg/kg) or higher (10 mg/kg) doses (Bell et al., 1997). Mild chronic food restriction of 15 g/day (90% of free-feeding body weight) enhances AMPH CPP for a moderate dose (0.85 mg/kg), but decreases preference for two higher doses (1.7 and 3.4 mg/kg) (Stuber et al., 2002). Mice previously exposed to repeated forced swim show a significantly greater preference for the side paired with COC (Mc Laughlin et al., 2003, 2006a; Kreibich et al., 2009).

Thus, stress induced by forced swim before COC conditioning augments the rewarding effects of this drug in the CPP paradigm. In addition, Schindler et al. (2010) found that previous exposure to repeated forced swim stress before the final preference test was enough to produce a potentiation of COC CPP. In their study, mice exposed to a 15 min swim 2-4h after completion of COC training on day 3, and those exposed to four 6 min swims 10 minutes before the final preference test on day 4 showed an increased acquisition of the CPP induced by COC, an effect that was not observed in mice exposed to acute forced swim stress (one 15 min swim on day 4, 10 or 45 min before the final preference test) (Schindler, Li, and Chavkin, 2010).

Table 2. Effect of stress on psychostimulant conditioned place preference

Authors	Year	Drug	Stressor	Process	Animal	Effect
Aldrich et al.	2009	COC	forced swim	reinstatement	mice	Reinstates CPP (Zyklophin prevents reinstatement)
Briand et al.	2010	COC	forced swim	reinstatement	mice	Reinstates CPP
Burke et al.	2011	AMPH	social defeat	acquisition	rats	Enhances CPP
Capriles & Cancela	1999	AMPH	restraint stress	acquisition	rat	Enhances CPP (haloperidol abolished this effect)
Carey et al.	2007	COC	forced swim	reinstatement	mice	Reinstates CPP (Arodyn prevents reinstatement)
Cruz et al.	2010	AMPH	restraint	reinstatement	rats	Reinstates CPP
Der-Avakian et al.	2007	COC	tailshock	acquisition	rats	Inhibits CPP
Faure et al.	2009	METH	maternal separation	acquisition	rats	No modify METH CPP
Grimwood et al.	2011	COC	forced swim	reinstatement	mice	Reinstates CPP (PF-04455242 prevents reinstatement)
Hays et al.	2012	COC	maternal separation	acquisition	mice	Reduces CPP
Kreibich et al.	2009	COC	forced swim	acquisition	mice	Enhances CPP (antalarmin prevents reinstatement)
Kreibich et al.	2004	COC	forced swim	reinstatement	mice	Reinstates CPP (not in CREB mutant mice)
Land et al.	2009	COC	social defeat	reinstatement	mice	Reinstates CPP (KOR antagonists prevents reinstatement)
Lu et al.	2001	COC	footshock	reinstatement	rat	Reinstates CPP (alpha-helical CRF 9-41 prevents reinstatement)
Lu et al.	2002	COC	footshock	reinstatement	rat	Reinstates CPP (L365,260 in Nacc s or amygdala prevents reinstatement)
Mantsch et al.	2010	COC	forced swim	reinstatement	mice	Reinstates CPP (clonidine prevents reinstatement)
McLaughlin et al.	2003	COC	forced swim	acquisition	mice	Enhances CPP (nor-binaltorphimine prevents reinstatement)
McLaughlin et al. (a)	2006	COC	forced swim	acquisition	mice	Enhances CPP (U50,488 15 blocks this effect)
McLaughlin et al. (b)	2006	COC	social defeat	acquisition	mice	Enhances CPP (nor-binaltorphimine blocks this effect)
Miller et al.	2008	COC	CUS	acquisition	mice	Enhanced CPP in CB1 KO
Qi et al.	2009	METH	restraint stress	reinstatement	mice	Reinstates CPP (oxytocin prevents reinstatement)
Redila & Chavkin	2008	COC	footshock forced swim	reinstatement	mice	Reinstates CPP (KOR antagonists prevents reinstatement)
Ribeiro Do Couto et al.	2009	COC	social defeat	acquisition reinstatement	mice	No modify COC CPP Enhanced priming-induced reinstatement
Richtand et al.	2012	AMPH	restraint	acquisition	rats	Inhibits CPP
Ross et al.	2011	COC	forced swim	reinstatement	mice	Reinstates CPP (D-Trp isomer prevents reinstatement)
Sanchez et al.	2003	COC	restraint	reinstatement	rat	Reinstates CPP (SKF 81297 and SCH 23390 prevents reinstatement)
Schindler et al.	2010	COC	forced swim	acquisition	mice	Enhances CPP (nor-binaltorphimine blocks this effect)
Vaughn et al.	2012	COC	forced swim	reinstatement	mice	Reinstates CPP (CB1 antagonist prevents reinstatement)
Vranjkovic et al.	2012	COC	forced swim	reinstatement	mice	Reinstates CPP (NA antagonist prevent reinstatement)

Neonatal stress (8h maternal separation per day from P5 to P9) in mice undermines adult COC CPP learning and increases adult hippocampal neurogenesis, effects that could be associated with a diminishing of adult arousal by neonatal stress (Hays et al., 2012). Moreover, stress during childhood in the form of maternal deprivation (3 h per day from PND 2 to PND 14) does not lead to a stronger METH CPP in adulthood. Rats exposed to stress in early life and normally reared controls have been shown to develop CPP after repeated METH exposure (Faure et al., 2009). This lack of a difference between deprived and non-deprived animals in the rewarding effects of METH could have been a result of the dose of METH used. According to the hypothesis that stress induced by maternal deprivation alters the motivational brain system, thereby reducing arousal and reward, a decreased CPP would only be observed with lower sub-threshold doses of drugs of abuse. In line with this, in a recent study in our laboratory we have observed that maternal deprivation impairs the rewarding effects of MDMA in rats (Llorente-Berzal et al., in press).

The rearing environment can also modify acquisition of CPP. Studies have housed rodents in isolation, in crowded conditions, or in an enriched environment and compared their acquisition of CPP with that of rodents reared in a standard environment. For example, it has been observed that COCCPP is maintained over long periods of abstinence in mice housed in a standard environment but disappears in mice housed in an enriched environment (Solinas, Chauvet, Thiriet, El Rawas, and Jaber, 2008). Studies carried out to explore the protective effects of different social environments are reviewed later on.

The chronic social stress induced by isolation during adolescence was shown to enhance the preference for AMPH in females at a dose of 1.0 mg/kg and induce a trend toward stronger preference in males at a dose of 0.25 mg/kg relative to control animals. When tested several weeks after adolescent stress, rats (both sexes) showed a decrease in preference for the 0.5 mg/kg dose of AMPH when compared to controls. These results suggest that the nature of the effects of chronic stress may depend in part on the developmental period in which the stress occurs, as well as the time lapse between stress exposure and testing (Mathews, Mills, and McCormick, 2008). On the other hand, Ribeiro Do Couto et al. (2009) found that housing conditions and social experiences do not affect the acquisition of CPP induced by COC in mice, though these experiences did produce effects on the reinstatement of COC CPP after extinction (see following section).

Social defeat stress-exposed mice (12-16 weeks old) conditioned with COC were found to exhibit significantly stronger CPP for the drug–paired chamber than unstressed mice (McLaughlin et al., 2006b). Another more recent study has investigated the effects of social defeat during adolescence on adult CPP induced by AMPH in male rats. Adolescent social defeat stress increases preference for AMPH-paired cues in adulthood, suggesting that social stress has a great impact on later drug behaviors (Burke et al., 2011). The rewarding efficacy of MDMA seems not to be modulated by social stress, since low and moderate doses are capable of inducing CPP in both non-confronted mice and mice exposed to aggressive social interactions (Rodriguez-Alarcon, Canales, and Salvador, 2007).

Effects of Stress on Reinstatement of the Conditioned Place Preference Induced by Psychostimulants

As many studies have confirmed, stress is a potent trigger for returning to drug use after long-term abstinence. In this context, we are going to examine evidence of how stress exposure promotes reinstatement of a previously extinguished psychostimulant-induced CPP. Studies have shown that exposing rodents to a variety of stressors, including electric footshock, forced swim and social stress, reinstates drug-induced CPP (see Table 2), which suggests that this procedure can be used to examine the neurobiological processes that contribute to stress-induced relapse (Aguilar et al., 2009).

Administration of 15-min footshock sessions prior to CPP testing reinstates preference for the previously COC-paired chamber in mice (Redila and Chavkin, 2008) and rats (Wang et al., 2000). Restraint, another kind of physical stressor, also induces reinstatement of psychostimulant CPP. Immobilization stress (15-min, administered within the CPP chamber) produces reinstatement of COC-seeking behavior in males rats (Sanchez et al., 2003). Acute exposure to restraint stress also reinstatesAMPH-induced CPP when tests are performed during adolescence (1 day following extinction), but not when animals are tested in adulthood (30 days after extinction) (Cruz, Leão, Marin, and Planeta, 2010). Restraint stress (15 min. immobilization) induces reinstatement of METH CPP in male mice (Qi et al., 2009), and, similarly, stress induced by forced swim reinstates COC CPP in male mice (Carey, Borozny, Aldrich, and McLaughlin, 2007; Grimwood et al., 2011; Kreibich and Blendy, 2004; Manstch et al., 2010; Redila and Chavkin, 2008; Ross, Reilley, Murray, Aldrich, and McLaughlin, 2012; Vaughn et al., 2012; Vranjkovic, Hang, Baker, and Mantsch, 2012).

Ribeiro Do Couto et al. (2009) reported that housing conditions and social experiences alter the reinstatement of COC CPP induced by COC priming. Isolation of animals or social defeat in an agonistic encounter prior to the reinstatement test increased susceptibility to COC-induced reinstatement (Ribeiro Do Couto et al., 2009). Indeed, a single social defeat has been shown to reinstate COC CPP in mice (Land et al. 2009, Titomanlio et al., submitted). Conversely, reinstatement of COC CPP is prevented by manipulation of housing conditions during acquisition of CPP or prior to the reinstatement test. Crowding in adolescent mice, isolation in adult mice, and cohabitation with a female in both age groups (when the animals were in the same conditions throughout the whole procedure) prevents COC-induced reinstatement. Cohabitating with a female or social interaction with another male before the reinstatement test also reduces priming-induced reinstatement of COC CPP (for more information about preventive factors, see section 9).

PHARMACOLOGICAL BLOCKADE OF THE POTENTIATING EFFECTS OF STRESS ON PSYCHOSTIMULANT REWARD

Stress exposure increases the risk of addictive drug use in human and animal models of drug addiction through mechanisms that are not completely understood. Some years ago, Capriles and Cancela (1999) demonstrated that restraint stress increases the rewarding effects of AMPH in the CPP and that the administration of D1 and D2 DA receptor antagonists (SCH 23390, sulpiride and haloperidol) abolished the sensitising effects of restraint stress on the reinforcing properties of AMPH. Later, McLaughlin et al. (2003, 2006a, b) showed that stress induced by social defeat enhanced the acquisition of COC CPP in mice (McLaughlin, Marton-Popovici, and Chavkin, 2003; McLaughlin, Land, Li, Pintar, and Chavkin, 2006a; McLaughlin, Li, Valdez, Chavkin, and Chavkin, 2006b). In addition, they found that daily pretreatment with the KOR antagonist norbinaltorphimine (nor-BNI) blocked stress-induced potentiation of COC CPP in male mice (McLaughlin et al., 2006a). Similarly, mice subjected to repeated forced swim stress before COC conditioning showed significantly stronger CPP than unstressed mice, and the same effect was observed when forced swim stress or the KOR agonist U50,488 were administered before testing for preference. Both effects were shown to be blocked by the KOR antagonist nor-BNI. These results suggest that stress enhances the rewarding value of COC-associated cues through a dynorphin-dependent mechanism (Schindler et al., 2010). In fact, accumulated evidence directly links the endogenous opioid neuropeptide dynorphin and the activation of dynorphin/KOR with the enhancing effect of stress on the rewarding properties of drugs of abuse (Bruchas et al., 2010). CRF and glutamate systems are also involved in the effects of stress on acquisition of COC SA. Intermittent social defeats augment COC SA and response rates during binges, and these effects are prevented when NMDA or AMPA receptor antagonists (Covington et al., 2008) or CRF1 receptor antagonists (Boyson et al., 2011) are administered before defeat.

With respect to the effects of stress on reinstatement, NA, CRF, kappa opioid, DA and cannabinoid receptors have been implicated, among other neurotransmitter receptors. Administration of the alpha2 adrenergic receptor (α2AR̡antagonist YOH induces the reinstatement of COC seeking. Some years ago, Erb et al. (2000) reported that footshock-induced reinstatement of COC SA was weakened by the α2AR agonists clonidine, lofexidine and guanabenz, while Leri et al. (2002) demonstrated that footshock-induced reinstatement of COC SA was attenuated by administration of a mixture of the beta(1)- and beta(2)-adrenergic receptor (β1AR, β2AR, respectively) antagonists betaxolol and ICI-118,551 to the BNST and CeA (Leri et al., 2002). The role of the different adrenergic receptors in stress-induced reinstatement has been studied by Mantsch et al. (2010). The most selective α2ARantagonist, BRL-44,408, induced the reinstatement of COC CPP. Suppression of noradrenergic neurotransmission by administration of the nonselective βAR antagonist propranolol, blocked reinstatement of COC CPP induced by both YOH and forced swim, an effect that was not achieved with the α-1 AR antagonist prazosin. The α2AR agonist clonidine and the β2AR antagonist ICI-118,551 also suppressed forced swim-induced reinstatement, while the selective β1AR antagonist betaxolol did not (Mantsch et al., 2010). More recently, Vranjkovic et al. (2012) reported that the administration of ICI-118,551 blocked reinstatement of COC CPP induced by forced swim, while betaxolol (at a high dose) interfered with swim-induced reinstatement. These data suggest that stress-induced reinstatement depends on NA signalling through β2ARs (Mantsch et al., 2010; Vranjkovic et al., 2012).

As occurs with YOH, the administration of *CRF* induces reinstatement of COC seeking (Erb et al., 2006, 2010). The non-selective CRF receptor antagonist, alpha-helical $CRF_{9\text{-}41}$, decreases footshock-induced reactivation of COC CPP reactivation (Lu, Liu, and Ceng, 2001), and administration of alpha-helical $CRF_{9\text{-}41}$ to the VTA (but not to the SN) decreases footshock-induced reinstatement of COC CPP (Wang et al., 2005). Similarly, the non-selective CRF antagonist D-Phe $CRF_{12\text{-}41}$ reducesCOC SA induced by footshock when administered icv (Erb et al., 2008), and to the BNST but not to the CeA (Erb and Stewart, 1999). However, it does not affect the reinstatement of COC SA induced by YOH (Brown et al., 2009). Recently, alpha helical $CRF_{9\text{-}41}$ was found to block footshock-induced reinstatement in rats with long-term access to COC SA (Graf et al., 2011) in a study which also demonstrated that when the adrenal response to SA was blocked before acquisition of SA by adrenalectomy with diurnal corticosterone replacement, subsequent footshock- and CRF-induced reinstatement was also blocked. However, adrenalectomy plus corticosterone before extinction and reinstatement failed to reduce reinstatement. The study in question suggested that adrenal-dependent neuroadaptations in CRF responsiveness underlie the increased susceptibility to stress-induced relapse that emerges with repeated COC use (Graf et al., 2011).

Similarly, stress-induced reinstatement of COC seeking is blocked by selective CRF1 receptor antagonists. CP-154,526 decreases footshock-induced reinstatement of COC SA (Shaham, 1998) and antalarmin blocks forced swim-induced reinstatement of COC CPP (Kreibich et al., 2009). However, in a study by Wang et al. administration of the selective CRF1 antagonists NBI-27914 and R121919 to the VTA did not block footshock-induced reinstatement of COC seeking (Wang et al., 2007). The same study also highlighted the important role of CRF2 receptors in the VTA in reinstatement of COC seeking, as antisauvagine-30, one such receptor antagonist decreased footshock-induced reinstatement of COC SA (Wang et al., 2007). Both CRF1 and CRF2 receptors seem to be important in CRF-dependent neuroadaptations, establishing stress-induced relapse to drug seeking behavior (Gysling, 2012).

In the last five years, data obtained regarding stress-induced reinstatement have corroborated the stress-like effect of KOR agonists (Wee and Koob, 2010) and demonstrated that KOR antagonists suppress stress-induced reinstatement of COC-seeking behavior in the CPP and SA paradigms. The KOR antagonists JDTic, nor-BNI and RTI-194 decrease footshock- or forced swim-induced reinstatement of COC SA (Beardsley et al., 2005, Beardsley, Shelton, Hendrick, and Johnson, 2010; Redila and Chavkin, 2008), while the KOR antagonists arodyn, zyklophin and PF-04455242 and the D-Trp isomer of CJ-15,208 diminish forced swim-induced reinstatement of COC CPP (Aldrich, Patkar, and McLaughlin, 2009; Carey et al., 2007; Grimwood et al., 2011; Ross et al., 2012). The inactivation of serotonergic KORs by injection of the KOR antagonist nor-BNI into the dorsal raphe nucleus also blocks social defeat-induced reinstatement of COC CPP (Land et al., 2009). Conversely, mu receptors are not involved in stress-induced reinstatement of COC seeking, since buprenorphine has no effect on footshock stress-induced reinstatement of COC SA (Sorge, Rajabi, and Stewart, 2005).

Transmission at DA receptors also seems to mediate the reinstatement of COC seeking CPP. The D1/5 receptor antagonist SCH23390 blocks reinstatement of COC SA induced by footshock when injected into the medial PFC and OFC (Capriles, Rodaros, Sorge, and Stewart, 2003) and the reinstatement of COC CPP induced by immobilization when injected into the medial FPC (Sanchez et al., 2003). The same effect is observed on CRF- and YOH-induced reinstatement when peripheral SCH23390 is administered (Brown et al., 2012). Similarly, the D1/D5 antagonist SCH31966 blocks YOH-induced reinstatement of COC SA (Brown et al., 2012), and the selective D3 antagonist SB-277011A attenuates footshock-induced reinstatement of COC seeking behavior when microinjected into the NAcc, but not into the dorsal striatum, of male rats (Xi et al., 2004). However, the D2/3 receptor antagonist raclopide does not block CRF- or YOH-induced reinstatement of COC seeking (Brown et al., 2012). In contrast, reinstatement of COC SA by footshock is undermined by administration of levo-tetrahydropalmatine, a tetrahydroprotoberberine isoquinoline with a pharmacological profile that includes antagonism of D1, D2 and D3 DA receptors (Figueroa-Guzman et al., 2011).

The role of endocannabinoid signaling has been studied in only two recent studies (Kupferschmidt et al., 2012; Vaughn et al., 2012). The cannabinoid CB1 receptor antagonist AM251 was found to block CRF-induced reinstatement of COC SA (Kupferschmidt et al. 2012) and forced swim-induced reinstatement of COC CPP (Vaughn et al., 2012). However, AM251 had no effect on footshock-induced reinstatement of COC SA (Kupferschmidt et al., 2012). On the other hand, the cannabinoid agonist CP 55,940 increases the reinstating effects of a low dose of the β2AR antagonist BRL-44408. Reinstatement COC CPP is observed when the two compounds are co-administered, but not when administered alone (Vaughn et al., 2012).

Other neurotransmitter systems, including brain neuropeptides, glutamate and GABA, have also been implicated in stress-induced reinstatement of COC seeking. The administration of the cholecystokinin (CCK) receptor antagonist L365, 260 to the amygdala and NAcc blocks stress-induced reinstatement of COC CPP (Lu et al., 2002). Similarly, the hypocretin type 1 receptor antagonist SB 334867 prevents footshock-induced reinstatement of COC SA (Boutrel et al., 2005). However, the administration of SB 408124, another hypocretin type 1 receptor antagonist, to the VTA has no effect on footshock-induced reinstatement (Wang et al., 2009) and YOH-induced reinstatement (Zhou et al., 2012) of COC SA. The neuropeptide oxytocin also obstructs the reinstatement of COC CPP induced by restraint stress (Qi et al., 2009), and an analog of theteneurin C-terminal-associated peptides (TCAP) blocks CRF-induced reinstatement of COC SA, though it has no effect on footshock-induced reinstatement of COC seeking (Kupferschmidt, Lovejoy, Rotzinger, and Erb, 2011). Recently, it has been demonstrated that footshock stress-induced reinstatement of COC SA is attenuated by the selective metbotropic glutamate receptor (mGluR)2/3 agonist LY379268 and by the selective mGluR5 antagonist MTEP (Martin-Fardon and Weiss, 2012). Moreover, the structural analog of GABA pregabalin suppresses the reinstatement of COC seeking induced by YOH (de Guglielmo et al., 2012). Finally, acupuncture applied for 1 min at bilateral Shenmen points after footshock stress suppresses the reinstatement of COC seeking behavior (Shoon Yoon et al., 2012).

Preventive Factors in Animal Models of Drug Addiction

The use of experimental animal models is essential to the study of the factors that determine vulnerability to drug addiction, such as stress, as they make it possible to isolate and control the genetic, environmental and social variables that contribute to the development of drug addiction. Similarly, the preventive effects of some variables, such as environmental enrichment, social interaction or cohabitation with females, and access to alternative rewards, on the vulnerability to drug addiction can be studied in animals.

Environmental Enrichment

An environmental factor that influences the behavioral and neurochemical effects of drugs of abuse and may provide protection against drug addiction is environmental enrichment (Bardo, Klebaur, Valone, and Deaton, 2001; Carroll, Anker, and Perry, 2009; El Rawas, Thiriet, Lardeux, Jaber, and Solinas, 2009; Jessor and Jessor, 1980; Solinas, Thiriet, El Rawas, Lardeux and Jaber, 2009; Solinas, Thiriet, Chauvet, and Jaber, 2010; Stairs and Bardo, 2009; Xu, Hou, Gao, He, and Zhang, 2007), which has been defined as "a combination of complex inanimate and social stimulation" (Rosenzweig, Bennett, Hebert, and Morimoto, 1978). With EE, animals are generally housed in large cages with running wheels and a few toys that are periodically changed to stimulate the curiosity of the animals and increase exploration (Laviola, Hannan, Macrì, Solinas, and Jaber, 2008; Nithianantharajah and Hannan, 2006; Rosenzweig and Bennett, 1996; van Praag, Kempermann, and Gage, 2000). In some cases, animals are exposed to EE for only a few hours for one or several days, in contrast to their normal housing conditions (Rampon et al., 2000). It has been hypothesized that EE provides animals with control and choice over their social and spatial environment (Baumans, 2005; Hutchinson, Avery, and Vandewoude, 2005).

To study the preventive effects of environmental enrichment (EE), animals are exposed before having any contact with the drug (Solinas et al., 2010). Accumulating evidence indicates that EE mimics positive life experiences and helps to prevent the development of drug addiction (Carroll, Anker, and Perry, 2009; Stairs and Bardo, 2009). In the SA paradigm, the reinforcing effects of the psychostimulants AMPH and COC are less pronounced in EE rats (Bardo et al., 2001; Green, Gehrke, and Bardo, 2002; Green et al.,

2010; Stairs, Klein, and Bardo, 2006). Rats reared with EE exhibit less drug taking behavior when measured by fixed ratio (FR1) schedules and less motivation for the drug when measured by progressive ratio (PR) schedules (Bardo et al., 2001; Green et al., 2002). A review of studies investigating the preventive effects of EE on drug addiction has been written by Stairs and Bardo (2009).

Other studies have shown that EE, as well as having preventive effects, is "curative" in cases of psychostimulant addiction. EE has also been shown to eliminate already developed addiction-related behaviours, decreasing resistance to the extinction of AMPH SA and reducing the propensity to relapse (Stairs et al., 2006). Exposure to EE during long periods of abstinence from COC SA also reduces drug seeking and attenuates reinstatement induced by conditioned cues and stress (Chauvet, Lardeux, Goldberg, Jaber, and Solinas, 2009).

The preventive and curative effects of EE have also been observed in the CPP paradigm. AMPH and COC produce CPP in EE rats but not in their isolated counterparts (Bardo et al., 1995a; Bowling and Bardo, 1994; Bowling, Rowlett, and Bardo, 1993; Green et al., 2009). The rewarding effects of COC in the CPP are blunted in mice reared with EE from weaning through to adulthood when compared with animals reared in standard environments (Solinas et al., 2009). Using in vivo microdialysis in mice, it has been demonstrated that EE does not exert its protective effects by reducing COC-induced increases in DA levels in the ventral or dorsal striatum, but rather by undermining COC-induced expression of the immediate early gene zif-268 in the NAcc (shell and core) and Delta-Fos B levels in the striatum (Solinas et al.,2009).

When mice are housed in an enriched environment after acquisition of COC CPP the reinstatement of CPP induced by COC priming is prevented, suggesting that environmental stimulation is a fundamental to facilitating abstinence and preventing relapse to COC addiction (Solinas et al., 2008). Moreover, EE reduces activation of the brain circuitry involved in COC-induced reinstatement. After CPP, COC increases c-FOS expression in the NAcc shell, VTA and BLA in mice housed in a standard environment but not in EE mice. In fact, COC-induced expression of c-FOS is significantly reduced in the NAcc core and infralimbic cortex of EE mice (Solinas et al., 2008). More recently, it has been demonstrated that EE undermines the maintenance of COC CPP, which is long-lasting in mice reared in a standard environment, and is associated with reduced expression of Fos in the anterior cingulate cortex, the lateral caudate putamen, the NAcc shell, the dentate gyrus of the hippocampus, the BLA and CeA, the BNST, and the VTA with respect to mice conditioned with COC and reared in a standard environment (Chauvet, Lardeux, Jaber, and Solinas, 2011).

Recent studies have shown that the expression of genes of the endocannabinoid system differ in mice reared with EE from the weaning stage until adulthood and those reared in a standard environment. EE increases CB1 mRNA levels in the hypothalamus and in the BLA, but decreases them in the basomedial amygdala. Similarly, FAAH mRNA levels are higher in the hypothalamus and the BLA of EE mice. Such changes in the endocannabinoid system could result in a reduced response to stress and, consequently, in a greater resistance to addiction (El Rawas, Thiriet, Nader, Lardeux, Jaber, and Solinas, 2011).

It is important to note that, contrary to that observed with COC, EE is incapable of reducing the rewarding effects of METH; mice reared with EE for 2 months during early stages of life develop CPP after conditioning with METH in adulthood (Thiriet et al., 2011). On the other hand, it has recently been demonstrated that if EE is not maintained into adulthood the risk of developing drug addiction increases. Mice reared with EE but then switched to a non-enriched standard environment experience stronger rewarding effects of COC and exhibit higher levels of CRF mRNA in the BNST and of CREB phosphorylation in the BNST and the NAcc shell. Indeed, increased sensitivity to the rewarding effects of COC is completely blocked by the CRF antagonist antalarmin, which points to the role of the CRF system in the negative consequences of environmental changes (Nader et al., 2012).

As discussed in the course of the present chapter, stress is known to play a crucial role in drug addiction (Goeders, 2003; Koob, 2008; Sinha, 2007, 2008) by increasing the rewarding effects of drugs and creating a negative emotional state that renders ex-users more vulnerable to relapse (Koob, 2008; Sinha, 2007, 2008). Studies showing that EE reverses already-established COC addiction suggest that levels of stress during abstinence influence the risk of relapse dramatically (Chauvet et al., 2009; Solinas et al., 2008; Thiel, Sanabria, Pentkowski, and Neisewander, 2009) and that EE acts as an anti-stress (Mora, Segovia, and del Arco, 2007; Segovia, del Arco, and Mora, 2009) or antidepressant (Laviola et al., 2008) mechanism whose function is to create a positive emotional state that protects against relapse. A recent study has demonstrated increased AMPH SA in socially isolated rats when compared to rats living in groups or with EE, and that this increase may involve enhanced reactivity of the HPA stress axis (Stairs et al., 2011). EE can be considered a functional opposite of stress. For example, in what is a protective role, the anti-stress effects of EE reduce the reinforcing effects of drugs and their ability to induce long-lasting neuroplastic changes, thus helping to prevent the development of drug addiction. In the case of the curative effects of EE, restoration of the normal, pre-drug functioning of the stress system facilitatesthe individual's resisting of the desire to take the drug, therefore lowering the risk of relapse (Solinas et al., 2010).

Another important mechanism that could underlie the positive effects of EE in facilitating abstinence and reducing COC seeking and reinstatement is its reversal of the cognitive deficits induced by chronic consumption of COC (Solinas et al., 2010). Psychostimulant addiction appears to be associated with deficits in decision making and other cognitive tasks that play an important role in relapse, such as behavioral inflexibility and perseverative behaviours (Verdejo-García and Bechara, 2009; Stalnaker, Takahashi, Roesch, and Schoenbaum, 2009). Therefore, environmental stimulation together with pharmacological treatment and behavioral therapy may be of fundamental importance to the success of drug addiction treatment programmes (Chauvet et al., 2009).

Social Interactions

There is compelling evidence that social experiences modify vulnerability to reinstatement, acting as prevention or risk factors in the development of drug addiction (Swadi, 1999). If negative environmental conditions render subjects more vulnerable to drug abuse, positive environmental conditions are likely to have protective effects against addiction. The presence of alternative nondrug reinforcers undermines acquisition and maintenance of COC use and abuse (for a review, see Higgins, 1997). Using animal models, several studies have investigated how different types of social interaction, if experienced in parallel to drug use, can prevent drug abuse and substance dependence (Fritz et al., 2011; Thiel, Okun, and Neisewander, 2008; Ribeiro Do Couto et al., 2009).

Social interaction with a coespecific animal is a rewarding experience. An environment previously paired with the presence of a rat induces CPP in adolescent rats, and social reward-CPP increases as the number of social pairings rises (Thiel et al., 2008). In addition, interaction between social and COC reward has been demonstrated; a low dose of COC (2 mg/kg, IP) and a low number of social pairings (2 pairings of an environment with a rat), insufficient for producing CPP in adolescent rats when administered alone, have been shown to produce a robust CPP when administered together (Thiel et al., 2008). On the other hand, in rats in the CPP paradigm concurrently trained to pair COC with one compartment and social interaction with the other, it has been demonstrated that four 15-min episodes of social interaction with a gender- and weight-matched male conspecific reversed CPP from COC to social interaction (Fritz et al., 2011a, b). Social interaction also reverses COC CPP-induced expression of the immediate-early gene zif268 in the NAcc shell, VTA, CeA and BLA (Fritz et al., 2011a), and the antagonism of sigma receptors with BD1047 decreased COC CPP in favour of social reward CPP (Fritz et al., 2011b). In addition, excitotoxic lesions of the NAcc core or the BLA shift CPP toward social interaction, whereas inactivation of the NAcc shell shifts CPP toward COC, demonstrating the differential involvement of these divisions of the NAcc in COC and social reward (Fritz et al., 2011c).

In our laboratory we have demonstrated that priming-induced reinstatement of a previously extinguished COC-induced CPP is blocked by exposing mice to different kinds of social interaction, such as exposure to a female, crowding during adolescence and a non-aggressive agonistic encounter (Ribeiro Do Couto et al., 2009). Cohabitation with a female seems to act as an alternative reinforcer by decreasing vulnerability to reinstatement, and contact with a female prior to a reinstatement test prevents reinstatement of heroine SA in rats (Shaham, Puddicombe, and Stewart, 1997). Similarly, we have observed that cohabitation with a female of the same age has a protective effect and reduces vulnerability to reinstatement of a COC CPP (Ribeiro Do Couto et al., 2009). Mating throughout the experimental procedure (during acquisition, extinction, and reinstatement of CPP) blocks the reinstatement induced by COC in adolescent and adult animals. Similarly, a brief mating episode 48 h before the reinstatement test blocks the reinstating effects of COC priming in adult male rats. However, no protective effects of mating are observed in adult grouped mice that are mated after acquisition of CPP (and which, thus, lived with a female for 9 days, during which extinction and reinstatement took place). These results suggest that exposure to female company only exerts a protective effect against reinstatement when cohabitation occurs during the acquisition, extinction and reinstatement of CPP, or before reinstatement. In the first case, mating may act as a natural reward that competes with the rewarding effects of COC, while in the second, the novelty of this natural reward interferes with the reinstating effects of COC. Therefore, the lack of reinstatement in mice with a mate could be due to the presence of an alternative reinforcer (the female) that prevents reinstatement after COC priming.

Crowding in adolescent mice (housing in groups of four from PND 21-PND 23 and from PND 24 onwards, and introducing another mouse into the cage every 2 days, until the cage houses eight mice) acts as a protective factor against reinstatement of COC CPP, but has the opposite effect in adult animals (Ribeiro Do Couto et al., 2009). In this way, crowded housing conditions produce different effects in adolescent and adult mice, blocking reinstatement in the former and increasing susceptibility to reinstatement in the latter. These differential effects may be due to the way in which animals perceive this housing condition and how it affects their emotional reactivity. It has been observed that crowding stresses adult male rats and increases their corticosterone levels (Brown and Grunberg, 1995) and ACTH response to noise, thus increasing their emotional reactivity (Armario, Castellanos, and Balasch, 1984). Stress induced in adult mice by crowding increases susceptibility to reinstatement, since CPP is reinstated in adult animals not only with 25 mg/kg but also with 12.5 mg/kg of COC, a dose that does not produce reinstatement in grouped animals. Conversely, it appears that crowded conditions are rewarding rather than stressing for adolescent mice. Periadolescent rodents are generally associated with a peculiar behavioral profile characterized by affiliative and playful behaviors. While crowding strengthens the corticosterone response to an acute stress challenge in adult male mice, a trend towards lower corticosterone levels is observed in periadolescent male mice (Laviola, Adriani, Morley-Fletcher, and Terranova, 2002). Indeed, a recent study has shown that social proximity is rewarding for juvenile mice (Panksepp and Lahvis, 2007). In this context, the rewarding effect of crowded conditions for adolescent mice may act as an alternative reinforcer that prevents reinstatement after COC priming (Ribeiro Do Couto, et al., 2009).

Social interaction with another male also decreases vulnerability to reinstatement of a COC CPP in rats (El Rawas et al., 2012; Fritz et al., 2011a, b) and mice (Ribeiro Do Couto et al., 2009). Four 15 min episodes of social interaction with a gender-and weight-matched male early-adult conspecific has been shown to inhibit COC-induced reinstatement of COC CPP (El Rawas et al., 2012; Fritz et al., 2011a, b). Similarly, we have observed that a single non-aggressive social encounter with a conspecific mouse (of equal age and body weight) in a neutral cage 30 min before the reinstatement test reduces priming-induced reinstatement of COC CPP. In the agonistic encounter in question experimental animals were confronted with opponents that had been housed in a group and made temporarily anosmic by intranasal lavage with 4% zinc sulfate solution one day before (Smoothy, Brain, Berry, and Haug, 1986). Since this type of opponent elicits attack but never initiates it, experimental animals do not suffer the experience of defeat. Thus, this type of agonistic encounter can be viewed as a normal social interaction between two conspecific animals with a similar low level of aggression. In fact, no aggressive behaviours were observed in these encounters. The fact that an agonistic encounter with a non-aggressive male before the reinstatement test blocks the reinstating effects of COC priming suggests that a brief social interaction also acts as an alternative reinforcer that prevents reinstatement of COC CPP (Ribeiro Do Couto et al., 2009).

Conclusion

As discussed throughout this chapter, exposure to stress stimulates psychostimulant consumption and vulnerability to relapse in animal models of addiction. Different types of stressors (physical, emotional and social) potentiate the rewarding effects of psychostimulants in the SA and CPP paradigms and induce reinstatement of drug seeking after extinction. However, it is important to note that a great number of the studies published about this subject have employed the SA paradigm, the footshock as stressor and adult rats as experimental subjects. In fact, current knowledge of the neural substrates of stress-induced reinstatement is derived mainly from this type of study, which may have created a somewhat limited perspective. In the last ten years, the use of the CPP paradigm, the application of stressful stimuli with more ethological relevance, such as emotional or social stressors, and the inclusion of mice as experimental animals have contributed to extending our understanding of how stress enhances vulnerability to relapse. It is now clear that SA and CPP evaluate different aspects of reward and that the results obtained with one paradigm must be complemented by studies performed in the other. Another limitation that becomes patent when reviewing the literature about the effects of stress on psychostimulant addiction is that most studies have been performed with COC, while the effects of stress on the rewarding properties of other psychostimulants have received little attention. Future work exploring the role of stress in psychostimulant addiction should focus on AMPH, METH or psychostimulant-related drugs such as MDMA. The way in which stress differentially affects adult and adolescent animals should also be an area of future research.

Pharmacological manipulation, particularly the antagonism of NA, CRF and kappa receptors, has shown potential in blocking stress-induced potentiation of acquisition of psychostimulant SA and CPP and stress-induced reinstatement of psychostimulant seeking. Future studies should test new drugs that act on the neurotransmitters and neuromodulator systems involved in stress and brain reward. The data obtained may be of great use in developing effective pharmacological treatments for addiction based on the mediation of stress triggers.

ACKNOWLEDGMENTS

This work was supported by the following grants: Ministerio de Economía y Competitividad: Dirección General de Investigación (PSI2011-24762), Instituto de Salud "Carlos III", RETICS, Red de Trastornos Adictivos (RD06/001/0016). Generalitat Valenciana, Conselleria de Educación (PROMETEO/2009/072 and Programa VALi+d for MP G-P), Spain.

We wish to thank Brian Normanly for his revision of the chapter´s English.

REFERENCES

Adriani, W., Macrì, S., Pacifici, R., and Laviola, G. (2002). Peculiar vulnerability to nicotine oral self-administration in mice during early adolescence. *Neuropsychopharmacology, 27* (2), 212-224.

Aguilar, M. A., Rodríguez-Arias, M., and Miñarro, J. (2009). Neurobiological mechanisms of the reinstatement of drug-conditioned place preference. *Brain Research Review, 59* (2), 253-277.

Ahmed, S. H. (2010). Validation crisis in animal models of drug addiction: beyond non-disordered drug use toward drug addiction. Neuroscience Biobehavior Reviews, 35 (2), 172-184.

Ahmed, S. H., and Koob, G. F. (1997). Cocaine- but not food-seeking behavior is reinstated by stress after extinction. *Psychopharmacology, 132* (3), 289-295.

Ahmed, S. H., and Koob, G. F. (1998). Transition from moderate to excessive drug intake: change in hedonic set point. *Science, 282* (5387), 298-300.

Ahmed, S. H., Kenny, P. J., Koob, G. F., and Markou, A. (2002). Neurobiological evidence for hedonic allostasis associated with escalating cocaine use. *Nature Neuroscience, 5* (7), 625-626.

Aldrich, J. V., Patkar, K. A., and McLaughlin, J. P. (2009). Zyklophin, a systemically active selective kappa opioid receptor peptide antagonist with short duration of action. *Proceedings of the National Academy of Sciences, 106* (43), 18396-18401.

Alheid, G. F., and Heimer, L. (1988). New perspectives in basal forebrain organization of special relevance for neuropsychiatric disorders: the striatopallidal, amygdaloid, and corticopetal components of substantia innominata. *Neuroscience, 27* (1), 1-39.

Anker, J. J., and Carroll, M. E. (2010a). Reinstatement of cocaine seeking induced by drugs, cues, and stress in adolescent and adult rats. *Psychopharmacology, 208* (2), 211-222.

Anker, J. J., and Carroll, M. E. (2010b). Sex differences in the effects of allopregnanolone on yohimbine-induced reinstatement of cocaine seeking in rats. *Drug Alcohol Dependence, 107* (2-3), 264-267.

Anstrom, K. K., Miczek, K. A., and Budygin, E. A. (2009). Increased phasic dopamine signaling in the mesolimbic pathway during social defeat in rats. *Neuroscience, 16;161* (1), 3-12.

Antelman, S. M., Szechtman, H., Chin, P., Fisher, A. E. (1975). Tail pinch-induced eating, gnawing and licking behavior in rats: dependence on the nigrostriatal dopamine system. *Brain Research, 99* (2), 319-337.

Antkiewicz-Michaluk, L., Filip, M., Michaluk, J., Romańska, I., Patsenka, A., Papla, I., Przegaliński, E.,…Vetulani, J. (2006). Conditioned rewarding stimulus associated with cocaine self-administration reverses the depression of catecholamine brain systems following cocaine withdrawal in rats. *International Journal of Neuropsycho-pharmacology, 9* (1), 37-50.

Armario, A., Castellanos, J. M., and Balasch, J. (1984). Effects of chronic noise or daily water restriction on the pituitary-adrenal axis in male rats. *Revista Española de Fisiologia, 40* (2), 153-157.

Aston-Jones, G., Rajkowski, J., Kubiak, P., Valentino, R. J., and Shipley, M. T. (1996). Role of the locus coeruleus in emotional activation. *Programme Brain Research, 107*, 379-402.

Ator, N. A., and Griffiths, R. R. (2003). Principles of drug abuse liability assessment in laboratory animals. *Drug Alcohol Dependence, 70* (S3), S55-72.

Bale, T. L., and Vale, W. W. (2004). CRF and CRF receptors: role in stress responsivity and other behaviors. *Annuals Reviews Pharmacology Toxicology, 44*, 525-557.

Banihashemi, L., Rinaman, L. (2006). Noradrenergic inputs to the bed nucleus of the stria terminalis and paraventricular nucleus of the hypothalamus underlie hypothalamic-pituitary-adrenal axis but not hypophagic or conditioned avoidance responses to systemic yohimbine. *Journal of Neuroscience.26* (44), 11442-11453.

Bardo, M. T., and Bevins, R. A. (2000). Conditioned place preference: what does it add to our preclinical understanding of drug reward? *Psychopharmacology, 153* (1), 31-43.

Bardo, M. T., Bowling, S. L., Rowlett, J. K., Manderscheid, P., Buxton, S. T., and Dwoskin, L. P. (1995). Environmental enrichment attenuates locomotor sensitization, but not in vitro dopamine release, induced by amphetamine. *Pharmacology Biochemistry and Behavior, 51* (2-3), 397-405.

Bardo, M. T., Klebaur, J. E., Valone, J. M., and Deaton, C. (2001). Environmental enrichment decreases intravenous self-administration of amphetamine in female and male rats. *Psychopharmacology, 155* (3), 278-284.

Baumans, V. (2005). Environmental enrichment for laboratory rodents and rabbits: requirements of rodents, rabbits, and research. *Institute for Laboratory Animal Reserach Journal, 46* (2), 162-170.

Beardsley, P. M., Howard, J. L., Shelton, K. L., and Carroll, F. I. (2005). Differential effects of the novel kappa opioid receptor antagonist, JDTic, on reinstatement of cocaine-seeking induced by footshock stressors vs cocaine primes and its antidepressant-like effects in rats. *Psychopharmacology, 183* (1), 118-126.

Beardsley, P. M., Pollard, G. T., Howard, J. L., and Carroll, F. I. (2010a). Effectiveness of analogs of the kappa opioid receptor antagonist (3R)-7-hydroxy-N-((1S)-1-{[(3R,4R)-4-(3-hydroxyphenyl)-3,4-dimethyl-1-piperidinyl]methyl}-2-methylpropyl)-1,2,3,4-tetrahydro-3-isoquinolinecarboxamide (JDTic) to reduce U50,488-induced diuresis and stress-induced cocaine reinstatement in rats. *Psychopharmacology, 210* (2), 189-198.

Beardsley, P. M., Shelton, K. L., Hendrick, E., and Johnson, K. W. (2010b). The glial cell modulator and phosphodiesterase inhibitor, AV411 (ibudilast), attenuates prime- and stress-induced methamphetamine relapse. *European Journal Pharmacology, 637* (1-3), 102-108.

Bell, S. M., Stewart, R. B., Thompson, S. C., and Meisch, R. A. (1997). Food-deprivation increases cocaine-induced conditioned place preference and locomotor activity in rats. *Psychopharmacology, 131* (1), 1-8.

Belujon, P., and Grace, A. A. (2011). Hippocampus, amygdala, and stress: interacting systems that affect susceptibility to addiction. *Annals of the New York Academy of Sciences, 1216*, 114-121.

Bijlsma, E. Y., de Jongh, R., Olivier, B., Groenink, L. (2010). Fear-potentiated startle, but not light-enhanced startle, is enhanced by anxiogenic drugs. *Pharmacology Biochemistry and Behavior, 96* (1), 24-31.

Blacktop, J. M., Seubert, C., Baker, D. A., Ferda, N., Lee, G., Graf, E. N., and Mantsch, J.R. (2011). Augmented cocaine seeking in response to stress or CRF delivered into the ventral tegmental area following long-access self-administration is mediated by CRF receptor type 1 but not CRF receptor type 2. *Journal of Neuroscience, 31* (31), 11396-11403.

Bolanos, C. A., Glatt, S. J., and Jackson, D. (1998). Subsensitivity to dopaminergic drugs in periadolescent rats: a behavioral and neurochemical analysis. *Brain Reserch Development, 111* (1), 25-33.

Bongiovanni, M., and See, R. E. (2008). A comparison of the effects of different operant training experiences and dietary restriction on the reinstatement of cocaine-seeking in rats. *Pharmacology Biochemistry and Behavior, 89* (2), 227-233.

Boutrel, B., Kenny, P. J., Specio, S. E., Martin-Fardon, R., Markou, A., Koob, G. F., and de Lecea, L. (2005). Role for hypocretin in mediating stress-induced reinstatement of cocaine-seeking behavior. *Proceedings of the National Academy of Sciences, 102* (52), 19168-19173.

Bowling, S. L., and Bardo, M. T. (1994). Locomotor and rewarding effects of amphetamine in enriched, social, and isolate reared rats. *Pharmacology Biochemistry and Behavior, 48* (2), 459-464.

Bowling, S. L., Rowlett, J. K., and Bardo, M. T. (1993). The effect of environmental enrichment on amphetamine-stimulated locomotor activity, dopamine synthesis and dopamine release. *Neuropharmacology, 32* (9), 885-893.

Boyson, C. O., Miguel, T. T., Quadros, I. M., Debold, J. F., and Miczek, K. A. (2011). Prevention of social stress-escalated cocaine self-administration by CRF-R1 antagonist in the rat VTA. *Psychopharmacology, 218* (1), 257-269.

Brady, K. T., and Sinha, R. (2005). Co-occurring mental and substance use disorders: the neurobiological effects of chronic stress. *American Journal Psychiatry, 162* (8), 1483-1493.

Brady, K. T., Dansky, B. S., Sonne, S. C., and Saladin, M. E. (1998). Posttraumatic stress disorder and cocaine dependence. Order of onset. *American Journal on Addiction, 7* (2), 128-135.

Brake, W. G., Zhang, T. Y., Diorio, J., Meaney, M. J., and Gratton, A. (2004). Influence of early postnatal rearing conditions on mesocorticolimbic dopamine and behavioural responses to psychostimulants and stressors in adult rats. *European Journal Neuroscience, 19* (7), 1863-1874.

Brebner, K., Phelan, R., and Roberts, D. C. (2000). Intra-VTA baclofen attenuates cocaine self-administration on a progressive ratio schedule of reinforcement. *Pharmacology Biochemistry and Behavior, 66* (4), 857-62.

Brebner, K., Froestl, W., and Roberts, D. C. (2002). The GABA(B) antagonist CGP56433A attenuates the effect of baclofen on cocaine but not heroin self-administration in the rat. *Psychopharmacology, 160* (1), 49-55.

Briand, L. A., Vassoler, F. M., Pierce, R. C., Valentino, R. J., and Blendy, J. A. (2010). Ventral tegmental afferents in stress-induced reinstatement: the role of cAMP response element-binding protein. *Journal Neuroscience, 1;30* (48), 16149-16159.

Brown, K. J., and Grunberg, N. E. (1995). Effects of housing on male and female rats: crowding stresses male but calm females. *Physiology Behavior, 58* (6), 1085-1089.

Brown, Z. J., and Erb, S. (2007). Footshock stress reinstates cocaine seeking in rats after extended post-stress delays. *Psychopharmacology, 195* (1), 61-70.

Brown, G., Jackson, A., and Stephens, D. N. (1998). Effects of repeated withdrawal from chronic ethanol on oral self-administration of ethanol on a progressive ratio schedule. *Behavioural Pharmacology, 9* (2), 149-161.

Brown, Z. J., Tribe, E., D'souza, N. A., and Erb, S. (2009). Interaction between noradrenaline and corticotrophin-releasing factor in the reinstatement of cocaine seeking in the rat.*Psychopharmacology, 203* (1), 121-130.

Brown, Z. J., Nobrega, J. N., and Erb, S. (2010). Central injections of noradrenaline induce reinstatement of cocaine seeking and increase c-fos mRNA expression in the extended amygdala. *Behavioural Brain Research, 217* (2), 472-476.

Brown, Z. J., Kupferschmidt , D. A., and Erb, S. (2012). Reinstatement of cocaine seeking in rats by the pharmacological stressors, corticotropin-releasing factor and yohimbine: role for D1/5 dopamine receptors. *Psychopharmacology,* (in press).

Bruchas, M. R., Land, B. B., and Chavkin, C. (2010). The dynorphin/kappa opioid system as a modulator of stress-induced and pro-addictive behaviors. *Brain Research, 1314*, 44-55.

Buffalari, D. M. and See, R. E. (2009). Footshock stress potentiates cue-induced cocaine-seeking in an animal model of relapse. *Physiology and Behavior, 98* (5), 614-617.

Buffalari, D. M., and Grace, A. A. (2009). Chronic cold stress increases excitatory effects of norepinephrine on spontaneous and evoked activity of basolateral amygdala neurons. *International Journal of Neuropsychopharmacology,* 12 (1), 95-107.

Buffalari, D. M., See, R. E. (2011). Inactivation of the bed nucleus of the stria terminalis in an animal model of relapse: effects on conditioned cue-induced reinstatement and its enhancement by yohimbine. *Psychopharmacology, 213* (1), 19-27.

Buffalari, D. M., Baldwin, C. K., Feltenstein, M. W., and See, R. E. (2012). Corticotrophin releasing factor (CRF) induced reinstatement of cocaine seeking in male and female rats. *Physiology and Behavior, 105* (2), 209-214.

Burke, A. R., Watt, M. J., andForster, G. L. (2011). Adolescent social defeat increases adult amphetamine conditioned place preference and alters D2 dopamine receptor expression. *Neuroscience, 197*, 269-279.

Cadoni, C., Solinas, M., Pisanu, A., Zernig, G., Acquas, E., and Di Chiara, G. (2005). Effect of 3,4-methylendioxymethamphetamine (MDMA, "ecstasy") on dopamine transmission in the nucleus accumbens shell and core. *Brain Research, 1055* (1-2), 143-148.

Caggiula, A. R., Donny, E. C., White, A. R., Chaudhri, N., Booth, S., Gharib, M. A., Hoffman, A., Perkins, K. A.,... Sved, A. F. (2002). Environmental stimuli promote the acquisition of nicotine self-administration in rats. *Psychopharmacology, 163* (2), 230-237.

Caine, S. B., and Koob, G. F. (1993). Modulation of cocaine self-administration in the rat through D-3 dopamine receptors. *Science, 260* (5115), 1814-1816.

Calipari, E. S, Ferris, M. J, Melchior, J. R, Bermejo, K., Salahpour, A., Roberts, D. C, and Jones, S. R. (2012).Methylphenidate and cocaine self-administration produce distinct dopamine terminal alterations. *Addiction Biology,* (in press).

Campbell, J., and Spear, L. P. (1999). Effects of early handling on amphetamine-induced locomotor activation and conditioned place preference in the adult rat.*Psycho-pharmacology, 143* (2), 183-189.

Campbell, U. C., and Carroll, M. E. (2001).Effects of ketoconazole on the acquisition of intravenous cocaine self-administration under different feeding conditions in rats.*Psychopharmacology, 154* (3), 311-318.

Campbell, U. C., Thompson, S. S., and Carroll, M. E. (1998). Acquisition of oral phencyclidine (PCP) self-administration in rhesus monkeys: effects of dose and an alternative non-drug reinforcer. *Psychopharmacology, 137* (2), 132-8.

Cannon, W. B. (1935). Stresses and strains of homeostasis. *American Journal Medicine Science, 189*,1-4.

Capriles, N., and Cancela, L. M. (1999). Effect of acute and chronic stress restraint on amphetamine-associated place preference: involvement of dopamine D(1) and D(2) receptors. *European Journal of Pharmacology, 386* (2-3), 127-134.

Capriles, N., Rodaros, D., Sorge, R. E., and Stewart, J. (2003). A role for the prefrontal cortex in stress- and cocaine-induced reinstatement of cocaine seeking in rats. *Psycho-pharmacology, 168* (1-2), 66-74.

Capuron, L., and Miller, A.H. (2011). Immune system to brain signaling: neuropsycho-pharmacological implications. *Pharmacology Therapy, 130* (2), 226-238.

Carey, A. N., Borozny, K., Aldrich, J.V., and McLaughlin, J. P. (2007). Reinstatement of cocaine place-conditioning prevented by the peptide kappa-opioid receptor antagonist arodyn. *European Journal of Pharmacology, 569* (1-2), 84-89.

Carlezon, W. A., and Thomas, M. J. (2009). Biological substrates of reward and aversion: a nucleus accumbens activity hypothesis. *Neuropharmacology, 1*, 122-132.

Carroll, M. E. (1984). Food deprivation produces persistent increases in self-administration behavior during cocaine extinction. *NIDA Research Monographs, 55*, 125-131.

Carroll, M. E. (1985). The role of food deprivation in the maintenance and reinstatement of cocaine-seeking behavior in rats. *Drug Alcohol Dependence, 16* (2), 95-109.

Carroll, M. E., and Lac, S. T. (1997). Acquisition of i.v. amphetamine and cocaine self-administration in rats as a function of dose. *Psychopharmacology, 129* (3), 206-214.

Carroll, M. E., France, C. P., and Meisch, R. A. (1981). Intravenous self-administration of etonitazene, cocaine and phencyclidine in rats during food deprivation and satiation. *The Journal Pharmacology Experimental Therapeutics, 217* (2), 241-247.

Carroll, M. E., Lac, S. T., Walker, M. J., Kragh, R., and Newman, T. (1986). Effects of naltrexone on intravenous cocaine self-administration in rats during food satiation and deprivation. *The Journal Pharmacology Experimental Therapeutics, 238* (1), 1-7.

Carroll, M. E., Anker, J. J., and Perry, J. L. (2009). Modeling risk factors for nicotine and other drug abuse in the preclinical laboratory. *Drug Alcohol Dependence, 104* (S1), S70-78.

Chauvet, C., Lardeux, V., Goldberg, S. R., Jaber, M., and Solinas, M. (2009). Environmental enrichment reduces cocaine seeking and reinstatement induced by cues and stress but not by cocaine. *Neuropsychopharmacology, 34* (13), 2767-278.

Chauvet, C., Lardeux, V., Jaber, M., and Solinas, M. (2011). Brain regions associated with the reversal of cocaine conditioned place preference by environmental enrichment. *Neuroscience, 16;184*, 88-96.

Chevrette, J., Stellar, J.R., Hesse, G.W., and Markou, A. (2002). Both the shell of the nucleus accumbens and the central nucleus of the amygdala support amphetamine self-administration in rats. *Pharmacology Biochemistry and Behavior, 71* (3), 501-7.

Chrousos, G. P., Gold, P. W. (1992). The concepts of stress and stress system disorders.Overview of physical and behavioral homeostasis. *Journal American Medical Association, 267* (9), 1244-1252.

Cleck, J. N., Ecke, L. E., and Blendy, J. A. (2008). Endocrine and gene expression changes following forced swim stress exposure during cocaine abstinence in mice. *Psychopharmacology, 201* (1), 15-28.

Collins, R. J., Weeks, J. R., Cooper, M. M., Good, P. I., and Russell RR. (1984). Prediction of abuse liability of drugs using IV self-administration by rats. *Psychopharmacology, 82* (1-2), 6-13.

Collins, S. L., and Izenwasser, S. (2002). Cocaine differentially alters behavior and neurochemistry in periadolescent versus adult rats. *Brain Research Development, 138* (1), 27-34.

Comer, S. D., Lac, S. T., Wyvell, C. L., Curtis, L. K., and Carroll, M. E. (1995). Food deprivation affects extinction and reinstatement of responding in rats. *Psychopharmacology, 121* (2), 150-157.

Conrad, K. L., McCutcheon, J. E., Cotterly, L. M., Ford, K. A., Beales, M., and Marinelli, M. (2010). Persistent increases in cocaine-seeking behavior after acute exposure to cold swim stress. *Biology Psychiatry, 68* (3), 303-305.

Costa-Pinto, F. A., and Palermo-Neto, J. (2010). Neuroimmune interactions in stress. *Neuroimmunomodulation, 17* (3), 196-199.

Covington, H. E., and Miczek, K. A. (2001). Repeated social-defeat stress, cocaine or morphine.Effects on behavioral sensitization and intravenous cocaine self-administration "binges". *Psychopharmacology, 158* (4), 388-398.

Covington, H. E.and Miczek, K. A. (2005). Intense cocaine self-administration after episodic social defeat stress, but not after aggressive behavior: dissociation from corticosterone activation. *Psychopharmacology, 183* (3), 331-340.

Covington, H. E., Kikusui, T., Goodhue, J., Nikulina, E. M., Hammer, R. P.and Miczek, K. A. (2005). Brief social defeat stress: long lasting effects on cocaine taking during a binge and zif268 mRNA expression in the amygdala and prefrontal cortex. *Neuropsychopharmacology, 30* (2), 310-321.

Covington, H. E., Tropea, T. F., Rajadhyaksha, A. M., Kosofsky, B. E., and Miczek, K. A. (2008). NMDA receptors in the rat VTA: a critical site for social stress to intensify cocaine taking. *Psychopharmacology, 197* (2), 203-216.

Cruz, F. C., Marin, M. T., and Planeta, C. S. (2008). The reinstatement of amphetamine-induced place preference is long-lasting and related to decreased expression of AMPA receptors in the nucleus accumbens. *Neuroscience, 151* (2), 313-319.

Cruz, F. C., Leão, R. M., Marin, M. T., and Planeta, C. S. (2010). Stress-induced reinstatement of amphetamine-conditioned place preference and changes in tyrosine hydroxylase in the nucleus accumbens in adolescent rats. *Pharmacology Biochemistry and Behavior, 96* (2), 160-165.

Cruz, F. C., Quadros, I. M., Hogenelst, K., Planeta, C. S., and Miczek, K. A. (2011). Social defeat stress in rats: escalation of cocaine and "speedball" binge self-administration, but not heroin. *Psychopharmacology, 215* (1), 165-175.

Dai, S., Corrigall, W. A., Coen, K. M., and Kalant, H. (1989). Heroin self-administration by rats: influence of dose and physical dependence. *Pharmacology Biochemistry and Behavior, 32* (4), 1009-10015.

Dalley, J. W, and Everitt, B. J. (2009). Dopamine receptors in the learning, memory and drug reward circuitry. *Seminars in Cell and Developmental Biology, 20* (4), 403-10.

Daza-Losada, M., Ribeiro Do Couto, B., Manzanedo, C., Aguilar, M. A., Rodríguez-Arias, M., and Miñarro, J. (2007). Rewarding effects and reinstatement of MDMA-induced CPP in adolescent mice. *Neuropsychopharmacology, 32* (8), 1750-1759.

de Guglielmo, G., Cippitelli, A., Somaini, L., Gerra, G., Li, H., Stopponi, S.,...Ciccocioppo, R. (2012). Pregabalin reduces cocaine self-administration and relapse to cocaine seeking in the rat. *Addiction Biology*, (in press).

de Oliveira, A. R., Reimer, A. E., and Brandão, M. L. (2006). Dopamine D2 receptor mechanisms in the expression of conditioned fear.*Pharmacology Biochemistry and Behavior, 84* (1), 102-111.

de Olmos, J. S., and Heimer, L. (1999). The concepts of the ventral striatopallidal system and extended amygdala. *Annals of the New York Academy of Sciences, 29;877*, 1-32.

De Vries, T. J., Schoffelmeer, A. N., Binnekade, R., Mulder, A. H., and Vanderschuren, L. J. (1998). Drug-induced reinstatement of heroin- and cocaine-seeking behaviour following long-term extinction is associated with expression of behavioural sensitization. *European Journal Neuroscience, 10* (11), 3565-3571.

De Vry, J., Donselaar, I., and Van Ree, J. M. (1989). Food deprivation and acquisition of intravenous cocaine self-administration in rats: effect of naltrexone and haloperidol. *The Journal of Pharmacology and Experimental Therapeutics, 251* (2), 735-740.

del Rosario Capriles, N., and Cancela, L. M. (2002). Motivational effects mu- and kappa-opioid agonists following acute and chronic restraint stress: involvement of dopamine D(1) and D(2) receptors. *Behavioural Brain Research, 132* (2), 159-169.

del Rosario, C. N., Pacchioni, A. M., and Cancela, L. M. (2002). Influence of acute or repeated restraint stress on morphine-induced locomotion: involvement of dopamine, opioid and glutamate receptors. *Behavioural Brain Research, 134* (1-2), 229-238.

Depoortere, R. Y., Li, D. H., Lane, J. D., Emmett-Oglesby, M. W. (1993). Parameters of self-administration of cocaine in rats under a progressive-ratio schedule. *Pharmacology Biochemistry and Behavior, 45* (3), 539-548.

Der-Avakian, A., and Markou, A. (2010). Neonatal maternal separation exacerbates the reward-enhancing effect of acute amphetamine administration and the anhedonic effect of repeated social defeat in adult rats. *Neuroscience, 170* (4), 1189-1198.

Der-Avakian, A.,Bland, S. T., Rozeske, R. R., Tamblyn, J. P., Hutchinson, M. R., Watkins, L. R., andMaier, S. F. (2007). The effects of a single exposure to uncontrollable stress on the subsequent conditioned place preference responses to oxycodone, cocaine, and ethanol in rats. *Psychopharmacology, 191* (4), 909-917.

Deroche, V., Marinelli, M., Maccari, S., Le Moal, M., Simon, H., and Piazza, P. V. (1995).Stress-induced sensitization and glucocorticoids. I. Sensitization of dopamine-dependent locomotor effects of amphetamine and morphine depends on stress-induced corticosterone secretion. *Journal of Neuroscience, 15* (11), 7181-8.

Deroche, V., Piazza, P. V., Casolini, P., Maccari, S., Le Moal, M., and Simon, H. (1992). Stress-induced sensitization to amphetamine and morphine psychomotor effects depend on stress-induced corticosterone secretion. *Brain Research, 598* (1-2), 343-348.

Deroche-Gamonet, V., Belin, D., and Piazza, P. V. (2004). Evidence for addiction-like behavior in the rat. *Science*, 305 (5686), 1014-1017.

Di Chiara, G., and Imperato A. (1988). Drugs abused by humans preferentially increase synaptic dopamine concentrations in the mesolimbic system of freely moving rats. *Proceeding of National Academy of Science, 85* (14), 5274-8.

Di Chiara, G., Bassareo, V., Fenu, S., De Luca, M.A, Spina, L., Cadoni ,C., Acquas, E., Carboni, E., Valentini, V., ... Lecca, D. (2004). Dopamine and drug addiction: the nucleus accumbens shell connection. *Neuropharmacology, 1*, 227-241.

Di Ciano, P., and Everitt, B. J. (2003). The GABA(B) receptor agonist baclofen attenuates cocaine- and heroin-seeking behavior by rats. *Neuropsychopharmacology,* 28 (3), 510-8.

Ding, Y., Kang, L., and Li, M. L. (2005). Enhanced cocaine self-administration in adult rats with adolescent isolation experience. *Pharmacology Biochemistry and Behavior, 82*, 673–677.

Donny, E. C., Caggiula, A. R., Rose, C., Jacobs, K. S., Mielke, M. M., and Sved, A. F. (2000). Differential effects of response-contingent and response-independent nicotine in rats. *European Journal of Pharmacology, 402* (3), 231-240.

El Rawas, R., Thiriet, N., Lardeux, V., Jaber,M.,and Solinas, M. (2009). Environmental enrichment decreases the rewarding but not the activating effects of heroin. *Psychopharmacology, 203* (3), 561-570.

El Rawas, R., Thiriet, N., Nader, J., Lardeux, V., Jaber,M., and Solinas, M. (2011). Early exposure to environmental enrichment alters the expression of genes of the endocannabinoid system. *Brain Research, 1390*, 80-89.

El Rawas, R., Klement, S., Kummer, K. K., Fritz, M., Dechant, G., Saria, A., and Zernig G. (2012). Brain regions associated with the acquisition of conditioned place preference for cocaine vs. social interaction. *Frontiers in Behavioral Neuroscience, 6*, 63.

Eliava, M., Yilmazer-Hanke, D., and Asan, E. (2003). Interrelations between monoaminergic afferents and corticotropin-releasing factor-immunoreactive neurons in the rat central amygdaloid nucleus: ultrastructural evidence for dopaminergic control of amygdaloid stress systems. *Histochemistry and Cell Biology, 120* (3), 183-197.

Ellenbroek, B. A., van der Kam, E. L., van der Elst, M. C., and Cools, A. R. (2005). Individual differences in drug dependence in rats: the role of genetic factors and life events. *European Journal of Pharmacology, 526* (1-3), 251-258.

Enoch, M.A. (2006). Genetic and environmental influences on the development of alcoholism: resilience vs. risk. *Annals of the New York Academy of Sciences, 1094*, 193-201.

Enoch, M. A., Hodgkinson, C. A., Yuan, Q., Shen, P. H., Goldman, D., and Roy, A. (2010). The influence of GABRA2, childhood trauma, and their interaction on alcohol, heroin, and cocaine dependence. *Biological Psychiatry, 67* (1), 20-27.

Epstein, D. H., Preston, K. L., Stewart, J., and Shaham, Y. (2006). Toward a model of drug relapse: an assessment of the validity of the reinstatement procedure. *Psychopharmacology, 189* (1), 1-16.

Erb, S. (2010). Evaluation of the relationship between anxiety during withdrawal and stress-induced reinstatement of cocaine seeking. *Progress in Neuro-Psychopharmacology and Biological Psychiatry, 34* (5), 798-807.

Erb, S., and Stewart, J. (1999).A role for the bed nucleus of the stria terminalis, but not the amygdala, in the effects of corticotropin-releasing factor on stress-induced reinstatement of cocaine seeking. *Journal of Neuroscience, 19* (20), RC35.

Erb, S., Shaham, Y., and Stewart, J. (1996). Stress reinstates cocaine-seeking behavior after prolonged extinction and a drug-free period. *Psychopharmacology, 128* (4), 408-412.

Erb, S., Hitchcott, P. K., Rajabi, H., Mueller, D., Shaham, Y., and Stewart, J. (2000). Alpha-2 adrenergic receptor agonists block stress-induced reinstatement of cocaine seeking. *Neuropsychopharmacology, 23* (2), 138-50.

Erb, S., Salmaso, N., Rodaros, D., and Stewart, J. (2001).A role for the CRF-containing pathway from central nucleus of the amygdala to bed nucleus of the stria terminalis in the stress-induced reinstatement of cocaine seeking in rats. *Psychopharmacology, 158* (4), 360-365.

Erb, S., Lopak, V., and Smith, C. (2004). Cocaine pre-exposure produces a sensitized and context-specific c-fos mRNA response to footshock stress in the central nucleus of the amygdala. *Neuroscience, 129* (3), 719-725.

Erb, S., Kayyali, H., and Romero, K. (2006). A study of the lasting effects of cocaine pre-exposure on anxiety-like behaviors under baseline conditions and in response to central injections of corticotropin-releasing factor. *Pharmacology Biochemistry and Behavior, 85* (1), 206-213.

Ettenberg, A., MacConell, L. A., and Geist, T. D. (1996). Effects of haloperidol in a response-reinstatement model of heroin relapse. *Psychopharmacology, 124* (3), 205-210.

Everitt, B. J., and Wolf, M. E. (2002). Psychomotor stimulant addiction: a neural systems perspective. *Journal Neuroscience, 22* (9), 3312-3320.

Everitt, B. J., Belin, D., Economidou, D., Pelloux, Y., Dalley, J. W., and Robbins, T. W. (2008). Review. Neural mechanisms underlying the vulnerability to develop compulsive drug-seeking habits and addiction. *Philosophical Transactions of the Royal Society of London B Biological Sciences, 363* (1507), 3125-3135.

Faure, J., Stein, D. J., and Daniels, W. (2009). Maternal separation fails to render animals more susceptible to methamphetamine-induced conditioned place preference. *Metabolic Brain Disease, 24* (4), 541-559.

Feltenstein, M. W., and See, R. E. (2006). Potentiation of cue-induced reinstatement of cocaine-seeking in rats by the anxiogenic drug yohimbine. *Behavioural Brain Research. 1;174* (1), 1-8.

Feltenstein, M. W., Henderson, A. R., and See, R. E. (2011). Enhancement of cue-induced reinstatement of cocaine-seeking in rats by yohimbine: sex differences and the role of the estrous cycle. *Psychopharmacology, 216* (1), 53-62.

Figueroa-Guzman, Y., Mueller, C., Vranjkovic, O., Wisniewski, S., Yang, Z., Li, S. J., Bohr, C., Graf, E. N., Baker, D. A.,... Mantsch, J. R. (2011). Oral administration of levo-tetrahydropalmatine attenuates reinstatement of extinguished cocaine seeking by cocaine, stress or drug-associated cues in rats. *Drug Alcohol Dependence, 116* (1-3), 72-79.

File, S. E. (1986). Aversive and appetitive properties of anxiogenic and anxiolytic agents. *Behavioural Brain Research, 21* (3), 189-194.

Fish, E. W., Faccidomo, S., and Miczek, K. A. (1999). Aggression heightened by alcohol or social instigation in mice: reduction by the 5-HT(1B) receptor agonist CP-94,253. *Psychopharmacology, 146* (4), 391-399.

Forray, M. I., Bustos, G., and Gysling, K. (1997). Regulation of norepinephrine release from the rat bed nucleus of the stria terminalis: in vivo microdialysis studies. *Journal of Neuroscience Research 50* (6), 1040-1046.

Franken, I. H., Booij, J., and van den Brink, W. (2005). The role of dopamine in human addiction: from reward to motivated attention. *European Journal of Pharmacology, 526* (1-3), 199-206.

Fritz, M., El Rawas, R., Salti, A., Klement, S., Bardo, M. T., Kemmler, G., Dechant, G., Saria, A., ... Zernig, G. (2011a). Reversal of cocaine-conditioned place preference and mesocorticolimbic Zif268 expression by social interaction in rats. *Addict Biology, 16* (2), 273-284.

Fritz, M., Klement, S., El Rawas, R., Saria, A., and Zernig, G. (2011b). Sigma1 receptor antagonist BD1047 enhances reversal of conditioned place preference from cocaine to social interaction. *Pharmacology, 87* (1-2), 45-48.

Fritz, M., El Rawas, R., Klement, S., Kummer, K., Mayr, M. J., Eggart, V., Salti, A., Bardo, M. T., Saria, A., ... Zernig, G. (2011c). Differential effects of accumbens core vs. shell lesions in a rat concurrent conditioned place preference paradigm for cocaine vs. social interaction. *Plos One, 6* (10), e26761.

Fuchs, E., Czéh, B., and Flügge, G. (2004). Examining novel concepts of the pathophysiology of depression in the chronic psychosocial stress paradigm in tree shrews. *Behavioural Pharmacology, 15* (5-6), 315-325.

Fuchs, R. A, Feltenstein, M. W, and See, R. E. (2006a). The role of the basolateral amygdala in stimulus-reward memory and extinction memory consolidation and in subsequent conditioned cued reinstatement of cocaine seeking. *European Journal Neuroscience, 23* (10), 2809-2813.

Fuchs, R. A., Branham, R. K., and See, R. E. (2006b). Different neural substrates mediate cocaine seeking after abstinence versus extinction training: a critical role for the dorsolateral caudate-putamen. *Journal Neuroscience, 26* (13), 3584-3588.

Fuchs, R. A., Ramirez, D. R., and Bell, G. H. (2008). Nucleus accumbens shell and core involvement in drug context-induced reinstatement of cocaine seeking in rats. *Psychopharmacology, 200* (4), 545-556.

Galvez, R., Mesches, M. H, McGaugh, J. L. (1996). Norepinephrine release in the amygdala in response to footshock stimulation.*Neurobiology of Learning and Memory, 66* (3), 253-257.

Garcia, A. S., Barrera, G., Burke, T. F., Ma, S., Hensler, J. G., and Morilak, D. A. (2004). Autoreceptor-mediated inhibition of norepinephrine release in rat medial prefrontal cortex is maintained after chronic desipramine treatment. *Journal of Neurochemistry, 91* (3), 683-693.

Gerber, G. J., and Stretch, R. (1975). Drug-induced reinstatement of extinguished self-administration behavior in monkeys. *Pharmacology Biochemistry and Behavior, 3* (6), 1055-1061.

Glick, S. D., Hinds, P. A., and Carlson, J. N. (1987). Food deprivation and stimulant self-administration in rats: differences between cocaine and d-amphetamine. *Psychopharmacology, 91* (3), 372-374.

Goddard, B., and Leri, F. (2006). Reinstatement of conditioned reinforcing properties of cocaine-conditioned stimuli. *Pharmacology Biochemistry and Behavior, 83* (4), 540-546.

Goeders, N. E. (2002a). Stress and cocaine addiction. *The Journal of Pharmacology and Experimental Therapeutics, 301* (3), 785-789.

Goeders, N. E. (2002b). The HPA axis and cocaine reinforcement. *Psychoneuro-endocrinology, 27* (1-2), 13-33.

Goeders, N. E. (2003). The impact of stress on addiction. *European Neuropsycho-pharmacology, 13* (6), 435-441.

Goeders, N. E., and Guerin, G. F. (1994). Non-contingent electric footshock facilitates the acquisition of intravenous cocaine self-administration in rats. *Psychopharmacology, 114* (1), 63-70.

Goeders, N. E., and Guerin, G. F. (1996). Role of corticosterone in intravenous cocaine self-administration in rats. *Neuroendocrinology, 64* (5), 337-348.

Graf, E. N., Hoks, M. A., Baumgardner, J., Sierra, J., Vranjkovic, O., Bohr, C., Baker, D. A., and Mantsch, J. R. (2011). Adrenal activity during repeated long-access cocaine self-administration is required for later CRF-Induced and CRF-dependent stressor-induced reinstatement in rats. *Neuropsychopharmacology, 36* (7), 1444-1454.

Green, T. A., Gehrke, B. J., and Bardo, M. T. (2002). Environmental enrichment decreases intravenous amphetamine self-administration in rats: dose-response functions for fixed- and progressive-ratio schedules. *Psychopharmacology, 162* (4), 373-378.

Green, T. A., Alibhai, I. N., Roybal, C. N., Winstanley, C. A., Theobald, D. E., Birnbaum, S. G., Graham, A. R., Unterberg, S., Graham, D. L., Vialou, V., Bass, C. E., Terwilliger, E. F., Bardo, M.T., ... Nestler, E. J. (2010). Environmental enrichment produces a behavioral phenotype mediated by low cyclic adenosine monophosphate response element binding (CREB) activity in the nucleus accumbens. *Biology Psychiatry, 67* (1), 28-35.

Grimm, J. W., Lu, L., Hayashi, T., Hope, B. T, Su, T. P, and Shaham, Y. (2003). Time-dependent increases in brain-derived neurotrophic factor protein levels within the mesolimbic dopamine system after withdrawal from cocaine: implications for incubation of cocaine craving. *Journal of Neuroscience, 23* (3), 742-747.

Grimwood, S., Lu, Y., Schmidt, A. W., Vanase-Frawley, M. A., Sawant-Basak, A., Miller, E., and Verhoest, P. R. (2011). Pharmacological characterization of 2-methyl-N-((2'-(pyrrolidin-1-ylsulfonyl)biphenyl-4-yl)methyl)propan-1-amine (PF-04455242), a high-affinity antagonist selective for κ-opioid receptors. *The Journal of Pharmacology and Experimental Therapeutics, 339* (2), 555-566.

Gysling, K. (2012). Relevance of both type-1 and type-2 corticotropin releasing factor receptors in stress-induced relapse to cocaine seeking behaviour. *Biochemical Pharmacology, 83* (1), 1-5.

Halbout, B., Quarta, D., Valerio, E., Heidbreder, C. A., and Hutcheson, D. M. (2011). The GABA-B positive modulator GS39783 decreases psychostimulant conditioned-reinforcement and conditioned-reward. *Addiction Biology, 16* (3), 416-427.

Hall, F. S., Wilkinson, L. S., Humby, T., Inglis, W., Kendall, D. A., Marsden, C. A, and Robbins T. W. (1998). Isolation rearing in rats: pre- and postsynaptic changes in striatal dopaminergic systems. *Pharmacology Biochemistry and Behavior, 59* (4), 859-872.

Haney, M., Maccari, S., Le Moal, M., Simon, H., and Piazza, P. V. (1995). Social stress increases the acquisition of cocaine self-administration in male and female rats. *Brain Research, 698* (1-2), 46-52.

Harris, A. P., Holmes, M. C., de Kloet, E. R., Chapman, K. E., and Seckl, J. R. (2012). Mineralocorticoid and glucocorticoid receptor balance in control of HPA axis and behaviour. *Psychoneuroendocrinology*, (in press).

Hasue, R. H., and Shammah-Lagnado, S. J. (2002). Origin of the dopaminergic innervation of the central extended amygdala and accumbens shell: a combined retrograde tracing and immunohistochemical study in the rat. *Journal of Comparative Neurology, 454* (1), 15-33.

Hays, S. L.,McPherson, R. J., Juul, S. E., Wallace, G., Schindler, A. G., Chavkin, C., and Gleason, C. A. (2012). Long-term effects of neonatal stress on adult conditioned place preference (CPP) and hippocampal neurogenesis. *Behavioural Brain Research, 227* (1), 7-11.

Herman, J. P., McKlveen, J. M., Solomon, M. B., Carvalho-Netto, E., and Myers, B. (2012). Neural regulation of the stress response: glucocorticoid feedback mechanisms. *Brazilian Journal of Medical and Biological Research, 45* (4), 292-298.

Higgins S. T. (1997). The influence of alternative reinforcers on cocaine use and abuse: a brief review. *Pharmacology Biochemistry and Behavior, 57* (3), 419-427.

Highfield, D., Clements, A., Shalev, U., McDonald, R., Featherstone, R., Stewart, J., and Shaham, Y. (2000). Involvement of the medial septum in stress-induced relapse to heroin seeking in rats. *European Journal of Neuroscience, 12* (5), 1705-1713.

Highfield, D.A., Mead, A.N., Grimm, J.W., Rocha, B.A.,and Shaham, Y. (2002). Reinstatement of cocaine seeking in 129X1/SvJ mice: effects of cocaine priming, cocaine cues and food deprivation. *Psychopharmacology, 161* (4), 417-424.

Hodos, W. (1961). Progressive ratio as a measure of reward strength. Science, 29;134 (3483), 943-944.

Hooks, M. S, Jones, G. H., Smith, A. D., Neill, D. B, and Justice, J. B. (1991). Response to novelty predicts the locomotor and nucleus accumbens dopamine response to cocaine. *Synapse, 9* (2), 121-128.

Hooks, M. S, Colvin, A. C., Juncos, J. L., and Justice, J. B. (1992). Individual differences in basal and cocaine-stimulated extracellular dopamine in the nucleus accumbens using quantitative microdialysis. *Brain Research, 587* (2), 306-312.

Howes, S. R., Dalley, J. W., Morrison, C. H., Robbins, T. W., and Everitt, B. J. (2000). Leftward shift in the acquisition of cocaine self-administration in isolation-reared rats: relationship to extracellular levels of dopamine, serotonin and glutamate in the nucleus accumbens and amygdala-striatal FOS expression. *Psychopharmacology, 151* (1), 55-63.

Hubbard, J. W., Pfister, S. L., Biediger, A. M., Herzig, T. C., Keeton, T. K. (1988). The pharmacokinetic properties of yohimbine in the conscious rat. *Naunyn Schmiedeberg´s Archives of Pharmacology, 337* (5), 583-587.

Hucklebridge, F. H., and Nowell, N. W. (1974). Plasma catecholamine response to physical and psychological aspects of fighting in mice. *Physiology and Behavior, 13* (1), 35-40.

Hunt, W. A., Barnett, L. W., and Branch, L. G. (1971). Relapse rates in addiction programs. *Journal Clinical Psychology, 27* (4), 455-456.

Hutchinson, E., Avery, A., and Vandewoude, S. (2005). Environmental enrichment for laboratory rodents. *Institute for Laboratory Animal Research Journal, 46* (2), 148-161.

Hyytiä, P., Bäckström, P., and Liljequist, S. (1999). Site-specific NMDA receptor antagonists produce differential effects on cocaine self-administration in rats. *European Journal Pharmacology, 378* (1), 9-16.

Jessor, R., and Jessor, S. (1980). A social-psychological framework for studying drug use. NIDA *Research Monograph, 30*, 102-109.

Johnston, A. L., File, S. E. (1989). Yohimbine's anxiogenic action: evidence for noradrenergic and dopaminergic sites. *Pharmacology Biochemistry and Behavior, 32* (1), 151-156.

Kabbaj, M., Norton, C. S., Kollack-Walker, S., Watson, S. J., Robinson, T. E., and Akil, H. (2001). Social defeat alters the acquisition of cocaine self-administration in rats: role of individual differences in cocaine-taking behavior. *Psychopharmacology, 158* (4), 382-387.

Kabbaj, M., Isgor, C., Watson, S. J., and Akil, H. (2002). Stress during adolescence alters behavioral sensitization to amphetamine. *Neuroscience, 113* (2), 395-400.

Kalivas, P. W., and Volkow, N. D. (2005). The neural basis of addiction: a pathology of motivation and choice. *American Journal of Psychiatry, 162* (8), 1403-1413.

Kalivas, P. W., Volkow, N., and Seamans, J. (2005). Unmanageable motivation in addiction: a pathology in prefrontal-accumbens glutamate transmission. *Neuron, 45* (5), 647-650.

Keller, R. W., Maisonneuve, I. M., Nuccio, D. M., Carlson, J. N., and Glick, S. D. (1994). Effects of prenatal cocaine exposure on the nigrostriatal dopamine system: an in vivo microdialysis study in the rat. *Brain Research, 634* (2), 266-274.

Kelley, A. E., and Berridge, K. C. (2002). The neuroscience of natural rewards: relevance to addictive drugs. *Journal of Neuroscience, 22* (9), 3306-3311.

Khoshbouei, H., Cecchi, M., Dove, S., Javors, M., and Morilak, D. A. (2002). Behavioral reactivity to stress: amplification of stress-induced noradrenergic activation elicits a galanin-mediated anxiolytic effect in central amygdala. *Pharmacology Biochemistry and Behavior, 71* (3), 407-417.

Kikusui, T., Faccidomo, S., and Miczek, K. A. (2005). Repeated maternal separation: differences in cocaine-induced behavioral sensitization in adult male and female mice. *Psychopharmacology, 178* (2-3), 202-210.

Kippin, T. E., Szumlinski, K. K., Kapasova, Z., Rezner, B., and See, R. E. (2008). Prenatal stress enhances responsiveness to cocaine. *Neuropsychopharmacology, 33* (4), 769-782.

Kiyatkin, E, A. (1993). Cocaine enhances the changes in extracellular dopamine in nucleus accumbens associated with reinforcing stimuli: a high-speed chronoamperometric study in freely moving rats. *European Journal of Neuroscience, 5* (3), 284-291.

Knackstedt, L. A., and Kalivas, P. W. (2007). Extended access to cocaine self-administration enhances drug-primed reinstatement but not behavioral sensitization. ? The *Journal of Pharmacology and Experimental Therapeutics, 322* (3), 1103-1109.

Koob, G. F. (2008). A role for brain stress systems in addiction. *Neuron, 59* (1), 11-34.

Koob, G. F. (2009). Brain stress systems in the amygdala and addiction.*Brain Research,* 1293, 61-75.

Koob, G. F. (2010). The role of CRF and CRF-related peptides in the dark side of addiction. *Brain Research, 1314*, 3-14.

Koob, G., and Kreek, M. J. (2007). Stress, dysregulation of drug reward pathways, and the transition to drug dependence, *American Journal of Psychiatry, 164* (8), 1149-1159.

Koob, G. F., and Volkow, N. D. (2010). Neurocircuitry of addiction. *Neuropsychopharmacology, 35* (1), 217-238.

Kosten, T. A., Miserendino, M. J., and Kehoe, P. (2000). Enhanced acquisition of cocaine self-administration in adult rats with neonatal isolation stress experience. *Brain Research,* 875 (1-2), 44-50.

Kozorovitskiy, Y., and Gould, E. (2004). Dominance hierarchy influences adult neurogenesis in the dentate gyrus. *Journal of Neuroscience, 24* (30), 6755-6759.

Kreibich, A. S., and Blendy, J. A. (2004). cAMP response element-binding protein is required for stress but not cocaine-induced reinstatement. *The Journal of Neuroscience*, *24* (30), 6686-6692.

Kreibich, A. S., Briand, L., Cleck, J. N., Ecke, L., Rice, K. C., and Blendy, J. A. (2009). Stress-induced potentiation of cocaine reward: a role for CRF R1 and CREB. *Neuropsychopharmacology, 34* (12), 2609-2617.

Kupfermann, I. (1991). Functional studies of cotransmission. *Physiology Reviews, 71* (3), 683-732.

Kupferschmidt, D. A., Tribe, E., andErb, S.(2009).Effects of repeated yohimbine on the extinction and reinstatement of cocaine seeking. *Pharmacology, Biochemistry and Behavior, 91* (3), 473-480.

Kupferschmidt, D. A., Brown, Z. J., and Erb, S. (2011a).A procedure for studying the footshock-induced reinstatement of cocaine seeking in laboratory rats. *Journal of Visualized Experiments, 6*, 47.

Kupferschmidt, D. A., Lovejoy, D. A., Rotzinger, S., and Erb, S. (2011b). Teneurin C-terminal associated peptide-1 blocks the effects of corticotropin-releasing factor on reinstatement of cocaine seeking and on cocaine-induced behavioural sensitization. *British Journal of Pharmacology, 162* (3), 574-583.

Kupferschmidt, D. A., Klas, P. G., and Erb, S. (2012). Cannabinoid CB1 receptors mediate the effects of corticotropin-releasing factor on the reinstatement of cocaine seeking and expression of cocaine-induced behavioural sensitization. *British Journal of Pharmacology, 167* (1), 196-206.

Land, B. B., Bruchas, M. R., Schattauer, S., Giardino, W. J., Aita, M., Messinger, D., Hnasko ,T. S., Palmiter, R. D.,... Chavkin, C. (2009). Activation of the kappa opioid receptor in the dorsal raphe nucleus mediates the aversive effects of stress and reinstates drug seeking. *Proceedings of the National Academy of Science USA, 106* (45), 19168-19173.

Lanier, L. P., and Isaacson, R. L. (1977). Early developmental changes in the locomotor response to amphetamine and their relation to hippocampal function. *Brain Research, 126* (3), 567-575.

Laviola, G., Adriani, W., Morley-Fletcher, S., and Terranova, M. L. (2002). Peculiar response of adolescent mice to acute and chronic stress and to amphetamine: evidence of sex differences. *Behavioural Brain Research, 130* (1-2), 117-125.

Laviola, G., Hannan, A. J., Macrì, S., Solinas, M., and Jaber, M. (2008). Effects of enriched environment on animal models of neurodegenerative diseases and psychiatric disorders. *Neurobiology of Disease, 31* (2), 159-168.

Lê, A. D., Harding, S., Juzytsch, W., Funk, D., and Shaham, Y. (2005). Role of alpha-2 adrenoceptors in stress-induced reinstatement of alcohol seeking and alcohol self-administration in rats. *Psychopharmacology, 179* (2), 366-373.

LeDoux, J. E. (2000). Emotion circuits in the brain. *Annual Reviews Neuroscience, 23*, 155-184.

Lee, A. L., Ogle, W. O., and Sapolsky, R. M. (2002). Stress and depression: possible links to neuron death in the hippocampus. *Bipolar Disorder, 4* (2), 117-128.

Lee, B., Tiefenbacher, S., Platt, D. M., Spealman, R. D. (2004). Pharmacological blockade of alpha2-adrenoceptors induces reinstatement of cocaine-seeking behavior in squirrel monkeys. *Neuropsychopharmacology, 29* (4), 686-693.

Leri, F., Flores, J., Rodaros, D., and Stewart, J. (2002).Blockade of stress-induced but not cocaine-induced reinstatement by infusion of noradrenergic antagonists into the bed nucleus of the stria terminalis or the central nucleus of the amygdala. *Journal Neuroscience, 1;22* (13), 5713-5718.

Leyton, M., and Stewart, J. (1990). Preexposure to foot-shock sensitizes the locomotor response to subsequent systemic morphine and intra-nucleus accumbens amphetamine. *Pharmacology Biochemistry and Behavior, 37* (2), 303-310.

Li, S. M., Ren, Y. H., and Zheng, J. W. (2002). Effect of 7-nitroindazole on drug-priming reinstatement of D-methamphetamine-induced conditioned place preference. *European Journal of Pharmacology, 443* (1-3), 205-206.

Llorente-Berzal, A., Manzanedo, C., Daza-Losada, M., Valero, M., López-Gallardo M., Aguilar, M. A., Rodríguez-Arias, M., Miñarro, J.,... Viveros, M. P.Sex-dependent effects of early maternal deprivation on MDMA-induced conditioned place preference in adolescent rats.Possible neurochemical correlates. *Toxicology* 2012 Dec 14. doi:pii: S0300-483X(12)00422-2.

Logrip, M.L., Koob, G.F., and Zorrilla, E.P. (2011). Role of corticotropin-releasing factor in drug addiction: potential for pharmacological intervention. *CNS Drugs, 25* (4), 271-287.

Logrip, M. L., Zorrilla, E. P., and Koob, G. F. (2012). Stress modulation of drug self-administration: implications for addiction comorbidity with post-traumatic stress disorder. *Neuropharmacology, 62* (2), 552-564.

Lu, L., Liu, D., and Ceng, X. (2001). Corticotropin-releasing factor receptor type 1 mediates stress-induced relapse to cocaine-conditioned place preference in rats. *European Journal of Pharmacology, 415* (2-3), 203-208.

Lu, L., Zhang, B., Liu, Z., and Zhang, Z. (2002). Reactivation of cocaine conditioned place preference induced by stress is reversed by cholecystokinin-B receptors antagonist in rats. Brain Research, 954 (1), 132-140.

Lu, L., Shepard, J. D., Hall, F. S., and Shaham, Y. (2003). Effect of environmental stressors on opiate and psychostimulant reinforcement, reinstatement and discrimination in rats: a review. *Neuroscience and Biobehavioral Reviews, 27* (5), 457-491.

Lynch, W. J., Kushner, M. G., Rawleigh, J.M., Fiszdon, J., and Carroll, M. E. (1999). The effects of restraint stress on voluntary ethanol consumption in rats. *Experimental and Clinical Psychopharmacology, 7* (4), 318-323.

Lynch, W. J., Mangini, L. D., and Taylor, J. R. (2005). Neonatal isolation stress potentiates cocaine seeking behavior in adult male and female rats. *Neuropsychopharmacology, 30* (2), 322-329.

Macedo, C. E., Martinez, R. C., Albrechet-Souza, L., Molina, V. A., and Brandão, M. L. (2007). 5-HT2- and D1-mechanisms of the basolateral nucleus of the amygdala enhance conditioned fear and impair unconditioned fear. *Behavioral Brain Research, 177* (1), 100-108.

Mahler, S. V., Moorman, D. E., Feltenstein, M. W., Cox, B. M., Ogburn, K. B., Bachar, M., McGonigal, J. T., Ghee, S. M., ... See ,R. E. (2012). A rodent "self-report" measure of methamphetamine craving?Rat ultrasonic vocalizations during methamphetamine self-administration, extinction, and reinstatement. *Behavioural Brain Research, 236C*, 78-89.

Maldonado, C., Rodríguez-Arias, M., Castillo, A., Aguilar, M. A., and Miñarro, J. (2007). Effect of memantine and CNQX in the acquisition, expression and reinstatement of cocaine-induced conditioned place preference. *Progress in Neuropsychopharmacology and Biology Psychiatry, 31* (4), 932-9.

Mantsch, J. R., and Katz, E. S. (2007). Elevation of glucocorticoids is necessary but not sufficient for the escalation of cocaine self-administration by chronic electric footshock stress in rats. *Neuropsychopharmacology, 32* (2), 367-376.

Mantsch, J. R., Baker, D. A., Francis, D. M., Katz, E. S., Hoks, M. A., and Serge, J. P. (2008). Stressor- and corticotropin releasing factor-induced reinstatement and active stress-related behavioral responses are augmented following long-access cocaine self-administration by rats. *Psychopharmacology, 195* (4), 591-603.

Mantsch, J. R., Weyer, A., Vranjkovic, O., Beyer, C. E., Baker, D. A, and Caretta, H. (2010). Involvement of noradrenergic neurotransmission in the stress- but not cocaine-induced reinstatement of extinguished cocaine-induced conditioned place preference in mice: role for β-2 adrenergic receptors. *Neuropsychopharmacology, 35* (11), 2165-2178.

Manzanedo, C., Aguilar, M. A., Rodríguez-Arias, M., and Miñarro, J. (2001). Effects of dopamine antagonists with different receptor blockade profiles on morphine-induced place preference in male mice. *Behavioural Brain Research, 121* (1-2), 189-197.

Manzanedo, C., Rodríguez-Arias, M., Daza-Losada, M., Maldonado, C., Aguilar, M. A., Miñarro, J. (2010). Effect of the CB1 cannabinoid agonist WIN 55212-2 on the acquisition and reinstatement of MDMA-induced conditioned place preference in mice. *Behavioral and Brain Functions, 6*, 19.

Marinelli, M., and Piazza, P. V. (2002). Interaction between glucocorticoid hormones, stress and psychostimulant drugs. *European Journal of Neuroscience, 16* (3), 387-394.

Marinelli, M., and White, F. J. (2000). Enhanced vulnerability to cocaine self-administration is associated with elevated impulse activity of midbrain dopamine neurons. *Journal of Neuroscience, 20* (23), 8876-8885.

Marinelli, P. W., Quirion, R., and Gianoulakis, C. (2004). An in vivo profile of beta-endorphin release in the arcuate nucleus and nucleus accumbens following exposure to stress or alcohol. *Neuroscience, 127* (3), 777-784.

Markou, A., and Koob, G. F. (1999). Bromocriptine reverses the elevation in intracranial self-stimulation thresholds observed in a rat model of cocaine withdrawal. *Neuropsychopharmacology, 7* (3), 213-224.

Markou, A., Weiss, F., Gold, L. H., Caine, S. B., Schulteis, G., and Koob, G. F. (1993). Animal models of drug craving. *Psychopharmacology, 112* (2-3), 163-182.

Martin-Fardon, R., and Weiss, F. (2012). (-)-2-oxa-4-aminobicylco[3.1.0]hexane-4,6-dicarboxylic acid (LY379268) and 3-[(2-methyl-1,3-thiazol-4-yl)ethynyl]piperidine (MTEP) similarly attenuate stress-induced reinstatement of cocaine seeking. *Addiction Biology, 17* (3), 557-564.

Martini, M., and Valverde, O. (2012). A single episode of maternal deprivation impairs the motivation for cocaine in adolescent mice. *Psychopharmacology, 219* (1), 149-158.

Mathews, I. Z., Mills, R. G., and McCormick, C. M. (2008). Chronic social stress in adolescence influenced both amphetamine conditioned place preference and locomotor sensitization. *Developmental Psychobiology, 50* (5), 451-459.

Matthews, K., Robbins, T. W., Everitt, B. J., and Caine, S. B. (1999). Repeated neonatal maternal separation alters intravenous cocaine self-administration in adult rats. *Psychopharmacology, 141* (2), 123-134.

McBride, W. J., Murphy, J. M., and Ikemoto, S. (1999). Localization of brain reinforcement mechanisms: intracranial self-administration and intracranial place-conditioning studies. *Behaviour Brain Research, 101* (2), 129-52.

McEwen, B. S. (2003). Mood disorders and allostatic load. *Biological Psychiatry, 54* (3), 200-207.

McFarland, K., and Ettenberg, A. (1997). Reinstatement of drug-seeking behavior produced by heroin-predictive environmental stimuli. *Psychopharmacology, 131* (1), 86-92.

McFarland, K., Davidge, S. B., Lapish, C. C., and Kalivas, P. W. (2004). Limbic and motor circuitry underlying footshock-induced reinstatement of cocaine-seeking behavior. *Journal of Neuroscience, 24* (7), 1551-1560.

McLaughlin, J. P., Marton-Popovici, M., and Chavkin, C. (2003). Kappa opioid receptor antagonism and prodynorphin gene disruption block stress-induced behavioral responses. *Journal of Neuroscience, 23* (13), 5674-5683.

McLaughlin, J. P., Land, B. B., Li, S., Pintar, J. E., and Chavkin, C. (2006a). Prior activation of kappa opioid receptors by U50,488 mimics repeated forced swim stress to potentiate cocaine place preference conditioning. *Neuropsychopharmacology, 31* (4), 787-794.

McLaughlin, J. P., Li, S., Valdez, J., Chavkin, T.A., and Chavkin, C. (2006b). Social defeat stress-induced behavioral responses are mediated by the endogenous kappa opioid system. *Neuropsychopharmacology, 31* (6), 1241-1248.

Miczek, K. A., and Mutschler, N. H. (1996). Activational effects of social stress on IV cocaine self-administration in rats. *Psychopharmacology, 128* (3), 256-264.

Miczek, K. A., Thompson, M. L., and Shuster, L. (1982). Opioid-like analgesia in defeated mice. *Science, 215* (4539), 1520-1522.

Miczek, K. A., Mutschler, N. H., van Erp, A. M., Blank, A. D., and McInerney, S. C. (1999a). d-amphetamine "cue" generalizes to social defeat stress: behavioral sensitization and attenuated accumbens dopamine. *Psychopharmacology, 147* (2), 190-199.

Miczek, K. A., Nikulina, E., Kream, R. M., Carter, G., and Espejo, E. F. (1999b). Behavioral sensitization to cocaine after a brief social defeat stress: c-fos expression in the PAG. *Psychopharmacology, 141* (3), 225-234.

Miczek, K. A., Covington, H. E., Nikulina, E. M. and Hammer, R. P. (2004). Aggression and defeat: persistent effects on cocaine self-administration and gene expression in peptidergic and aminergic mesocorticolimbic circuits. *Neuroscience and Biobehavioral Reviews, 27* (8), 787-802.

Miczek, K. A., Yap, J. J., and Covington, H. E. (2008). Social stress, therapeutics and drug abuse: preclinical models of escalated and depressed intake. *Pharmacology and Therapeutics, 120* (2), 102-128.

Miczek, K. A., Nikulina, E. M., Shimamoto, A., and Covington, H. E. (2011). Escalated or suppressed cocaine reward, tegmental BDNF, and accumbal dopamine caused by episodic versus continuous social stress in rats. *Journal of Neuroscience, 31* (27), 9848-9857.

Millan, M. J., Newman-Tancredi, A., Audinot, V., Cussac, D., Lejeune, F., Nicolas, J. P., Cogé, F., Galizzi, J. P., Boutin, J. A. , Rivet, J. M. , Dekeyne, A., ... Gobert, A. (2000). Agonist and antagonist actions of yohimbine as compared to fluparoxan at alpha(2)-adrenergic receptors (AR)s, serotonin (5-HT)(1A), 5-HT(1B), 5-HT(1D) and dopamine D(2) and D(3) receptors. Significance for the modulation of frontocortical monoaminergic transmission and depressive states. *Synapse, 35 (2),* 79-95.

Miller, L. L., Ward, S. J., and Dykstra, L. A. (2008). Chronic unpredictable stress enhances cocaine-conditioned place preference in type 1 cannabinoid receptor knockout mice. *Behavioural Pharmacology, 19* (5-6), 575-581.

Moffett, M. C., and Goeders, N. E. (2005). Neither non-contingent electric footshock nor administered corticosterone facilitate the acquisition of methamphetamine self-administration. *Pharmacology Biochemistry and Behavior, 80* (2), 333-339.

Moffett, M. C., Harley, J., Francis, D., Sanghani, S. P., Davis, W. I., and Kuhar, M. J. (2006). Maternal separation and handling affects cocaine self-administration in both the treated pups as adults and the dams. *The Journal Pharmacology and Experimental Therapeutics, 317* (3), 1210-1218.

Moffett, M. C., Vicentic, A., Kozel, M., Plotsky, P., Francis, D. D., and Kuhar, M. J. (2007). Maternal separation alters drug intake patterns in adulthood in rats. *Biochemical Pharmacology, 73* (3), 321-30.

Moore, R. Y., and Bloom, F. E. (1979). Central catecholamine neuron systems: anatomy and physiology of the norepinephrine and epinephrine systems. *Annual Reviews of Neuroscience, 2*, 113-168.

Mora, F., Segovia, G., and del Arco, A. (2007). Aging, plasticity and environmental enrichment: structural changes and neurotransmitter dynamics in several areas of the brain. *Brain Research Reviews, 55* (1), 78-88.

Moser, P., Wolinsky, T., Duxon, M., and Porsolt, R. D. (2011). How good are current approaches to nonclinical evaluation of abuse and dependence? *Journal Pharmacology Experimental Therapeutics, 336* (3), 588-595.

Nader, J., Claudia, C., Rawas, R. E., Favot, L., Jaber, M., Thiriet, N., and Solinas, M. (2012). Loss of environmental enrichment increases vulnerability to cocaine addiction. *Neuropsychopharmacology, 37* (7), 1579-87.

Nawata, Y., Kitaichi, K., and Yamamoto, T. (2012). Increases of CRF in the amygdala are responsible for reinstatement of methamphetamine-seeking behavior induced by footshock. *Pharmacology Biochemistry and Behavior, 101* (2), 297-302.

Nestler, E. J. (2004). Molecular mechanisms of drug addiction. *Neuropharmacology, 1,* 24-32.

Nikulina, E. M., Marchand, J. E., Kream, R. M., and Miczek, K. A. (1998). Behavioral sensitization to cocaine after a brief social stress is accompanied by changes in fos expression in the murine brainstem. *Brain Research, 9;810* (1-2), 200-210.

Nikulina, E. M., Covington, H. E., Ganschow, L., Hammer, R. P. and Miczek, K. A. (2004). Long-term behavioral and neuronal cross-sensitization to amphetamine induced by repeated brief social defeat stress: Fos in the ventral tegmental area and amygdala. *Neuroscience, 123* (4), 857-865.

Nikulina, E. M., Miczek, K. A., and Hammer, R. P. (2005). Prolonged effects of repeated social defeat stress on mRNA expression and function of mu-opioid receptors in the ventral tegmental area of rats. *Neuropsychopharmacology, 30* (6), 1096-1103.

Nithianantharajah, J., and Hannan, A. J. (2006). Enriched environments, experience-dependent plasticity and disorders of the nervous system. *Nature Reviews Neuroscience, 7* (9), 697-709.

O'Brien, C. P. (1997). A range of research-based pharmacotherapies for Addiction. *Science, 278*, 66–70.

O'Connor, E. C., Chapman, K., Butler, P., and Mead, A. N. (2011). The predictive validity of the rat-self administration model for abuse liability. *Neuroscience and Biobehavioural Reviews, 35*, 912-938.

Oleson, E. B., and Roberts, D. C. (2008). Behavioral economic assessment of price and cocaine consumption following self-administration histories that produce escalation of either final ratios or intake. *Neuropsychopharmacology, 34* (3), 796-804.

Osborne, M. P., and Olive, M. F. (2008). A role for mGluR5 receptors in intravenous methamphetamine self-administration. *Annals of the New York Academy of Sciences USA, 1139*, 206-211.

Owens, M. J., and Nemeroff, C. B. (1991). Physiology and pharmacology of corticotropin-releasing factor. *Pharmacology Reviews, 43* (4), 425-473.

Pacchioni, A. M., Gioino, G., Assis, A., and Cancela, L. M. (2002). A single exposure to restraint stress induces behavioral and neurochemical sensitization to stimulating effects of amphetamine: involvement of NMDA receptors. *Annals of the New York Academy of Sciences USA, 965*, 233-246.

Pacchioni, A. M., Cador, M., Bregonzio, C., and Cancela, L. M. (2007). A glutamate-dopamine interaction in the persistent enhanced response to amphetamine in nucleus accumbens core but not shell following a single restraint stress. *Neuropsychopharmacology, 32* (3), 682-692.

Panksepp, J. B., and Lahvis, G. P. (2007). Social reward among juvenile mice. *Genes, Brain and Behavior, 6* (7), 661-671.

Pañeda, C., Huitron-Resendiz, S., Frago, L. M., Chowen, J. A., Picetti, R., de Lecea, L., and Roberts, A. J. (2009). Neuropeptide S reinstates cocaine-seeking behavior and increases locomotor activity through corticotropin-releasing factor receptor 1 in mice. *Journal of Neuroscience, 29* (13), 4155-4161.

Papasava, M., and Singer, G. (1985). Self-administration of low-dose cocaine by rats at reduced and recovered body weight. *Psychopharmacology, 85* (4), 419-425.

Parker, L. A., and McDonald, R. V. (2000). Reinstatement of both a conditioned place preference and a conditioned place aversion with drug primes. *Pharmacology Biochemistry and Behavior, 66* (3), 559-561.

Paterson, N. E., and Markou A. (2003). Increased motivation for self-administered cocaine after escalated cocaine intake. *Neuroreport, 14* (17), 2229-2232.

Paterson, N. E., and Markou, A. (2004). Prolonged nicotine dependence associated with extended access to nicotine self-administration in rats. *Psychopharmacology, 173* (1-2), 64-72.

Pavlov, I. P. (1927). *Conditioned Reflexes*. Oxford University Press, Oxford.

Pezze, M. A., and Feldon, J. (2004). Mesolimbic dopaminergic pathways in fear conditioning. *Progress in Neurobiology, 74* (5), 301-20.

Phelix, C. F., Liposits, Z., and Paull, W. K. (1994). Catecholamine-CRF synaptic interaction in a septal bed nucleus: afferents of neurons in the bed nucleus of the stria terminalis. *Brain Research Bulletin, 33* (1), 109-119.

Piazza, P. V., and Le Moal, M. (1997). Glucocorticoids as a biological substrate of reward: physiological and pathophysiological implications. *Brain Research, 25* (3), 359-372.

Piazza, P. V., and Le Moal, M. (1998).The role of stress in drug self-administration. *Trends in Pharmacological Sciences, 19* (2), 67-74.

Piazza, P. V., Deminière, J. M., Le Moal, M., and Simon, H. (1989). Factors that predict individual vulnerability to amphetamine self-administration. *Science, 245* (4925), 1511-1513.

Piazza, P. V., Deminiere, J. M., Le Moal, M., and Simon, H. (1990). Stress- and pharmacologically-induced behavioral sensitization increases vulnerability to acquisition of amphetamine self-administration. *Brain Research, 23;514* (1), 22-26.

Qi, J., Yang, J. Y., Wang, F., Zhao, Y. N., Song, M., and Wu, C. F. (2009).Effects of oxytocin on methamphetamine-induced conditioned place preference and the possible role of glutamatergic neurotransmission in the medial prefrontal cortex of mice in reinstatement. *Neuropharmacology, 56* (5), 856-865.

Quadros, I. M., and Miczek, K. A. (2009). Two modes of intense cocaine bingeing: increased persistence after social defeat stress and increased rate of intake due to extended access conditions in rats. *Psychopharmacology, 206* (1), 109-120.

Rampon, C., Jiang, C. H., Dong, H., Tang, Y. P., Lockhart, D. J., Schultz, P. G., Tsien, J. Z.,... Hu, Y. (2000). Effects of environmental enrichment on gene expression in the brain. *Proceedings of the National Academy of Science, 97* (23), 12880-12884.

Ramsey, N. F., and Van Ree, J. M. (1993). Emotional but not physical stress enhances intravenous cocaine self-administration in drug-naive rats. *Brain Research, 608* (2), 216-222.

Razzoli, M., Carboni, L., Guidi, A., Gerrard, P., and Arban, R. (2007). Social defeat-induced contextual conditioning differentially imprints behavioral and adrenal reactivity: a time-course study in the rat. *Physiology and Behavior, 92* (4), 734-740.

Redila, V. A., and Chavkin, C. (2008). Stress-induced reinstatement of cocaine seeking is mediated by the kappa opioid system. *Psychopharmacology, 200* (1), 59-70.

Reis, F. L., Masson, S., de Oliveira, A. R., and Brandão, M. L. (2004). Dopaminergic mechanisms in the conditioned and unconditioned fear as assessed by the two-way avoidance and light switch-off tests. *Pharmacology Biochemistry and Behavior, 79* (2), 359-365.

Ribeiro Do Couto, B., Aguilar, M. A., Manzanedo, C., Rodríguez-Arias, M., Armario, A., and Miñarro, J. (2006). Social stress is as effective as physical stress in reinstating morphine-induced place preference in mice. *Psychopharmacology, 185* (4), 459-470.

Ribeiro Do Couto, B., Aguilar, M. A., Lluch, J., Rodríguez-Arias, M., and Miñarro, J. (2009). Social experiences affect reinstatement of cocaine-induced place preference in mice. *Psychopharmacology, 207* (3), 485-498.

Richtand, N. M., Ahlbrand, R., Horn, P.S., Chambers, B., Davis, J., and Benoit, S. (2012). Effects of prenatal immune activation and peri-adolescent stress on amphetamine-induced conditioned place preference in the rat. *Psychopharmacology, 222 (*2), 313-324.

Ripley, T. L., and Stephens, D. N. (2011). Critical thoughts on current rodent models for evaluating potential treatments of alcohol addiction and withdrawal. *British Journal of Pharmacology, 164* (4), 1335-1356.

Robbins, T. W. (1978). The acquisition of responding with conditioned reinforcement: effects of pipradrol, methylphenidate, d-amphetamine, and nomifensine. *Psychopharmacology, 58* (1), 79-87.

Roberts, D. C., Andrews, M. M., and Vickers, G. J. (1996). Baclofen attenuates the reinforcing effects of cocaine in rats. *Neuropsychopharmacology, 15* (4), 417-423.

Rodaros, D., Caruana, D. A., Amir, S., and Stewart, J. (2007). Corticotropin-releasing factor projections from limbic forebrain and paraventricular nucleus of the hypothalamus to the region of the ventral tegmental area. *Neuroscience, 150* (1), 8-13.

Rodriguez-Alarcón, G., Canales, J. J., and Salvador, A. (2007). Rewarding effects of 3,4-methylenedioxymethamphetamine ("Ecstasy") in dominant and subordinate OF-1 mice in the place preference conditioning paradigm. *Progress in Neuropsychopharmacology and Biological Psychiatry, 31* (1), 191-199.

Rodríguez-Arias, M., Miñarro, J., Aguilar, M. A., Pinazo, J., and Simón, V. M. (1998). Effects of risperidone and SCH 23390 on isolation-induced aggression in male mice. *European Neuropsychopharmacology, 8* (2), 95-103.

Rodríguez-Arias, M., Castillo, A., Daza-Losada, M., Aguilar, M. A., and Miñarro, J. (2009). Effects of extended cocaine conditioning in the reinstatement of place preference. *Physiology and Behavior, 96* (4-5), 620-630.

Rosenkranz, J. A., and Grace, A. A. (2002). Cellular mechanisms of infralimbic and prelimbic prefrontal cortical inhibition and dopaminergic modulation of basolateral amygdala neurons in vivo. *Journal of Neuroscience, 22* (1), 324-337.

Rosenkranz, J. A., and Grace, A. A. (2002). Dopamine-mediated modulation of odour-evoked amygdala potentials during pavlovian conditioning. *Nature, 417* (6886), 282-287.

Rosenkranz, J. A., Moore, H., and Grace, A. A. (2003). The prefrontal cortex regulates lateral amygdala neuronal plasticity and responses to previously conditioned stimuli. *Journal of Neuroscience, 23* (35), 11054-11064.

Rosenzweig, M. R., and Bennett, E. L. (1996). Psychobiology of plasticity: effects of training and experience on brain and behavior. *Behavioral Brain Research, 78* (1), 57-65.

Rosenzweig, M. R., Bennett, E. L., Hebert, M., and Morimoto, H. (1978). Social grouping cannot account for cerebral effects of enriched environments. *Brain Research, 153* (3), 563-576.

Ross, N. C., Reilley, K. J., Murray, T. F., Aldrich, J. V., and McLaughlin, J. P. (2012). Novel opioid cyclic tetrapeptides: Trp isomers of CJ-15,208 exhibit distinct opioid receptor agonism and short-acting κ opioid receptor antagonism. *British Journal of Pharmacology, 165* (4b), 1097-1108.

Rougé-Pont, F., Piazza, P. V., Kharouby, M., Le Moal, M., and Simon, H. (1993). Higher and longer stress-induced increase in dopamine concentrations in the nucleus accumbens of animals predisposed to amphetamine self-administration. A microdialysis study. *Brain Research, 602* (1), 169-174.

Rougé-Pont, F., Marinelli, M., Le Moal, M., Simon, H., and Piazza, P. V. (1995).Stress-induced sensitization and glucocorticoids. II. Sensitization of the increase in extracellular dopamine induced by cocaine depends on stress-induced corticosterone secretion. *Journal of Neuroscience, 15* (11), 7189-7195.

Sakanaka, M., Shibasaki, T., and Lederis, K. (1986).Distribution and efferent projections of corticotropin-releasing factor-like immunoreactivity in the rat amygdaloid complex.*Brain Research, 382* (2), 213-38.

Sanchez, C. J., and Sorg, B. A. (2001). Conditioned fear stimuli reinstate cocaine-induced conditioned place preference. *Brain Research, 908* (1), 86-92.

Sanchez, C. J., Bailie, T. M., Wu, W. R., Li, N., and Sorg, B. A. (2003). Manipulation of dopamine d1-like receptor activation in the rat medial prefrontal cortex alters stress- and cocaine-induced reinstatement of conditioned place preference behavior. *Neuroscience, 119* (2), 497-505.

Sanchis-Segura, C., and Spanagel, R. (2006). Behavioural assessment of drug reinforcement and addictive features in rodents: an overview. *Addiction Biology, 11* (1), 2-38.

Sapolsky, R. M., Uno, H., Rebert, C. S., and Finch, C. E. (1990). Hippocampal damage associated with prolonged glucocorticoid exposure in primates. *Journal of Neuroscience, 10* (9), 2897-902.

Sapolsky, R. M. (2000). Glucocorticoids and hippocampal atrophy in neuropsychiatric disorders. *Archives of General Psychiatry, 57* (10), 925-35.

Sarnyai, Z., Shaham, Y., and Heinrichs, S. C. (2001). The role of corticotropin-releasing factor in drug addiction. *Pharmacology Reviews, 53* (2), 209-243.

Scatton, B., Zivkovic, B., and Dedek, J. (1980). Antidopaminergic properties of yohimbine. The *Journal Pharmacology and Experimental Therapeutics, 215* (2):494-499.

Schenk, S., Lacelle, G., Gorman, K,,and Amit, Z. (1987). Cocaine self-administration in rats influenced by environmental conditions: implications for the etiology of drug abuse. *Neuroscience Letters, 81* (1-2), 227-231.

Schindler, A. G., Li, S., and Chavkin, C. (2010). Behavioral stress may increase the rewarding valence of cocaine-associated cues through a dynorphin/kappa-opioid receptor-mediated mechanism without affecting associative learning or memory retrieval mechanisms. *Neuropsychopharmacology, 35* (9), 1932-1942.

Schramm-Sapyta, N. L., Walker, Q. D., Caster, J. M., Levin, E. D., and Kuhn, C. M. (2009). Are adolescents more vulnerable to drug addiction than adults? Evidence from animal models. *Psychopharmacology, 206* (1), 1-21.

See, R. E. (2005). Neural substrates of cocaine-cue associations that trigger relapse. *European Journal Pharmacology, 526* (1-3), 140-146.

See, R. E., Fuchs, R. A., Ledford, C. C., and McLaughlin, J. (2003). Drug addiction, relapse, and the amygdala. *Annals of the New York Academy of Sciences, 985*, 294-307.

See, R. E., Waters, R. P. (2010). Pharmacologically-induced stress: a cross-species probe for translational research in drug addiction and relapse. *American Journal of Translational Research, 3* (1), 81-89.

Segovia, G., del Arco, A., and Mora, F. (2009). Environmental enrichment, prefrontal cortex, stress, and aging of the brain. *Journal of Neural Transmission, 116* (8), 1007-1016.

Self, D. W. (1998). Neural substrates of drug craving and relapse in drug addiction.*Annals of Internal Medicine, 30* (4), 379-389.

Selye, H. (1956). *The Stress of Life*. McGraw-Hill Book Company, Inc. New York.

Selye, H. (1975). *Stress Without Distress*. Penguin Group. Canada.

Sgoifo, A., Koolhaas, J., Alleva, E., Musso, E., and Parmigiani, S. (2001). Social stress. Acute and long-term effects on physiology and behavior. *Physiology and Behavior, 73* (3), 253-254.

Shaham, Y., and Stewart, J. (1994). Exposure to mild stress enhances the reinforcing efficacy of intravenous heroin self-administration in rats. *Psychopharmacology, 114* (3), 523-527.

Shaham, Y., Rajabi, H., and Stewart, J. (1996). Relapse to heroin-seeking in rats under opioid maintenance: the effects of stress, heroin priming, and withdrawal. *Journal of Neuroscience, 16* (5), 1957-1963.

Shaham, Y., Puddicombe, J., and Stewart, J. (1997). Sexually arousing events and relapse to heroin-seeking in sexually experienced male rats. *Physiology and Behavior, 61* (2), 337-341.

Shaham, Y., Erb, S., Leung, S., Buczek, Y., and Stewart, J. (1998). CP-154,526, a selective, non-peptide antagonist of the corticotropin-releasing factor1 receptor attenuates stress-induced relapse to drug seeking in cocaine- and heroin-trained rats. *Psychopharmacology, 137* (2), 184-190.

Shaham, Y., Erb, S., and Stewart, J. (2000). Stress-induced relapse to heroin and cocaine seeking in rats. *Brain Research Reviews, 33* (1), 13-33.

Shaham, Y., Shalev, U., Lu, L., De Wit, H., and Stewart J. (2003). The reinstatement model of drug relapse: history, methodology and major findings. *Psychopharmacology, 168* (1-2), 3-20.

Shalev, U., Highfield, D., Yap, J., and Shaham, Y. (2000). Y. Stress and relapse to drug seeking in rats: studies on the generality of the effect. *Psychopharmacology, 150* (3), 337-346.

Shalev, U., Grimm, J. W., and Shaham, Y. (2002). Neurobiology of relapse to heroin and cocaine seeking: a review. *Pharmacological Reviews, 54* (1), 1-42.

Shalev, U., Marinelli, M., Baumann, M. H., Piazza, P. V., and Shaham, Y. (2003).The role of corticosterone in food deprivation-induced reinstatement of cocaine seeking in the rat. *Psychopharmacology, 168* (1-2), 170-176.

Shalev, U., Erb, S., and Shaham, Y. (2010). Role of CRF and other neuropeptides in stress-induced reinstatement of drug seeking. *Brain Research, 1314*, 15-28.

Shepard, J. D., Bossert, J. M., Liu, S. Y., and Shaham, Y. (2004). The anxiogenic drug yohimbine reinstates methamphetamine seeking in a rat model of drug relapse. *Biological Psychiatry, 55* (11), 1082-1089.

Shippenberg, T. S., and Koob, G. F. (2002). Recent advances in animal models of drug addiction and alcoholism. In K. L. Davis, D. Charney, J. T. Coyle, C. Nemeroff (Eds.), Neuropsychopharmacology: the fifth generation of progress. (pp. 1381–1397). Philadelphia, PA: Lippincott Williams and Wilkins.

Shoaib, M., Schindler, C. W., and Goldberg, S. R. (1997). Nicotine self-administration in rats: strain and nicotine pre-exposure effects on acquisition. *Psychopharmacology, 129* (1), 35-43.

Shoaib, M., Swanner, L. S., Beyer, C. E., Goldberg, S. R., and Schindler, C. W. (1998). The GABAB agonist baclofen modifies cocaine self-administration in rats. *Behavioral Pharmacology, 9* (3), 195-206.

Sinha, R. (2001). How does stress increase risk of drug abuse and relapse? *Psychopharmacology, 158* (4), 343-359.

Sinha, R. (2007). The role of stress in addiction relapse. *Current Psychiatry Reports, 9* (5), 388-395.

Sinha, R. (2008). Chronic stress, drug use, and vulnerability to addiction. *Annals of the New York Academy of Sciences, 1141,* 105-130.

Sinha, R. (2011). New findings on biological factors predicting addiction relapse vulnerability. *Current Psychiatry Reports, 13* (5), 398-405.

Sinha, R., Garcia, M., Paliwal, P., Kreek, M. J., and Rounsaville, B. J. (2006). Stress-induced cocaine craving and hypothalamic-pituitary-adrenal responses are predictive of cocaine relapse outcomes. *Archives of General Psychiatry, 63* (3), 324-331.

Sinha, R., Shaham, Y., and Heilig, M. (2011). Translational and reverse translational research on the role of stress in drug craving and relapse. *Psychopharmacology, 218* (1), 69-82.

Smith, R. J., and Aston-Jones, G. (2008). Noradrenergic transmission in the extended amygdala: role in increased drug-seeking and relapse during protracted drug abstinence. *Brain Structure and Function, 213* (1-2), 43-61.

Smith, J. K., Neill, J. C., and Costall, B. (1997). Post-weaning housing conditions influence the behavioural effects of cocaine and d-amphetamine. *Psychopharmacology, 131* (1), 23-33.

Smoothy, R., Brain, P. F., Berry, M. S., and Haug, M. (1986). Alcohol and social behaviour in group-housed female mice. *Physiology and Behavior, 37* (5), 689-694.

Solinas, M., Chauvet, C., Thiriet, N., El Rawas, R., and Jaber, M. (2008). Reversal of cocaine addiction by environmental enrichment. *Proceedings of the National Academy of Sciences, 105* (44), 17145-17150.

Solinas, M., Thiriet, N., El Rawas, R., Lardeux,V., and Jaber, M. (2009). Environmental enrichment during early stages of life reduces the behavioral, neurochemical, and molecular effects of cocaine. *Neuropsychopharmacology, 34* (5), 1102-1111.

Solinas, M., Thiriet, N., Chauvet, C., and Jaber, M. (2010). Prevention and treatment of drug addiction by environmental enrichment. *Progress in Neurobiology, 92* (4), 572-592.

Sorge, R. E., and Stewart, J. (2005). The contribution of drug history and time since termination of drug taking to footshock stress-induced cocaine seeking in rats. *Psychopharmacology, 183* (2), 210-217.

Sorge, R. E., Rajabi, H., and Stewart, J. (2005). Rats maintained chronically on buprenorphine show reduced heroin and cocaine seeking in tests of extinction and drug-induced reinstatement. *Neuropsychopharmacology, 30* (9), 1681-1692.

Soria, G., Barbano, M. F., Maldonado, R., and Valverde, O. (2008). A reliable method to study cue-, priming-, and stress-induced reinstatement of cocaine self-administration in mice. *Psychopharmacology*, 199 (4), 593-603.

Southwick, S. M., Morgan, C. A., Charney, D. S., andHigh, J. R. (1999). Yohimbine use in a natural setting: effects on posttraumatic stress disorder. *Biological Psychiatry, 46* (3), 442-444.

Stairs, D. J., and Bardo, M. T. (2009). Neurobehavioral effects of environmental enrichment and drug abuse vulnerability. *Pharmacology Biochemistry and Behavior, 92* (3), 377-382.

Stairs, D. J., Klein, E. D., and Bardo, M. T. (2006). Effects of environmental enrichment on extinction and reinstatement of amphetamine self-administration and sucrose-maintained responding. *Behavior Pharmacology, 17* (7), 597-604.

Stalnaker, T. A., Takahashi, Y., Roesch, M. R., and Schoenbaum, G. (2009). Neural substrates of cognitive inflexibility after chronic cocaine exposure. *Neuropharmacology, 1*, 63-72.

Stewart, J. (2000). Pathways to relapse: the neurobiology of drug- and stress-induced relapse to drug-taking. *Journal of Psychiatry & Neuroscience, 25* (2), 125-136.

Stöhr, T., Almeida, O. F., Landgraf, R., Shippenberg, T. S, Holsboer, F., and Spanagel, R. (1999). Stress- and corticosteroid-induced modulation of the locomotor response to morphine in rats. *Behavioural Brain Research, 103* (1), 85-93.

Stratakis, C. A, and Chrousos, G. P. (1995). Neuroendocrinology and pathophysiology of the stress system. *Annals of the New York Academy of Sciences, 29*, 771, 1-18.

Stuber, G. D., Evans, S. B., Higgins, M. S., Pu, Y., and Figlewicz, D. P. (2002). Food restriction modulates amphetamine-conditioned place preference and nucleus accumbens dopamine release in the rat. *Synapse, 46* (2), 83-90.

Sun, W. (2011). Dopamine neurons in the ventral tegmental area: drug-induced synaptic plasticity and its role in relapse to drug-seeking behavior. *Current Drug Abuse, 4* (4), 270-85.

Swadi, H. (1999). Individual risk factors for adolescent substance use. *Drug Alcohol Dependence, 55* (3), 209-224.

Tabakoff, B., and Hoffman, P. L. (2000). Animal models in alcohol research. *Alcohol Research Health, 24* (2), 77-84.

Thiel, K. J., Okun, A. C., and Neisewander, J. L. (2008). Social reward-conditioned place preference: a model revealing an interaction between cocaine and social context rewards in rats. *Drug and Alcohol Dependence, 96* (3), 202-212.

Thiel, K. J., Sanabria, F., Pentkowski, N. S., and Neisewander, J. L. (2009). Anti-craving effects of environmental enrichment. *International Journal of Neuropsychopharmacology, 12* (9), 1151-11516.

Thiriet, N., Gennequin, B., Lardeux ,V., Chauvet, C., Decressac, M., Janet, T., Jaber, M., ... Solinas, M. (2011). Environmental enrichment does not reduce the rewarding and neurotoxic effects of methamphetamine. *Neurotoxicity Research, 19* (1), 172-182.

Tidey, J. W., and Miczek, K. A. (1997). Acquisition of cocaine self-administration after social stress: role of accumbens dopamine. *Psychopharmacology, 130* (3), 203-212.

Titomanlio, F., Manzanedo, C., Rodríguez-Arias, M., Mattioli, L., Perfumi, M., Miñarro, J., and Aguilar, M. A. Effects of Rhodiola rosea on cocaine-induced hyperactivity and conditioned place preference. Phytomedicine (submitted).

Tjurmina, O. A., Goldstein, D. S., Palkovits, M., and Kopin, I. J. (1999). Alpha2-adrenoceptor-mediated restraint of norepinephrine synthesis, release, and turnover during immobilization in rats. *Brain Research, 826* (2), 243-252.

Tornatzky, W., and Miczek, K. A. (2000). Cocaine self-administration "binges": transition from behavioral and autonomic regulation toward homeostatic dysregulation in rats. *Psychopharmacology, 148* (3), 289-298.

Tornatzky, W., andMiczek, K. A. (1993).Long-term impairment of autonomic circadian rhythms after brief intermittent social stress.*Physiology and Behavior, 53* (5), 983-993.

Triffleman, E. G., Marmar, C. R., Delucchi, K. L., and Ronfeldt, H. (1995). Childhood trauma and posttraumatic stress disorder in substance abuse inpatients. *Journal of Nervous Mental Disease,* 183 (3), 172-176.

Trzcińska, M., Bergh, J., DeLeon, K., Stellar, J. R., and Melloni, R. H. (2002). Social stress does not alter the expression of sensitization to cocaine. *Physiology Behavior, 76* (4-5), 457-463.

Turnbull, A. V., and Rivier, C. (1997). Corticotropin-releasing factor (CRF) and endocrine responses to stress: CRF receptors, binding protein, and related peptides. *Proceedings of the Society for Experimental Biology and Medicine*, 215 (1), 1-10.

Tzschentke, T. M. (1998). Measuring reward with the conditioned place preference paradigm: a comprehensive review of drug effects, recent progress and new issues. *Progress in Neurobiology, 56* (6), 613-672.

Tzschentke, T. M. (2007). Measuring reward with the conditioned place preference (CPP) paradigm: update of the last decade. *Addiction Biology, 12* (3-4), 227-462.

Ungless, M. A., Argilli, E., and Bonci, A. (2010). Effects of stress and aversion on dopamine neurons: implications for addiction. *Neuroscience Biobehavior Reviews, 35* (2), 151-156.

Valdez, G. R., Platt, D. M., Rowlett, J. K., Rüedi-Bettschen, D., and Spealman, R. D. (2007). Kappa agonist-induced reinstatement of cocaine seeking in squirrel monkeys: a role for opioid and stress-related mechanisms. *The Journal of Pharmacology and Experimental Therapeutics, 323* (2), 525-533.

Van den Oever, M. C, Spijker, S, Smit, A. B, andDe Vries, T. J. (2010).Prefrontal cortex plasticity mechanisms in drug seeking and relapse. *Neuroscience and Biobehavioral Reviews, 35* (2), 276-84.

Van Praag, H., Kempermann, G., and Gage, F. H. (2000). Neural consequences of environmental enrichment. *Nature Reviews Neuroscience,* 1 (3), 191-198.

Vanderschuren, L. J., and Everitt, B. J. (2004). Drug seeking becomes compulsive after prolonged cocaine self-administration. *Science, 305* (5686), 1017-1019.

Vaughn, L. K., Mantsch, J. R., Vranjkovic, O., Stroh, G., Lacourt, M., Kreutter, M., and Hillard, C. J. (2012). Cannabinoid receptor involvement in stress-induced cocaine reinstatement: potential interaction with noradrenergic pathways. *Neuroscience, 204*, 117-124.

Verdejo-García, A., and Bechara, A. (2009). A somatic marker theory of addiction. *Neuropharmacology, 1*, 48-62.

Vranjkovic, O., Hang, S., Baker, D. A., and Mantsch, J. R. (2012). β-adrenergic receptor mediation of stress-induced reinstatement of extinguished cocaine-induced conditioned place preference in mice: roles for β1 and β2 adrenergic receptors. *The Journal of Pharmacology and Experimental Therapeutics, 342* (2), 541-551.

Wang, B., Luo, F., Zhang, W. T., and Han, J. S. (2000). Stress or drug priming induces reinstatement of extinguished conditioned place preference. *Neuroreport, 11* (12), 2781-2784.

Wang, X., Cen, X.,and Lu, L. (2001). Noradrenaline in the bed nucleus of the stria terminalis is critical for stress-induced reactivation of morphine-conditioned place preference in rats. *European Journal Pharmacology, 432* (2-3), 153-161.

Wang, B., Luo, F., Ge, X. C., Fu, A. H., and Han, J. S. (2002). Effects of lesions of various brain areas on drug priming or footshock-induced reactivation of extinguished conditioned place preference. *Brain Research, 950* (1-2), 1-9.

Wang, B., Shaham, Y., Zitzman, D., Azari, S., Wise, R. A., and You, Z. B. (2005). Cocaine experience establishes control of midbrain glutamate and dopamine by corticotropin-releasing factor: a role in stress-induced relapse to drug seeking. *Journal of Neuroscience, 25* (22), 5389-5396.

Wang, B., You, Z. B., Rice, K. C., and Wise, R. A. (2007). Stress-induced relapse to cocaine seeking: roles for the CRF(2) receptor and CRF-binding protein in the ventral tegmental area of the rat. *Psychopharmacology, 193* (2), 283-294.

Wang, B., You, Z. B., and Wise, R. A. (2009). Reinstatement of cocaine seeking by hypocretin (orexin) in the ventral tegmental area: independence from the local corticotropin-releasing factor network. *Biological Psychiatry, 65* (10), 857-862.

Wee, S., and Koob, G. F. (2010).The role of the dynorphin-kappa opioid system in the reinforcing effects of drugs of abuse. *Psychopharmacology, 210* (2), 121-135.

Weiss, F. (2005). Neurobiology of craving, conditioned reward and relapse. *Current Opinion Pharmacology, 5* (1), 9-19.

Weiss, F. (2010). Advances in Animal Models of Relapse for Addiction Research. In: C. M. Kuhn, G. F. Koob (Eds). Advances in the Neuroscience of Addiction (pp. 1-25). Boca Raton (FL): CRC Press.

Weiss, I. C., Domeney, A. M., Heidbreder , C. A., Moreau, J. L, and Feldon, J. (2001). Early social isolation, but not maternal separation, affects behavioral sensitization to amphetamine in male and female adult rats. *Pharmacology Biochemistry and Behavior, 70* (2-3), 397-409.

Willner, P. (2005). Chronic mild stress (CMS) revisited: consistency and behavioural-neurobiological concordance in the effects of CMS. *Neuropsychobiology, 52* (2), 90-110.

Willner, P., Towell, A., Sampson, D., Sophokleous, S., and Muscat, R. (1987). Reduction of sucrose preference by chronic unpredictable mild stress, and its restoration by a tricyclic antidepressant. *Psychopharmacology, 93* (3), 358-364.

Wise, R. A. (1998). Drug-activation of brain reward pathways. *Drug and Alcohol Dependence, 51* (1-2), 13-22.

Wise, R. A. (2005). Forebrain substrates of reward and motivation. *Journal of Comparative Neurology, 493* (1), 115-121.

Wise, R. A. (2008). Dopamine and reward: the anhedonia hypothesis 30 years on. *Neurotoxicity Research, 14* (2-3), 169-183.

Wise, R. A. (2009). Ventral tegmental glutamate: a role in stress-, cue-, and cocaine-induced reinstatement of cocaine-seeking. *Neuropharmacology, 1*, 174-176.

Wise, R. A., and Morales, M. (2010). A ventral tegmental CRF-glutamate-dopamine interaction in addiction. *Brain Research, 16;1314*, 38-43.

Xi, Z. X., and Stein, E. A. (1999). Baclofen inhibits heroin self-administration behavior and mesolimbic dopamine release. *The Journal of Pharmacology and Experimental Therapeutics, 290* (3), 1369-1374.

Xi, Z. X., and Stein, E. A. (2000).Increased mesolimbic GABA concentration blocks heroin self-administration in the rat. *The Journal of Pharmacology and Experimental Therapeutics,* 294 (2), 613-619.

Xi, Z. X., Gilbert, J., Campos, A. C., Kline, N., Ashby, C. R. Jr, Hagan, J. J., Heidbreder, C. A., ... Gardner, E. L. (2004). Blockade of mesolimbic dopamine D3 receptors inhibits stress-induced reinstatement of cocaine-seeking in rats. *Psychopharmacology, 176* (1), 57-65.

Xu, Z., Hou, B., Gao, Y., He, F., and Zhang, C. (2007). Effects of enriched environment on morphine-induced reward in mice. *Experimental Neurology, 204* (2), 714-719.

Yahyavi-Firouz-Abadi, N., and See, R. E. (2009). Anti-relapse medications: preclinical models for drug addiction treatment. *Pharmacology Therapeutics, 124* (2), 235-247.

Yan, Y., and Nabeshima, T. (2009). Mouse model of relapse to the abuse of drugs: procedural considerations and characterizations. *Behavioural Brain Research, 196* (1), 1-10.

Yap, J. J., and Miczek, K. A. (2007). Social defeat stress, sensitization, and intravenous cocaine self-administration in mice. *Psychopharmacology, 192* (2), 261-273.

Yap, J. J., and Miczek, K. A. (2008). Stress and Rodent Models of Drug Addiction: Role of VTA-Accumbens-PFC-Amygdala Circuit. *Drug Discovery Today Disease Models, 5* (4), 259-270.

Yoon, S. S., Yang, E. J., Lee, B. H., Jang, E. Y., Kim. H. Y., Choi, S. M., Steffensen, S. C.,...Yang, C. H. (2012). Effects of acupuncture on stress-induced relapse to cocaine-seeking in rats. *Psychopharmacology, 222* (2), 303-311.

Zhang, X. Y, Sanchez, H., Kehoe, P., and Kosten, T. A. (2005). Neonatal isolation enhances maintenance but not reinstatement of cocaine self-administration in adult male rats. *Psychopharmacology, 177* (4), 391-399.

Zhou, L., Ghee, S. M., Chan, C., Lin, L., Cameron, M. D., Kenny, P. J., See, R. E. (2012). Orexin-1 receptor mediation of cocaine seeking in male and female rats. The *Journal Pharmacology and Experimental Therapeutics, 340* (3), 801-809.

Zhou, Y., Spangler, R., LaForge, K. S., Maggos, C. E., Ho, A., and Kreek, M. J. (1996). Modulation of CRF-R1 mRNA in rat anterior pituitary by dexamethasone: correlation with POMC mRNA. *Peptides, 17* (3), 435-441.

In: Drug Use and Abuse
Editor: Marie Claire Van Hout

ISBN: 978-1-62618-232-5

Chapter 11

GENDER SENSITIVITY AND MENTAL HEALTH CARE PROVISION

Michael Bergin**, *John Wells and Sara Owen

Department of Nursing, Waterford Institute of Technology,
College of Social Science, University of Lincoln

ABSTRACT

This chapter examines gender and mental health service provision with particular reference to alcohol related disorders and sensitivity of care. The theoretical and empirical literature in relation to gender, mental health care provision and alcohol related issues is explored.

The Irish Government has adopted *Gender Mainstreaming* as a strategy to promote equal opportunities between women and men in its National Development Plan. However, while current mental health policy addresses the principle of *partnership* and *social inclusiveness* as a way forward for mental health service provision, it still does not explicitly deal with the notion of gender and gender sensitivity. Irish mental health policy and service provision is criticised for being gender-neutral. Research exploring the gendered needs of service users is lacking and this further compounds any attempt in the provision of care that is gender sensitive. Drinking alcohol is considered a gendered activity and impacts upon gender sensitivity and mental health care provision. Gender differences exist and the literature suggests that there is less social acceptability for women with alcohol related problems as traditional codes of femininity are seen to be broken, and such behaviour patterns are largely viewed as deviant. This mirrors dominant societal expectations for women and alcohol use. Drinking alcohol and related problems are viewed as belonging within a masculine domain and such practices are still more socially acceptable for men.

Keywords: Gender, Care Provision, Alcohol, Ireland

---

* Corresponding author: Michael Bergin, mbergin@wit.ie.

Introduction

Gender is considered significant in the transformation of the physical body to the social and it is this gendered identity that allows for a gender analysis of mental illnesses (Lorber and Moore, 2002). Indeed, there is a growing recognition for the inclusion of both '*sex*' and '*gender*' sensitivity within health service delivery, policy development and research (World Health Organisation (WHO), 2004).

While mental health policy in Ireland promotes the provision of services that are comprehensive and community based, such services are criticised for being 'gender-neutral' (Women's Health Council, 2005). Research exploring the gendered needs of service users is lacking and this further compounds any attempt in the provision of care that is gender sensitive. This chapter therefore explores gender and mental health care provision with particular reference to alcohol related disorders and sensitivity of care. Key issues in relation to the lives of women and men in Ireland are presented with an exploration of the gendered landscape for mental illnesses.

Women and Men in Ireland: Some Key Issues

The Irish Government has adopted *'Gender Mainstreaming'* as a strategy to promote equal opportunities between women and men within its National Development Plan (NDP) (Government of Ireland, 2003). 'Gender Mainstreaming' is the process of assessing the implications for women and men of any planned action, legislation, policies or programmes in any area and at all levels. It is a strategy for making women's and men's concerns and experiences a central dimension in the design, implementation, monitoring and evaluation of policies and programmes in all political, economic and social spheres, such that inequality between men and women is not continued. The ultimate goal is gender equality (United Nations (UN), 1997; WHO, 2007).

A recent report by the Irish Central Statistics Office (Government of Ireland, 2011) entitled '*Women and Men in Ireland 2010*' outlines some key issues of interest arising in the analysis of the lives of men and women in Ireland. For example, Irish women work fewer hours, earn less and are under-represented in local and regional authorities and in the Oireachtais. Men are more likely to be in the labour force and the vast majority of those looking after the home and family members are women. More men are emigrating and men are more likely to die young. Most workers in the health and education sectors are women. Women are more likely to be admitted to hospital with depression and men are more likely to be admitted with schizophrenia and alcohol related disorders. These figures demonstrate advantages and disadvantages for both women and men in relation to each other. Most notable are in areas relating to health, education and socio-economics.

Mental Illness in Ireland: A Gendered Landscape

At the request of the Commission of Inquiry on Mental Illness an inpatient reporting system was initiated in psychiatric hospitals in Ireland (Departrment of Health (DoH), 1966).

During the period 1965 to 2002, all admission numbers increased, from 15,440 in 1965 to 23,736 in 2002. However, within this time span there were considerable fluctuations – see table 1.

Historically, more men than women were admitted to Irish psychiatric hospitals and this phenomenon remained relatively unchanged during the decades (Finnane, 1986). Male admission rates were higher than female admission rates during the entire period from 1965-2002 (Health Research Board (HRB), 2004). Over this period, the male rate increased from 551.2 in 1965, its lowest point, to 629.2 per 100,000 population in 2002.

Recent psychiatric inpatient reports (HRB, 2010, 2009, 2005) suggest that there is now virtually no difference between men and women in admission numbers for all or first admissions. Figures in relation to the rate of male and female all admissions in 2009 was almost equal (476.8 per 100,000 population for males and 475.9 for females), in contrast to the trend observed for many years (HRB, 2010). Admissions for depressive disorders, schizophrenia, mania and alcohol related disorders accounted for 71% of all admissions in 2009 (HRB, 2010).

Depressive disorders were the most common cause of all admissions, accounting for 30%. Also, more women are admitted for mood and personality disorders whilst men are admitted more frequently for alcohol and drug related disorders (HRB, 2010, 2009, 2005). Schizophrenia accounted for 20% of all admissions, mania-11% and alcohol related disorders-10%.

It is important to recognize that the lack of any community-based survey of psychiatric morbidity in Ireland, apart from some local assessments, notably of the elderly (Lawlor, Radic, Bruce, Swanwick and Gregory, 1994) limits the extent for true morbidity figures. This is in contrast to other jurisdictions, for example the DHSS in the UK (Meltzer, Gil, Petticrew and Hinds, 1995) and the Epidemiological Catchment Area (ECA) study in the US (Reiger et al., 1984) who has carried out such studies. Arguably this type of information needs to be available for the future rational planning of services (HRB, 2004). However, figures for gender differences in the admission rates for mental illnesses in Ireland present an interesting gendered landscape and challenge mental health services in providing care that is gender sensitive.

Table 1. All and first admissions by sex for various years 1965–2002. Rates per 100,000 total population (Health Research Board, 2004)

		All			First	
Year	*Male*	*Female*	*Total*	*Male*	*Female*	*Total*
1965	551.2	519.4	535.4	226.2	204.3	215.3
1970	736.6	670.0	705.3	283.4	248.5	266.9
1975	930.4	807.7	869.3	321.9	273.6	297.9
1980	875.9	732.2	804.5	280.3	221.6	251.1
1985	918.0	770.4	844.5	279.2	210.7	245.1
1990	850.7	717.7	784.2	242.6	185.4	214.0
1995	819.8	680.9	749.9	230.8	180.5	205.5
2000	721.9	621.5	671.3	228.7	176.4	202.4
2002	629.2	583.0	605.9	201.3	162.0	181.5

GENDER SENSITIVE CARE

Bowden (1997) argues that gender is truly associated with caring practices, and as a result, understanding and make sense of such practices requires a gendered analysis. She suggests that an awareness of the social, political and historical contexts of caring activities and the circumstances between individuals are central for individualised care. There is a need to capture the individual experiences of men and women to determine the level of gender sensitive care received.

Based upon Bowden's (1997) analysis of gender sensitive ethics, Miers (2002, p.72) states that a gender sensitive approach to health care should involve *'an understanding of the socio-political context in which the need for, and nature of, health care takes place'*. She suggests that a gender sensitive approach requires an understanding of the frequencies of men's and women's morbidity and mortality rates as well as the specifics and uniqueness of individual experiences. Individuals and the particular context in which health care takes place; the subjective experiences of men and women of their illnesses; and the relationships between health care professionals and users need to be explicitly recognised and explored (Miers, 2002). Therefore, gender sensitive care is informed by a knowledge and understanding of gender differences in women and men and their inter-relationship with life experiences; social, family and economic realities; expression and experiences of mental ill health; pathways into services and treatment needs and responses (DoH (UK), 2003).

A gender sensitive approach requires a knowledge base about how *'sex'* and *'gender'* affect the health of both women and men (Bird and Rieker, 1999; Khoury and Weisman, 2002). While research in relation to sex specific illnesses (for example, ovarian and prostate cancer) will be required, the health problems that are shared by both women and men need to move beyond controlling for *'sex'*, and focus analysis on how such conditions are experienced by individuals (Payne, 2006).

An integrated approach to research is required that explores both the biological and social processes of health and illness, and that biased assumptions towards any one approach need to be challenged and reduced (Bird and Rieker 1999). Debates in relation to the division of labour, income, caring, power, production, reproduction and how they affect health, ill health, illness and health care provision need to be explored (Im and Meleis, 2001; Khoury and Weisman, 2002; Miers 2002, 2000).

In relation to mental health, Busfield (1996) argues that gender permeates categories of mental disorders and emphasises the importance of inequities of power not only between men and women, but also among groups of men and women. An awareness and knowledge of the ways women and men live their lives and the connections and arrangements between them need to be more explicitly understood, so that any future developments for gender sensitive health care can occur (Miers 2002, 2000).

Gender sensitive care requires a knowledge base that explores a continuous and evolving understanding of gender that is informed by morbidity and mortality disparities both between and within the sexes (Fausto-Sterling, 2000; 1992). Such disparities are influenced by socio-economics, the public and private roles of men and women, power and social relationships, gendered experiences and prevailing beliefs of sexuality and body image (Lorber and Moore, 2002; Miers, 2002).

Gender Sensitivity and Service Provision

In the past women patients in psychiatric institutions experienced an inferior position compared to that of men, mirroring prevailing social mores, prejudices and stereotypes (see Busfield, 1996; Showalter, 1987; Ussher, 1991). For example, Padgett (1997) found that mental health services tend to view older women as a homogenous group, underpinned by a convergent ageist and sexist view of their needs, leading to an inaccurate assessment of need and the provision of inappropriate services. Since the 1980s a consistent finding of much research is that services and options offered to women with mental health problems is often limited and fails to meet their needs or aspirations. These service responses can be rationalised by professionals as protecting women from stress, having lower expectations of women and generally seeing their social role and value as less important than that of men (Kohen, 2000).

Mental health services may be the only source of potential support available to women and men with mental health problems to help them in their multiple roles. This is particularly important since the functional disabilities experienced by women with mental health problems impact on social and domestic roles unique to female identity and social expectations (Women's Health Council, 2002).

The area of motherhood has been examined in this regard. The majority of women with a *'chronic mental illness'* are mothers but services often pay little attention to the specific needs of this group in relation to their parenting roles (Diaz-Caneja and Johnson, 2004). A number of studies have found that there is no child support and care made available to women who have to be hospitalised because of their mental health difficulties or specialist visiting arrangements, leading to great distress for all concerned (Nicholson, Sweeney and Geller 1998).

Yet it has been found that lone parents with mental health problems (the vast majority of whom are women) are over three times less likely to be employed than mothers without a mental health problem (Social Exclusion Unit, 2004). The consequent social and material stressors experienced by mothers with mental health problems may not only exacerbate their current mental health difficulties but lead them into a vicious cycle of poverty, social isolation and mental illness (Chandola et al. 2004). The degree to which mental health services are configured to engage in supportive activity beyond regulatory and treatment/occupational activity has been questioned. For example, even in mental health services that engage in active consultation with women users about services it has been found that whilst listening took place service planners sometimes failed to act on what they had been told (Barnes, Davis, Guru, Lewis and Rogers, 2002; Owen and Milburn, 2001).

In the UK, the Department of Health responded to concerns about the overall lack of gender sensitivity within mainstream mental health services. A consultation process occurred with *'Mainstreaming Gender and Women's Mental Health: The Implementation Guidance'* (DoH (UK) 2003) being issued. This document was targeted towards all organizations involved in the planning, commissioning, delivery, performance, management, research and evaluation of mental health care in England and Wales. It recommended that gender sensitive mental health services need to take account of the differences experienced in a range of areas both between and within men and women (see Box 1).

Childhood and adult life experiences
e.g women are more likely to experience violence and abuse; young male victims of abuse have a propensity to become abusers.

Day-to-day social, family and economic realities
e.g. women are more likely to live in poverty, be lone parents; men are more likely to be in full-time employment and not be primary carers.

Expression and experience of mental ill health;
e.g. women are more likely to self harm, suffer from depression and anxiety; men are more likely to receive a diagnosis of anti-social personality disorder, experience an earlier onset and more disabling course of schizophrenia; women are more likely to attempt suicide and men more likely to succeed.

Pathways into services
e.g. women with dual diagnosis with substance misuse are more likely to be seen initially in mental health or primary care services; men are more likely to present at drug/alcohol services.

Treatment needs and responses
e.g. women are more likely than men to actively seek 'talking therapies' and benefit from self help.

Figure 1. Differentiating Gender Experience Domains (Department of Health (UK) 2003).

The Department of Health (UK) states that individual differences must be paramount in terms of treatment approach but that this should be informed by an awareness of gender issues (DoH (UK) 2003). For example, the Royal College of Psychiatrists (2000) recommends that health authorities have perinatal mental health strategies, including policies on providing immediate care and skills, a specialist consultant and multi-disciplinary team and specialist mental health mother and baby units.

An evaluation of the literature exploring men's and women's experiences of mental health services have identified issues in relation to (1) *'treatment specifically related to women'*; (2) *'to keep a façade'* and (3) *'single-sex or mixed wards'* (Määttä, 2009). Women expected a broad range of treatment options, such as therapy groups, writing activities and various kinds of complimentary therapies. They also felt the need to share their experiences with other women and felt more vulnerable if discussing their feelings with men. Being with other women helped them to cope better by listening to and sharing problems with each other (Cutting and Henderson, 2002). A number of women felt that being in mixed acute care units mirrored relationships in society and that it was problematic and an extra burden for them (ibid). This led many women to keep up a façade of femininity and normality.

Morrow and Chappell (1999) suggest that many women are still patronized by male medical professionals and that many of their claims surrounding sensitive issues are not responded to or adequately dealt with. This reflects a gender-role ideology where health care providers sometimes hold less than favourable attitudes (negative stereotypes) towards women, as compared to men, especially in relation to judgements about different aspects of care required and care to be given (Salgado, Vogt, King and King 2002, Vogt, Barry and King 2008). For example, women with alcohol related problems are more readily stigmatised and negatively stereotyped as deviant and are seen as not conforming to appropriate female behaviours, when compared to that of males (Angove and Fothergill, 2003). This may hinder women from seeking help and is often further compounded by a lack in childcare facilities and feelings of shame and guilt surrounding their alcohol related problems.

Women and Men with a Mental Illness in Ireland and Gender Sensitivity

In Ireland, people with a mental illness now have their mental health and social needs met in the community by their families, the provision of day services, primary care and through community residences (Daly and Walsh, 2003). Admission data would suggest that whilst generally men are more likely to be admitted to public psychiatric hospitals, women form the majority of users of community services (ibid).

Issues in relation to health and women are highlighted and prioritised within current Irish policy (DoHC, 2001; DoH, 1997). The Plan for Women's Health 1997-1999 (DoH 1997) emphasised a need to maximise women's health and social gain through developing services in which women are consulted and represented. More recently, Schizophrenia Ireland (2004) emphasised the importance of women participating in policy formulation and service provision in relation to *'gender specific'* issues as they relate to mental health problems.

More recently, a National Men's Health Policy 2008-2013 was published in response to a growing awareness and concern about the burden of ill-health experienced by men. Among the many recommendations made, is a call for an increased focus on the gendered nature of mental health and men in Ireland (DoHC, 2008).

Although mental health policy in Ireland promotes the provision of services that are comprehensive and community based, as already stated such services are criticised for being *'gender-neutral'* (Women's Health Council, 2005).To date published research in relation to gender and mental health is limited in Ireland. The available literature has focused on the family burden of mental illness (Keogh, 1997); needs of people with schizophrenia (Keogh et al. 2003); support for families who have members with an enduring mental illness (O Doherty, Doherty and Walsh 2006); gender differences in diagnosis and admission rates (Daly and Walsh, 2003); adult service users views of public services (Mental Health Commission 2011, 2006) and the personal experiences of recovering from mental health problems (HRB 2010). There appears to be no published work that explores how gender aware psychiatric services are for women and men that engage with such services.

Gender and Alcohol Use in Ireland

There is a long history of alcohol consumption and its predominance within Irish society (Molloy, 2002). Ireland has been unusual in relation to alcohol use due to extreme cultural expressions from one of abstinence to over-use (Cassidy, 1997; Ferriter, 1999).

Arguably, Ireland has had ambivalent views towards alcohol that could be attributed to a Catholic dominated culture and resistances to such authoritarianism (Tovey and Share, 2003). Traditionally, the pub has been recognised as a masculine place with women's access often being confined to specialist areas in the past – the snug or lounge with women's drinking often being poorly understood (Ferriter, 1999).

Masculinity, particularly hegemonic masculinity means that '*doing gender*' frequently involves behaving in ways that puts men's health at risk (Courtenay, 2000). For example, excess alcohol consumption and not seeking professional help for health related issues are well cited in the literature (Mahalik, Burns and Syzdek, 2007).

Furthermore, being a woman and having an alcohol related problem is still viewed as unfeminine by society (Jakobsson, Hensing and Spak, 2008), and contravenes societal expectations for women and the norms and values associated with their roles in society (Measham, 2002). Therefore, drinking alcohol is a gendered activity (Lyons, 2009) and impacts upon the gender sensitivity of care provision.

GENDER SENSITIVITY, ALCOHOL RELATED PROBLEMS AND CARE PROVISION

Internationally, cross-cultural research shows that men continue to drink more often and more heavily than women (Rahav, Wilsnack, Bloomfield, Gmel and Kuntsche, 2006). Having an alcohol related problem is still viewed as unfeminine and this may cause women to avoid exposing their alcohol problems to others; whereas an inability to handle alcohol is viewed as unmasculine (Jakobsson et al., 2008).

In Ireland, more women are admitted for mood and personality disorders whilst men are admitted more frequently for alcohol and drug related disorders (HRB 2010, 2009, 2005). A recent study of Irish mental health service providers suggests that they try not to view men and women with alcohol related problems differently. However, gender differences do exist (Bergin, 2012). Findings suggest that there is less social acceptability for women with alcohol related problems as traditional codes of femininity are seen to be broken, and such behaviour patterns are largely viewed as deviant. For men, their drinking '*just spiralled out of control*'.

There are some indications that as social positions for women are changing as a result of greater freedoms and gender equality, that traditional stereotypical thinking in relation to women that drink problematically is changing (Busfield, 2002). As Busfield (2010) recently suggested that such changes can be explained whereby when social expectations (behaviours and emotions) for males and females within a society change over a period of time, gender differences for mental illnesses may change also. For example, she cites how women's greater participation in the work place and greater public freedoms can impact on them when they are confronted with psychological difficulties, whereby they may resort to excessive alcohol and drug use rather than becoming depressed. However, such changes in the patterns of illnesses and gender are both '*a source of hope, and a threat, because historical change is not all progress*' (Connell 2012, p.2792). While there is evidence of some changes in the gender order in relation to women and men with alcohol related problems in Ireland; such changes are not a dominant view (Bergin, 2012).

Research exploring how women perform gender through their drinking identifies alternate versions of femininities, with women and men constructing women who drink as empowered, independent, pleasure-seeking social beings, which is linked to their changing position in society (Emslie and Hunt, 2008; Lyons and Willott, 2008). In the United Kingdom, young women have been found to drink heavily but show self-restraint and self policing around intoxication for fear of social disapproval, ensuring they stay within the boundaries of traditional femininity (Measham, 2002).

One of the most threatening aspects of women drinking heavily or problematically in public is '*her disruption of dominant discourses on gender and on women as carer*' (Jackson and Tinkler 2007, p.264). This is likely to explain the double standards that continue to exist around when, what and how much drinking women should be engaging in (Lyons and Willott, 2008). Men and women might engage in similar drinking behaviours for the same reasons but this plays out in very different ways for masculinities, femininities and gender relations (O'Connor and Kelly, 2006). Women's drinking generates concern because it is viewed as leading to problems for children, homes and the traditional moral order (Holmila and Raitasalo, 2005).

Bergin (2012) identified how mental health service providers in Ireland treated women with alcohol problems differently to men in relation to parenting, with their treatment plans often prioritising and centring on their responsibilities for children. This was not the case for men with a similar diagnosis. Arguably, such views mirror dominant societal expectations for women that are acquired as a result of an individual's lay socialisation. Other findings from this study identify that drinking alcohol and related problems are viewed by service providers as belonging within a masculine domain and such practices are still more socially acceptable for men.

Capraro (2000) argues that alcohol drinking must be understood as behaviour embedded in masculinity that is linked to systems of attitudes, values and structures in men's lives that constitute masculinity and men's social position relative to women. For women, drinking must be understood within broader and continuously changing structures and gender relations, an understanding that is apparent in lay people's talk about gender and health (Emslie and Hunt, 2008). Targeting drinking patterns needs to tackle the complex issues around the functions of drinking for gendered identities (Lyons, 2009), and how such gendered identities are perceived by health care workers. This is an issue that requires consideration by Irish mental health care workers in providing care that is gender sensitive for women and men (marginalised).

CONCLUSION

This chapter examined gender and mental health service provision with particular reference to alcohol related disorders and sensitivity of care. The theoretical and empirical literature in relation to gender sensitivity, mental health care provision and alcohol related issues was explored. The research literature indicates that generic mental health services often fail to address the specific gendered needs of women and men.

In part, this may be due to a combination of gender stereotyping sometimes based on epidemiological data, insufficient recognition of the unique social and situated experience of women and men with mental health problems, a lack of consultation with service users about their needs or the absence of a gender framework that assesses and evaluates services. This may reinforce a feeling of being disempowered by their mental health problems and their previous experiences of mental health services, thereby, feeling unable to articulate their gender sensitive views.

Drinking alcohol is considered a gendered activity and impacts upon gender sensitivity and mental health care provision. Gender differences exist and the literature suggests that there is less social acceptability for women with alcohol related problems as traditional codes of femininity are seen to be broken, and such behaviour patterns are largely viewed as deviant. This mirrors dominant societal expectations for women and alcohol use. Drinking alcohol and related problems are viewed as belonging within a masculine domain and such practices are still more socially acceptable for men.

REFERENCES

Angove, R., and Fothergill, A. (2003). Women and alcohol: misrepresented and misunderstood. *Journal of Psychiatric and Mental Health Nursing, 10*, 213-219.

Barnes, M., Davis, A., Guru, S., Lewis, L., and Rogers, H. (2002). *Women-only and women sensitive mental health services: an expert paper* Final report to the Department of Health. Department of Health, London.

Bergin, M. (2012). *Realist Social Theory, Gender Awareness and Irish Mental Health Care – An Exploratory Analysis,* unpublished PhD thesis. Lincoln (UK), University of Lincoln.

Bird, C.E., and Rieker ,P.P. (1999). Gender matters: an integrated model for understanding men's and women's health. *Social Science and Medicine, 48,* 745-755.

Bowden, P. (1997). Caring: Gender Sensitive Ethics. London, Routledge.

Busfield, J. (2010). Gender and mental health: In *The Palgrave Handbook of Gender and Healthcare,* (eds. Kuhlmann E and Annandale E.), pp.172-188. Hampshire, Palgrave Macmillan.

Busfield, J. (2002). The archaeology of psychiatric disorder: gender and disorders of thought, emotion and behaviour. In: *Gender, Health and Healing: The Public/Private Divide,* (eds. Bendelow, G., Carpenter M., Vautier C. and Williams S.), pp.144-162. London, Routledge.

Busfield, J. (1996) *Men Women and Madness, Understanding Gender and Mental Disorder.* Hampshire, Palgrave Macmillan.

Capraro, R.L. (2000). Why college men drink: alcohol, adventure, and the paradox of masculinity. *Journal of American College Health, 48,* 307-315.

Cassidy, T.M. (1997). Sober for the Sake of the Children: The Church, The State and Alcohol Use amongst Women in Ireland. In: *Women and Irish Society, A Sociological Reader* (Byrne A. and Leonard M. eds.), pp.447-464. Belfast, Beyond the Pale Productions.

Chandola, T., Martikainen, P., Bartley, M., Lahelma, E., Marmot, M., Michikazu, S., and Nasermoaddeli, A. (2004). Does conflict between home and work explain the effect of multiple roles on mental health? A comparative study of Finland, Japan, and the UK. *International Journal of Epidemiology, 33* (4), 884-893.

Connell, R. (2012). Gender, health and theory: conceptualizing the issue, in local and world perspective. *Social Science and Medicine, 74*(11), 1675-1683.

Courtenay, W.H. (2000). Constructions of masculinity and their influence on men's well-being: a theory of gender and health. *Social Science and Medicine, 50* (10), 1385-1401.

Cutting, P., and Henderson, C. (2002). Women's experiences of hospital admission. *Journal of Psychiatric and Mental Health Nursing, 9,* 705–712.

Daly, A., and Walsh, D. (2003). *Activities of Irish Psychiatric Services 2001*. Dublin: Health Research Board.

Department of Health (DoH), (1997). *A Plan for Women's Health.* Dublin: Stationery Office.

Department of Health (DoH), (1966). *Commission of Inquiry on Mental Illness.* Dublin: The Stationery Office.

Department of Health (UK), (2003). *Mainstreaming Gender and Women's Mental Health Implementation Guidance*. London: Department of Health.

Department of Health and Children (DoHC), (2008). *National Men's Health Policy 2008-2013: Working with Men in Ireland to Achieve Optimum Health and Well Being*. Dublin: Stationery Office.

Department of Health and Children (DoHC), (2001). *Quality and Fairness: A Health System for You*. Dublin: The Stationery Office.

Diaz-Caneja, A., and Johnson, A. (2004). The views and experiences of severely mentally ill mothers – a qualitative study. *Social Psychiatry and Psychiatric Epidemiology, 39*(6), 472-82.

Emslie, C., and Hunt, K. (2008). The weaker sex? Exploring lay understandings of gender differences in life expectancy: a qualitative study. *Social Science and Medicine, 67*, 808-816.

Fausto-Sterling, A. (2000). *Sexing the Boby: Gender Politics and the Construction of Sexuality*. New York: Basic Books.

Fausto-Sterling, A. (1992). *Myths of Gender: Biological Theories about Men and Women*. New York: Basic Books.

Ferriter, D. (1999). *A Nation of Extremes: The Pioneers in Twentieth Century Ireland*. Dublin: Irish Academic Press.

Finnane, M. (1986). Law and the social uses of the asylum in nineteenth century Ireland. In: *Asylum in the Community*, (eds. Tomlinson D. and Carrier J.), pp.91-110), London: Routledge.

Government of Ireland, (2011). *Women and Men in Ireland 2010*. Central Statistics Office. Dublin: Stationery Office.

Government of Ireland, (2003). *Sustaining progress: Social Partnership Agreement 2003–05*. Dublin: Stationery Office.

Health Research Board (HRB), (2010). *HRB Statistics Series 9, Activities of Irish Psychiatric Units and Hospitals 2009*, Main Findings. Dublin; Health Research Board.

Health Research Board (HRB), (2009). *HRB Statistics Series 7, Activities of Irish Psychiatric Units and Hospitals 2008*. Dublin: Health Research Board.

Health Research Board (HRB), (2005) *Activities of Irish Psychiatric Units and Hospitals 2004*. Mental Health Research Division, Dublin: Health Research Board.

Health Research Board (HRB), (2004). *Mental Illness in Ireland 1750-2002, Reflections on the Rise and Fall of Institutional Care*. Dublin: Health Research Board.

Holmila, M., and Raitasalo, K. (2005). Gender differences in drinking: why do they still exist? *Addiction, 100*, 1763–1769.

Im, E.O., and Meleis, A.I. (2001). An international imperative for gender sensitive theories in women's health. *Journal of Nursing Scholarship, 33* (4), 309-314.

Jackson, C., and Tinkler, P., (2007). 'Ladettes' and 'modern girls': 'troublesome' young femininities. Sociological Review, 55, 251-272.

Jakobsson, A., Hensing, G., and Spak, F. (2008). The role of gendered conceptions in treatment seeking for alcohol problems. *Scandinavian Journal of Caring Sciences, 22*, 196-202.

Keogh, F. (1997). *Family Burden and Mental Illness in Ireland*. Unpublished PhD thesis, Trinity College, Dublin.

Keogh, F., Finnerty, A., O'Grady-Walshe, A., Daly, I., Murphy, D., Lane, A., and Walsh, D. (2003). Meeting the needs of people with schizophrenia living in the community: a report from a European collaboration. *Irish Journal of Psychological Medicine, 20* (2), 45-51.

Khoury, A.J., and Weisman, C.S. (2002). Thinking about women's health: the case for gender sensitivity. *Women's Health Issues, 12* (2), 61-65.

Kohen, D. (2000). Psychiatric services for women. In: *Women and Mental Health,* (ed. Kohen D.), pp.218-232, London: Routledge.

Lawlor, B., Radic, A., Bruce, I., Swanwick, I. and Gregory, R. J.(1994). Prevalence of mental illness in the community-dwelling elderly in Dublin using AGECAT. *Irish Journal of Psychological Medicine, 11* (4), 157-160.

Lorber, J. and Moore, L.J. (2002). *Gender and the Social Construction of Illness*. Aalta Mira Press, Oxford.

Lyons, A.C. (2009). Masculinities, femininities, behaviour and health. *Social and Personality Psychology Compass, 3* (4), 394-412.

Lyons, A.C., and Willott, S.A. (2008). Alcohol consumption, gender identities and women's changing social positions. *Sex Roles, 59,* 694-712.

Määttä, S. (2009). Exploring male and female patients' experiences of psychiatric hospital care: a critical analysis of the literature. *Issues in Mental Health Nursing, 30,* 174-180.

Mahalik, J.R., Burns, S.M., and Syzdek, M. (2007). Masculinity and perceived normative health behaviours as predictors of men's health behaviours. *Social Science and Medicine, 64*, 2201-2209.

McClelland, R., Webb, M., and Mock, G. (2000). Mental Health Services In Ireland. *International Journal of Law and Psychiatry, 23* (3-4), 309-328.

Measham, F. (2002). 'Doing gender'–'doing drugs': conceptualizing the gendering of drugs cultures. *Contemporary Drug Problems, 29*, 335-373.

Meltzer, H., Gill, B., Petticrew, M., and Hinds, K. (1995). *OPCS Surveys of Psychiatric Morbidity in Great Britain. Report 1. The Prevalence of Psychiatry Morbidity among Adults Living in Private Households.* London: HMSO.

Mental Health Commission, (2011). Your Views of Mental Health Inpatient Services, Inpatient Survey 2011. Dublin, Mental Health Commission.

Mental Health Commission, (2006). *The Views of Adult Users of the Public Sector Mental Health Services.* Dublin: Mental Health Commission.

Miers, M. (2002). Developing an understanding of gender sensitive care: exploring concepts and knowledge. *Journal of Advanced Nursing, 40*, (1), 69-77.

Miers, M. (2000). *Gender Issues and Nursing Practice, Sociology and Nursing Practice Series.* Hampshire: MacMillan Press Ltd.

Molloy, C. (2002). *The Story of the Irish Pub.* Dublin: Liffey.

Morrow, M., and Chappell, M. (1999). *Hearing Women's Voices. Mental Health Care for Women.* Vancouver: British Columbia Centre for Excellence for Women's Health.

Nicholson, J., Sweeney, E. M., and Geller, J. L. (1998). Mothers with mental illness: the competing demands of parenting and living with mental illness. *Psychiatric Services, 49* (5), 635-642.

O'Connor, C. and Kelly, K. (2006). Auto theft and youth culture: a nexus of masculinities, femininities and car culture. *Journal of Youth Studies, 9,* 247-267.

O Doherty, Y.R., Doherty, T.D., and Walsh D. (2006). *Family Support Study: A Study of Experiences Needs and Support Requirements of Families with Enduring Mental Illness in Ireland.* Dublin: Health Research Board.

Owen, S., and Milburn, C. (2001). Implementing research findings into practice: improving and developing services for women with serious and enduring mental health problems. *Journal of Psychiatric and Mental Health Nursing, 8* (3), 221-231.

Padgett, D.K. (1997). Women's mental health: some directions for research. *American Journal of Orthopsychiatry, 67* (4), 522-534.

Payne, S. (2006). *The Health of Men and Women*. Cambridge: Polity Press.

Rahav, G., Wilsnack, R., Bloomfield, K., Gmel, G., and Kuntsche, S. (2006). The influence of societal level factors on men's and women's alcohol consumption and alcohol problems. *Alcohol and Alcoholism, 41,* 147-155.

Reiger D.A., Myers J.K., Kramer M., Robins L.N., Blazer D.G., Hough R.L., Eaton W.W., and Locke, B.Z. (1984). The NIMH Epidemiologic Catchment Area Program. Historical Context, Major Objectives, and Study Population Characteristics. *Archives of General Psychiatry, 41*, 934-941.

Royal College of Psychiatrists, (2000). *Perinatal Maternal Mental Health Services Council Report CR88.* London: Royal College of Psychiatrists.

Salgado, D.M., Vogt, D.S., King, L., and King, D.W. (2002). Gender awareness inventory – VA: A measure of ideology, sensitivity and knowledge related to women veterans' health care. *Sex Roles, 46* (7/8), 247-262.

Schizophrenia Ireland, (2004). SI News, Summer, issue 65, Dublin.

Showalter, E. (1987). *The Female Malady: Women, Madness and English Culture, 1830-1980.* London: Virago.

Social Exclusion Unit, (2004). *Mental Health and Social Exclusion, Social Exclusion Unit Report.* London: Office of the Deputy Prime Minister.

Tovey, H., and Share, P. (2003). *A Sociology of Ireland*, second edition. Dublin: Gill and MacMillan.

United Nations (UN), (1997). *Mainstreaming the Gender Perspective into all Policies and Programmes in the United Nations*. New York: United Nations.

Ussher, J. (1991). *Women's Madness, Misogyny or Mental Illness?* Hertfordshire: Harvester Wheatsheaf.

Vogt, D., Barry, A., and King, L. (2008). Toward gender-aware health care: evaluation of an intervention to enhance care female patients in the VA Setting. Journal of *Health Psychology, 13* (5), 624-638.

Women's Health Council, (2005). *Women's Mental Health: Promoting a Gendered Approach to Policy and Service Provision.* Dublin: The Women's Health Council.

Women's Health Council, (2002). *Promoting Women's Health, A Population Investment for Ireland's Future. A Position Paper of the Women's Health Council,* Dublin.

World Health Organisation (WHO), (2007) Glossary, at www.euro.who.int/GEM/strategy/20070426-7, accessed 19 August 2012.

World Health Organisation (WHO), (2004) *Gender in Mental Health Research.* Geneva: World Health Organisation.

In: Drug Use and Abuse
Editor: Marie Claire Van Hout

ISBN: 978-1-62618-232-5

Chapter 12

MOTIVATIONAL INTERVIEWING: A MODEL IN A STORY

Colin O'Driscoll
Glyndŵr University, Institute of Health,
Medical Sciences and Society

ABSTRACT

Motivational Interviewing, as a way of being with a person, a style of conversation and treatment model, has demonstrated a significant and compelling evidence base across 30 years of rigorous scientific evaluation. The evidence base presenting the efficacy for this intervention is ranging far beyond the original target behaviour (alcohol misuse), and the breadth of literature becomes richer and more compelling with each decade of research. Where did this model come from? How was it developed? The current chapter explores its origins, presenting the story as a valid and effective means of representing its essence. The story, therefore, is purported to hold the keys. Consequently the story may be suggested to be a means of conveying the enduring cornerstones of a model that is today regarded highly, in peer-reviewed journals, clinical contexts and in education settings, as a valid and rich approach that resonates with good instincts as well as efficacious practice. This chapter also considers what comes next and outlines a potential gap in this literature, namely the clear sense of why this model works; the internal processing in response to the intervention.

Keywords: Motivational Interviewing, evidence based treatment, history of MI

INTRODUCTION

Motivational Interviewing (MI) was developed (or in fact evoked) initially as a treatment approach for addictions. It was evoked in the sense that it emanated out of conversations that William R. Miller had whilst supervising psychologists (Miller and Rose, 2009). Miller was already applying this method. It was not considered a method other than his own particular approach to working with people who struggle with addiction. The formulation of the structure of this intervention came later and was first articulated in an article written by Miller in 1983 (Miller, 1983). Since that time Motivational Interviewing has vastly expanded regarding literature publications and has been researched prolifically, via clinical control trials (>180)(Corbett, 2008), a wide variety of research papers and articles in various academic journals, and has an equally impressive expansion of application variety. Initially designed for problem drinkers (Miller, 1983) Motivational Interviewing now demonstrates a wide remit and evidence base for a wide range of issues. See table 1 below for an outline of examples of research and investigation of motivational interviewing across a range of areas.

Motivational Interviewing was initially developed for problem drinking and whilst the research has significantly diversified across the years, alcohol and substance misuse remain the stronger research focus with smoking cessation growing significantly also. MI has shown a strong and convincing empirical evidence base in a range of studies over the last 25 years. As a therapeutic strategy it is relatively simplistic, however proficiency in demonstrating the spirit and skills remains quite complex in that it is difficult to learn. Training workshops demonstrate poor outcome relating to proficient practice (Miller and Mount, 2001).

The current chapter will present the base of evidence and published literature pertinent to MI, and will frame the essence and evidence through the history and model structure respectively.

Table 1. Topical MI Literature examples

Treatment area	Literature example
Anxiety	Westraand Phoenix, 2003
Asthma	Schmaling, Blume, and Afari, 2001
Binge Eating	Dunn, Neighbors, and Larimer, 2006
Brain Injury	Bombardier and Rimmele, 1999
Cardiac rehabilitation	Scales, 1998
Dentistry	Weinstein, Harrison, and Benton, 2004
Diabetes	Channon, Smith, and Gregory, 2003
Diet	Berg-Smith et al., 1999
Domestic violence	Kistenmacher, 2000
Dual Diagnosis	Baker et al., 2002
Eating disorders	Feld, Woodside, Kaplan, Olmsted, and Carter, 2001
Exercise	Hillsdon, Thorogood, White, and Foster, 2002
Family / relationships	Kelly, Halford, and Young, 2000
Gambling	Hodgins, Currie, el-Guebaly, and Peden, 2004
Health promotion	Harland et al., 1999
HIV / AIDS	Carey et al., 2000
Injury Prevention	Johnston, Rivara, and Droesch, 2002
Medical Adherence	Aliotta, Vlasnik, and Delor, 2004
Medication adherence	Ogedegbe et al., 2006
Mental Health	Humphress et al., 2002
Obesity	Smith, Heckemeyer, Kratt, and Mason, 1997
Offending	Sinha, Easton, Renee-Aubin, and Carroll, 2003
Sexual behaviour	Yahne, Miller, Irvin-Vitela, and Tonigan, 2002
Speech therapy	Behrman, 2006
Tobacco	Brown et al., 2003
Trauma	Zatzick et al., 2004

Overview

Motivational Interviewing (MI) is defined as a client-centred, directive therapeutic style to enhance readiness for change by helping clients explore and resolve ambivalence (Miller and Rollnick, 2002). Essentially MI was a strategy that Miller used to help an individual to develop a sense of the interference in their values by their behaviour (developing discrepancy) and consequently helping the client to therefore articulate their own argument for change by generating utterances that are self-motivating (e.g. Miller, 1983; Miller and Rollnick, 2002).

MI was developed by William Miller through a number of different stags and these arguably best describe the core elements of what Motivational Interviewing actually is; the essence of it's evolution. Therefore the current chapter will follow these phases in explanation of the evolution of the research and contextual base for the model itself. These phases may be represented as follows:

Phase 1 (Resistance and Ambivalence)

Miller established his career working in addiction treatment settings in The United States of America. Miller in his years of study and clinical work was, as with so many new professionals in the area of addiction, working within a field that tended to predominantly view alcoholism as a disease and thus taking the view point that you either were or were not an alcoholic; that moderating drinking for instance was not a possibility. Yet Miller found in some of his early investigations that controlled drinking promotion was in control trials demonstrating some success (e.g. Miller, 1978).

Miller found that in a fairly empathic conversation people were willing to discuss their behaviour openly and explore their thoughts, feelings and fears about their behaviour, and the future.

He found a very strong relationship in fact between empathy and outcome and demonstrated this well in his early research (e.g. Miller, 1980). This was of course contrary to the predominant view that often refer to such ideas of core empathy as little more than naivety; being pulled into the game; the gullible enabler serving little more than collusion with the client, who would buy and sell the therapist through an elaborate system of denial that the therapist is now reinforcing. But again, this was just not what Miller found. It was not a convincing picture and certainly did not reflect reality in relation to his experience and encounters with his clients.

It may be obvious in general psychotherapy and its clinicians that if the approach is more efficacious (as indeed fidelity to it), the benefit will be greater to the client. Of course this may be clear.

Otherwise training clinicians to a high level would be pointless. However in the treatment of addiction, most of the exhibited behaviour and thinking patterns of the *addict*, is put down to them almost exclusively and is rarely related to the behaviour or thought patterns of the clinician.

This is rarely considered to be reinforced or reduced according to the engagement style of the therapist in this area. Yet it may be considered obvious that it must be not only important, but actually inevitably determinant of outcomes, which indeed it is.

Therefore, for Miller the actual way of being with a person in a clinical setting directly determined how the client would engage (or not engage) the therapist and indeed the process itself. In other words, it was clear to him that how he was with the client directly influenced how the client would be with him, and that determined whether or not they would meaningfully engage in an integral therapeutic process. The revelation here is that Miller was very clear, from very early on that the *resistance, often interpreted traditionally as denial,* that so many professionals had warned about, was actually interpersonally based. Therefore what the clinician does influences what the client does. Again, this may appear straightforward, but when one understands this comprehensively it becomes clearer that when resistance is experienced, rather than that telling the professional something about the client (e.g. denial), it is actually telling them something about themselves (or more poignantly the relationship), and what they are doing. Miller played around with this and quickly discovered that specific conversational approaches elicit specific response styles. E.g. confrontation tends to promote resistance (e.g. White and Miller, 2007); empathy tends to promote reduced anxiety and increased elaboration (e.g. Angus and Kagan, 2009), and so on. Therefore it seemed clear that resistance, an angry push back was, rather than being related to client personality deficits, was actually quite a normal human response to confrontation (Miller, 2009).

Therefore Miller suggested that when an individual feels safe enough, and that they are not in a situation where they will be judged, criticised, pressured or cajoled into changing before they are ready, they simply tend to be more likely to discuss the issue (e.g. Miller and Rollnick, 2004). They tend to be more likely to put their thoughts and feelings about it onto the table. They are less worried that the therapist will use this information against them as the therapist is reassuring them that these decisions are absolutely for them.

Therefore when this happened there were some very interesting therapeutic processes that took place. Clients did not invest energy in lying and manipulating. Rather they considered the issue, and with support, at length. In doing so Miller realised that they more or less talked themselves into changing (Miller and Rollnick, 2004). He found that when they continued to think and talk about it, without switching off, or simply stopping thinking about due to the discomfort associated with the mismatch of their own values and behaviour, they explored both sides of the picture: why they want to do this and why they don't. It seemed clear that as this process continued, people became ultimately ready to change, and then simply found a way. This process is referred to as exploring and resolving ambivalence (e.g. Miller and Rollnick, 2002). Ambivalence is a state of wanting to change and wanting to stay the same at the same time; experiencing both conflicting desires. The essence here is that the person struggling with addiction, and indeed their lies and denials that are traditionally front of focus from a therapeutic point of view, was not actually apparent to a Miller that was simply aware of the fact that people can feel two ways about something and be in internal conflict on this basis (ambivalence). It was apparent to Miller therefore that if one rolls with resistance (Miller and Rollnick, 2002) one is more likely to facilitate the exploration about ambivalence and thus the resolution, resulting in engaging intrinsic motivation to change. The task in MI is to express empathy for the conflict that exists in-between these two states; being 'stuck' in ambivalence, in order to facilitate momentum and movement through this state.

Phase 2 (Motivational Interviewing)

Whilst Miller was visiting Norway on a sabbatical where he was lecturing in Bergen University and supervising a group of Psychologists (Miller, 2009). This supervision provided some rich discussions on the various mechanisms involved in the promotion of behavioural change. Through analytic role plays which Miller and the psychologists engaged in the psychologists evoked from Miller the technical elements of what he was doing, and Miller began to articulate the set of decision rules he was using to determined specific responses; what he was doing and why (Miller, 2009). This group evaluated and reflected upon these ideas and concepts, and found great synchronicity in terms of style of therapeutic engagement. The Psychologists were very animated by what they saw. It was clear to them that there was something new and very exciting that they were being exposed to. To Miller, really it was just good clinical practice; a good common sense humanistic application of a fairly client-centred form of therapy. Yet to those that were witnessing it, these Norwegian Psychologists, there was a fascinating and quite revolutionary picture revealing itself to them. This was an innovation in Psychotherapy that required much more attention and evaluation. That was clear.

What was it that they saw that excited them so? They saw a very respectful, seemingly gentle and robustly empathic approach. They saw a Psychologist dare to centrally attend to the autonomy of the individual, even when the stakes were high and where most would fear to let go of a certain level of therapeutic control. They saw a partnership form, quickly and easily between therapist and client. They saw a positive alliance established effortlessly; the sense of complete safety where the client was simply more likely to confide thoughts and feelings, and indeed fears in a productive setting. Yet what was most compelling was how quickly in this context clients moved from being quite resistant to any notion of change, to speaking in definitive terms about change. This directly resonated with their own concepts of change dynamics and they applied these techniques (and style) clinically in supervision with Miller. The supervision involved a kind of linguistic analysis of what influence specific therapist language had on an individual's expressed desire for change.

These psychologists passionately dissected Miller's ideas and suggested interventions; "What are you thinking now at this moment in this session?" "You asked a question there. Why did you ask that question, because there are other things you could have asked?" etc. (Miller, 2009) Miller responded with honesty to these clever questions and in the truest spirit of the approach itself, a model was born. Following this experience Miller wrote an article summarising these articulations, which became the first published document on MI: "Motivational Interviewing with Problem Drinkers" (Miller, 1983)

Phase 3 (Miller and Rollnick)

Motivational Interviewing (MI) was formally established in its earliest form in 1982. What was always clear about this approach of Miller's was that it worked. Not only did it work, but it did so in empowering ways and in relatively brief periods (e.g. Hettema, Steele, and Miller, 2005; Amrhein, Miller, Yahne, Palmer, and Fulcher, 2003; Moyers et al., 2007; Vasilaki, Hosier, and Cox, 2006; Rubak, Sandbaek, Lauritzen, and Christensen, 2005; Knight, McGowan, Dickens, and Bundy, 2006).

Enter Steven Rollnick. Miller met Rollnick in Australia on Miller's second sabbatical. Rollnick had been busy teaching this model which he was relying exclusively on the 1983 article to inform. He was excited to meet Miller who was surprised that Rollnick (or indeed anybody he was not immediately associated with) had read the paper (Miller, 2009). Rollnick understood immediately the importance of what Miller was doing. He resonated with the essence of this model and was extremely eager to formalise this theory. Straightaway they got to work developing the framework and theory behind this model. The crystallisation, and continued theory evocation from within Miller, matched with Rollnick's tenacious insight and theoretical drive, reached new levels of clarity and formal establishment. It began to become clear what the mechanism of MI actually was, and more importantly, how it worked. It was clear that there were two pieces to this puzzle and they indeed required their respective attention. One relates to the mechanistic components; the other the relational elements; in other words, the tools and principles (mechanistic), and the spirit (relational) of MI. This partnership resulted in publication of the first book on MI: Motivational Interviewing. Preparing People to Change (Miller and Rollnick, 1991).

MI Components

Motivational Interviewing (MI) is defined as a "client-centered, directive method for enhancing intrinsic motivation to change by exploring and resolving ambivalence." (Miller and Rollnick, 2002). In latter years this definition evolved into a "collaborative, person-centered form of guiding to elicit and strengthen motivation for change" (Miller and Rollnick, 2009), placing a greater emphasis on the element of guiding collaboratively as a means of developing an argument for change. Today, in the recently published 3rd edition of the Motivational Interviewing textbook, we see it as "...a collaborative conversation style for strengthening a person's own motivation and commitment to change" (Miller and Rollnick, 2013). Essentially MI is a means of assisting an individual to resolve ambivalent ideas (desire to both change and remain the same concurrently) about change in order to release motivation. It is a means of supporting individuals in the development of their own unique argument for change. This has three essential components: The Spirit, which creates the right environment for one to safely explore their often ambivalent ideas about change; The principles which represent a sort of map for the therapist to follow; and the Skills which are the utterance by utterance techniques that the therapist relies upon.

Spirit

There are three parts to the spirit of MI (later amended to four), which is often described as the essence. Many argue this to be the most important part (e.g. Miller, 2009); the spirit of MI is arguably influenced by (or informed by) the client-centred theory of Carl Rogers (1959). It is at its heart working with somebody; alongside them, honouring their autonomy and right to choose for themselves in addition to their wisdom to do so which is evoked rather than instilled (Rollnick and Miller, 1995; Miller and Rollnick, 2002). Motivational Interviewing spirit is framed as follows:

Figure 1. Spirit of MI[1].

The client is seen to be an equal. The process of motivational interviewing is so-named as it relates to an interaction where two people dually inter-view upon the same thing. The term interviewing was selected in this context. It is where two people sit down side by side (metaphorically) and join in their analysis of a particular issue. This is in contrast with sitting opposite on another where one knows the answers and the other needs to learn them (e.g. skills based therapies, CBT, etc.). Therefore collaboration relates to addressing somebody in an equal way and working with them in partnership to explore their struggle and guiding them to their conclusions about both their behaviour and what they may need to think about and do next (e.g. Miller and Rollnick, 2002).

As previously stated MI supports and directly promotes the autonomy of the individuals over their own process. This is ultimately their decision to change their behaviour, or not. However important the change may be, it is found that when a person wants to change (and believes that they can) that they are simply more likely to do so (e.g. Amrhein, 2003 and Bandurra, 1977 respectively). Avoiding arguing for change and allowing (and trusting) the client to do so facilitates this, and thus this is what grows. People are most poignantly convinced by their own voice (Bem, 1972) and therefore through this course of intervention the individual is more convinced by the argument to change that is their own. They catch themselves articulating it therefore it must be true. It emerges therefore as a better idea to follow; more so than it seemed before the therapy session.

Motivational Interviewing is a therapeutic strategy that is primarily about evoking ideas about change (and indeed homeostasis) from an individual. Rather than instilling ideas from one person into another, the goal of this approach is to work within the context of the internal thoughts ideas and feelings about a specific issue within the individual. The skills are geared towards naturally evoking the clients' ideas on the subject as these tend to translate more into the development of motivation then the therapist providing the argument, as evidenced by Paul Amrhein's research (e.g. Amrhein et al., 2003).

It is therefore the task of the MI therapist to seek to elicit (evocation) from the client their ideas about the behaviour in order to work together with them (collaboration) in any psychological movement towards a better life for them, as per their design, if they choose to allow it (autonomy).

Principles

In addition to providing the right kind of space within which a client is likely to talk themselves into changing (Miller, 2004), MI is about more strategic components. Therefore in

[1] With the publication of the 3rd edition of the Motivational interviewing text book (Miller and Rollnick, 2013) we see the introduciton of compassion, essentially ensuring that this is not misunderstood as a means for manipultaion, such as in a sales context. Therefore one embodies the spirit by embracing the central point of wanting on behalf of another; To give priority to others' needs (Miller and Rollnick, 2013).

addition to creating the right way of being with a client (the spirit), MI follows various principles in the specific mechanism of this technique, and they are as follows:

Figure 2. Principles of MI.

As discussed previously resistance is considered quite normal and based on the interpersonal dynamic. It is essential that when resistance is detected that there is not an opposition to that resistance. Opposition to resistance tends to set up opposition to the process itself, and this tends to increase the chances of the client arguing against change. Resistance in the client is often an indication of the behaviour of the therapist. The resistance tells us something about what we are doing. Resistance therefore is a signal to do something different (e.g. Rubak, et al., 2005).

How confident one is in their ability to successfully implement and maintain change is a crucial factor in determining how likely they are to allow themselves to take on the risk (of trying and failing). One's belief in their ability to do something (self-efficacy) is key to allowing themselves to reflect upon how important the change may be, and fundamental in terms of how successful they are likely to be. Those whom believe that they can are more likely to articulate this and are more likely to change (Amrhein et al., 2003). Supporting the development of self-efficacy is integral to the MI process and is acutely achieved through skilful affirmations, which are discussed further below.

Discrepancy refers to the gap between where one is and where they want to be. This specifically relates to one's current behaviour pattern, contrasted with one's system of goals and/or values. Motivational Interviewing conversations are specifically effective for developing perception of this gap and when it happens, people develop an argument to themselves to change on this basis (e.g. Lundahl, Kunz, Brownell, Tollefson, and Burke, 2010).

As previously discussed Empathy is centrally important to therapeutic outcomes (e.g. Miller, 1980). Fundamental to this interaction, is not only the experience of empathy, but the expression of it. Having a generally empathic air is crucial, as is the necessity to actually express this to the client. When we express empathy it tends to contribute to a more trustful and safe environment, within which the client is more likely to feel safe enough to address their concerns about their own behaviour. When people allow themselves to do this they are more likely to develop arguments for change, and thus are more likely to (e.g. Miller and Rollnick, 2004).

Resolving Ambivalence

As previously mentioned, one of the cornerstones of this model is the insight that it provides to professionals (and individuals alike) in relation to the processes involved in change and in particular those involved in resistance to change. Perhaps traditionally understood as deliberate denial and a manipulation, the concept of ambivalence shines from the core of this theory. For the first time it seemed, a theory of why resistance exists in relation to change emerged. The apparent mystery being unfolded therefore is rather than people manipulating reality and other people in order to facilitate continued self destructive behaviour (e.g. addiction), they are actually fairly ambivalent about it: they both want to change and want to stay the same, at once. This creates a deep discomfort, and the human condition being comprehensively opposed to discomfort, people tend to simply stop thinking about the issue, and indeed stop talking about it, especially if (1) the listener is pushing in one direction (change) and (2) the individual lacks in self-efficacy (their confidence in their ability) to successfully change.

Ambivalence therefore relates to having conflicting ideas about a behavioural change. Having valid reasons to change, yet equally valid, and conflicting ideas about not changing. Resolving this process is key to enhancing the possibility of change. The resolution takes place in a non-judgemental atmosphere that simply allows one to explore this ambivalence and thus begin to develop an argument towards a particular course of action; a direction of change. Ambivalence is seen as completely normal (e.g. Miller and Rollnick, 2002).

Processes

The latest material being developed by Miller and Rollnick (2013) is developing a newer focus on the four processes of motivational interviewing which span the interpersonal process. These are articulated as follows:

Figure 3. Processes of MI.

One may see the life of the conversational context here, where the practitioner pays primary attention to engaging the individual as outlined in the spirit. Then collaboratively focuses on the subject of the conversation, essentially the direction. From this point the practitioner evokes selectively an argument for change and then having done so plans how this may evolve. Each phase, once activated remains active throughout (one does not stop one to do the other).

One may see how the principles, as outlined, map onto these processes sequentially.

Techniques

There are various tools associated with Motivational interviewing. Whilst a therapist is embodying the Spirit and ensuring that the principles are being met, and adhered to, what one may hear happening in the dialogue are the actual techniques of MI, and they are possibly best described by the acronym OARS:

Figure 4. Skills of MI.

It has been suggested (Thomas Gordon, 1970) that questions are like roadblocks to a flowing therapeutic conversation. It is certainly suggested in Motivational Interviewing that one avoids (other than in information gathering and clarifying of detail) closed questions. Open-ended questions are much more likely to allow the client to develop their points, articulate and elaborate further and thus process their own thinking at a more flowing pace. It is specifically characteristic of MI to affirm the client; to articulate to the client that the efforts that they are making are noticed and acknowledged; the struggle that they experience and the progress that they are making. This directly reinforces the client and helps them to feel supported by both the process and the therapist engaged in it with them.

Reflecting what a person is articulating is at the heart of MI. Essentially the MI therapist evokes what the individual is saying by repeating it back to them in their own words rather than asking questions *per se.* There are various types of reflections between simple and complex (e.g. double-sided, paraphrasing, repeating, amplified, of felling, etc.), and they are various ways of communicating to the client that they are being understood and that this can be communicated back to them in different words (and ways). This is in keeping with the spirit of evocation; drawing out from the person rather than instilling ideas in them, on the basis that, as previously stated, the individual is more likely to be convinced by their own arguments than those of others (Bem, 1972).

Reflecting tends to be general early on in the conversation however as momentum develops reflection content (what the therapist reflects specifically) tends to be more selective (Miller, 2009), demonstrating preference for the agreed direction of change. Every 20-30 utterances the therapist may make some sort of summary, a monologue detailing what the therapist understands from what has been said. This is a mechanism to convey understanding, provide further opportunity for affirmation, convey to the client that the therapist is on their side and paying attention to every word, provide the opportunity for reframes, and allow the therapist orchestrate some sort of direction change in the dialogue.

Change talk

Change talk is any articulation of a desire, ability, reason or need to change (DARN), and indeed an expression of commitment, activation and taking steps. Change talk and in particular commitment language demonstrates a significant link to therapeutic outcomes in motivational interviewing conversations (e.g. Moyers and Martin, 2006; Moyers et al., 2007; Amrhein et al., 2003;Moyers, Martin, Catley, Harris, and Ahluwalia, 2003). In other words those who develop an argument for change, tend to. This is the reason that the principles and techniques hold this particular design: to facilitate the development of this argument for change.

Therefore the ultimate objective of a Motivational Interviewing conversation is to elicit this argument; to establish a greater incidence of change talk (DARN). When this occurs (therapist hears change talk) it is imperative to seek elaboration, request explanation, examples and further discussion. When there is more DARN there tends to be more CATS (commitment, activation and taking steps), and this is directly linked to change itself (e.g. Amrhein et al., 2003; Moyers et al., 2007).

CONCLUSION

In summary therefore, it has become clear in Miller's continued analysis (and indeed that of Rollnick and countless other professionals and academics) that when somebody is caught in this area of addiction, they tend to be fairly ambivalent about it. They tend to want to change and want to not change at the same time creating a significant internal struggle that usually results in them stopping thinking about it and resisting the encouragements of others to face it, often appearing like they have no idea that there is an issue at all (traditionally understood as denial). Then, once there is a space that is safe and non-judgementally supportive enough (facilitated by the spirit of MI) they are more likely to look at this ambivalence. Whenever they feel like resisting that is also facilitated (and treated as normal) and consequently there is less need to defend against the judgement (as there is none). Thus resistance is often short-lived and they continue to explore their ambivalent feelings about the behaviour.

They then begin to both resolve the ambivalence and develop an argument for change, based on their own ideas, values and reasons, which is actively guided and reinforced through the various techniques and principles of MI. They develop commitment and seem to simply find a way to change, despite for instance previously feeling that there was little chance of succeeding in this.

Table 2. Empirical examples of key assumptions

	Key assumption	Empirical examples
1	MI works	Hettema et al., 2005; Amrhein et al., 2003; Moyers, et al., 2007; Vasilaki et al., 2006; Rubak et al., 2005; Knight et al., 2006
2	Empathy is essential and strongly linked to therapeutic outcome	Miller, 1980
3	Treatment fidelity is a pre-requisite	Hettema et al., 2005
4	MI interventions (relational and technical) are linked to client language change	Moyers et al., 2007
5	Client language (amount and frequency of change talk and sustain talk) is a crucial indicator	Moyers et al., 2007; Moyers and Martin, 2006; Moyers et al., 2003
6	Reinforcement of client language results in commitment language	Amrhein et al., 2003
7	Commitment language is strongly related to successful and meaningful change	Amrhein et al., 2003

Table 2 above shows a summary of some key assumptions provided by empirical research into the efficacy of MI as articulated in the previous sections. Therefore it appears reasonable that Motivational Interviewing has been established as an evidence based model. We know that when one affirms clients, supports their self-efficacy, helps them to develop discrepancy between values and behaviour, rolls with any resistance (treating it as normal), and expresses empathy, the individual tends to resolve ambivalence (reasons to change and reasons to stay the same) in favour of healthy behavioural change (in an agreed direction). There is a wide range of empirical research testifying to this as outlined in the current chapter. There is a range of Systematic Reviews and Meta-Analyses on the subject that are very well documented and evidenced (e.g. Hettema et al., 2005; Rubak et al., 2005; Knight et al., 2006; Dunn et al., 2001; Lundahl et al., 2010; Vasilaki et al., 2006; Burke, Dunn and Atkins, 2004). However in relation to the essences as to *why* MI demonstrates this evidence base and what it is that the interventions cause in relation to the internal experience of the individual client, there is very little documented evidence or research.

What Next?

The literature is quite clear and comprehensive regarding both the efficacy of this model, the mechanisms involved (relational and technical; Miller and Rose, 2009) and therefore the means of teaching it. What is not clear essentially is why, beyond the structure of the interventions themselves. Although one can be clear that when one engages people therapeutically using these techniques, and embodying the required style and way of being, people are simply more likely to respond by (1) resolving ambivalence (2) developing an articulated argument for change and (3) strengthening commitment for change, and (4) successfully doing so.

However one does not necessarily know in the realm of the clients' perception, how this process is experienced and thus essentially why it works. In other words, when the therapist emulates good efficacious MI practice (how) the client language shifts, yet there is little knowledge of why this shift occurs in response to these specific interventions. The words of the therapist themselves, it may be argued, does not cause the shift. The internalisation of those words on the part of the client does and the only access the research(er) may have to this process is by asking the client.

The research base of MI is quite strong and comprehensive, yet there is precious little that examines this piece (client perspective), which may be suggested to be fundamental to understanding the process and the effectiveness of the model itself. It has been found that clients' internal experience of discrepancy has been significantly related to therapeutic outcomes in MI sessions (alongside some other therapist behaviours), which is a rare finding that points towards the experience of the client (Apodaca, 2009). Otherwise this may be considered to be a significant gap in the literature. Whilst arguably this would not necessarily change how one uses the model, as any deviations are found to compromise treatment outcomes (e.g. Amrhein et al., 2003; Moyers et al., 2007); it may add significant meaning to the therapist's understanding of the essence of MI and possibly increase the ease with which the model can be learned.

REFERENCES

Aliotta, S. L., Vlasnik, J. J., and Delor, B. (2004). Enhancing adherence to long-term medical therapy: A new approach to assessing and treating patients. *Advances in Therapy, 21,* 214-231.

Amrhein PC, Miller WR, Yahne CE, Palmer M, and Fulcher L. (2003). Client commitment language during motivational interviewing predicts drug use outcomes. *J. Consult. Clin. Psychol. 71:862–78.*

Angus, L. E., and Kagan, F. (2009). Therapist empathy and client anxiety reduction in motivational interviewing: 'She carries with me, the experience. *Journal of Clinical-Psychology, 65,* 1156-1167.

Apodaca, T. R., and Longabaugh, R. (2009). Mechanisms of change in motivational interviewing: A review and preliminary evaluation of the evidence. *Addiction, 104,* 705–715.

Baker, A., Lewin, T., Reichler, H., Clancy, R., Carr, V., Garrett, R., ...Terry, M. (2002). Evaluation of a motivational interview for substance use within psychiatric in-patient services. *Addiction, 97*(10), 1329-1337.

Bandura, A. (1977). Self-efficacy: Towards a unifying theory of behavior change. *Psychological Review, 84,* 191–215.

Behrman, A. (2006). Facilitating behavioral change in voice therapy: The relevance of motivational interviewing. *American Journal of Speech-Language Pathology, 15*, 215-225.

Bem DJ. (1972). Self-perception theory. In *Advances in Experimental Social Psychology,* ed. L Berkowitz, 6:1–62. New York: Academic.

Berg-Smith, S. M., Stevens, V. J., Brown, K. M., Van Horn, L., Gernhofer, N., Peters, E., ... Smith, K. (1999). A brief motivational intervention to improve dietary adherence in adolescents. *Health Education Research, 14*, 399-410.

Bombardier, C. H., and Rimmele, C. T. (1999). Motivational interviewing to prevent alcohol abuse after traumatic brain injury: A case series. *Rehabilitation Psychology, 44*, 52-67.

Brown, R. A., Ramsey, S. E., Strong, D. R., Myers, M. G., Kahler, C. W., Lejuez, C. W., ... Abrams, D. (2003).Effects of motivational interviewing on smoking cessation in adolescents with psychiatric disorders. *Tobacco Control, 12*(Suppl. 4), 3-10.

Burke B.L., Dunn C.W., Atkins D.C., *and Phelps, J.S.* (2004) The emerging evidence base for motivational interviewing: a meta-analytic and qualitative inquiry. *Journal of Cognitive Psychotherapy* 18, 309–322.

Carey, M. P., Braaten, L. S., Maisto, S. A., GLeason, J. R., Forsyth, A. D., Durant, L. E., ... Beth, C. (2000). Using information, motivational enhancement, and skills training to reduce the risk of HIV infection for low-income urban women: A second randomized clinical trial. *Health Psychology, 19*, 3-11.

Channon, S., Smith, V. J., and Gregory, J. W. (2003).A pilot study of motivational interviewing in adolescents with diabetes. *Archives of Disease in Childhood, 88*(8), 680-683.

Corbett, G. (2008). What The Research Says About MI... Where Do You Start? MINT Bulletin, Vol 14. No. 1.

Dunn, C., Deroo, L., and Rivara, F.P. (2001) The use of brief interventions adapted from motivational interviewing across behavioural domains: A Systematic Review. Addiction, 96 (12), 1725-1742.

Dunn, E. C., Neighbors, C., and Larimer, M. (2006). Motivational enhancement therapy and self-help treatment for binge eaters. *Psychology of Addictive Behaviors, 20*, 44-52.

Feld, R., Woodside, D. B., Kaplan, A. S., Olmsted, M. P., and Carter, J. C. (2001). Pretreatment motivational enhancement therapy for eating disorders: A pilot study. *International Journal of Eating Disorders, 29*, 393-400.

Gordon, T. (1970). Parent effectiveness training. New York: Wyden.

Harland, J., White, M., Drinkwater, C., Chinn, D., Farr, L., and Howel, D. (1999). The Newcastle Exercise Project: A randomised controlled trial of methods, to promote physical activity in primary care. *British Medical Journal, 319*, 828-832.

Hettema, J., Steele, J., and Miller, W.R., (2005). Motivational Interviewing. *Annu. Rev. Clin. Psychol. 2005. 1:91–111.*

Hillsdon, M., Thorogood, N., White, I., and Foster, C. (2002). Advising people to take more exercise is ineffective: A randomised controlled trial of physical activity promotion in primary care. *International Journal of Epidemiology, 31*, 808-815.

Hodgins, D. C., Currie, S., el-Guebaly, N., and Peden, N. (2004). Brief motivational treatment for problem gambling: A 24-month follow-up. *Psychology of Addictive Behaviors, 18*, 293-296.

Humphress, H., Igel, V., Lamont, A., Tanner, M., Morgan, J., and Schmidt, U. (2002). The effect of a brief motivational intervention on community psychiatric patients' attitudes to their care, motivation to change, compliance and outcome: A case control study. *Journal of Mental Health, 11*, 155-166.

Johnston, B. D., Rivara, F. P., and Droesch, R. M. (2002). Behavior change counseling in the emergency department to reduce injury risk: A randomized, controlled trial. *Pediatrics, 110*, 267-274.

Kelly, A. B., Halford, W. K., and Young, R. M. (2000). Maritally distressed women with alcohol problems: The impact of a short-term alcohol-focused intervention on drinking behaviour and marital satisfaction. *Addiction, 95*, 1537-1549.

Kistenmacher, B. R. (2000). *Motivational interviewing as a mechanism for change in men who batter: A randomized controlled trial.* Unpublished Doctoral Dissertation, University of Oregon.

Knight, K. M., McGowan, L., Dickens, C., and Bundy, C. (2006).A systematic review of motivational interviewing in physical health care settings. *British Journal of Health Psychology, 11,* 319–332.

Lundahl B.W., Kunz C., Brownell C., Tollefson, D., and Burke, B. L.(2010) A meta-analysis of motivational interviewing: twenty-five years of empirical studies. *Research on Social Work Practice* 20, 137–160.

Miller W. R. (1978) Behavioral treatment of problem drinkers: a comparative outcome study of three controlled drinking therapies. *J Consult ClinPsychol*; 46: 74–86.

Miller W. R. (1983) Motivational interviewing with problem drinkers. *BehavPsychother.* 11: 147–72.

Miller, W. R. (2009), Conversation with William R. Miller. Addiction, 104: 883–893.doi: 10.1111/j.1360-0443.2009.02544.x.

Miller WR, Mount KA. (2001). A small study of training in motivational interviewing: Does one workshop change clinician and client behavior. *Behav. Cogn. Psychother.* 29:457–71.

Miller WR, and Rollnick S. (1991). *Motivational Interviewing: Preparing People to Change Addictive Behavior.* New York: Guilford.

Miller, W. and Rollnick, S. (2002) *Motivational Interviewing- Preparing People For Change",* 2nd Ed., Published by The Guilford Press, NY, USA.

Miller, W. and Rollnick, S. (2013) *Motivational Interviewing- Helping People Change, 3rd* Ed., Published by The Guilford Press, NY, USA.

Miller W. R., and Rollnick S. (2004) Talking oneself into change: motivational interviewing, stages of change, and therapeutic process. *J Cognitive Psychotherapy.*18: 299–308.

Miller, W. R., and Rollnick, S. (2009). Ten Things That Motivational Interviewing Is Not. *Behavioural and Cognitive Psychotherapy, 37(2), 129-140.*

Miller W. R., Taylor C. A., West J. C. (1980) Focused versus broad spectrum behavior therapy for problem drinkers. *J Consult Clin Psychol.* 48: 590–601.

Miller, W. R., and Rose, G. S. (2009). Toward a theory of motivational interviewing. American Psychologist, 64, 527-537.

Moyers, T. B., and Martin, T. (2006). Therapist influence on client language during motivational interviewing sessions: Support for a potential causal mechanism. *Journal of Substance Abuse Treatment, 30,* 245– 251.

Moyers, T. B., Martin, T., Catley, D., Harris, K. J., and Ahluwalia, J. S. (2003). Assessing the integrity of motivational interventions: Reliability of the Motivational Interviewing Skills Code. *Behavioural and Cognitive Psychotherapy, 31,* 177–184.

Moyers, T.B., Martin, T., Christopher, P.J., Houck, J.M., Tonigan, J.S., and Amrhein, P.C. (2007). Client Language as a Mediator of Motivational Interviewing Efficacy: Where is the Evidence? *Alcoholism: Clinical and Experimental Research Vol. 31.*

Ogedegbe, G., Schoenthaler, A., Richardson, T., Lewis, L., Belue, R., Espinosa, E., ... Charlson, M.E. (2007). An RCT of the effect of motivational interviewing on medication adherence in hypertensive African Americans: Rationale and design. *Contemporary Clinical Trials, 28, 169-181.*

Rollnick S., Miller W. R. (1995). What is motivational interviewing? *BehavCognPsychother*; 23: 325–34.

Rubak S., Sandbaek A., Lauritzen T., and Christensen, B.(2005) Motivational interviewing: a systematic reviewand meta-analysis. *British Journal of GeneralPractice* 55, 305–312.

Schmaling, K. B., Blume, A. W., and Afari, N. (2001). A randomized controlled pilot study of motivational interviewing to change attitudes about adherence to medications for asthma. *Journal of Clinical Psychology in Medical Settings, 8,* 167-172.

Scales, R. (1998). Motivational interviewing and skills-based counseling in cardiac rehabilitation: The Cardiovascular Health Initiative and Lifestyle Education (CHILE) study. Unpublished Doctoral dissertation, University of New Mexico.

Sinha, R., Easton, C., Renee-Aubin, L., and Carroll, K. M. (2003). Engaging young probation-referred marijuana-abusing individuals in treatment: A pilot trial. *American Journal on Addictions, 12*(4), 314-323.

Smith, D. E., Heckemeyer, C. M., Kratt, P. P., and Mason, D. A. (1997). Motivational interviewing to improve adherence to a behavioral weight-control program for older obese women with NIDDM: A pilot study. *Diabetes Care, 20,* 52-54.

Vasilaki, E., Hosier, S., and Cox, W. (2006). The efficacy of motivational interviewing as a brief intervention for excessive drinking: A meta-analytic review. Alcohol and Alcoholism, 41, 328-335.

Weinstein, P., Harrison, R., and Benton, T. (2004). Motivating parents to prevent caries in their young children: One-year findings. *Journal of the American Dental Association, 135*(6), 731-738.

Westra, H. A., and Phoenix, E. (2003). Motivational enhancement therapy in two cases of anxiety disorder: New responses to treatment refractoriness. *Clinical Case Studies, 2*(4), 306-322.

White W.L. and Miller W.R. (2007) The use of confrontation in addiction treatment: history, sciences and time for change. *Counselor* 8, 12–30.

Yahne, C. E., Miller, W. R., Irvin-Vitela, L., and Tonigan, J. S. (2002). Magdalena pilot project: Motivational outreach to substance abusing women street sex workers. *Journal of Substance Abuse Treatment, 23*(1), 49-53.

Zatzick, D., Roy-Byrne, P., Russo, J., Rivara, F., Droesch, R., Wagner, A., ... Katon, W. (2004). A randomized effectiveness trial of stepped collaborative care for acutely injured trauma survivors. *Archives of General Psychiatry, 61*(5), 498-506.

INDEX

S

T

W

Y